Lecture Notes
in Business Information Proc

G000155244

Series Editors

Wil van der Aalst
  Eindhoven Technical University, Eindhoven, The Netherlands
John Mylopoulos
  University of Trento, Povo, Italy
Michael Rosemann
  Queensland University of Technology, Brisbane, QLD, Australia
Michael J. Shaw
  University of Illinois, Urbana-Champaign, IL, USA
Clemens Szyperski
  Microsoft Research, Redmond, WA, USA

More information about this series at http://www.springer.com/series/7911

Ilan Oshri · Julia Kotlarsky
Leslie P. Willcocks (Eds.)

Achieving Success and Innovation in Global Sourcing: Perspectives and Practices

9th Global Sourcing Workshop 2015
La Thuile, Italy, February 18–21, 2015
Revised Selected Papers

 Springer

Editors
Ilan Oshri
School of Business and Economics
Loughborough University
Loughborough
UK

Leslie P. Willcocks
London School of Economics
London
UK

Julia Kotlarsky
Aston Business School
Aston University
Birmingham
UK

ISSN 1865-1348   ISSN 1865-1356 (electronic)
Lecture Notes in Business Information Processing
ISBN 978-3-319-26738-8   ISBN 978-3-319-26739-5 (eBook)
DOI 10.1007/978-3-319-26739-5

Library of Congress Control Number: 2015954976

Springer Cham Heidelberg New York Dordrecht London

Springer International Publishing AG Switzerland is part of Springer Science+Business Media
(www.springer.com)

Preface

This edited book is intended for use by students, academics, and practitioners who take interest in outsourcing and offshoring of information technology and business services. The book offers a review of the key topics in outsourcing and offshoring, populated with practical frameworks that serve as a toolkit to students and managers. The range of topics covered in this book is wide and diverse, but predominately focused on how to achieve success and innovation in global sourcing. More specifically the book examines sourcing models giving specific attention to strategic aspects of global sourcing. The interplay between contractual and relational governance is studied by focusing on contract design, social capital, and relationship quality. The book also explores challenges associated with achieving innovation in outsourcing and offshoring settings. Last but not least, collaboration and governance in multi-sourcing and other interorganizational arrangements are studied in depth. Topics discussed in this book combine theoretical and practical insights regarding challenges that industry leaders, policy makers, and professionals face. Case studies from various organizations, industries, and countries are used extensively throughout the book.

The book is based on a vast empirical base brought together through years of extensive research by leading researchers in information systems, strategic management, international business, and operations.

August 2015

Ilan Oshri
Julia Kotlarsky
Leslie P. Willcocks

Organization

Global Sourcing Workshop is an annual gathering of academics and practitioners.

Program Committee

Julia Kotlarsky	Aston Business School, UK
Ilan Oshri	Loughborough Centre for Global Sourcing and Services, UK
Leslie P. Willcocks	London School of Economics, London, UK

Contents

Software Sourcing Modes and Software Sourcing Gestalts

Marko Nöhren, Armin Heinzl, and Thomas Kude(✉)

University of Mannheim, Schloss, 68131 Mannheim, Germany
mnoehren@googlemail.com, {heinzl,kude}@uni-mannheim.de

Abstract. Enterprise systems offer the potential of integrating corporate functions as well as enabling business process improvements. These systems can be deployed in three different software sourcing modes: in-house, on-premises, and on-demand. This study examines whether software sourcing gestalts, i.e., combinations of IT resources and organisational resources involved, are able to absorb changes in the firm's environment. If this is the case, the prevailing gestalts of IT and organisational resources parsimoniously "fit" the chosen software sourcing mode in response to changing forces in the firm's environment.

Keywords: Software · Sourcing · Mode · On-demand · On-premises · In-house · Gestalt · Technical resources · Organisational resources

1 Introduction

1.1 Problem Statement

Enterprise systems have been crucial for companies' daily operations. They offer the potential of integrating corporate functions as well as enabling business process improvements [1]. Companies can choose among three types of software sourcing modes: custom-built in-house applications, on-premises packaged applications as well as on-demand applications. While process-centric enterprise systems – such as Enterprise Resource Planning (ERP), Customer Relationship Management (CRM), or Supplier Relationship (SCM) software – were traditionally sourced in an in-house setting or as packaged on-premises applications, cloud based on demand solutions, including ERP-as-a-Service or CRM-as-a-Service, are on the rise [2]. Although on-demand services cut clients' cost and speed up access to systems and software upgrades, on-premises and on-demand solutions are considered less customizable which in turn impacts integrability and performance [3, 4]. As a consequence, enterprise systems may fail to deliver the expected value if the properties of the software sourcing mode chosen does not fit the prevailing organisational requirements [5, 6].

One stream of the literature focuses on the role of software alignment as a central mediator between the enterprise software implemented and its performance outcomes [5–8]. These studies analyse what constitutes organisational fit of applications, how it is achieved, and how fit (or misfit) emerges across organisational subunits. Nevertheless,

© Springer International Publishing Switzerland 2015
I. Oshri et al. (Eds.): Global Sourcing 2015, LNBIP 236, pp. 1–28, 2015.
DOI: 10.1007/978-3-319-26739-5_1

these studies pose three significant shortcomings. First, most studies are rather conceptual, i.e. not empirical in nature. Second, their main focus is on packaged applications only, not considering on-demand sourcing modes or in-house applications. Third, these studies do not systematically take into account how combinations of IT resources and complementary organisational structures [9] do look like and how well they fit with the respective software sourcing modes and how they impact outcome measures.

Despite a long tradition of IT value research [9, 10] there is still uncertainty with respect to an enterprise system's contribution to organisational performance. Previous research in the field of process-centric enterprise software frequently investigated the outcomes of each of the sourcing modes individually [11–15]. So far, no study has incorporated all three software sourcing modes simultaneously or considered whether combinations of IT resources and organisational resources form intermediating patterns. This is rather surprising because these modes imply different magnitudes of customisability and control, which in turn may impact the value delivered.

1.2   Research Objective

This study intends to address the reported research gap by analysing the existence of coherent patterns of IT resources and complementary organisational resources [9] which may impact the value creation of the adopted software sourcing modes (i.e., in-house, on-premises, and on-demand). The focus of this paper is, first, to explore the existence of such patterns that we refer to as software sourcing gestalts. Second, we will analyse how well these gestalts fit with the software sourcing mode chosen.

As IT resources, we will analyse the software structure of business applications (including ERP, CRM, or SRM systems), which are referred to as technological resources in the literature [9]. As the key complementary organisational resources, we focus on the adaptability of the business process structure, which is induced by pressures and changes of the organisational environment [9].

If the software sourcing mode is well mirrored by combinations of IT resources and complementary organisational resources as sound responses to changing forces in the environment, we refer to these patterns as gestalts. In contrast, combinations of IT resources and complementary organisational resources, which are not well aligned with environmental changes, are referred to as non-gestalts.

Consequently, the major objective of this paper is to explore, identify, and describe combinations or gestalt patterns which inhibit a high level of fit between the business process structure and software structure of a firm in response to changing forces in the environment.

Our research is theoretical, empirical, and descriptive in nature. We first develop a framework based on Institutional Theory, which captures key dimensions for gestalts on the basis of the existing literature. Based on these dimensions, we will develop four gestalts, which incorporate a high level of resource fit. Subsequently, we will provide empirical evidence of the gestalts developed. Finally, we will explore the relationship between those gestalts and software sourcing modes (see Fig. 1).

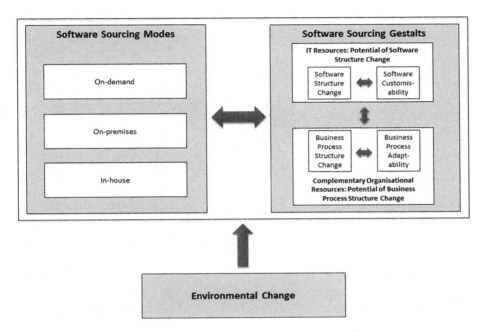

Fig. 1. "Fit" between Software Sourcing Modes and Software Sourcing Gestalts

2   Theoretical and Conceptual Foundations

2.1   Refinement of Core Concepts

Environmental Change. Changes in the external and internal environment of an organisation are key stimuli for adaptation strategies and behaviours of a firm. Institutional Theory differentiates between imposed and voluntary change [5, 16, 17]. Imposed change is a response to external forces such as government regulations or established industry practices [5, 18]. A distinction between a firm-specific, an industry-specific, and a country-specific imposed change is made [5, 16]. While these changes result from outside an organisation and can be considered reactive in nature, voluntary change results from internal forces [16]. It is rather proactive in nature. Table 1 provides an overview of the respective change types including its definitions and examples. Environmental change can be a stimulus for business process and software change.

Business Process Structure Change. A business process represents a distinct sequence of corporate activities, which need to be accomplished in order to achieve a certain business outcome [20, 21]. According to Institutional Theory, business processes are considered as a set of organised and established structures of activities [5, 22]. Unlike data structures, business processes structures are not static in nature. In fact, the structure of business process changes often over time. Thus, they are dynamic in nature.

Table 1. Environmental change

Construct		Definition	Sources
Macro envi-ronmental change	Imposed country context	Changes in the socio-political system, economic configuration, or cultural practices within a country.	[5, 16, 17, 19]
	Imposed industry context	Changes in practices specific to firm's industrial sector.	
Micro environ-mental change	Imposed firm context	Changes in structures related to a firm's trading partners.	
	Voluntary context	Changes in the idiosyncratic organisational structures.	

Institutional Theory takes up this argument as well. It posits that most business process structures are exposed to change over time [16, 22, 23]. Table 2 provides a definition of business process structure change.

Table 2. Business process structure change

Construct	Definition	Sources
Business process structure change	Business process structure change occurs when an organisation transforms the structure of its tasks (i.e., activities), rules, and procedures.	[19], based on [24]

Software Structure Change. Software structure change is usually a reaction to environmental change as well as business process change. It refers to situations where novel software features will be introduced [25]. These novel features usually involve adding, removing, or improving functional modules or user interfaces. The origin of the software structure change could be inside or outside the organisation. Thus, it could be either client-driven, i.e., demand pull, or vendor-driven, i.e., technology push [26–29]. Demand pull describes a situation in which a structure transformation of an enterprise system is either performed by a corporate IT unit or by a subcontracted service provider. In this scenario, software structure innovation is largely governed within a firm's hierarchy. Technology push describes a situation in which a software vendor conducts feature changes of an enterprise system. Thus, software structure change is governed outside a firm's hierarchy.

There may be situations where client organisations are trying to adapt to changes in the environment through a combination of demand pull and technology push. This form of ambidexterity can be found in situations where an organisation utilizes an on-premises enterprise systems platform from a software vendor, but adds specific in-house developed functionalities to better support its business process. This type of software structure change can be regarded as a push-pull-innovation-strategy. The taxonomy of a software structure change is summarised in Table 3.

Table 3. Software structure change

Construct		Definition	Sources
Software structure change	Technology push innovation	Technology push innovation occurs when software innovation developed by a software vendor is implemented within a firm.	based on [26], based on [27–29]
	Business (demand) pull innovation	Business pull innovation occurs when software innovation developed by a client is implemented within its firm.	

Business Process Adaptability. To remain competitive, firms must be able to adapt to (environmental or voluntary) change. Companies reconfigure their key business processes independent of their software structures as changing (market) conditions require to do so [30]. Thus, business process adaptability serves as a concept for business process structure flexibility and its ease of adaptation [31]. The adaptation of business processes to changing conditions can be considered as an important capability, which evolves out of a rigorous organisational learning process. This capability is likely to be heterogeneously distributed between firms and can be a source of sustained competitive advantage [32, 33]. The conceptualisation of business process adaptability is summarised in Table 4.

Table 4. Business process adaptability

Construct	Definition	Sources
Business process adaptability	Degree/extent to which structures of business processes can be rapidly and extensively modified and adapted.	[30, 31], based on [34]

Software Customisability. If a firm experiences an environmental or voluntary change, which results in a business process transformation (i.e., a business process structure change), its enterprise systems need to change equipollently and isochronally [5, 16, 19, 22]. Consequently, software structures need to be flexible and customisable. Software is flexible or customisable, if it can rapidly and efficiently be adapted in case of a business change [35]. Software sourcing modes facilitate different degrees of customisability and integrability. Whereas in-house applications allow for the support and integration of highly specific and idiosyncratic requirements through changes in the software code, on-premises packages offer reduced customisability and integrability through parametrisation options, customisation languages and application programming interfaces (APIs) for every client installation [25]. On-demand solutions offer the lowest degree of customisability and integrability because the service provider operates them in a multi-tenancy mode, which implies that customisations have to be implemented without affecting the running core of the fully standardized system. Thus, software sourcing modes differentiate themselves from each other by the degree to which the respective applications allow client-specific customisations. The conceptualisation of the construct software customisability is provided in Table 5.

Table 5. Software customisability

Construct	Definition	Sources
Software Customisability	Degree/extent to which deep and surface structures of software can be rapidly and extensively customized by a client.	[35], based on [36, 37]

The dimensions are summarized in Fig. 2. Based on these dimensions, we derive a framework of software sourcing gestalts and non-gestalts.

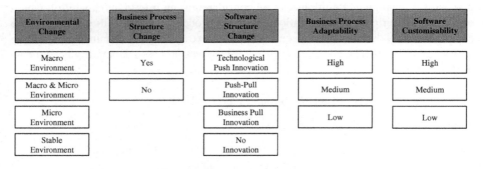

Fig. 2. Taxonomy for software sourcing gestalts.

2.2   Conceptualization of Software Sourcing Gestalts

Based on the developed taxonomy, this section develops a conceptualization of software sourcing mode gestalts. A "gestalt" is a collection of physical, biological, psychological, and symbolic elements that creates a whole, unified concept or pattern which is other than the sum of its parts, due to the relationship between its parts [38, 39].

Software sourcing gestalts are coherent patterns of environmental change, business process structure change, software structure change, software customisability, and business process adaptability. As outlined above, it is assumed that alterations in the structure of the business process and software are reactions to environmental changes, whereas the software customisability as well as the business process adaptability capture the resource potentials to respond to these requirements changes.

Pioneer Gestalt. Pioneers rely on enterprise software solutions which are developed outside the client's organisation. These solutions are purchased over the market. Thus, the change momentum resides with the software vendor.

The change impetus of this gestalt is triggered in the macro environment of the firm. Companies in this gestalt pattern experience ongoing changes within their imposed industry and country context. These environmental pressures are constantly addressed by adapting the structure of the business processes as well as ongoing changes in the software structure. The latter requires a pro-active and continuous release management by an external software vendor.

The environmental pressures are not idiosyncratic on a corporate level. Multiple firms within a country or within the same industry do face similar change pressures. Thus, this situation favours a market governance of software structure change or - in other words - a technology push logic of the vendors which regularly offer new software releases in order to cope with the changes of the macro environment.

In order to absorb the vendor induced software structure changes, client organisations may have to adapt their business processes. According to the magnitude of the macro environmental change, the requirements for adapting the firm's business processes can be high as well. Since the vendor has to implement the software structure changes, it will make the required software functionality available. From the perspective of the client organisation, the software is hard to customize. It usually does not allow for customisations of the micro environment. The resulting gestalt pattern is documented in Fig. 3.

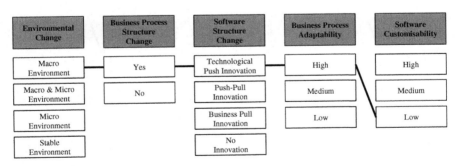

Fig. 3. Pioneer Gestalt

Patterns where changes in the macro environment do not require business process adaptations and where the required software structure change is conducted inside the client organisation (demand pull) are *not* considered as well-aligned. Thus, we refer to such a pattern as a macro environmental *non-gestalt*. If changes in the macro environment are not absorbed by adaptations in the business process structure, a firm is putting its organisational integrity at risk. Furthermore, if the software structure is changed internally as a response to macro environmental changes, a client organisation is likely to choose a suboptimal governance structure because a vendor can redistribute his development costs amongst multiple clients. Furthermore, if business process adaptability is low, it will not be able to absorb the required process changes. If the software customisability is too high, the client is likely to pay for a functionality it does not necessarily require.

Cautious Gestalt. The Cautious Gestalt describes the antipode of the Pioneer Gestalt. In this profile, a firm has to react on changes in the micro environment. Companies experience constant changes within their imposed firm environment or their voluntary context. These environmental shifts are addressed by constant efforts of business process redesign and software adaptations. The latter are primarily conducted within the firm. Thus, the focal firm can be considered as a cautious innovator that relies primarily on hierarchical governance with respect to software structure changes.

Usually, firms, which adhere to this gestalt face micro environmental changes, which are highly idiosyncratic to them. No other or only very few firms within that industry or country do face these change requirements. Highly idiosyncratic pressures favour a hierarchical governance of the implied software changes. Along these lines, the business processes are adapted incrementally rather than radically. Thus, the processes' adaptability is solely required to be medium to low. In order to support these highly specific and constantly changing business processes, the software customisability has to be very high. The resulting gestalt pattern is documented in Fig. 4.

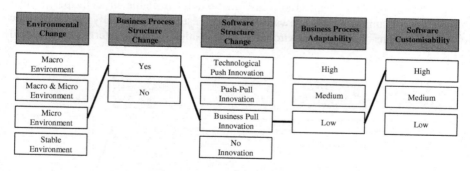

Fig. 4. Cautious Gestalt

Profiles where changes in the highly idiosyncratic micro environment lead to no change requirements in the process structure are contradictious. Furthermore, if a firm intends to address the process changes through the deployment of packaged enterprise software, it may not be able to account for the highly specific and idiosyncratic processes. The same holds true for process adaptability and software customisability. Since the software can be tailored to the business process needs, high process adaptability is not required. Thus, the in-house built software needs to be highly customisable. Any other profile, which intends to respond to micro environmental changes can be considered as a cautious non-gestalt.

Ambidextrous Gestalt. The third gestalt in our paper refers to an amalgamation of the Pioneer and the Cautious Gestalt. Thus, we frame it as the Ambidextrous Gestalt. This profile deploys its enterprise software from a combination of packaged software and in-house built solutions. Thus, it relies on a combination of market governance and hierarchical governance.

The change impetus of the Ambidextrous Gestalt results from stimuli in the macro and micro environment. Firms that underlie this gestalt experience changes within their imposed industry and country context as well as constant changes within their imposed firm context and their voluntary context. These environmental shifts require constant changes in the business process structure as well as software structure.

These changes are addressed by combining technology push with demand pull innovation. Firms intend to address macro environmental changes with the help of packaged solutions, which in turn demand a high adaptability of the available business processes. These packaged solutions represent the core enterprise system functionality of the firm, which is continuously updated with the help of novel releases from external software vendors. This functional core is complemented by in-house built add-on applications or modules, which support highly idiosyncratic business processes. These business processes often differentiate the firm's value chain or value system in the respective industry. Thus, the externally sourced software requires highly flexible business processes whereas the custom-built add-on software requires highly customisable software. The resulting profile is captured in Fig. 5.

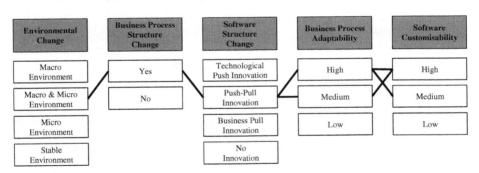

Fig. 5. Ambidextrous Gestalt

Specifications which respond to changes in the macro and micro environment that do not entail the described ambidextrous properties are considered as a non-gestalts since they contradict the logic described. For instance, a firm that intends to react to macro and micro environmental change by deploying packaged software only neglects its idiosyncratic and differentiation business processes. A company, which attempts to address both changes by in-house software only runs the risk of devoting too many resources which will have a negative effect on its cost position.

Conservative Gestalt. The final profile is referred to as the Conservative Gestalt. It is embedded in a stable environment and does not experience significant changes within its macro and micro environment over a longer period of time. As a consequence, it requires little or no changes in the business processes and software structure. Thus, this archetype relies on structural persistence. The systems landscape is historically grown and entails either in-house built applications or - in some instances - standardized packages from external vendors. For these reasons, the role of business process adaptability and software customisability are negligible or low. The resulting profile is illustrated in Fig. 6.

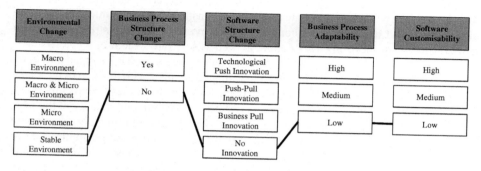

Fig. 6. Conservative gestalt

Firms that respond to a stable environment by pro-actively changing the structure of its business processes or software may put its organisational or technological stability at risk. Consequently, there is little need for adaptive business processes or customisable software functions.

3   Research Design

The presented work aims to increase our understanding of how existing software sourcing modes are interrelated with software sourcing gestalts. Thus, we are interested in demonstrating its empirical viability. For this reason, a qualitative exploratory field study has been conducted which attempts to combine a traditional in-depth case study investigation with quantitative large-scale survey study [40, 41]. Thus, it allows for an incorporation of a larger number of empirical profiles than traditional case study research [40, 41]. In doing so, it reduces the risk of overweighting the idiosyncrasies of a few specific empirical profiles and increases the generalisability of our findings [42].

Our units of analysis are process-centric enterprise systems as a part of the corporate IT function. Consequently, key informants were executives responsible for managing the enterprise software artefact under study [40]. In outlining the restrictions of this study, temporal and spatial boundaries are defined [43]. According to Swanson and Ramiller [44], the process of organisational innovation – such as the implementation of an enterprise system – proceeds in four consecutive steps.

It starts with a comprehension phase, in which a firm becomes aware of the potential benefits of an enterprise system. In a second stage, a business case is created. This business case can result in an implementation of an enterprise system, which constitutes the third step in the innovation process. Following the implementation phase, the final assimilation (or use) phase starts, when the enterprise system "begins to be absorbed into the work life of the firm and to demonstrate its usefulness" [44, p. 558].

In order to understand the dynamic nature of software performance in the post-implementation phase, only such empirical profiles were incorporated that completed the implementation phase and entered the final stage of the innovation process. The presented study focuses on enterprise systems designed to support primary and secondary business processes within a firm [12, 45, 46]. Therefore, ERP systems as well as functional modules for CRM, warehousing, or procurement were investigated. The decision was made in close cooperation with the key informants based on whether an organisation has implemented a comprehensive enterprise system or relied on heterogeneous process-centric software landscape.

In contrast to quantitative methods, case and field study design relies on a theoretical sampling of a population instead of a statistical one [42]. Researchers are able to focus on cases that extend existing theories [41, 42, 47]. Consequently, a central goal of this exploratory field study was to include data points as long as new insights emerged from the findings [42]. Three stopping criteria had been defined. First, a sufficiently large number of field study data had to be collected. Due to the fact that this study draws heavily on the qualitative field study design by Guillemette and Paré [40], the minimum number of empirical profiles was set to be 33. The larger the empirical data set, the sounder the derived patterns [48]. Second, data should be observed under a wide variety of conditions [48]. Therefore, data was gathered for all three software sourcing modes, in different industrial sectors, within companies of different sizes, and for different process-centric applications. Third, empirical profiles that challenge the preliminary research model were included in order to extent existing literature.

Data was collected through semi-structured interviews using pre-formulated questions as well as new questions that emerged during the conversations [49]. Each interview started with broad questions that asked the respondent to describe the IT function in general and his or her responsibility in software management. Then the interviewer asked more specific questions to ensure that the company has completed the implementation phase and that all constructs of the preliminary research model were covered. In the second part of the interview, open questions were asked to capture data on all concepts under study. In order to differentiate between gestalts and non-gestalts which occurred during the implementation phase and those that arose over time, a detailed description of the software implementation process and how the software evolved since entering the assimilation phase [44] was asked for. In the last part of the interview, open questions to evaluate software's value in terms of alignment and performance were asked. After each interview, transcripts were coded and interpreted.

The qualitative data from the field study was analysed using the software tools NVivo, Microsoft Excel, and Microsoft Access. This analysis implies "identifying, coding, categorizing, classifying, and labeling the primary patterns in the data [by] analyzing the core content of interviews" [50, p. 463]. Such codes are "labels for assigning units of meaning to the descriptive or inferential information compiled during a study. Codes usually are attached to 'chunks' of varying size – words, phrases, sentences, or whole paragraphs" [51, p. 56] reflecting the constructs within a study.

Data has been gathered within 43 field study companies, comprising a large variety of industries (Fig. 7), of size (Fig. 8.A), and interviewee roles (Fig. 8.B). In total, 51 interviews were conducted within the 43 case companies. It has to be noted that due to missing values, two interviewees were interrogated twice. Consequently, 49 respondents participated in the field study as indicated in Fig. 8.B. Among the respondents, 19 were chief information officers (CIOs), 14 were high-level IT executives on the second tier of IT management, seven were C-level executives and chief executive officers (CEOs), seven were high-level key users and business process owner, one was an assistant to the board of directors, and one was a chief operations officer (COO).

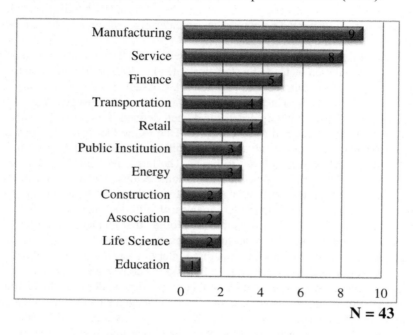

N = 43

Fig. 7. Industry of field study companies

Empirical profiles within this study reflect process-centric enterprise systems. Interviewees in four organisations provided an in-depth description of not only one but two enterprise systems. As shown in Fig. 9.A, 30 ERP systems, 14 CRM applications and three other systems including one warehousing application, one procurement software, and one campus management system have been observed. With respect to the software sourcing mode, six applications were sourced in an in-house setting (≈ 13 %), whereas 41 enterprise system were packaged applications (see Fig. 9.B). Out of them, 26 applications were provided on-premises (≈ 55 %) and 15 on-demand (≈ 32 %).

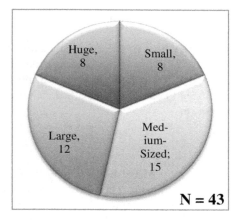 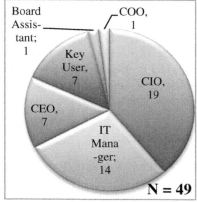

A. Company size (headcount)   B. Respondents roles

Fig. 8. Company size and roles of the respondents

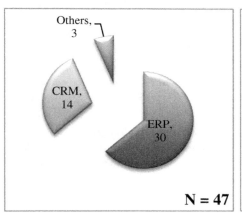 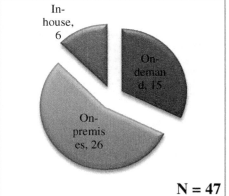

A. Software Systems   B. Software Sourcing Modes

Fig. 9. Empirical profiles

ERP systems were most frequently sourced in an on-premises mode. In particular, out of 30 ERP systems, 20 were provided on-premises, nine were provided on-demand, and one ERP system was sourced in-house. In contrast, a bigger share of on-demand software was found with respect to CRM applications. In particular six out of 14 CRM applications were provided on-demand, four in-house, and four were deployed in an on-premises mode.

4   Empirical Investigation of the Software Sourcing Gestalts

This section offers findings from our single-case analysis in order to demonstrate the viability of software sourcing mode gestalts [41, 42]. An in-depth investigation of all 44 empirical profiles would be beyond the scope of this paper. Thus, we will present four exemplary empirical profiles, which are linked to one of the gestalts developed in chapter two in order to demonstrate their existence.

4.1   Pioneer Gestalt

An exemplary case of a pioneer innovator is given by ALPHA-FINANCE. ALPHA-FINANCE is a German statutory health insurance company. The German health care market is separated in private health insurance – for self-employed people and those with higher incomes – and in statutory health insurance by which all other people are insured [53]. Approximately 90 % of the German population is protected by statutory health insurances [53]. Among them, more than five million people are insured by ALPHA-FINANCE. As the interviewees reported, APLHA-FINANCE is primarily driven by macro environmental changes in terms of shifts in their imposed country context.

> *"Health insurance companies depend on the legislator and there are several changes per year. Of course, the extent of these changes varies from year to year. Typically we see two regulatory changes within a one year time frame. Take SEPA as an example. (…) Health insurance is a financial service, so SEPA impacts our cash flows. We need SEPA functionalities within the system and we need to provide information on our customers' bank accounts."* IT Manager, *ALPHA-FINANCE*

These change requirements are addressed by solely relying on pure technological push innovation. ALPHA-FINANCE's ERP system is deployed in a private cloud setting. An external service provider is responsible for operating and updating the ERP system. ALPHA-FINANCE does not conduct any client-driven software structure changes internally.

> *"[The provider] is responsible for all updates. It is standard software. (…) We get new releases two times a year with new features and functionalities. (…) Those updates are very extensive ones. (…)"* IT Manager, *ALPHA-FINANCE*
> *"It is standard software. We do not adapt it."* IT Manager, *ALPHA-FINANCE*

In order to act in conformance with shifts in the imposed country context, ALPHA-FINANCE adapts its business processes frequently.

> *"There is a certain standard that all health insurance companies rely on. So there is little room for individuality. So if a new law comes into force, we have to adapt to it."* Key User, *ALPHA-FINANCE*

Business process adaptability turned out to be high at ALPHA-FINANCE. The interviewees reported that frequently software structure changes in terms of technology push innovation induce business process modifications. These variations are conducted to align business processes in the light of changing software structures.

"With [the packaged software], we are highly restricted to what the software offers (...) When software change takes place, we get the opportunity to reassess our processes. (...) Frequently, this leads to process adaptations." Key-User, ALPHA-FINANCE
"Software drives our processes more than our processes drive software. (...) Our standard software offers certain processes and it is in our interest to adapt to these processes." IT Manager, ALPHA-FINANCE

The IT manager at ALPHA-FINANCE conveyed that technological push innovation is accountable for preventing the company from the occurrence of software structure misfits.

"The releases [provided by the vendor] are necessary to ensure our ability to act in conformance with the law. (...) We get those releases on the first of January and the first of July each year because – in general – these are the dates when new laws for health insurance companies come into force." IT Manager, ALPHA-FINANCE

By relying on a pioneer innovator gestalt, ALPHA-FINANCE's ERP system was found to be in line with business process structures. This situation results in a positive impact on business process performance.

"[The ERP system] supports the efficiency and effectiveness of our processes. Efficiency is always influenced by software. In our case, the influence is very strong. There are two key aspects when talking about efficiency: First, the agent who works with this software. How efficiently can he or she navigate through the software and how fast does he or she get the information he or she needs. How intuitive is the software? How many steps does he or she need to do a certain task. A second point of efficiency is: How much – we call it bad processing – can the software prevent? How good are the plausibility checks, etc. (...) That is what we get from the software. So that is why this software is essential for us." Key User, ALPHA-FINANCE

In addition, the established fit situation impacts sourcing performance. As stated by ALPHA-FINANCE, the chosen gestalt related to its deployment of the ERP system positively impacts IT efficiency.

"We only need a few people for software maintenance." IT Manager, ALPHA-FINANCE
"IT efficiency is influenced significantly. (...) In the end, it must be said that the economic benefits are just great." IT Manager, ALPHA-FINANCE
"The advantage is: The software is always developed proactively by the vendor. So we do not have to worry about it." Key User, ALPHA-FINANCE

To sum up, changes in the macro environment are encountered with external technology push innovations in the form of new software releases in a private cloud, which in turn trigger significant business process adaptations in the client firm. Given that the software structure changes offered by the external vendor are able to highly match the legislator's demands, the client firm does not require a high level of software customisability. Environmental change, software structure change, and business process change are highly congruent in this situation, yielding empirical evidence for the Pioneer Gestalt (see also Fig. 10).

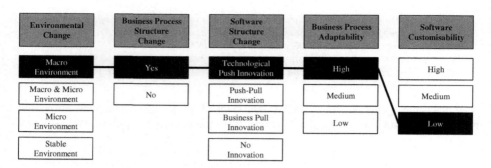

Fig. 10. Exemplification of the Pioneer Gestalt at ALPHA-FINANCE

4.2 Cautious Gestalt

An example of a Cautious Gestalt is given by BETA-FINANCE. This firm is a leading international provider of tangible assets in the areas of real estate and aviation with a total investment volume of more than 15 billion Euros. Looking at the CRM process, the company is primarily impacted by shifts in the imposed firm context. Constant changes within the legal framework influence BETA-FINANCE indirectly. In particular, these changes do not affect the financial service provider itself but their clients and thereby the company's financial products.

> *"As mentioned before, we are in a niche segment. That means, we form the end of the entire investment portfolio. We always had a market environment with only few competitors. Since the financial crisis in 2009 and 2010, the number of competitors has decreased. But nevertheless there are a couple of key players on the market that compete with us. (...) Most of the changes that we have to face are regulatory ones. The legislation – especially in our market segment – is in a permanent flow. (...) These legal changes impact us indirectly. That means, we have to adapt our service offerings. (...) To give you another example: From the 90 s of last century until the early 2000s, our products were rather a tax saving opportunity for wealthy customers. They could spread their tax charges over many years." CIO, BETA-FINANCE*

These legal changes influence BETA-FINANCE's idiosyncratic offerings. With each regulatory change, BETA-FINANCE has to adapt its financial products and, thereby, its CRM process.

> *"Regulatory changes impact our clients. This, in turn, means that we have to adapt our financial products and our CRM process." CIO, BETA-FINANCE*

The required software structure change of the on-premises CRM system relies on pure business pull innovation. *No vendor-driven software structure changes occurred in more than one decade.*

> *"Of course there is this entirely new version of the system available on the market, but we are not going to implement it; at least not before 2015. That would then be the first major disruption of the package. In fact, it would be like implementing a whole new system. You can certainly take over some of the things we have, but it would be the first upgrade in eleven or twelve years." CIO, BETA-FINANCE*

"We conduct all adjustments of the CRM system ourselves. That is the most important thing for us (...) You simply have to know the system well." CIO, BETA-FINANCE

This internally executed software structure change is supported by a high customisability of the on-premises enterprise system. The interviewee at BETA-FINANCE reported on multiple opportunities to adapt the system according to the company's very specific needs.

"This is why we have decided in favour of this system. It is completely parameterizable without traditional programming or development activities. That means that I can control workflows, extensions, and the entire business logic of it with a simple parameterizing tool. This is manageable with simple technical IT know-how. (...) That – ultimately – is the crucial strength of our CRM system." CIO, BETA-FINANCE

A high level of software customisability supports the financial service provider in rapidly addressing required software structure changes as a result of shifts within the imposed firm context. Thereby, the company avoids the occurrence of deficiencies within their on-premises CRM system.

"So, every regulatory change finds a complete echo within the system. From a system's side, changing competition and the regulatory environment influence us intensively. (...) Timeliness is the most important thing for us. So, these changes often occur very short-dated. Due to the fact that all of these changes impact our funding concepts, it has to be implemented within a few days. As you have already heard, it is simply not acceptable that we cannot get a fund on the market on time due to technical reasons. That is an absolute 'no go'" CIO, BETA-FINANCE

By relying on a Cautious Gestalt, BETA-FINANCE's ERP system is in line with its business process structure. The software helps to address constant environmental changes in a timely manner. This has a positive impact on the efficiency and effectiveness of BETA-FINANCE's CRM process.

"The CRM system supports efficiency and effectiveness of our processes. Take the following example: A large international banking house decides to distribute an Airbus A380. That means, we talk about 300 to 350 million Euros. Imagine the amount of data that has to be handled if they decide to issue a public fund with a minimum amount of 10,000 Euros. (...) Once the partner [banking institution] agreed to sign a contract with us, we typically have less than two weeks to get the fund on the market. That means we change the system to support our sales processes. (...) So yes, the software contributes to efficiency and effectiveness of our sales process." CIO, BETA-FINANCE

Looking at sourcing performance, software-business process fit impacts outcomes related to BETA-FINANCE's IT function. The CRM system positively influences strategic benefits because it enables BETA-FINANCE to be faster than its competitors with respect to highly customer specific financial products and services, economic benefits in terms of gaining economies of scale through automation, and technological benefits by reducing the risk of cost explosions and technological obsolescence.

"And within our system, we can perfectly perform all these [required changes] ourselves. Actually, we can meet every interface requirement – no matter how obscure it is – relatively fast and with very small IT capabilities. So I would conclude: 'No matter what you need, you get it in less than two weeks." CIO, BETA-FINANCE

"The software meets all our expectations. I am also responsible for business organisation in my company. So I am aware of what is going on in the market. So far, we were able to satisfy all those requirements from changing business processes in a very, very effective manner." CIO, BETA-FINANCE

"From an economic point of view, we are highly satisfied with the system. We have been using this system for more than ten years now. We made several large adaptations to it without having any costs for external programmers and without having high development costs. This is just great." CIO, BETA-FINANCE

To sum up, changes in the micro environment require changes in the business process structure which are tackled with internal business (demand) pull innovations in the form of software customisations in the utilized on-premises CRM system. With the help of the rapid internal software customisations, the client firm is able to respond effectively to the highly specific business partner needs. Thus, the example of BETA-FINANCE provides empirical evidence for the Cautious Gestalt (see also Fig. 11).

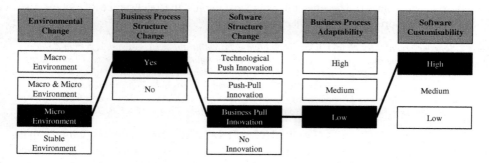

Fig. 11. Exemplification of the Cautious Gestalt at BETA-FINANCE

4.3   Ambidextrous Gestalt

BETA-MANUFACTURING is a medium-sized provider of foam plastics within the automotive, the construction, and the transportation industry. With a workforce of approximately 350 employees, the German-based company realized an annual turnover of more than 30 million Euros in 2013. While being active in different industries, the BETA-MANUFACTURING's key accounts are large global car manufacturers. One impetus for structural change has come from these companies. As reported by the CIO, key accounts constantly demand for software and business process adaptations that have to be implemented immediately. Besides such shifts within the imposed firm context, BETA-MANUFACTURING experiences several changes within their imposed country context throughout the year. As a consequence, the provider of foam plastics is impacted by both, micro and macro environmental changes.

"Our market segment is quite challenging. We are a supplier within the automotive industry. Automotive companies are very huge organisations. (...) Automotive companies have very high and complex requirements with respect to quality, documentation, and several other things. (...) Nowadays, we do not only deliver products, we also deliver information to Daimler, BMW, and

all the other companies. (...) We have to keep pace with changing electronic data transfer requirements of the automotive companies. In recent years, this is getting more and more challenging. For instance, in 1988, Daimler asked whether we could deliver some information electronically. Back in the days, electronic data transfer was a foreign word for us, so we told them: 'Yes, we take care of it and we will get back to you in one and a half years. Today, they say we need this or that change and you have fourteen days to get your system ready." CIO, BETA-MANUFACTURING*

"There are a lot of legal changes throughout the year. Especially in the area of human resources." CIO, BETA-MANUFACTURING*

These macro and micro environmental shifts force BETA-MANUFACTURING to adapt its business processes frequently. The interviewee reported that changes in the structure of their business processes occurred more often in recent years.

"We have to adapt ourselves to changing requirements quite often. Such changes occur more frequently nowadays and it is even getting worse. (...) It is getting more complex. Often, when an automotive company demands for a particular adaptation to our [ERP system], our business units have to work differently because they have to provide other data or something like that." CIO, BETA-MANUFACTURING*

An on-premises ERP system was implemented by BETA-MANUFACTURING in 2000. Since that time, software structure change has been realized by combining technology push innovation with business pull innovation. All ERP updates available are implemented by BETA-MANUFACTURING. However, due to micro environmental changes within the imposed firm context, the provider of foam plastics has to perform client-driven software adaptations as well.

"(...) there are 'Enhancement Packages' adding new features to the current version. (...) We implement all these 'Enhancement Packages' available." CIO, BETA-MANUFACTURING*

"From time to time, we have to adapt the system. (...) If necessary, we do some reprogramming. (...) That is always a huge effort for us." CIO, BETA-MANUFACTURING*

A medium level of software customisability supports business pull innovation. BETA-MANUFACTURING ramped up their internal IT capabilities in order to perform those required software structure changes.

"Last year, we learned that we had too little knowledge to make all those modifications to [the ERP system] that we would require. So we hired an additional [ERP system] programmer, who had several years of experience with the software. Since then, we have been able to make lots of adaptations on our own." CIO, BETA-MANUFACTURING*

At the same time, business process adaptability was found to be high at BETA-MANUFACTURING. The interviewee reported that business processes are rather adjusted to the inherent software standard than vice versa.

"Our philosophy is to stick as close as possible to the standard. We rather adapt ourselves than [the ERP system]. (...) We use a lot of the standard functionalities. (...)" CIO, BETA-MANU-FACTURING*

BETA-MANUFACTURING is highly satisfied with the dynamic nature of their on-premises ERP system. Vendor-driven software structure change in combination with client-driven software structure change prevents the company from suffering from deficiencies.

"In the face of a potential production line standstill of our clients, we have to adapt our ERP system immediately. Our all-time record was that we did 800 kilometres in three hours. We got a call from the Hungarian site of one of our clients that all of our goods were consumed. We had three hours to deliver the raw materials to this site. We did it, but it was very expensive. There are a lot of these situations where something goes wrong, which could get expensive for us. So it is a good thing that we can adapt the system quite fast in order to prevent such things in the future. (...) [The software vendor] provides lots of updates when there are bugs within the system or if a new legislation comes into force." CIO, BETA-MANUFACTURING

Consequently, BETA-MANUFACTURING has been able to carefully orchestrate the advantages of technology push and demand pull. Software add-ons from the external vendor help to respond to changes in the macro environment, while internal software customisations address idiosyncratic change requirements from business partners, in particular the OEM. Thus, software structure is in line with business process structure, which contributes to business process performance.

"Processes became more agile and easier to handle (...) The biggest advantage of [the ERP system] is the automation within the production and the delivery department. It is way easier to link our internal units with those units of our clients." CIO, BETA-MANUFACTURING

The interviewee has been satisfied with the technological benefits of their on-premises ERP system. The technology push innovation dimension reduces the risk of software obsolescence at BETA-MANUFACTURING in this Ambidextrous Gestalt.

"It is no longer how it was once. [The software vendor] improved its update strategy. In the past, we got a new release every second or third year. Now there are 'Enhancement Packages' adding new features to the current version. This is way easier for us, because we get these updates more often." CIO, BETA-MANUFACTURING

A somewhat different picture was found with respect to the outcome of this approach. The interviewee reported no increase in the organisations' IT competence with respect to the external sourcing of the on-premises ERP system. In addition, client-driven software structure change turned out to be complex and resource consuming for BETA-MANUFACTURING, indicating that such a strategy requires additional resources. Only if the invested resources for idiosyncratic software structure customisation yield positive outcomes, the Ambidextrous Gestalt can be justified. Instead of focusing on its core competencies, BETA-MANUFACTURING has to focus on its IT resources as well.

"Our IT competence did not increase. Of course, it is quite difficult to assess what would have been if there was a crisis, but I think we could have managed it with the old software as well (...) If we have to move one comma within the system, we need three man-days. Like I said, the system offers a lot of opportunities for us to adapt it to our needs, but we have to make changes at multiple locations within the system simultaneously and this is a huge effort for us." CIO, BETA-MANUFACTURING

Looking at the economic outcomes, the CIO at BETA-MANUFACTURING has provided evidence that the company is not able to perform all required software structure changes internally. In some situations, external consultants have to support the firm's IT unit, which is quite costly.

"Often, the software lacks important features and we have to build them on our own. To give you an example – despite the fact that we sourced the automotive version of [the ERP system]

– form printouts are really bad within the system. In fact, dozens of forms are missing, (...) In such situations, we hire external consultants and this is really expensive." CIO, BETA-MANU-FACTURING

To sum up, changes in the macro *and* micro environment are encountered with external technology push innovations in the form of new software add-ons as well as internal software customisations. This is the reason why this gestalt can be considered as ambidextrous. Changes in the macro logic of the software are provided by the vendor with the help of short release cycles. Changes in the micro logic according to idiosyncratic requirements of business partners are absorbed by internal software patches. Thus, the vendor provides a structural framework for internal customisations. The changes in the macro logic may have a profound impact on the adaptability of the firm's business processes, whereas the degree of software customisability is medium, since the major software structure changes are left to the vendor. The resulting pattern of BETA-MANUFACTURING is visualized in Fig. 12.

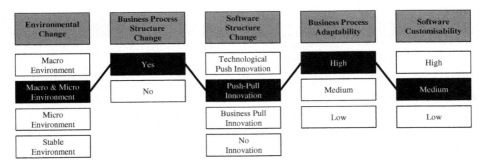

Fig. 12. Exemplification of the Ambidextrous Gestalt at BETA-MANUFACTURING

4.4   Conservative Gestalt

ALPHA-ASSOCIATION is a German-based sports federation. The company has jurisdiction on a league system and is responsible for the management and execution of national and international sport events. Looking at the CRM process, the sports federation was found to be in a very stable market position. Due to its quasi-monopolistic position, ALPHA-ASSOCIATION does not have to face competition on the domestic market with respect to organizing events and selling tickets. The interviewee reported that neither micro nor macro environmental shifts serve as impetus for structural change.

"We are in a very stable and static market. (...) We do not have any competitors in our domestic market." CIO, ALPHA-ASSOCIATION

As a consequence of ALPHA-ASSOCIATION's stable market position, no change to the structures of the company's CRM process occurs. The interviewee reported on structural persistence since the completion of the software implementation phase.

"We do not have to adapt to any market changes." CIO, ALPHA-ASSOCIATION

An on-premises CRM system was implemented. This system is responsible for supporting the business in managing marketing campaigns, in selling tickets, and in realizing cross-selling potentials. ALPHA-ASSOCIATION neither underwent technology push innovation, nor business pull innovation of software structures. Their on-premises CRM system was adapted to the company's very specific needs during the implementation phase. An external consulting firm executed these adaptations. This consulting firm was eventually phased-out by entering the assimilation phase (Swanson and Ramiller 2004). No further software structure changes are intended.

"We were supported by a consulting company [during system implementation phase]. This company was responsible for project management and especially for change management. (...) We phased-out the consulting firm. (...) We have not changed the system since that time." CIO, ALPHA-ASSOCIATION

The interviewee reported no deficiencies. Due to the absence of business process structure change, the initial software structure adaptation in the software implementation phase is still sufficient.

"The initial analysis [of our processes] was very intensive. This supported us in communicating change requests to the software vendor and the consulting firm. (...) In the end, we got what we needed." CIO, ALPHA-ASSOCIATION

ALPHA-ASSOCIATION provides an example of a Conservative Gestalt. Non-existence of environmental change, business process structure change, and software structure changes have induced no need for software customisations as well as business process adaptations. In this stable environment, ALPHA-ASSOCIATION's CRM system adds to the performance of the supported business process.

"For instance, several employees contacted the same customers about the same marketing campaign. That is something that we can better manage and control now (...) So, these [ticketing] processes had been executed manually before implementing the CRM software." CIO, ALPHA-ASSOCIATION

In addition, the CRM system positively impacts sourcing performance. The system has increased IT competence of the sports federation. Moreover, ALPHA-ASSOCIATION established a new technological agenda and increased software landscape's interoperability by linking its CRM system to a novel database system provided by the software vendor. Thereby, the company is able to handle a large number of customer data records while increasing its own efficiency.

"In the past, our ticketing was operated by an external partner. We had no possibility to integrate it into our ERP system." CIO, ALPHA-ASSOCIATION
"And I am convinced that we achieved an economic benefit simply through the structure of our entire data." CIO, ALPHA-ASSOCIATION
"We are a flagship project of [the software vendor] because we are the first company that runs [the CRM system] on [software vendor's novel database system]. The system helps us to handle our customer data." CIO, ALPHA-ASSOCIATION

By relying on a Conservative Gestalt, the software structure of ALPHA-ASSOCIATION is in line with its business process structure. It was found that the CRM system contributes to business process performance as well as sourcing performance in terms of technological benefits. The resulting pattern of ALPHA-ASSOCIATION is visualized in Fig. 13.

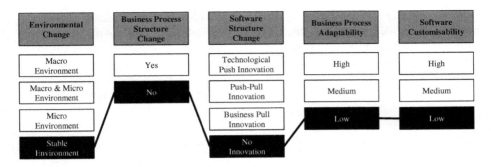

Fig. 13. Exemplification of the Conservative Gestalt of ALPHA-ASSOCIATION

5   Software Sourcing Modes and Software Sourcing Gestalts

In order to further demonstrate the viability of software sourcing gestalts, we will subsequently analyse its association with sourcing modes. The idea is to better understand whether sourcing modes fit the four gestalts which reflect meaningful combinations of IT and organisational resources in response to changing forces in the environment.

In order to analyse this association, we will conduct two types of analysis. First, we will relate the software sourcing modes to patterns from our empirical data. If the cases are reflecting one of the four suggested combinations, we refer to them as gestalts. If this is not the case, i.e., the pattern observed contradicts the suggested logic, we will classify them as non-gestalts. Second, in order to get a more thorough view, we will extract the four specific gestalts and associate them directly with the respective software sourcing mode. In doing so, we will apply Chi-Square tests in order to understand whether there is a significant relationship between the variables involved.

The contingency table of software sourcing modes and gestalt patterns can be found in Table 6. The 2 * 3 matrix indicates that 20 out of 44 cases analysed reflect patterns where the business structure and software structure is well aligned with its salient environmental forces. The relationship between these two categorical variables is not significant (Chi-Square = 1.305, Significance Level = 0.521).

Table 6. Assocation of software sourcing modes and gestalts/non-gestalts

	Gestalts	Non-gestalts	Total
On-demand	6	9	15
On-premises	10	13	23
In-house	4	2	6
Total	20	24	44

From this finding we can conclude that the analysed firms do not follow meaningful patterns of IT and organisational resources, which we refer to as gestalts or non-gestalts to software sourcing modes.

If we now take a closer look at the identified gestalts, our analysis yields a 3 * 4 table, which indicates the association of the four distinct gestalt types and the software sourcing modes (see Table 7). Based on this analysis, however, it becomes evident that the majority of Pioneer Gestalts favour on-demand software sourcing modes whereas Ambidextrous Gestalts do solely deploy enterprise systems in an on-premises mode. Furthermore, Cautious Gestalts deploy on-premises and in-house modes, whereas Conservative Gestalts inhibit all types of software sourcing modes.

Table 7. Assocation of software sourcing modes and specific gestalt types

	Pioneer	Ambidex-trous	Cautious	Conser-vative	Total
On-demand	5			1	6
On-premises	2	5	2	1	10
In-house			3	1	4
Total	7	5	5	3	20

The relationship is significant (Chi-Square = 17.092, Significance Level = 0.009), but is has to be noted that our results have to be treated with some caution since 20 % of the expected frequencies are smaller than five due to a too small data set. On this basis, we can prudently assert that there is an association between the deployed software sourcing modes and the postulated gestalts. Those firms that come up with gestalts, i.e., meaningful arrangements of IT and organisational resources to absorb changes from the environment, deploy different software sourcing modes.

6   Discussion

Contributions. The findings presented are among the first ones that analyse three different software sourcing modes in one study on a comprehensive empirical basis. Previous studies had been rather conceptual in nature or did focus on one software sourcing mode only. Furthermore, we drew on Institutional Theory as a conceptual framework for understanding complex arrangements of IT resources and complementary organisational resources. We described these arrangements as gestalts and we have been able to elaborate that these patterns attempt to absorb changing environmental forces. Those organisations, which were able to respond to environmental changes with coherent patterns of IT and organisational resources were referred to as gestalts. Based on different environmental forces, we identified four meaningful and comprehensive gestalts. Furthermore, we were able to demonstrate that different gestalt types are associated with different sourcing modes. Although this has to be treated with some caution due to a small data set, we believe that this key finding is quite novel and intriguing in the light to the extant literature. We also assume that we have been providing an explanatory logic for these phenomena.

Limitations. As almost every empirical study, we have to report some inherent limitations. First, the companies involved resided in Germany, Austria, and Switzerland. Thus, we are not fully able to repudiate a certain cultural bias of our results. Second, although our gestalts followed the conceptualisations of Institutional Theory as well as IT Business Value, their structure and composition followed a qualitative, i.e., subjective approach. Third, due to quantitative limitations in our data set, the association between the four gestalts presented and the prevailing software sourcing modes has to be treated with some caution. Finally, demonstrating certain levels of fit between software sourcing modes and software sourcing gestalts is probably not a merit of its own. We have not yet analysed how congruent patterns of sourcing modes and gestalts impact certain outcome measures like business process performance. This has to be conducted in the future.

7 Summary and Outlook

Our intention was to explore and reveal software sourcing gestalts, which are associated with software sourcing modes. Thus, we deduced four gestalt types based on the arguments of the institutional logic and demonstrated the empirical viability of the proposed patterns. In addition, we linked these gestalt patterns to software sourcing modes. We used a data set of 44 case studies to corroborate the existences of software sourcing gestalts as well as their association with software sourcing modes.

We are confident that our study offers significant potential for further analyses. First, we plan to explore the fit properties from a time variant, i.e., dynamic perspective. We intend to study gestalt changes over time in order to find out how firms are (not) able to achieve a dynamic fit [54]. Second, we want to understand whether higher levels of fit between software sourcing modes and gestalts have an impact on outcome measures, following the conceptualisations of Melville et al. [9]. In other words, software sourcing gestalts are not considered as a value per se but are likely to represent a complex arrangement of IT resources and complementary organisational resources which induce a higher level of IT business value, in particular better business process performance.

References

1. Cotteleer, M.J., Bendoly, E.: Order lead-time improvement following enterprise information technology implementation: an empirical study. MIS Q. **30**(3), 643–660 (2006)
2. Koslowski, T., Strüker, J.: ERP-On-demand-plattform: komplementäreffekte am beispiel eines nachhaltigkeits-benchmarking-dienstes. Wirtschaftsinformatik **53**(6), 347–356 (2011)
3. Lacity, M.C., Willcocks, L.P.: Strange bedfellows no more: researching business process outsourcing and dynamic innovation. In: Forth International Conference on the Outsourcing of Information Systems (ICOIS), no 2013
4. Stuckenberg, S., Kude, T., Heinzl, A.: Understanding the role of organizational integration in developing and operating Software-as-a-Service. J. Bus. Econ. **84**(8), 1019–1050 (2014)

5. Sia, S., Soh, C.: An assessment of package-organisation misalignment: institutional and ontological structures. Eur. J. Inf. Syst. **16**(5), 568–583 (2007)
6. Strong, D.M., Volkoff, O.: Understanding organization-enterprise system fit: a path to theorizing the information technology artifact. MIS Q. **34**(4), 731–756 (2010)
7. Cao, L.: The misalignment between packaged enterprise systems and chinese context: a context study of packaged ES adoption in China. In: Pacific Conference on Information Systems (PACIS), no. 1, pp. 1596–1603 (2010)
8. Maurer, C., Berente, N., Goodhue, D.: Are enterprise system related misfits always a bad thing?. Hawaii Int. Conf. Syst. Sci., 4652–4661 (2012)
9. Melville, N., Kraemer, K., Gurbaxani, V.: Review: information technology and organizational performance: an integrated model of IT business value. MIS Q. **28**(2), 283–322 (2004)
10. Dehning, B., Richardson, V.J.: Returns on investments in information technology: a research synthesis. J. Inf. Syst. **16**(1), 7–30 (2002)
11. Houdeshel, G., Watson, H.J.: The management information and decision support (MIDS) system at lockheed-georgia. MIS Q. **11**(1), 127–141 (1987)
12. Shang, S., Seddon, P.B.: Assessing and managing the benefits of enterprise systems: the business manager's perspective. Inf. Syst. J. **12**(4), 271–299 (2002)
13. Ranganathan, C., Brown, C.V.: ERP investments and the market value of firms: toward an understanding of influential ERP project variables. Inf. Syst. Res. **17**(2), 145–161 (2006)
14. Schwarz, A., Jayatilaka, B., Hischheim, R., Goles, T.: A conjoint approach to understanding IT application services outsourcing. J. Assoc. Inf. Syst. **10**(10), 748–781 (2009)
15. Zhang, J., Seidmann, A.: Perpetual versus subscription licensing under quality uncertainty and network externality effects. J. Manag. Inf. Syst. **27**(1), 39–68 (2010)
16. Scott, W.R.: The adolescence of institutional theory. Adm. Sci. Q. **32**(4), 493–511 (1987)
17. Soh, C., Sia, S.: An institutional perspective on sources of ERP package-organisation misalignments. J. Strateg. Inf. Syst. **13**(4), 375–397 (2004)
18. DiMaggio, P.J., Powell, W.W.: The iron cage revisited: institutional isomorphism and collective rationality in organizational fields. Am. Sociol. Rev. **48**(2), 147–160 (1983)
19. Maltz, E., Kohli, A.K.: Market intelligence dissemination across functional boundaries. J. Mark. Res. **33**(1), 47–61 (1996)
20. van der Aalst, W., Hee, K.: Workflow Management: Models, Methods, and Systems. MIT Press, Cambridge (2004)
21. Davenport, T.H., Stoddard, D.B.: Reengineering: business change of mythic proportions? MIS Q. **18**(2), 121–127 (1994)
22. Berente, N., Yoo, Y.: Institutional contradictions and loose coupling: postimplementation of NASA's enterprise information system. Inf. Syst. Res. **23**(2), 376–396 (2012)
23. Jones, M.R., Karsten, H.: Giddens's structuration theory and information systems research. MIS Q. **32**(1), 127–157 (2008)
24. Blum, H.S.: Logistik-Contolling. Kontext, Ausgestaltung und Erfolgswirkungen. Deutscher Universitätsverlag, Wiesbaden (2006)
25. Brehm, L., Heinzl, A., Markus, L.: Tailoring ERP systems: a spectrum of choices and their implications. In: Hawaii International Conference on System Sciences (HICSS) (2001)
26. Carmel, E., Sawyer, S.: Packaged software development teams: what makes them different? Inf. Technol. People **11**(1), 7–19 (1998)
27. Davern, M.J., Kauffman, R.J.: Discovering potential and realizing value from information technology investments. J. Manag. Inf. Syst. **16**(4), 121–143 (2000)

28. Kim, D.J., Yue, K.B., Hall, S.P., Gates, T.: Global diffusion of the internet XV: web 2.0 technologies, principles, and applications: a conceptual framework from technology push and demand pull perspective. Commun. Assoc. Inf. Syst. **24**, 657–672 (2009)

29. Lin, A., Chen, N.C.: Cloud computing as an innovation: percepetion, attitude, and adoption. Int. J. Inf. Manage. **32**(2012), 533–540 (2012)

30. Yang, J., Papazoglou, M.P.: Interoperation support for electronic business. Commun. ACM **43**(6), 39–47 (2000)

31. Tatikonda, M.V., Montoya-Weiss, M.M.: Integrating operations and marketing perspectives of product innovation: the influence of organizational process factors and capabilities on development performance. Manage. Sci. **47**(1), 151–172 (2001)

32. Barney, J.B.: Firm resources and sustained competitive advantage. J. Manage. **17**(1), 99–120 (1991)

33. Mata, F.J., Fuerst, W.L., Barney, J.B.: Information technology and sustained competitive advantage: a resource-based analysis. MIS Q. **19**(4), 487–506 (1995)

34. Lacity, M.C., Solomon, S., Yan, A., Willcocks, L.P.: Business process outsourcing studies: a critical review and research directions. J. Inf. Technol. **26**(4), 221–258 (2011)

35. Wang, E., Ju, P., Jiang, J.J., Klein, G.: The effects of change control and management review on software flexibility and project performance. Inf. Manag. **45**(7), 438–443 (2008)

36. Benlian, A., Hess, T., Buxmann, P.: Drivers of SaaS-adoption – an empirical study of different application types. Bus. Inf. Syst. Eng. **1**(5), 357–369 (2009)

37. Winkler, T., Brown, C.: Horizontal allocation of decision rights for on-premise applications and software-as-a-service. J. Manag. Inf. Syst. **30**(3), 13–48 (2014)

38. Wertheimer, M.: Laws of organization in perceptual forms. First published as Untersuchungen zur Lehre von der Gestalt II. Psycologische Forschung, 4, 301–350 (1923); Translation published in Ellis, W. (ed.) A Source Book of G. Psychology, pp. 71–88. Routledge & Kegan Paul, London (1938)

39. Ellis, V.D.: A Source Book of Gestalt Psychology. Harcourt, Brace & World, New York (1938)

40. Guillemette, M.G., Paré, G.: Towards a new theory of the contribution of the IT function in organizations. MIS Q. **36**(2), 529–551 (2012)

41. Yin, R.K.: Case Study Research - Design and Methods, 4th edn. Gage Inc., Thousand Oaks (2009)

42. Eisenhardt, K.M.: Building theories from case study research. Acad. Manag. Rev. **14**(4), 532–550 (1989)

43. Bacharach, S.B.: Organizational theories: some criteria for evaluation. Acad. Manag. Rev. **14**(4), 496–515 (1989)

44. Swanson, E.B., Ramiller, N.C.: Innovating mindfully with information technology. MIS Q. **28**(4), 553–583 (2004)

45. Grant, G.G.: Strategic alignment and enterprise systems implementation: the case of metalco. J. Inf. Technol. **18**(3), 159–175 (2003)

46. Swanson, E.B.: Information systems innovation among organizations. Manage. Sci. **40**(9), 1069–1092 (1994)

47. Kirsch, L.J.: Deploying common systems globally: the dynamics of control. Inf. Syst. Res. **15**(4), 374–395 (2004)

48. Chalmers, A.: What is this thing called Science?, 3rd edn. McGraw-Hill Education, United Kingdom (1999)

49. Myers, M.D.: Qualitative Research in Business and Management, 1st edn. Sage Publications Ltd, London (2009)

50. Patton, M.Q.: Qualitative Research and Evaluation Methods, 3rd edn. Sage Publications Ltd, Thousand Oaks (2002)
51. Miles, M.B., Huberman, M.A.: Qualitative Data Analysis: An Expanded Sourcebook. Sage Publications Ltd, Thousand Oaks (1994)
52. Niemann, F.: ERP aus der Cloud kommt langsam in Fahrt. Computerwoche (51–52), 14–15 (2013)
53. Roeder, F.C., Labrie, Y.: The private sector within a public health care system: the german example (2012)
54. Noehren, M., Heinzl, A., Kude, T.: Structural and behavioral fit in software sourcing alignment. In: 47th Hawaii Conference on System Sciences (HICSS), pp. 3949–3958 (2014)

Towards Model-Based Strategic Sourcing

Laleh Rafati[(✉)] and Geert Poels

Center for Service Intelligence, Faculty of Economics and Business
Administration, Ghent University, Tweekerkenstraat 2, 9000 Ghent, Belgium
{laleh.rafati,geert.poels}@UGent.be

Abstract. Strategic sourcing recognizes that procurement is not just a cost
function, but supports the firm's effort to achieve its long-term objectives.
Strategic sourcing has become a critical area of strategic management that is
centered on decision-making regarding an organization's procurement activities
such as spend analysis, capability sourcing, supplier selection and evaluation,
contract management and relationship management. Many companies face
challenges in obtaining the benefits associated with effective strategic sourcing.
From an organizational perspective, procurement data management is a core
organizational challenge for chief procurement officers (CPOs) for fact-based
strategic sourcing decision-making. To address this challenge, we define
research objectives to design a holistic view on strategic sourcing orientations
and to develop a conceptual basis for enabling centralization of procurement
data and enabling the systemic exploration of sourcing alternatives. From a
service ecosystem perspective as a holistic view on strategic sourcing, we define
a model driven approach to explore sourcing alternatives based on a common
language (C.A.R.S) that enables companies to achieve procurement data management and analytics competencies for fact-based decision-making.

Keywords: Model based strategic sourcing · Strategic sourcing and procurement · Service-dominant conceptual modeling · Procurement data management · Procurement analytics · Strategic sourcing decision-making · Fact-based
decision-making

1 Introduction

Procurement has gained importance in supply chain management due to factors such as
globalization, increased added value in the supply chain, and accelerated technological
change. Vice versa, the growing importance of supply chain management has led to an
increasing recognition of the strategic role of procurement [1]. Procurement has
evolved from mere buying into strategic sourcing [2, 3] and has recently been recognized as a critical driving force in the strategic management of supply chains [4–6].
Strategic sourcing recognizes that procurement is not just a cost function, but supports
the firm's effort to achieve its long-term objectives [7]. Strategic sourcing has become a
critical area of strategic management that is centered on decision-making regarding an
organization's procurement activities such as spend analysis, capability sourcing,
supplier selection and evaluation, contract management and relationship management.

© Springer International Publishing Switzerland 2015
I. Oshri et al. (Eds.): Global Sourcing 2015, LNBIP 236, pp. 29–51, 2015.
DOI: 10.1007/978-3-319-26739-5_2

Because of the increasing significance of procurement, strategic sourcing decisions become more important. Sourcing decisions are strategic decisions at the management level about finding opportunities for and delivering sustainable savings; choosing the right sourcing alternatives like outsourcing, insourcing and co-sourcing (i.e., the typical make-versus-buy decisions) to achieve (sustained) competitive advantage; selecting the right suppliers and evaluate their strategic and performance dimension for long-term and short-term partnerships; identifying solutions for mitigating supplier risk, improving supplier governance and enforcing supplier compliance. These decisions are critical for various procurement decision-makers such as chief procurement officers (CPOs), chief strategic officers (CSOs), strategic sourcing managers, category managers, product managers, purchasing managers, contract managers and supplier/customer relationship managers.

This chapter demonstrates how a model-based approach that we characterize as "service-dominant conceptual modeling" can support companies to achieve two key competencies, procurement data management and analytics, which allow moving the company toward fact-based strategic sourcing decision-making. The chapter is organized as follows: Sect. 2 describes the results of our literature review on fact-based decision-making in strategic sourcing and subsequently elaborates on our research objectives; Sect. 3 introduces the proposed approach to achieve these research objectives; Sect. 4 discusses the research methodology, which is Design Science Research; Sect. 5 introduces the theoretical foundation of the research as "the way of thinking"; Sect. 6 defines a strategic sourcing conceptualization and viewpoints as "the way of modeling"; Sect. 7 presents a model-based approach for exploring strategic sourcing alternatives as "the way of working"; and Sect. 8 outlines "the way of supporting" the proposed model-based strategic sourcing approach; Finally, Sect. 9 concludes the chapter.

2   Procurement Data Management and Analytics

To drive fact-based decision-making, organizations require two critical competencies, data management and data analytics. The data management competency is the ability to address issues of data architecture, extraction, transformation, movement, storage, integration, and governance. The data analytics competency is the ability to analyze data for answering key business questions through applying advanced techniques such as modeling (e.g. statistical, contextual, quantitative, predictive, cognitive, other emerging models), deep computing, simulation, data mining, and optimization. Procurement analytics uses procurement data systematically through techniques from applied analytical disciplines to drive strategic sourcing decision-making for planning, management, measurement and learning. Advanced procurement analytics provides the fuel for an organization to make better sourcing decisions faster [8, 9].

Many companies face challenges in obtaining the benefits associated with effective strategic sourcing. From an organizational perspective, procurement data management is a core organizational challenge for CPOs and CSOs [10, 11]. A number of businesses have insufficient accurate and timely information about their spending patterns and suppliers. Most businesses are challenged with spend analysis and need to manage vast volumes of internal and external supplier data due to the disparate nature of systems and data sources [10, 11]. With a large and increasingly global supply base and scattered data, most companies are overwhelmed with supplier information management and challenged to apply that information for procurement analytics to drive fact-based decision-making [12, 13].

Based on our literature review, we have analyzed the observed challenge in obtaining procurement data management and analytics competencies by identifying problems at different organizational layers of procurement and strategic sourcing (Fig. 1). The first organizational layer is the application layer that consists of various software applications and information systems such as Accounts Payable, ERP and SAP applications; corporate purchasing cards; e-Procurement and e-Auctions systems; and online RFx (i.e. RFI, RFP and RFQ) applications to support operational procurement activities. Our review indicates that, due to the disparate nature of these applications, procurement data is often scattered across disconnected and diverse systems and data sources. The second layer is the process layer that consists of key procurement activities for strategic sourcing such as spend management, sourcing management, supplier selection and evaluation, contract management and relational management. Here our review learns that not all procurement processes are adequately supported by applications resulting in data that is not available in electronic form for analysis. Further, as decision-making within these processes could be better supported, there is an opportunity to integrate analytics into procurement processes to enable accurate and quick action. The third organizational layer is the data layer, which should be the core layer in the architecture for managing procurement data such as spends data, sourcing data, supplier data, contract data and relational data. Our review indicates that there is a lack of platform to consolidate all sources of data from the application layer and the process layer to enable creative discovery and a lack of shared operational data store to accelerate the ability to ingest and analyze procurement data. The fourth, analytics layer of procurement includes techniques for spend analysis, cost-benefit analysis, market analysis, demand analysis, capability analysis and performance analysis, risk analysis and value chain analysis. This layer thus focuses on analyzing the procurement data and identifying the insights most likely to create a positive business impact. Here, due to the lack of advanced analytical techniques (e.g. descriptive, diagnose, predictive and prescriptive), tools and skills, procurement data cannot be translated into insights that can inform decision-making. Finally, the last layer is the decision layer that uses the insights derived from procurement data to create value for the organization. Here the need is felt to use visualization techniques to quickly understand and act on data for fact-based decision-making [8–10, 14].

To address the above organizational challenge and enable companies to obtain competencies with respect to procurement data management and procurement analytics, our research objectives have been defined as below:

Objective 1: Design a holistic view on strategic sourcing.

Objective 2: Develop a conceptual basis for enabling centralization of procurement data.

Objective 3: Develop a conceptual basis for enabling the systemic exploration and evaluation of strategic sourcing alternatives.

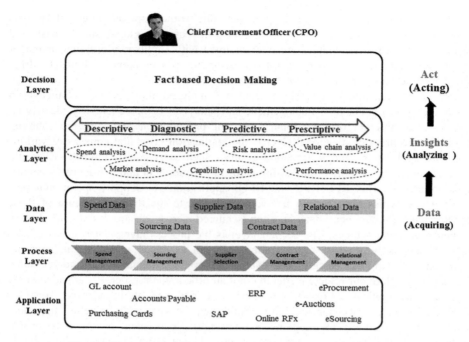

Fig. 1. Organizational layers of procurement and strategic sourcing

The first research objective is designing a holistic view on the multidimensional phenomenon of strategic sourcing. Eltantawy et al. (2014) [15] distinguish four strategic sourcing orientations: learning, performance, planning, and the relational orientation. The learning orientation focuses on exploiting opportunities for new capabilities and products through capability and resource analysis. This means learning about how a firm's internal capabilities and resources can be combined with external (supplier) capabilities and resources to create competitive advantage. The performance orientation focuses on exploiting opportunities for value creation and cost saving through cost-benefit analysis, spend analysis, value chain analysis, demand analysis, and market analysis in order to achieve bottom-line results (operational goals). The planning orientation focuses on defining sourcing objectives through strategic analysis in order to achieve long-term strategic goals. Finally, the relational orientation focuses on managing the supply base and structuring the supply network through strategic and performance analysis to maintain beneficial long-term and short-term relationships. A holistic view on strategic sourcing is needed to integrate these various strategic sourcing orientations, which is a prerequisite to develop solutions for the centralization of procurement data.

The second research objective is elaborating this holistic view into a conceptual basis for enabling the centralization of procurement data. Integration of procurement data from disparate sources and getting the data in the right form for analysis is a perennial challenge in organizations. A lot of time is wasted trying to collate data from various systems and cleansing and organizing it. A common language and model of procurement data facilitates such centralization that is required for efficient and effective data architecture, storage, extraction, integration, governance, and hence enabling companies to obtain competency in procurement data management.

The third research objective is a further elaboration of our solution for enabling a systemic exploration and evaluation of strategic sourcing alternatives. A systemic exploration is a prerequisite for identifying multiple strategic sourcing alternatives and choosing the right sourcing alternative. We define strategic sourcing alternatives according to the four strategic sourcing orientations as performance alternatives, learning alternatives, relational alternatives and planning alternatives. Performances alternatives are multiple options about spend costs, captured value (profit) and perceived value for what and by whom. Learning alternatives are various options based on the actor's abilities, capacities and assets to achieve (sustainable) competitive advantage by participation in a value network. Planning alternatives are options about sourcing objectives for operational, strategic, short-term and long-term goals. Finally, relational alternatives are procurement options for choosing suppliers for long-term and short-term partnerships and finding new customers to seize the market. Such systemic exploration is required for effective use of procurement data to compare and choose the right sourcing alternatives and support companies to obtain competency in procurement analytics.

3   Service-Dominant Conceptual Modeling

We present in this chapter a model-based strategic sourcing approach, which we characterize as *service-dominant conceptual modeling*, as the proposed solution approach for achieving our research objectives. The main properties of our solution approach can be described as follows:

– **Service ecosystem perspective as a holistic view on strategic sourcing orientations**: As will be explained in Sect. 5, we propose a service ecosystem perspective as a holistic view on complex sourcing interactions such as resource integration, capability configuration, service exchange, value creation and capture, innovation, competitive advantage, profitability and sustainability. The proposed view integrates various strategic sourcing orientations, which is a prerequisite to develop solutions for centralization of procurement data and systemic exploration of sourcing alternatives.

– **Strategic sourcing conceptualization for procurement data modeling:** We propose the construction of a conceptualization of strategic sourcing that can be used as a language for modeling procurement data. We designed the strategic sourcing conceptualization by referring to Service-Dominant Logic as the foundation theory of our service ecosystem perspective as will be explained in Sect. 5. Different kinds of procurement data (e.g. spend cost data, sourcing data, supplier data, contract data and relational data) can be identified based on the core procurement concepts and their attributes and relations. We believe that such identification through the proposed conceptualization based on an holistic view of strategic sourcing will help developing solutions for procurement data centralization, integration and standardization, thus enabling companies to achieve procurement data management competency.

– **Conceptual modeling as a way of exploring strategic sourcing alternatives:** We propose conceptual modeling as a technique for exploring strategic sourcing alternatives. We introduce conceptual models as schematic descriptions [16] of sourcing alternatives and apply the proposed conceptualization as a common language for describing these models. The exploration of the alternatives is systemic as the underlying conceptualization of the models offers a holistic view of strategic sourcing according to the various orientations (i.e. learning, planning, performance and relational). Through the proposed conceptual modeling of strategic sourcing alternatives, procurement data can be identified for evaluating the sourcing alternatives, which enables companies to achieve procurement analytic competency by applying model-based analytical techniques and tools.

The solution approach is described in the rest of the chapter according to the four different perspectives proposed by Seligmann et al. (1989) [17]: as a way of thinking (i.e. principles for a systemic view of strategic sourcing) which addresses the first research objective, as a way of modeling (i.e. conceptualization of strategic sourcing) which addresses (partially) the second research objective, as a way of working (model-based exploration of strategic sourcing alternatives) which addresses the second and third research objectives, and as a way of supporting (model-based analytical techniques and tools) which we present as future research to further address the third research objective.

4   Research Methodology

The research methodology that was applied to develop our solution approach was the Design Science Research Method (DSRM), which is the standard research methodology used in the Information Systems discipline for designing new artifacts that solve unsolved problems or improve upon existing solutions. Design science research artifacts include constructs, models, methods and instantiations of these [18]. Referring to the DSRM process model we distinguish the following research phases [19]: (1) **Problem Analysis Phase**: we conducted a literature review of theoretical and conceptual studies in various procurement and strategic sourcing domains to explore the research problem, justify the value of a solution, and define the research objectives. (2) **Solution Analysis Phase**: state-of-the-art Service Science research contributions to Strategic Sourcing [15, 20] and Information Systems research contributions to Strategic Management [21] were investigated to shape a solution approach that has the potential to address the research problem. (3) **Design and Demonstration Phase**: we designed a model-based approach that can be characterized as *service-dominant conceptual modeling* to achieve the research objectives. We developed a proof-of-concept case based on a literature review in the healthcare domain to demonstrate the use of the proposed approach for exploring strategic sourcing alternatives in an outsourcing scenario; (4) **Evaluation Phase**: the goal of this phase is to observe and measure how well the proposed approach supports companies to achieve procurement data management and analytics competencies for fact-based strategic sourcing decision-making. This evaluation will be performed through conducting case-study research. The evaluation phase is the next level of our research as we aim at translating our conceptual solution into a practical solution through the application of the envisioned tool support (part of our ongoing research). The current chapter is mainly focused on the first level of research (conceptual solution) through problem formulation, solution definition, design and demonstration, and a minimal scenario-based evaluation of the proposed conceptual solution.

In the remainder of this chapter, the emphasis is on the results of our Design Science Research study, which we present according to the four perspectives of Seligmann et al. (1989) [17] as discussed in the previous section.

5   Way of Thinking: Service Ecosystem

A systemic view on complex sourcing interactions (e.g. resourcing, capability configuration, service exchange and innovation, sustainability, value co-creation) is needed to integrate various strategic sourcing orientations (e.g. learning, planning, performance and relationship management orientations). Without such overview, it is difficult identifying the right procurement data and exploring various sourcing alternatives.

The interpretation of complex emerging phenomena is greatly facilitated by a systems view that synthesizes both a reductionist perspective (i.e. analyzing elements and their relations) and a holistic perspective (i.e. being capable of observing the whole) [22]. The Viable Systems Approach (vSa) is a Systems Theory that is linked to complexity theories and has been developed as a behavioral approach to interpret business and its interactions with the environment [23, 24]. A viable system is defined as a system that survives, that is both internally and externally balanced, and that has mechanisms and opportunities to develop and adapt, and hence to become more and more efficient within its environment [23, 24]. The vSa is also increasingly getting attention in service research due to their contribution to understanding complex phenomena of the service (eco)system such as resource integration, value co-creation, service exchange and win-win interactions [25, 26]. A service ecosystem is defined as a system of service systems connected (internally and externally) by mutual value creation interactions realized through service exchanges [27]. This ecosystem view is founded on Service-Dominant Logic (S-D Logic), which is an important theoretical framework for the study of service systems [28, 29]. The S-D Logic views (Fig. 2) a service system (SS) as a dynamic value co-creation configuration of resources, with at least one operant resource, that is connected internally and externally to other service systems by value propositions through service exchanges [30]. It highlights a paradigm shift away from the Goods-Dominant Logic (G-D Logic) in the service science. This paradigm shift from the G-D Logic to the S-D Logic implies a change in the service perspective from a static view to a dynamic view, which is formalized in the vSa as a structure-system approach [31, 32]. According to the vSa, the complex phenomena of a service system (e.g. resource integration, service exchange, value co-creation) can be observed from a dual perspective focusing on a structure-based view (StBV) or a systems-based view (SyBV). The StBV is a static and objective perspective that is useful for describing and measuring a phenomenon by focusing on its components and relations. The SyBV is a dynamic and subjective perspective that is useful for interpreting the dynamic nature of a phenomenon by focusing on its interactions [33].

Consequently, we apply a *service ecosystem perspective (founded on S-D Logic)* as a system-structure view *(according to vSa)* on complex strategic sourcing interactions at micro levels (e.g. dyadic exchange encounter), meso levels (e.g. local), and macro levels (e.g. global) [34]. According to this perspective, vSa provides a structure-system view on strategic sourcing to describe and interpret its static and dynamic nature (e.g. sourcing components, relations and interactions). Moreover, S-D Logic provides a framework for thinking more clearly about the service system and its role in competition [15] and survivability [35]. The traditional view on (tactical) sourcing was a G-D Logic view that suppliers and customers were merely senders and receivers of goods. On the contrary, today's view on (strategic) sourcing derives from value co-creation as a central premise to the S-D Logic [15].

A service ecosystem perspective of strategic sourcing introduces a way of thinking about strategic sourcing in terms of S-D Logic. We observe a clear similarity between S-D Logic concepts (Fig. 2) and strategic sourcing concepts, as defined below in Table 1 [20, 36–40].

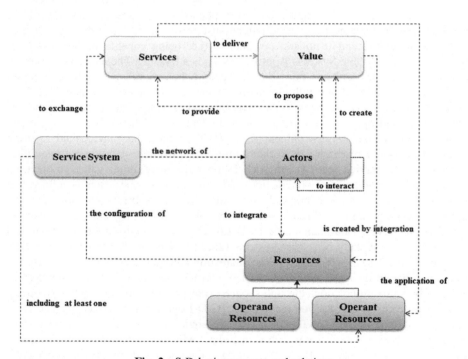

Fig. 2. S-D logic concepts and relations

Table 1. S-D logic and strategic sourcing mapping of concepts

S-D logic concepts	Strategic sourcing concepts
Operand Resources as usually tangible, static and passive resources that must be acted on to be beneficial, e.g., natural resources, goods, and money [30, 41].	**Resources** as the firm's assets that require action to make them valuable and beneficial for the firm to sustain competitive advantage. Strategic resources enable organizations to sustain competitive advantage, if the resources are Valuable, Rare, Inimitable, and Non-substitutable (VRIN) [42, 43].
Operant Resources as usually intangible, dynamic and active resources that act upon other resources to create benefits, e.g., knowledge, skills [30, 41]. They are the essential component of differentiation and the fundamental source of competitive advantage [20].	**Competencies** are the firm's specific strengths that allow a company to gain competitive advantage. *Threshold competencies* are needed to meet the necessary requirements to compete in a given market and achieve parity competitive advantage, whereas *distinctive competencies* allow the firm to achieve sustainable competitive advantage [44].
Service System as a configuration of resources (at least one operant resource) that is capable of providing benefit to other service systems and itself [30]. The ability to configure best in class operant resources from different organizations increases the ability to gain competitive advantage or increase viability.	**Capability** is a configuration of the firm's resources and competencies that makes the firm able to achieve and sustain competitive advantage. *Dynamic capabilities* are the firm's capacities and abilities to reconfigure its resource base internally and externally to achieve the sustainable competitive advantage [45]. Dynamic capability act on operational capabilities [46]. *Operational capabilities* can be broken into technical, administrative, and governance capabilities for producing and selling a defined (and static) set of products and services [47].
Service is the application of operant resources for the benefit of another party [30]; Service is the fundamental basis of value creation through economic exchange. *Competitive advantage* is a function of how one firm exchanges its services to meet the needs of the customer relative to how another firm exchanges its services" [20]. *Surviving* is a function of how the firm exchanges its services to be able to survive and thrive in its surrounding environment" [35]. Service is the primary source of competitive advantage and survivability. However,	**Service** is the application of competencies to achieve competitive advantage or survivability. *Competitive advantage* is the ability to create more economic value than competitors. It is a firm's profitability that is greater than the average profitability for all firms in its industry. Furthermore, *sustained competitive advantage* is a firm maintaining above average and superior profitability for a number of years [44]. The primary objective of strategic sourcing is to achieve a sustained competitive advantage (in a commercial domain) or survivability (in a noncommercial domain)

(Continued)

Table 1. (*Continued*)

S-D logic concepts	Strategic sourcing concepts
"the only true source of sustainable competitive advantage and survivability is the operant resources that make the service possible" [20].	which in turn results in superior profit or long-term viability.
Actors are engaged in the services exchange as value co-creators through *actor-to-actor (A2A) relations* [48] at the micro, meso, micro level [34, 49]. They are essentially doing the same thing: creating value for themselves and others through resource integration [50]. An actor can only offer a value proposition concerning some services and cannot solely create value for the beneficiary actor [41, 51].	**Supply chain members** as the focal firm, buyers, suppliers, internal customers and external customers are able to create value in the supply network through sourcing relations like supplier-buyer relationship and customer- provider relationship [15].
Value is an increase in the viability (survivability, well-being) of the system. Value comes from the ability to act in a manner that is beneficial to a party [52]. A *value proposition* establishes connections and relationships among actors [41, 51]. The process of co-creating value is driven by **value-in-use** (actualization), but mediated and monitored by **value-in-exchange** (capturing) [35].	**Perceived value** is defined by customers, based on their perceptions of the usefulness of the product on offer. **Exchange value** is realized when the product is sold. It is the amount paid by the buyer to the producer for the perceived value [53]. Strategic sourcing derives from value co-creation, which in the provider role serves as value proposition to customers, in the supplier role serves as value facilitation to customers, and in the customer role serves as value actualization [15].

As a result, to create a systemic procurement and strategic sourcing view, we consider the firm's organization as a system of interconnections and interdependencies (e.g. service exchange, capability configuration, resource integration and value creation), both internally (sub-systems) and externally (supra-systems) balanced, that has mechanisms (e.g. outsourcing, global sourcing and co-sourcing) and opportunities (e.g. learning, reconfiguration, seizing and sensing) to achieve (sustainable) competitive advantage and survivability. Therefore, we define sourcing as a strategic process for organizing and fine-tuning the focal firm's capabilities and resources internally and externally through A2A interactions (e.g. resource integration, capability configuration and service exchange) with suppliers, buyers, internal and external customers, at the different sourcing levels (e.g. local, international and global) to achieve (sustainable) competitive advantage or survivability, which in turn results in value as superior profit or long-term viability.

6   Way of Modeling: The C.A.R.S Conceptualization

Conceptual modeling is our proposed approach for exploring strategic sourcing alternatives in the four strategic sourcing orientations or decision areas of learning, performance, planning and relational management. Conceptual modeling [54] is a technique used in several research and application fields in Information Systems such as requirements engineering, database and information system design, knowledge management and enterprise modeling. Conceptual modeling has also been introduced in the Strategic Management and Business Model Innovation literature as a technique to generate business models [55]. To create conceptual models that describe sourcing alternatives, a domain-specific modeling language [16] for strategic sourcing is needed. Such language is defined by a conceptualization of the strategic sourcing domain and associated viewpoints that specify conventions for constructing and using different sourcing views. A view is a representation (i.e. conceptual model) of a system from the perspective of one or more decision makers to address specific concerns [56].

We introduce the C.A.R.S (Capability – Actor – Resource – Service) conceptualization as a language for strategic sourcing modeling. There is a clear mapping between the C.A.R.S concepts and core concepts of S-D Logic as we apply them in the way of thinking to strategic sourcing (Fig. 3). The C.A.R.S concepts capability, resource and competency are interpreted as their corresponding S-D Logic concepts, i.e. service system, operand resource and operant resource. We chose to retain the more specific strategic sourcing terminology instead of employing general S-D Logic terminology, though the meaning of the concepts is derived from S-D Logic. C.A.R.S further employs the service concept to interpret the primary objective of strategic sourcing that is competitive advantage or survivability. Furthermore, the actor notion is used to describe the role of the focal firm, suppliers, buyers and customers in a supply network for value co-creation. The C.A.R.S concepts are defined as follows:

- *Capability* is *'What the actor Can do'* for competitiveness and survivability. The capability notion can illustrate the abilities of firm, buyer and supplier to achieve long-term objectives. The capability of an actor represents its potential long-term effects on the achievement of sourcing objectives.
- *Actor* is *'Who is the Resource Integrator'* that provides service, proposes value, creates value and captures value.
- *Resource base* is *'What the actor Has'* that is capable to create value. The resource base notion includes tangible and static resources (e.g. goods), as well as intangible and dynamic resources (e.g. competencies and skills), hence both *resources* (i.e. S-D Logic operand resources) and *competencies* (i.e. S-D Logic operant resources) are included in the resource base.
- *Service* is *'What the actor Does'* that is exchanged with other actors for competitiveness and survivability. The service notion can illustrate the performance dimension of actors to achieve operational objectives (bottom-line results). Performance of an actor represents short-term effects on the achievement of sourcing objectives.

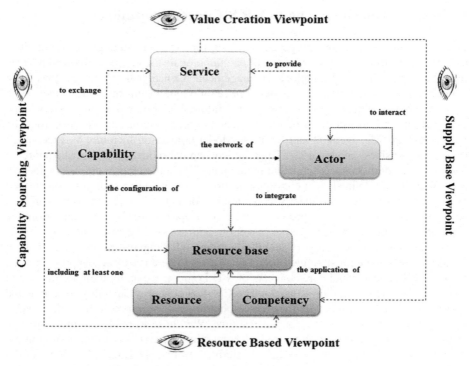

Fig. 3. C.A.R.S conceptualization and viewpoints

The C.A.R.S conceptualization is extended by considering viewpoints (Fig. 3) that relate to different strategic sourcing orientations and associated decision-making areas and decision-makers. The *value creation viewpoint* focuses on the firm's profitability that is derived by the participation of its network members to co-create value. The value creation viewpoint's concern is performance-oriented sourcing decisions about determining how much cost is being spent, with which suppliers, for what and by whom; how much value is perceived or captured, with whom, and for what. The *capability sourcing viewpoint* focuses on the firm's abilities (strategic dimension), its supplier's abilities and its customer's abilities to configure its resources and competencies internally and externally to achieve competitive advantage and to survive in a rapidly changing environment. The capability sourcing viewpoint's concerns are (a) learning-oriented sourcing decisions to choose the right sourcing alternatives like outsourcing, insourcing and co-sourcing (make-versus-buy decisions) to achieve (sustained) competitive advantage; (b) planning-oriented sourcing decisions about identifying sourcing objectives (e.g. cost saving, mitigating risk, ensuring delivery availability, enforcing compliance, driving innovation and making long-term partnership) and aligning these objectives with long-term organizational goals. The *resource based viewpoint* focuses on the firm-specific strengths (superior resources and core competencies) that are capable of creating value and allow a firm to gain competitive advantage. The resource based viewpoint's concern is learning-oriented sourcing decisions about integrating superior resources and turning into a specific benefit. Finally, the *supply base viewpoint* focuses on the firm's interactions with suppliers and internal and external customers to achieve long-term or short-term partnerships. This viewpoint's concern is relational-oriented sourcing decisions (a) to select the right suppliers and evaluate their strategic and performance dimensions for long term and short-term partnerships; (b) to find new customer to create more value and innovation.

The purpose of the C.A.R.S conceptualization and its viewpoints is to support strategic-sourcing decision-makers by offering a common language to model procurement data such as *spend data, sourcing data, supplier data, contract data* and *relational data* that reside in disparate systems and data sources. The capability notion, its attributes and other supplementary concepts defined in the capability sourcing viewpoint can be used to model the (strategic) sourcing data about outsourced, insourced and co-sourced capabilities, operational, organizational and technical capabilities and also data about capacities to leverage the existing resource base, to reconfigure the existing resource base, to integrate the resources, to develop new products and capabilities, to absorb the external resource base and to take advantage of market opportunities (adapting). The service notion, its attributes and other supplementary concepts defined in the value creation viewpoint can be used: (a) to model the performance (operational) data about the spend cost, the total cost of ownership, the transaction cost, the captured value (profit) and the perceived value; (b) to model the contract (operational) data about the quality of service, the service level agreements and the service delivery time, the contract's clauses, RFx (e.g. RFI, RFQ, RFP) and KPIs for evaluating supplier performance. The actor notion, its attributes and other supplementary concepts of the supply base viewpoint can be used to model the relational data about the suppliers and their classification such as registered, approved, active, partner, strategic partner, undesirable and blocked and also data about the (strategic and non-strategic) customers. The resource notion, its attributes and other supplementary concepts defined in the resource-based viewpoint can be used to model sourcing data about the internal and external resource base, interconnected resources, composite resources, threshold and distinctive competencies and VRIN resources.

The next section illustrates an instantiation of C.A.R.S based on an outsourcing scenario, employing a model driven approach as way of working.

7 Way of Working: Model Driven Approach

We propose a model driven approach to explore strategic sourcing alternatives in various orientations (e.g. learning, planning, performance and relational) for three distinct purposes: descriptive, predictive or prescriptive. In this paper, the proposed approach has been defined and limited by focusing on the upstream procurement activities (Fig. 4) from spend analysis to contracting- as the Source to Contract (S2C) process- that include spend analysis, sourcing management and relationship management.

According to the first step of S2C process, *category spend management* is a main sub-process of spend analysis to determine the category baseline spend costs and then identify potential cost saving opportunities. A category is a grouping of resources or

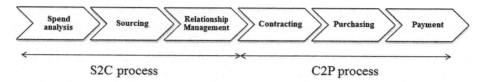

S2C process   C2P process

Fig. 4. Source to Contract (S2C) process Vs. Contract to Pay (C2P) process

services that have similar supply and usage characteristics to meet business objectives. In the second step, *capability sourcing* is a core sub-process of sourcing management to achieve sourcing goals and objectives. Capability sourcing is a course of action to execute strategic sourcing goals through gaining access to best-in-class capabilities in the value chain to achieve sourcing objectives such as increasing quality, capturing saving, mitigating risk, ensuring delivery availability, enforcing compliance, driving innovation and making long-term partnership [38–40, 57]. Finally, in the last step, *supplier lifecycle management* is a sub process of relationship management for supplier discovery, supplier engagement, supplier qualification, supplier performance management, and supplier classification and supplier risk assessment to achieve sourcing objectives such as supply base reduction, optimization and rationalization. Referring to the S2C process and its sub-processes, we define the model driven exploration based on the C.A.R.S conceptualization in three executive steps as below:

1. *Spend exploration* to determine how much cost is being spent, with whom, and for what.
2. *Sourcing exploration* to identify sourcing objectives and choose the right sourcing model alternatives (e.g. outsourcing, co-sourcing and insourcing) to achieve objectives through capability sourcing.
3. *Supply base exploration* to identify, evaluate and qualify of suppliers for long time or short time partnership.

We take a hypothetical case for illustrating our model-based exploration through a literature review [58–60] on strategic sourcing in the healthcare domain. Healthcare costs are increasing and hospitals are facing fierce competition to provide high quality services, continued lower operating margins, increased risks and potentially once-in-a-lifetime health care reform. With this backdrop, there is an increasing focus on supply chain management as a means to minimize risk, optimize operating costs, improve revenue, improve operating margins and hence enable the hospital to better serve the patient. Now more than ever, hospitals need strategic sourcing in order to survive within the sector. Strategic sourcing can play a key role in creating a more efficient hospital by decreasing the total cost of ownership of resources (e.g., capital equipment) through tracking the sales prices of equipment sold by suppliers; differentiating the hospital's services through hiring specialists and purchasing or renting equipment; improving supply chain management through decreasing negotiation times in the new vendors contracts by providing the necessary information to streamline the process; defining and reviewing the Preferred Supplier List; obtaining QDC objectives (Quality-Delivery-Cost) for all projects; managing strategic long-term relationships with the global suppliers. We focus our example to find cost saving opportunities in "Healthcare Information Management". The proposed model-driven approach should be able to support decision makers to answer the business questions as below through three executive exploration steps (e.g. spend exploration, sourcing exploration and supply base exploration) based on the C.A.R.S conceptualization.

- How much is being spent on "information system management" by the hospital?
- What could be the right sourcing model (e.g. outsourcing, co-sourcing and insourcing) of "information system management" for saving cost in the hospital?
- What should be the hospital's resource base that enables the hospital to have a core "information system management" capability to achieve sustainable competitive advantage?
- Who is the preferred provider for "information system management" in the hospital?

Step 1: Spend Exploration Based on the C.A.R.S Conceptualization. In the first step, the value creation view (Fig. 5) as a descriptive representation illustrates (1) how much cost is being spent on "information system management" (as a category of healthcare information management) to improve the hospital operational efficiency; (2) how much value is being perceived by the end users of information systems; (3) what is the value proposition of the IT department (as the internal service provider) to improve the hospital operational efficiency; and (4) how much profit is being captured by the hospital through improving operational efficiency. Value as "*What the actor Perceives*" and profit as "*What the actor Captures*" are two supplementary concepts in the value creation viewpoint. Consequently, Total Cost of Ownership (TCO), Net Perceived Value (NPV) and Net Captured Value (NCV) are operational metrics to measure the cost, value and profit. The profit of improving operational efficiency as the captured value by hospital is determined after perceiving value by beneficiary actor (users) as "NCV = NPV - TCO" [61]. Here, the cost of "information system management" is more than its profit that is being captured by hospital. Hence, there is the opportunity for saving cost in "information system management" through a right sourcing decision-making.

Step 2: Sourcing Exploration Based on the C.A.R.S Conceptualization. In the second step, the capability sourcing view (Fig. 6) as a predictive representation shows what could be the right sourcing model of "information system management" for saving cost in the hospital. Referring to the view, the right sourcing model of "information system management" could be an outsourcing model. Two metrics for choosing the right sourcing models are (1) the strategic metrics such as operational capabilities (e.g. technical, administrative, organizational) and dynamic capability (e.g. leveraging and reconfiguration); and (2) the operational metrics such as Production Costs (PC) and transaction costs (TC) of service. The hospital's ability to leverage the existing resources and competencies for "information system management" is a non-core capability that results in a parity competition, not competitive advantage. Therefore, the "information system management" can be outsourced to a preferred supplier in the value network based on the low transaction costs. Dynamic capability as "*the actor's capacity and ability to alter its resource base*" and operational capability as "*the actor's capacity and ability to configure its resource base*" are two supplementary

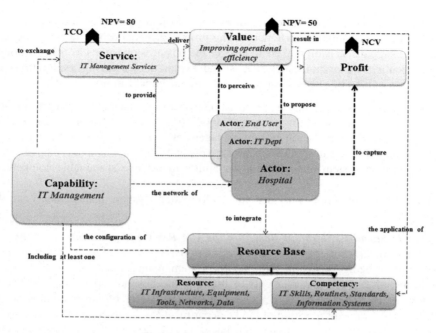

Fig. 5. A value creation view

concepts in the capability sourcing view. Operational capabilities constituted by valuable resources and distinctive competencies are critically underpinning competitive advantage that others cannot imitate and obtain. These core operational capabilities are deeply embedded in the firm and therefore difficult to transfer and likely to be performed internally. Capabilities involved by non-valuable resources and threshold competencies are non-core operational capabilities, which can be outsourced without any serious compromise to the firm competitive position.

Furthermore, in this step, the resource based view (Fig. 7) as a prescriptive representation illustrates what should be the hospital's resource base to have a core capability in "healthcare information management" to achieve sustainable competitive advantage as a long-term goal. Referring to the view, the hospital needs a knowledge creation and integration capability to manage its information. This capability as an interconnected operant resource is the hospital's ability to create, absorb, acquire and integrate information through internal and external networks. This interconnected operant resource is constituted by technological competence (e.g. technological expertise), network competence (e.g. the ability of network management execution) and quality management competence (e.g. the ability of quality management execution) that are Composite Operant Resources (CORs). These resources are a composition of IT infrastructure and systems, individual skills (e.g. IT security, CRM) and quality audit routines and policies as the Basic Operant Resources (BORs). By integration of composite operant resources (CORs), the hospital is able to achieve a temporary competitive advantage and by integration of basic operant resources (BORs), the

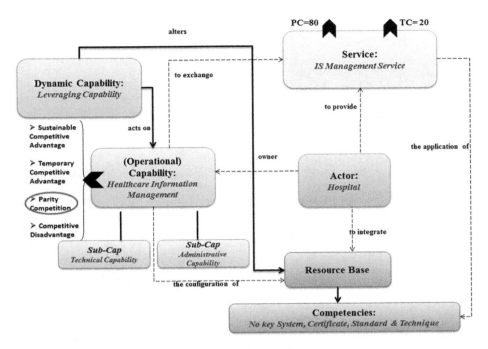

Fig. 6. A capability sourcing view

hospital is able to achieve parity competitive but no advantage. The hospital is able to achieve a sustainable competitive advantage through integrating interconnected operant resources (IORs) as a combination of BORs. Valuable, Rare, Inimitable, and Non-substitutable (VRIN) attributes are metrics to evaluate the actor's resource base to achieve (sustainable) competitive advantage. Valuable common resources can lead to competitive parity but no advantage such as basic operant resources. Non-value-adding resources lead to competitive disadvantage. Rare resources are those possessed uniquely by one organization or by a few others only. Valuable rare resources can provide, at best, temporary competitive advantage such as composite operant resources. Inimitable resources are those that competitors find difficult to imitate or obtain. Non-substitutable resources are resources that do not have a strategic equivalent. Only valuable, rare, hard-to-imitate and non-substitutable resources can provide sustained competitive advantage such as interconnected operant resources [62].

Step 3: Supply Base Exploration Based on the C.A.R.S Conceptualization. In this step, the supply base view (Fig. 8) as a descriptive-predictive representation illustrates (1) what are the service providers operations and capabilities in "information system management"; and (2) who can be a preferred provider for long-term partnership in an outsourcing contract. Referring to the view, the service provider B with the high-level capabilities (e.g. information quality management, documentation and cost reduction) and the high-level performance (e.g. the cost of service, the delivery time of service and the quality of service) can be a candidate for long-term relationship. Two measurements are defined for supplier selection and evaluation as operational and strategic

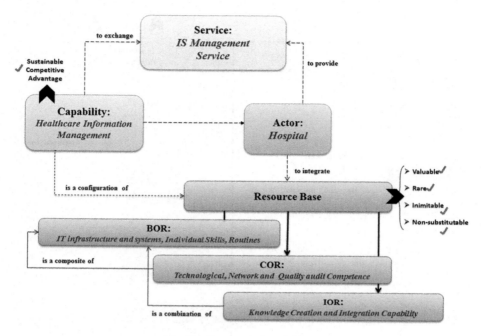

Fig. 7. A resource based view

metrics [63]. Operational metrics are indicators related to the performance dimension of a supplier (i.e. quality, cost and delivery time). Strategic metrics are indicators related to the capability dimension of suppliers such as technical, managerial, and operational capabilities. Consequently, service providers characterized by high-level performance and high-level capability are strategic providers, which the firm needs to develop a long-term relationship with. Service providers with a high-level performance and a low-level capability are candidates for further development to improve their capabilities. Service providers with a low-level performance and a high-level capability are unable to use their capability efficiently. Service providers with low-level performance and capability are candidates for "pruning".

The purpose of model driven exploration based on the C.A.R.S conceptualization is a systemic representation (descriptive, predictive and prescriptive) of the procurement data to explore sourcing alternatives and enabling companies to achieve procurement analytic competency by applying model-based analytical techniques as way of supporting.

8   Way of Supporting: Model Based Analytical Tools

Procurement analytics is the process of using advanced techniques such as modeling, deep computing, simulation, data mining, and optimization to derive actionable insights and outcomes from procurement data. Analytical techniques for procurement

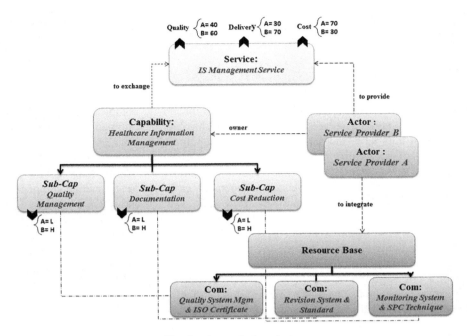

Fig. 8. A supply based view

and strategic sourcing have ranged from simple weighted scoring models to complex mathematical programming approaches. These approaches may include (1) mathematical techniques such as AHP, TCO, and linear programming; (2) artificial intelligence techniques such as neural networks, software agent and fuzzy set theory; and (3) complex techniques based on a single analysis method like cluster analysis and principal component analysis or involve combined methods like AHP with linear programming [64]. The analytical techniques used are usually performance outcome based techniques for evaluating "point-in-time" procurement data [65]. Although, these approaches have their own relative advantages, the procurement analytics needs to involve more than the consideration of current operational characteristics. Strategic sourcing decision-making needs to incorporate tangible, intangible, strategic, and operational factors into any analysis [66]. Furthermore, the lack of reliable data, intelligent tools and analytics skills to interpret data are other important issues in the procurement analytics.

A model based analytical technique can be integrated into our approach to support the way of modeling (C.A.R.S conceptual modeling) and the way of working (model driven approach) for enabling fact-based decision-making. Such analytical technique based on C.A.R.S conceptualization would be capable of (1) extracting the most data from applications and operations (i.e. application and process layers in Fig. 1) to deliver outcomes that matter; (2) integration the procurement analytics into procurement processes; (3) considering tangible, intangible, strategic, and operational metrics into any (descriptive, predictive and prescriptive) analysis based on the historical procurement data; and finally (4) visualizing insights and results derived from procurement data.

9 Conclusion

Companies are acting in an increasingly volatile, uncertain, complex and ambiguous world. Hence, more and more they expect from the chief procurement officers (CPOs) to develop long-term and short-term plans in supply chain management. Generating and measuring savings, safeguarding quality, ensuring delivery availability and enhancing value creation, making partnership and innovation will be remained the top priorities of CPOs in the supply chain management until 2017 [11]. Leading companies need to transform their supply network from static, isolated and internally focused to externally collaborative to achieve the today's procurement objectives and priorities. To create a new business model of supply network, organizations should adopt a strategic sourcing approach that includes initiatives designed to drive above priorities. By applying a systemic view (service ecosystem) on the supply network, we consider the strategic sourcing as a strategic process for fine-tuning the organization's capabilities and resources internally and externally through interactions with suppliers, buyers, internal and external customers to achieve procurement and sourcing objectives. According to this systemic view, a model driven approach has been defined to explore sourcing alternatives based on a common language (C.A.R.S) that enables fact-based decision-making through procurement data management and analytics competencies. As future work, we will evaluate the proposed model-based strategic sourcing around important sourcing trends such as shared service centers, business process outsourcing and global sourcing.

References

1. Anderson, P.H., Rask, M.: Supply chain management: new organizational practices for changing procurement realities. J. Purchasing Supply Manag. **9**(2), 83–95 (2003)
2. Ellram, L.M., Carr, A.S.: Strategic purchasing: a history and review of the literature. Int. J. Phys. Distrib. Mater. Manag. **30**(2), 10–18 (1994)
3. Cooper, M.C., Ellram, L.M.: Characteristics of supply chain management and the implications for purchasing and logistics strategy. Int. J. Logistics Manag. **4**(2), 13–24 (1993)
4. Chen, I.J., Paulraj, A., Lado, A.: Strategic purchasing, supply management and firm performance. J. Oper. Manag. **22**(5), 505–523 (2004)
5. Ellram, L.M., Liu, B.: The financial impact of supply management. Supply Chain Manag. Rev. **6**(6), 30–37 (2002)
6. Paulraj, A., Chen, I.J., Flynn, J.: Levels of strategic purchasing: Impact on supply integration and performance. J. Purchasing Supply Manag. **12**, 107–122 (2006)
7. Weelec, A.: Purchasing and Supply Chain Management. Analysis, Startegy, Planning and Practise, 5th edn. Cengage Learning EMEA, Hampshire (2010)

8. Finch, G., Davidson, S., Kirschniak, C., Weikersheimer, M., Reese, C., Shockley, R.: Analytics: The Speed Advantage; Why Data-Driven Organizations are Winning the Race in Today's Marketplace. IBM Global Business Services (2014)

9. LaValle, S., Hopkins, M., Lesser, E., Shockley, R., Kruschwitz, N.: Analytics: The New Path to Value; How the Smartest Organizations are Embedding Analytics to Transform Insights into Action. IBM Global Business Services (2010)

10. Procurement: optimizing savings and mitigating risk in a complex world. Technical report, IBM Smarter Commerce (2013)

11. The CPO's Agenda for 2014… and Beyond. Technical report, Aberdeen Group (2014)

12. Dhawan, R., Walters, D., Bhattacharjya, J.: Procurement models for the future. In: The SMART Supply Chain Conference, Australia (2011)

13. Dhawan, R.: Procurement analytics. In: The CIPS Conference, Australia (2010)

14. Butner, B.: Sourcing in a Demanding Economic Environment. IBM Global Business Services (2009)

15. Eltantawy, R., Giunipero, L., Handfield, R.: Strategic sourcing management's mindset: strategic sourcing orientation and its implications. Int. J. Phys. Distrib. Logistics Manag. 21 (2014)

16. Thalheim, B.: The science and art of conceptual modeling. In: Hameurlain, A., et al. (eds.) TLDKS VI. LNCS, vol. 7600, pp. 76–105. Springer, Heidelberg (2012)

17. Seligmann, P.S., Wijers, G.M., Sol, H.G.: Analyzing the structure of IS methodologies, an alternative approach. In: Proceedings of the First Dutch Conference on Information Systems, Amersfoort, The Netherlands (1989)

18. March, S.T., Smith, G.F.: Design and natural science research on information technology. Decis. Support Syst. 15(4), 251–266 (1995)

19. Peffers, K., Tuunanen, T., Rothenberger, M., Chatterjee, S.: A design science research methodology for information systems research. J. Manag. Inf. Syst. 24(3), 45–77 (2007)

20. Lusch, R.F., Stephen, L., Vargo, S.L., Matthew, O.: Competing through service: insights from service-dominant logic. J. Retail. 83(1), 2–18 (2007)

21. Osterwalder, A., Pigneur, Y.: Designing business models and similar strategic objects: the contribution of IS. J. Assoc. Inf. Syst. 14(5), Article 3 (2013)

22. Von Bertalanffy, L.: General system theory (1969)

23. Beer, S.: Brain of the Firm. The Penguin Press, London (1972)

24. Beer, S.: The viable system model: its provenance, development, methodology and pathology. J. Oper. Res. Soc. 35(1), 7–25 (1984)

25. Ng, I.C.L., Parry, G., Maull, R., McFarlane, D.: Complex engineering service systems: a grand challenge. In: Ng, I.C.L., Parry, G., Wild, P., McFarlane, D., Tasker, P. (eds.) Complex Engineering Service Systems. Springer, New York (2010). doi:10.1007/978-0-85729-189-9_23

26. Barile, S., Polese, F.: Smart service systems and viable service systems. In: Service Science, vol. 2, no. 1/2 (2010)

27. Vargo, S.L., Lusch, R.F.: From repeat patronage to value co-creation in service ecosystems: a transcending conceptualization of relationship. J. Bus. Mark. Manag. 4(4), 169–179 (2010)

28. Maglio, P., Spohrer, J.: Fundamentals of service science. J. Acad. Mark. Sci. 36(1), 18–20 (2008)

29. Vargo, S.L., Lusch, R.F., Akaka, M.A.: Advancing service science with service-dominant logic: clarifications and conceptual development. In: Maglio, P.P., Kieliszewski, J.A., Spohrer, J.C. (eds.) Handbook of Service Science. Springer, New York (2010)

30. Vargo, S.L., Akaka, M.A.: Service-dominant logic as a foundation for service science: clarifications. Serv. Sci. 1(1), 32–41 (2009)

31. Barile, S., Saviano, M.: A new perspective of systems complexity in service science. Coll. BARILE, S., Impresa, Ambiente, Manag. **3**(3) (2010)
32. Barile, S., Polese, F.: Linking the viable system and many-to-many network approaches to service-dominant logic and service science. Int. J. Q. Serv. Sci. **2**(1), 23–42 (2010)
33. Barile, S., Saviano, M.: Foundations of systems thinking: the structure systems paradigm, in Aa, Vv. Contributions to Theoretical and Practical Advances in Management. A Viable Systems Approach (VSA). International Printing (2011)
34. Vargo, S.L., Akaka, M.A.: Value co-creation and service systems (Re)formation: a service ecosystems view. Inf. Serv. Sci. **4**(3), 207–217 (2012)
35. Vargo, S.L., Maglio, P.P., Akaka, M.A.: On value and value co-creation: a service systems and service logic perspective. Eur. Manag. J. **26**(3), 145–152 (2008)
36. Dobrzykowski, D., Tran, O., Tarafdar, M.: Value co-creation and resource based perspectives for strategic sourcing. Strat. Outsourcing: Int. J. **3**(2), 106–127 (2010)
37. Mele, C., Della Corte, V.: Resource-based view and service-dominant logic: similarities, differences and further research. JBM – J. Bus. Mark. Manag. **6**(4), 192–213 (2013)
38. Rafati, L.: Capability sourcing: a service-dominant logic view. In: Proceedings of the 8th Mediterranean Conference on Information Systems (2014)
39. Rafati, L., Poels, G.: Introducing service-oriented organizational structure for capability sourcing. In: Snene, M., Leonard, M. (eds.) IESS 2014. LNBIP, vol. 169, pp. 82–91. Springer, Heidelberg (2014)
40. Rafati, L., Poels, G.: Capability sourcing modeling. In: Iliadis, L., Papazoglou, M., Pohl, K. (eds.) CAiSE Workshops 2014. LNBIP, vol. 178, pp. 77–87. Springer, Heidelberg (2014)
41. Poels, G.: The resource-service-system model for service science. In: Trujillo, J., et al. (eds.) ER 2010. LNCS, vol. 6413, pp. 117–126. Springer, Heidelberg (2010)
42. Barney, J.: Firm resources and sustained competitive advantage. J. Manag. **17**(1), 99–120 (1991)
43. Barney, J.: Gaining and sustaining competitive advantage, 2nd edn. Prentice Hall, Upper Saddle River (2002)
44. Hill, C., Jones, G.: Strategic Management: An Integrated Approach, 10th edn. Cengage Learning, Boston (2012)
45. Helfat, C., Finkelstein, S., Mitchell, W., Peteraf, M., Singh, H., Teece, D., Winter, S.: Dynamic Capabilities: Understanding Strategic Change in Organizations. Blackwell, Malden (2007)
46. Zollo, M., Winter, S.G.: Deliberate learning and the evolution of dynamic capabilities. Organ. Sci. **13**(3), 339–351 (2002)
47. Teece, D.: A dynamic capabilities-based entrepreneurial theory of the multinational enterprise. J. Int. Bus. Stud. 01/2014 **45**(1), 8–37 (2014)
48. Vargo, S.L., Lusch, R.F.: It's all B2B…and beyond: toward a systems perspective of the market. Indus. Mark. Manag. **40**(2), 181–187 (2011)
49. Akaka, M.A., Vargo, S.L., Lusch, R.F.: An exploration of networks in value cocreation: a service-ecosystems view. Rev. Marketing Res. **9**(Special issue), 13–50 (2012)
50. Wieland, H., Polese, F., Vargo, S.L., Lusch, R.F.: Toward a service (eco) systems perspective on value creation. Int. J. Serv. Sci. Manag. Eng. Technol. **3**(3), 12–24 (2012)
51. Cardoso, J., Lopes, R., Poels, G.: Service Systems: Concepts, Modeling, and Programming. Springer Briefs in Computer Science. Springer, Heidelberg (2014)
52. Vargo, S.L., Lusch, R.F.: Service-dominant logic: looking ahead. Presentation at the Naples Forum on Service, Isle of Capri, Italy, 14–17 June 2011
53. Bowman, C., Ambrosini, V.: Value creation versus value capture: towards a coherent definition of value in strategy. Br. J. Manag. **11**, 1–15 (2000)
54. Olive, A.: Conceptual Modeling of Information Systems. Springer, Berlin (2007)

55. Teece, D.: Business models, business strategy and innovation. Long Range Plan. **43**, 172–194 (2010)
56. IEEE recommended practice for architectural description of software-intensive systems. IEEE, New York (2000)
57. Loftin, R., Lync, R., Calhoun, J.: The Sourcing Canvas: A Strategic Approach to Sourcing Decisions, p. 13. Accelare Inc., USA (2011)
58. Cortada, J.W., Gordon, D., Lenihan, B.: The Value of Analytics in Healthcare, from Insights to Outcomes. IBM Global Business Services, New York (2012)
59. Brennan, C.D.: Integrating the healthcare supply chain. Healthc. Fin. Manag. **52**(1), 31–34 (1998)
60. Chakraborty, S., Dobrzykowski, D.: Linking service-dominant logic and healthcare supply chain (2013)
61. Golnam, A., Viswanathan, V., Moser, C.I., Ritala, P., Wegmann, A.: Designing value-oriented service systems by value map. In: Shishkov, B. (ed.) BMSD 2013. LNBIP, vol. 173, pp. 150–173. Springer, Heidelberg (2014)
62. Madhavaram, S., Hunt, S.D.: The service-dominant logic and a hierarchy of operant resources: developing masterful operant resources and implications for marketing strategy. J. Acad. Mark. Sci. **36**(1), 67–82 (2008)
63. Ashutosh, S., Pratap, K.M.: Evaluation of supplier capability and performance: a method for supply base reduction. J. Purchasing Supply Manag. **12**(3), 148–163 (2006)
64. Chen, Y.J.: Structured methodology for supplier selection and evaluation in a supply chain. Inf. Sci. **181**, 1651–1670 (2011)
65. Narasimhan, R., Talluri, S., Mendez, D.: Supplier evaluation and rationalization via data envelopment analysis: an empirical examination. J. Supply Chain Manag.: Glob. Rev. Purchasing Supply **37**(3), 28–37 (2001)
66. Sarkis, J., Talluri, S.: A model for strategic supplier selection. J. Supply Chain Manag. **38**(4), 18–28 (2002)

The Mediating Effect of Formal Contractual Controls in the Relationship Between Experience and Contract Design

Kiron Ravindran[1(✉)], Anjana Susarla[2], Ranjani Krishnan[2],
and Deepa Mani[3]

[1] IE Business School, Madrid, Spain
Kiron.Ravindran@ie.edu
[2] Michigan State University, East Lansing, MI, USA
{asusarla,krishnan}@broad.msu.edu
[3] Indian School of Business, Hyderabad, India
Deepa_Mani@isb.edu

Abstract. An underlying assumption in the literature on inter-firm contracting has been that relational governance is better than formal controls at mitigating contractual hazards. If formal controls are at best inadequate and at worst useless, then it are hard to reconcile the practical observation that most firms continue to write detailed contracts that include a rich set of formal controls.

Formal controls weaken under two conditions: first, conventional, accounting-based performance measures are not effective when uncertainty is high. Second, as parties accumulate contracting experience "specialized language develops" enabling less expensive options than formal ones. We therefore question the logic that formal controls can only be useful if they strengthen relational governance.

In this paper, we posit that noisy performance measurement problem continues to exist in relational contracting as well as in formal contracting. And the purpose of such contractual controls therefore lies in mediating experience and contract design.

Keywords: IT · Outsourcing · Contracting · Experience · Mediation

1 Introduction

A considerable amount of prior literature has examined the challenges in contracts for outsourced IT services. In particular, contracting for complex IT services, which are interlinked with organizational processes and require considerable knowledge of the organizational context, are fraught with exchange hazards such as holdup [1]. Given the difficulty in specifying contractual contingencies upfront in such outsourcing initiatives, an underlying assumption has been that relational governance is better than formal controls at mitigating contractual hazards (e.g., [2]). If contractual controls are at best inadequate and at worst useless, then it are hard to reconcile the practical observation that most firms continue to write detailed contracts that include a rich set of formal controls. The pervasiveness of formal contractual controls is even more puzzling

© Springer International Publishing Switzerland 2015
I. Oshri et al. (Eds.): Global Sourcing 2015, LNBIP 236, pp. 52–61, 2015.
DOI: 10.1007/978-3-319-26739-5_3

when we observe experienced contracting parties who should, presumably, have evolved to relational contracting.

Extant argument that formal contracts serve as a base over which relational contracts can more effectively function [2] appears less credible considering that the cost of formal contract design and maintenance can account for up to 10 % of the total contracting costs[1] of multi-million dollar contracts.

In this study, we examine the interplay between formal, i.e., contractual controls and relational governance on contract design in contracting for complex IT services between experienced contracting parties.

2 Related Literature and Theory

Literature has explored the relationship between formal controls and relational governance [2–4]. The typical assertion is that formal controls and relational governance mechanisms such as trust should be substitutes because formal controls are not necessary when there is relational capital. Some authors such as [5, p. 495] are emphatic about this: "trust not only cannot be a control mechanism but it also implies the exclusion of deliberate control over the behavior of others... Control comes into play only when adequate trust is not present." [24, p. 982] see "Contracts and trust as alternative means by which parties can manage risk in exchange relationships." The empirical evidence that formal controls and relational governance co-exist even in partners that contract repeatedly is usually met with skepticism. Often, the conclusion is that formal controls are used to strengthen relational governance. For example, Poppo and Zenger [2, p. 708] state: "well-specified contracts may actually promote more cooperative, long-term, trusting exchange relationships." Ryall and Sampson [4, p. 923] arrive at a similar conclusion that formal controls may be positively associated with relational governance "not due to their usefulness in court, but instead, their usefulness in maintaining a smoothly functioning relational contract."

The focus of extant literature on relational governance arises in part because formal controls lose their efficacy in the presence of uncertainty. This failure of formal controls arises from two factors: first, conventional, accounting-based performance measures are not effective when uncertainty is high [6–8]. Uncertainty increases the noise in performance measures, which reduces their use for control purposes (the performance measure noise factor). Uncertainty increases the chances of renegotiation, leading to transaction costs, especially in the presence of fixed-price contracts (ex post transaction hazard factor). Second, as parties accumulate contracting experience, it is posited that "specialized language develops as experience accumulates and nuances are signaled and received in a sensitive way," [9, p. 240], making individuals less likely to engage in opportunism. Williamson also posits that as experience accumulates, parties can realize transaction-specific savings "as contracts are successfully adapted to unfolding events," in other words, inter-firm contracting experience. This often leads researchers to conclude that formal controls are less relevant for experienced transactors, especially

---

[1] The Real Cost of Outsourcing, 2012 by OSF Global Services http://www.osf-global.com/assets/uploaded_files/en/outsourcing-costs-OSF-white-paper.pdf.

in the presence of uncertainty, unless these controls have some role to play in relational governance.

We question the logic that formal controls can only be useful if they strengthen relational governance – if formal controls have no value because of their limited signal power or reduced ability to mitigate transaction hazards, then why do they continue to be extensively used?

In this study, we offer an alternate perspective for the co-existence of formal controls and relational governance in contracting between experienced parties. We use contract and transaction cost theories and develop arguments that there is a role for formal controls that is independent of their relation-strengthening role. We posit that although relational governance can reduce ex post transaction hazards, the risk of moral hazard, i.e., the likelihood that the vendor shirks by exerting lower efficiency enhancing (unobservable) effort remains a problem. That is, the noisy performance measurement problem continues to exist even in relational contracting. Using insights from agency theory, we suggest that experience arising from repeated contracting helps the client to obtain a better assessment of the uncontrollable risks that could arise in the future from environmental uncertainty. Assuming that cost efficiency of the project is a function of vendor effort and a random environmental error [10], experience allows better assessment of the distribution of the random error term, reduces information asymmetry, and improves the understanding of the relation between effort and outcome. That is, experience helps in reducing the noise of contractual performance measures thereby increasing the efficacy of formal control systems and allowing the client to place greater reliance on contractual controls. The net effect is that experience allows contracting parties to develop more efficient formal contractual controls. Thus creating an independent reason for the existence of formal contractual controls in the presence of experienced vendors.

The direction of our analysis is to explore if indeed experience is associated with formal contracts and in turn formal contracts mediate the relationship between experience and contract design elements.

3   Theoretical Model

In the presence of uncertainty, trading partners adopt alternate approaches to mitigate the risk of uncertainty. The arguments built on transaction cost economics suggest that firms resort to moving transactions from the market to within the organization [11]. However alternatively firms might choose to mitigate the risks of uncertainty by relying on exclusive dyadic relationships based on prior experience [12]. Podolny's argues that in times of uncertainty firms are likely to lock themselves into exclusive relationships as such prior experience offers a social cue of predictable outcomes. The limits of exclusivity are not restricted to the dyad, but he also show how firms might exclusively trade only with other firms of similar status, similar being defined as those possessing similar levels of social embeddedness in the market. This link between uncertainty and visible indications of experience has been elaborated also by Granovetter [13].

We use a standard contracting setting where the observed performance outcome for a project implemented by vendor i is a function of unobservable vendor effort (μi), and three sources of uncertaintyθ, ζi, and δij. The first type of uncertainty,θ (with variance $\sigma\theta 2$) arises from industry-level risk factors and is common to all vendors with whom the client can transact. The second uncertainty, ζi (with variance $\sigma\zeta 2$) denotes idiosyncratic uncertainty and varies among vendors [14, 15] and arises from factors such as the vendor's ability and skills [14] also include the agent's luck as an element of idiosyncratic uncertainty). The third uncertainty, δij (with variance $\sigma\delta 2$) arises from random factors that are specific to the buyer-seller relationship such as culture, communication styles, and coordination patterns.

Client experience with other vendors in the same industry allows contracting parties to obtain a better assessment of the industry level uncertainty factors (θ). Vendor experience with other clients in the same industry provides the client with larger information set to assess the vendor's actions in different situations contingencies arise, which is a measure of idiosyncratic uncertainty (ζi,). Dyadic experience allows contracting parties to obtain a better assessment of the uncertainty arising from the buyer-seller relationship (δij). Therefore each of the above three types of experience reduce noise in contractual performance measures and facilitates their use in formal contracts. Therefore, we are likely to observe a positive association between experience and contractual controls.

With effective controls in place, it is likely that both vendors and clients would avail the reduced transaction costs associated with long term contracts. While long term contracts raise a risk of hold-up, the reduced costs of repeated renegotiations are likely to appeal to both clients and vendors. Taking in isolation, the link between contractual controls and the contract design element of duration is likely to be positive. However, this raises the research question whether such contractual controls act as mediators in the link between experience and contract duration.

Our overall model is provided in Fig. 1.

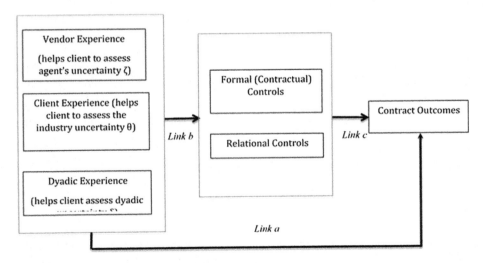

Fig. 1. Theoretical model

We examine the effect of formal and relational controls on contract duration. Contract duration is an important factor, especially in complex projects that involve relationship-specific capital [23]. Contracting parties need to tradeoff the negotiation cost of a series of shorter-term projects with the relationship hazards that arise from commitment to a long-term project [16]. Additionally, in complex projects, long-term contracts reduce the risk of business disruptions [17]. Contract duration plays a dual role in meeting the needs of the clients and the vendors in a typical outsourcing arrangement. Longer contracts lower the renegotiation costs, offer incentives to vendors to invest, and help mitigate the risk of opportunism from vendors adopting a short-term perspective. Shorter contracts on the other hand allow clients to leverage market efficiencies [11] and contain project slippage in software projects [18]. From a vendor's perspective a longer term contract is favorable as it indicates a longer stream of revenue and a longer window to recoup relationship specific investments. However, a longer term contract can raise the risk of vendors shirking as there is less immediate threat of termination. Therefore clients might find it more favorable to limit contract duration to avoid the risk of lock-in. Even if contract termination and re-initiation is costly clients may prefer the option to leverage market efficiencies with greater frequency. The contract duration decision is therefore a complex decision that balances risks and incentives of both clients and vendors.

4 Hypotheses Development

A deeper industry level experience allows the client to specify more explicit contracts and thus adopt formal contracts to limit their uncertainty. Similarly a vendor's exposure to multiple clients assures clients of vendors' ability to deal with the idiosyncratic uncertainties specific to the client industry. Given this understanding of the clients' idiosyncratic risks, vendors are more amenable to formal contracts as they are now more able than otherwise to predict uncertainties.

At the same time, dyadic experience could also improve relational contracting and the development of trust, as posited in prior literature. Increased trust is also likely to have an effect on formal controls and this effect can be positive if formal controls improve the smooth functioning of a relational contract [4] or supplant the need for formal controls [19]. We therefore expect contracting experience to increase formal controls as well as trust.

Hypothesis 1. Prior experience is likely to be positively associated with Formal and Relational Controls

However, we argue that the effect of experience on the efficacy of formal controls via its effect on the performance measure precision role is independent of its effects in improving relational contracting. The conclusion in prior literature that the positive association between relational and formal controls is exclusively driven by the facilitating role of formal controls in relational contracting is incomplete. The positive association arises from two separate mechanisms and combining them under the umbrella of relational contracting confounds the role of repeated contracting in improving formal controls. Therefore we are likely to see a direct effect of experience on the contract design and an indirect effect mediated by the formal control mechanisms.

Hypothesis 2. *The relation between prior experience and contract design is likely to be mediated by control mechanisms.*

5   Empirical Analysis

We use data from 22,039 multi-year contracts for the period 1989 – 2009 to test the above predictions. The data were obtained from International Data Corporation, a leading market intelligence and advisory services firm that tracks public announcements of outsourcing arrangements. A typical observation contains various details of the outsourcing arrangement. For our analysis we focus on the name of the client firm, the vendor firm, the year the contract was signed, a brief description of the outsourcing deal, information whether the deal was fixed or flexible price deal, and whether the contract was won through a process of competitive bidding or not.

As a measure for formal contractual controls we use the pricing scheme of the contract – i.e., fixed-price (FP) versus cost-plus (CP). The method of pricing can influence risk, efficiency, and profit [20]. FP contracts provide higher incentives for vendor efficiency, but carry the risk of hold up and transaction costs of renegotiation and adaptation. In contrast, CP contracts reduce transaction costs, but increase the likelihood of vendor inefficiency. Formal contractual relationships, we assume, reflect a higher chance of having the pricing terms fixed up front. In contrast, as a measure of relational contractual controls, we rely on whether the contract was awarded in an open competitive bid or was it awarded to a previously chosen party. Contracts when not awarded through a competitive bid are awarded to incumbents, or are sole-sourced with the winning vendor chosen by an advisory firm or from a pool of preferred vendors. When contracts are awarded in non-competitive ways, we assume the contract includes measures of relational governance.

To examine if the control system mediates the relation between experience and contractual outcomes, we use a formal mediation test as described by Baron and Kenny [21] and the Sobel [25] test. First, we test whether experience is associated with contractual outcomes (link a). Second, we test whether experience influences the mediators, that is, control systems (link b). Third, we include control systems as an additional explanatory variable in the equation that tests the association between experience and outcomes. To establish mediation the following must occur. First, control systems (the mediator variable) must have an effect on contract outcomes (link c) after controlling for the effect of experience. Second, including control systems should reduce the magnitude of the effect of experience on outcomes. We implemented the mediation analysis in the STATA package where the mediators are modeled using probit regressions (with an independent and identically distributed error term) and the outcome variable as a continuous variable with standard normal distribution [e.g., 22].

Results of the mediation models are presented in Table 1. We estimate the four equations using a Seemingly Unrelated Regression Estimation (SURE) that accounts

Table 1. Mediation Model estimates (using SUR estimation)

	Coef.	Std. Err.	P > |z|
1. DV: Duration			
Vendors' experience	0.7811	0.0611	0.0000
Clients' experience	0.0071	0.0010	0.0000
Dyad experience	0.0001	0.0001	0.3130
Intercept	27.9409	0.6934	0.0000
2. DV: Formal Controls (FP)			
Vendors' experience	0.0398	0.0061	0.0000
Clients' experience	0.0013	0.0001	0.0000
Dyad experience	0.0000	0.0000	0.2740
Intercept	1.3949	0.0744	0.0000
3. DV: Trust			
Vendors' experience	0.0531	0.0069	0.0000
Clients' experience	-0.0007	0.0001	0.0000
Dyad experience	0.0001	0.0000	0.0000
Intercept	-2.2159	0.0895	0.0000
4. DV: Duration			
Formal Controls (FP)	-6.1951	0.5387	0.0000
Relational controls	-4.2613	0.5941	0.0000
Vendors' experience	0.6424	0.0812	0.0000
Clients' experience	0.0057	0.0011	0.0000
Dyad experience	0.0002	0.0001	0.1610
Intercept	38.3528	1.0755	0.0000

for possible correlation between the error terms of the different models. Table 2 lists the direct and indirect effects due to mediation by the contractual controls.

6   Results

First, greater vendor experience in terms of breadth in industries is associated with a longer contract duration. Similarly, customers that have traded with a greater number of vendors are likely to enter into longer-term contracts. Greater vendor experience is also associated with a higher likelihood of formal and relational contractual controls. With greater client experience, the likelihood of formal contractual controls is greater however the likelihood of relational contracts (or non-competitive bids) drops with greater experience of clients[2]. As expected experience is associated with longer

---

[2] However, in an alternate model not reported where we eliminated government contracts, this relationship is positive. This suggests a specific approach of government contract allocation.

Table 2. Direct and Indirect effects

	Coef.	Std. Err.	P > |z|
Vendor experience via FP	-0.2464	0.0425	0.0000
Client experience via FP	-0.0083	0.0010	0.0000
Dyad experience via FP	0.0001	0.0001	0.2760
Vendor experience via trust	-0.2261	0.0431	0.0000
Client experience via trust	0.0031	0.0007	0.0000
Dyad experience via trust	-0.0002	0.0001	0.0000
Total indirect vendor experience	-0.4724	0.0601	0.0000
Total indirect client experience	-0.0052	0.0012	0.0000
Total indirect dyad experience	-0.0002	0.0001	0.0810
Direct vendor experience	0.6424	0.0812	0.0000
Direct client experience	0.0057	0.0011	0.0000
Direct dyad experience	0.0002	0.0001	0.1610

contracts as experience is likely to indicate lesser risk in entering into longer term arrangements.

Control Variables: Annual Contract Value, Contract region, Service types, Industry

Both formal controls and relational controls significantly affect contract duration. While formal contracts are negatively associated with contract duration as expected, we find it interesting that contracts which have a relational governance mechanism are also associated with shorter contract duration controlling for experience. However, the drop in coefficient values of experience in the model including a mediator (comparing models (1) and (4) in Table 1) is the indication that a mediation effect does exist.

The direct and indirect effects are presented in Table 2. The negative coefficient of experience mediated by FP (−0.246 and −0.008) suggests that Fixed Pricing mutes the relationship between experience and duration. Vendor experience and dyadic experience is similarly muted by relational contractual controls (−0.226) however client experience is accentuated (0.003). Including the mediating paths of both formal and relational controls, the total indirect effect of vendor experience is negative while the total direct effect is positive and greater. This seems to suggest that while greater vendor experience can help vendors win longer contracts, greater experience can also permit vendors to agree to more formal contractual controls favorable to the client. Client experience works in a similar fashion. Greater client experience is associated with longer duration on the whole but the total indirect effect is negative w.r.t. duration. However, if clients are indeed happier with shorter contracts, then the combined effect of formal and relational contracts is to enable the clients to sign even shorter contracts. Further, this effect is more strongly enforced through formal contractual controls. The justification of why firms would indeed draft expensive formal contracts lies is the result that independent of its role as a base which smooths the running of relational contracts, they also offer a tool for clients and vendors to exhibit their prior stock of experience.

7   Contribution and Conclusion

Our paper makes a number of contributions to the literature. First, extant literature has generally used the term "uncertainty" to refer to a large set of heterogeneous factors that influence the extent to which outcome is driven by effort. We contribute to the literature by decomposing uncertainty into three types: one that is driven by uncertainty in the industry (industry uncertainty), second that is driven by uncertainty in the vendor's action-outcome mapping (vendor uncertainty), and the third that is driven by the uncertainty in the relationship (dyadic uncertainty). Second, the results from this study can potentially shed light on the debate regarding the relationship between contractual and relational controls. Literature considers formal (i.e. contractual) and relational controls as alternative mechanisms to manage exchange hazards. At the same time, empirical evidence has been equivocal. Evidence of a positive association is often interpreted as the complementary role of contractual controls in facilitating relational governance. In this paper we provide evidence that contracting experience facilitates the development of contractual controls independent of whether relational mechanisms have developed between parties. Finally, we show a credible mechanism for why firms consider costly formal contracting. We have an extensive database, which spans the entire population of inter-firm repeated contracts as opposed to other studies that use smaller, and potentially less representative sample sizes.

References

1. Susarla, A., Subramanyam, R., Karhade, P.: Contractual provisions to mitigate holdup: evidence from information technology outsourcing. Inf. Syst. Res. **21**(1), 37–55 (2010)
2. Poppo, L., Zenger, T.: Do formal contracts and relational governance function as substitutes or complements? Strateg. Manag. J. **23**(8), 707–725 (2002)
3. Mayer, K.J., Argyres, N.S.: Learning to contract: evidence from The personal computer industry. Organ. Sci. **15**, 394–410 (2004)
4. Ryall, M.D., Sampson, R.C.: Formal contracts in the presence of relational enforcement mechanisms: evidence from technology development projects. Manag. Sci. **55**(6), 906–925 (2009)
5. Das, T.K., Teng, B.: Between trust and control: developing confidence in partner cooperation in alliances. Acad. Manag. Rev. **23**, 491–512 (1998)
6. Banker, R., Datar, S.: Sensitivity, precision and linear aggregation of signals for performance evaluation. J. Acc. Res. **27**, 21–39 (1989)
7. Feltham, G.A., Xie, J.: Performance measure congruity and diversity in multi-task principal-agent relations. Acc. Rev. **69**, 429–453 (1994)
8. Lambert, R.A.: Contracting theory and accounting. J. Acc. Econ. **32**(1–3), 3–87 (2001)
9. Williamson, O.E.: Transaction-cost economics: the governance of contractual relations. J. Law Econ. **22**(2), 233–261 (1979)
10. Prendergast, P.: Uncertainty and incentives. Journal of Labor Economics **20**(2), 115–137 (2002)
11. Williamson, O.E.: The economic institutions of capitalism. Simon and Schuster, New York (1985)

12. Podolny, J.M.: Market uncertainty and the social character of economic exchange. Adm. Sci. Q. **39**, 458–483 (1994)
13. Granovetter, M.: Economic action and social structure: the problem of embeddedness. Am. J. Sociol. **91**, 481–510 (1985)
14. Lazear, E.P., Rosen, S.: Rank-order tournaments as optimum labor contracts. J. Polit. Econ. **89**, 841–864 (1981)
15. Nalebuff, B.J., Stiglitz, J.E.: Prizes and incentives: towards a general theory of compensation and competition. Bell J. Econ. **14**, 21–43 (1983)
16. Crocker, K.J., Masten, S.E.: Mitigating contractual hazards: Unilateral options and contract length. RAND J. Econ. **19**(3), 327–343 (1988)
17. Ravindran, K., et al.: Social capital and contract duration in buyer-supplier networks for information technology outsourcing. Inf. Syst. Res. **26**(2), 379–397 (2015)
18. Pressman, R.S.: Software Engineering: A practical approach. McGraw-Hill, New York (1997)
19. Dyer, J.H., Singh, H.: The relational view: cooperative strategy and sources of inter-organizational competitive advantage. Acad. Manag. Rev. **23**, 660–679 (1998)
20. Gopal, A., Sivaramakrishnan, K.: On vendor preferences for contract types in offshore software projects: the case of fixed price versus time and materials contracts. Inf. Syst. Res. **19**(2), 202–220 (2008)
21. Baron, R.M., Kenny, D.A.: The moderator-mediator variable distinction in social psychological research: conceptual, strategic, And Statistical Considerations. J. Pers. Soc. Psychol. **51**, 1173–1182 (1986)
22. Imai, K., Keele, L., Yamamoto, T.: Identification, inference, and sensitivity analysis for causal mediation effects. Stat. Sci. **25**, 51–71 (2010)
23. Joskow, P.L.: Price adjustment in long-term contracts: the case of coal. J. Law Econ. **31**(1), 47–83 (1988)
24. Malhotra, D., Lumineau, F.: Trust and collaboration in the aftermath of conflict: the effects of contract structure. Acad. Manag. J. **54**(5), 981–998 (2011)
25. Sobel, M.E.: Asymptotic confidence intervals for indirect effects in structural equation models. Sociol. Methodol. **13**, 290–312 (1982)

Applying a Configurational Approach for Explaining the Role of Relationship Quality for Successful Outsourcing Arrangements

Christian Jentsch[1](✉), Frank Schlosser[1], and Daniel Beimborn[2]

[1] Department of Information Systems and Services, University of Bamberg,
An der Weberei 5, 96049 Bamberg, Germany
{christian.jentsch,frank.schlosser}@uni-bamberg.de
[2] Management Department of Frankfurt School of Finance and Management,
Sonnemannstr. 9-11, 60314 Frankfurt am Main, Germany
d.beimborn@fs.de

Abstract. Relationship quality dimensions like trust or commitment have been proven to be crucial determinants for the success of outsourcing arrangements. Most previous empirical studies focus on the success of relationship quality dimensions within a specific contextual outsourcing arrangement. We argue that the importance and formation of each relationship quality dimension highly depend on the contextual background of the particular study. To substantiate this contingency argument, we conducted 16 interviews with managers in different types of outsourcing arrangements and questioned them about their understanding of relationship quality. Linking managers' statements with their outsourcing background, we found several configurational patterns that describe the different roles of relationship quality for successful outsourcing.

Keywords: IT outsourcing · Relationship quality · Configurational perspective · Explorative approach

1 Introduction

Managing high-quality relationships with IT service providers is one of the key challenges in outsourcing arrangements and often a source of failure [1–3]. Various outsourcing studies have analyzed these challenges by focusing on different dimensions of relationship quality (RQ), such as trust, commitment or mutual understanding, and their management [4]. Empirically, these studies usually focus on specific types of outsourcing arrangements, which raises the presumption that the role or importance of certain RQ dimensions depends on such contextual factors. Research tries to gain a richer understanding in this field by developing a generic conceptualization of the RQ dimensions and then relating them to different contexts.

Thus, our research question is: *How does the importance of the dimensions of relationship quality differ in various IT outsourcing contexts?*

To answer this question we applied an explorative approach and conducted 16 interviews with outsourcing managers responsible for relationship management between IT provider and IT client. In the following, this paper proceeds with providing

© Springer International Publishing Switzerland 2015
I. Oshri et al. (Eds.): Global Sourcing 2015, LNBIP 236, pp. 62–82, 2015.
DOI: 10.1007/978-3-319-26739-5_4

an overview about the multi-dimensional concept of relationship quality and about the applied configurational perspective (Sect. 2). Then we present our research approach and describe the data collection and coding process (Sect. 3). As a result of the interviews we first specify the relationship quality construct from the practitioners' point of view (Sect. 4.1) and then develop a configurational framework which links the identified RQ dimensions to the particular configurations of outsourcing arrangements with regard to project and collaboration type. Thus, the resulting model highlights the *contextual* description of relationship quality dimensions enabling detailed insights into the differential importance of relational aspects in IT outsourcing.

2 Theoretical Background

2.1 Relationship Quality in Outsourcing Projects

According to Lacity, Khan and Willcocks [3], determinants for Information Technology Outsourcing (ITO) success can be categorized into: ITO decision, contractual governance and relational governance. Relational governance attempts to manage relationship variables like trust, commitment or mutual understanding. Altogether, these variables form the outsourcing relationship quality (RQ). The importance of RQ on ITO success has been shown in various studies [e.g. 2, 5]. In a review of the ITO literature regarding relationship quality, we compiled a list of 17 dimensions which have been mentioned as being crucial components of relationship quality in previous studies (see Appendix). This list gives an impression of the diverse discussion on relationship quality. Within this discussion, scholars discuss which dimensions are the most relevant for ITO success. For example, Beimborn [6] showed in a study on outsourcing of application management that "commitment and communication quality are the most important RQ dimensions." (p. 9). Another study clusters the different client types (e.g. "Business-efficiency clients" or "Strategists and innovation seekers") and identifies the differential importance of RQ dimensions like trust or vendor proactivity for these client types [7]. Even though this study highlights the importance of different RQ dimensions, it does not include possible differences in the meaning of the RQ dimension within a certain cluster of client types. Thus, it remains open if, for example, a 'strategist' has the same understanding of the RQ dimensions (like 'cultural similarity') like a 'business-efficiency client'.

2.2 Configurational Explanation

The contextual influence on ITO has already been considered in previous studies. Most studies focus on the link between ITO strategies and ITO success [e.g. 7, 8]. An important study in this context has been conducted by Lee, Miranda and Kim [9] who apply three possible perspectives to explain the success of ITO strategies – namely the universalistic, contingency and configurational perspective. While the universalistic perspective seeks for best practices in the explanation of project success, the contingency perspective assumes that there exist different environmental factors which drive the success of ITO. A list of such contingency factors has been developed in a literature review on IT project portfolio management by Frey and Buxmann [10]. This list includes factors like geographical location, project type or organizational environment. The contextual explanation extends the universalistic theory by linking the contextual factors to specific strategies which allows multiple pathways in the explanation of success.

The empirical findings of Lee, Miranda and Kim [9] "indicate the superiority of the configurational approach over universalistic and contingency perspectives in explain outsourcing success." (p. 110). Along this perspective, the success of an ITO strategy lies mainly in the configurational patterns of the organization (i.e. gestalts). Because we assume the configurations of different contextual factors as being critical for the relevance of certain RQ dimensions, we apply this configurational perspective. The aspects that form the configurational pattern can be based on previous studies on contingency factors such as the outsourcing object [7], duration of partnership [9] or organizational structure [8]. In our study, we will focus on the set of contingency factors identified by the literature review of Frey and Buxmann [10], referred to above.

In our study, the configuration patterns will be described by several contingency factors, which in combination with the RQ statements lead to the contextual description of the RQ dimensions. Because the specification of the pattern has been one of the results of the interviews, the pattern will be presented later in the findings.

3   Research Approach

3.1   Data Collection

The objective of this explorative study is to find out more about the concept of relationship quality in different outsourcing arrangements. To do so we first compiled a list of the commonly adopted RQ dimensions. A team of five researchers and two practitioners reviewed the list of previously applied RQ dimensions (see Appendix) and compiled a short list of the most critical dimensions consisting of 15 dimensions[1].

Due to the explorative nature of our study, we did not prepare any further guideline for the interviews, which took 80 min on average. The main objective was to expose the interviewees' understanding of the relationship quality concept. To conduct the second step of adjusting the statement to the context, we first asked the interviewees to provide some insight into their previous and current responsibilities and experiences in outsourcing and relationship management. Important aspects were duration of the current job position, type and duration of previous outsourcing-related positions, and experiences in current and previous projects in terms of outsourcing object, geography (e.g. offshoring), and organizational structure of the arrangements. All 16 interviewees have been responsible for managing IT outsourcing relationships for 3 to 22 years. Common outsourcing objects cover the development of applications and firmware, management and support of existing applications, or the maintenance and support of existing IT infrastructure. Most of the projects are farshore or nearshore projects. In one

---

[1] The 15 dimensions are: Trust, Fairness, Mutual Understanding, Vision, Control, Consensus, Identification, Communication, Cultural Values, Flexibility, Forbearance, Commitment, Extra Mile, Openness, Respect.

case the provider is located next to the client's site. The partnership forms vary from highly embedded partnerships to independent and output-oriented partnerships. Table 1 highlights the key attributes that give a short overview of the general interviewee's background.

Table 1.   Interview participants

ID	Industry	Outsourcing experience [in years]	Role, responsibility	Geographical range
A	Consultant	15	Strategic sourcing advisory	Farshore, nearshore, onshore
B	Software engineering	15	Managing director	Farshore, nearshore, onshore
C	Railway	>10	Platform and application management	Farshore, nearshore
D	Banking	10	Vendor management	Onshore
E	Aerospace	20	Data center services; IT operations	Nearshore
F	Telecomm-unication	>10	Strategic provider management in ISD	Focus on farshore, nearshore
G	Telecomm-unication	10	Relationship and escalation management	Farshore, nearshore
H	Banking	>10	Relationship manager on provider side	Farshore
I	Software engineering	>20	Relationship and program management	Farshore, nearshore
J	Railway	>10	Application development and integration	Farshore
K	Banking	>15	Global head of product sourcing; Commodity management	Farshore, nearshore
L	Aerospace	>10	Head of service delivery;	Nearshore
M	Telecomm-unication	–	Carry-on partner management	Nearshore, onshore
N	Aerospace	>10	Companywide IT infrastructure	Farshore, focus on nearshore, onshore
O	Health care	>15	Global IS development	Farshore, nearshore, onshore
P	Pharma and biotech	–	Relationship management	Farshore, nearshore

After the description of their responsibilities, the interviewees were asked to describe their understanding of RQ. If necessary, we applied the prepared 15 dimensions of RQ and asked the managers for their understanding of each particular dimension. To underpin the statements we asked the interviewees to present specific examples from existing projects in which they experienced different aspects of RQ. These examples were later used to confirm the description of the responsibilities given at the beginning of the interviews.

3.2 Coding

The coding process has been conducted by four researchers. In a first step, the transcribed interviews were reviewed by every researcher individually. In addition to the full transcript, a list of interviewee statements related to the different relationship quality dimensions was compiled and handed out to the researchers. In a first discussion session, the concept of relationship quality as perceived by the interviewees was discussed in detail and without any association to any particular (outsourcing) context. First, we discussed every single RQ dimension that had been part of the interviews. Then we tried to uncover overlaps and similarities between the RQ dimensions. The results of this step reduced the initial 15 literature-based dimensions of RQ to five comprehensive RQ dimensions. The results of this analysis are presented in Sect. 4.1. In a next session, we then focused explicitly on the context of the outsourcing arrangements and projects the interviewees had been referring to. First, we compiled a list of background information of the interviewee and characterized the project responsibilities. Items in this list have been, e.g., position in the company, types of responsibilities or specific partnerships mentioned in the interviews. We discussed each item in the list and evaluated the potential influence of each item as well as a combination of items on the statements of the interviewee. The results of this discussion are presented in Sect. 4.2. In the last step, we linked the findings of Sects. 4.1 and 4.2. We documented the key statements of every interview about the determined RQ dimensions and allocated them to the configurational pattern resulting from Sect. 4.2. The results of this allocation are presented in Sect. 4.3.

4 Results

This section consists of three sub-sections. First, we present the generic description of the relationship quality variable which arose from the interviews. Second, we develop the configurational framework that is based on the different characteristics of the projects discussed in the interviews. In the last step, we merge the findings of the two previous sections and present an evaluation of relationship quality within the different contextual situations in which the project are embedded.

4.1   The Dimensions of Relationship Quality

As a result, we distilled a five-dimensional relationship quality construct, consisting of mutual understanding, trust, commitment, communication, and fairness. Each of these dimensions consists of several characteristics to further specify the respective dimension (Fig. 1).

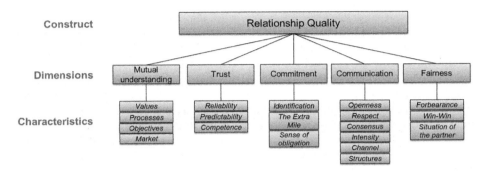

Fig. 1. Characteristics of the RQ Dimensions

In the following, we present a description of the five dimensions as a first result of the interviews.

Mutual Understanding. Mutual understanding is defined as "the ability of IT and business [...], at a deep level, to understand and be able to participate in the other's key processes" [11, p. 86] and is important to enable knowledge transfer and to make the vendor staff able to provide effective services to the client.

In the interviews, mutual understanding has been discussed through an organizational perspective, focusing on organizational processes, objectives and the market environment, and through a social perspective, referring to the level of understanding regarding each other's values. The latter helps to understand the values and beliefs that drive an individual's behavior and to deeply understand the intentional actions of the partner. The values are mostly formed by the individual's experiences in the social environment. With a focus on the importance of mutual understanding about the values, we need to distinguish between two context-related scenarios. While in the context of standardized services some interviewees named mutual understanding to be of only minor importance, high importance was reported for understanding the client's/provider's values in projects and more specific services.

By contrast, organizational mutual understanding focuses less on interpersonal interactions and understanding but more on the general understanding of the mutual tasks within the collaboration. Thereby, three aspects are important. First, understanding the partner's business and processes helps to understand the consequences of delivery failures. As an example two interviewees mentioned that they try to involve their partners as much as possible into the overall business domain, so that they fully understand both the relevant processes to be supported and the consequences of late or low quality service deliveries (system failures etc.) (e.g. interviewee L). Second, an understanding of the partner's objectives refers to knowledge about what both partners try to achieve in the collaboration. In general, there exist several reasons and the partners have to understand each other's motives to act accordingly. The third aspect of organizational mutual understanding is an understanding of the market environment like regulations or competition. This type of understanding helps to comprehend the formal possibilities and boundaries of the partner's scope for action.

Trust. Trust can be defined as "the firm's belief that another company will perform actions that will result in positive outcomes for the firm, as well as not take unexpected actions that would result in negative outcomes for the firm" [12, p. 326].

Similar to previous research, we found evidence for the conceptualization of trust into relational trust (like reliability and predictability) and competence-related trust [13, 14]. At the beginning of each relationship there is a high need for competence-based trust, meaning that the provider needs to rely on the word and fairness of the client, and the client needs to rely on the competence and capabilities of the provider (interviewees H, C). Nevertheless, this competence-based trust should be highly tightened to the specific project context. For example, one interviewee (interviewee G) mentioned a collaboration in which the client trusted in the competence of the provider because of a previous project. However, the context of the project objectives changed for which reason the provider could not deliver its service at the expected quality level. Hence it is important to take the specific environment into account when developing competence-based trust.

In the ongoing collaboration, relational trust becomes more important. The experts agreed that reliability is the most important factor for generating trust. The second layer of social trust is predictability which reflects the extent of unexpected changes in the behavior or service delivery (e.g., the client can rely on the steady service delivery of the provider in application maintenance arrangement). Some experts argued that it is necessary for the parties to not show varying behaviors. Frequent changes in behavior lead to a situation in which the parties are not able to assess the partner's behavior.

Commitment. "Commitment refers to an implicit or explicit pledge of relational continuity between exchange partners. In an outsourcing partnership, both the vendor and the client can and should allocate sufficient resources and signal bearing sufficient or even extra efforts in order to sustain and improve the relationship over time" [6].

Commitment can be captured by (1) the identification with both the partner and the task; (2) "going the extra mile"; and (3) the sense of obligation. First of all, identification focuses on the vendor´s company/brand (does the provider show identification with the vendor´s company/brand) and/or on the task (is the provider enthusiastic for the task). Depending on the contextual situation some interviewees extended the unidirectional into bidirectional identification. Identification requires closeness to the partner and appraisal. Effective means to increase identification are therefore, e.g., visits at the partner's office or teambuilding events (e.g. O, J). However, some of the interviewed experts sharply rejected the importance of identification (G, M). Bound to the context, we found a higher importance of identification in close and highly dependent relationships.

Second, high commitment on both sides of the sourcing arrangement will increase the possibility that the provider delivers more than agreed-on as per the contract obligations, e.g., working long/extra hours or at the weekend, when necessary. Hence commitment leads to a greater willingness for going the extra mile.

The third layer consists of the sense of obligation one party feels for the other. This can either be because of moral values (the values of both parties are consistent with each other), emotional binding (sense of emotional closeness to the partner) or financial aspects (high salary). Highly obligated parties are less likely to leave the project but to invest time and effort into the relationship. As a negative example, an expert mentioned a situation in which a lot of the partner's employees left the project because the application development project was not interesting enough (J). In this specific case, the organization even reacted by stopping collaboration projects which were not interesting enough for the partner.

Communication. Communication is viewed in terms of both communication quality and communication intensity. Communication quality "describes the efficiency and effectiveness of information exchange between partners" [15, p. 3]. The first aspect of communication quality is openness. Occurring problems and unexpected events need to be addressed as soon as the provider cannot handle the problem alone without performance declines. Several interviewees noticed that the problems need to be addressed in an open communication. Second, the communication has to be respectful. The experts agreed that a relationship only harmonizes if the parties respect each other and do not assume that the partner is "too stupid". In problematic situations, each party has to keep a professional attitude and focus on jointly solving the problem in a respectful manner. The communication process of finding consensus refers to reaching a situation which is suitable for both parties. In the interviews, most experts agreed that the process of achieving consensus is more important than just having a consensus as an end in itself. Only if the partners spend sufficient time to understand the others' problems and intentions, both can achieve an effective and sustainable consensus.

Communication intensity is characterized by three layers – intensity, channel and structure. The first layer (intensity) focuses on the regularity of communication which also incorporates the proactivity. We found that the level of communication intensity needs to be aligned to the specific context. On the one hand the optimal level of communication intensity depends on the maturity of the relationship and on the other hand on the complexity of the project. Communication channels (which form the second layer of communication quantity) determine how information is transferred and how it is perceived by the recipient. Possible channels may be face-to-face, email or telephone. The experts agreed that the major channel in complex collaboration tasks is face-to-face communication but also mentioned that it again depends on the context of the collaboration, i.e., simple or standardized tasks can be coordinated through digital communication channels. One interviewee argued that a sudden switch between communication channels is often a sign of deeper problems in a relationship (O). Communication quantity, as the third layer, reflects the communication structure, meaning who is speaking to whom and sharing which information. By analyzing the structure we can identify actual roles, responsibilities and contact persons. The experts noticed that the formalized structure of responsibilities and contact persons does not always match to the one used in practice. Similar to communication channels we recognized that the sudden change from informal communication structures to formal structures may be a signal for significant problems within the collaboration.

Fairness. Fairness addresses an important facet of the perception of a partner's specific actions. "An action is perceived as fair if the intention that is behind the action is kind, and as unfair if the intention is hostile" [16, p. 819f.]. In addition, "people determine the fairness of others according to their motives, not solely according to actions taken" [17, p. 1289].

According to our findings, fairness consists of three layers – situation of the partner, forbearance, and win-win. The first layer describes the behavior in situations which were not anticipated at the beginning of the relationship and therefore require specific behavior. The parties should try to understand any unexpected situation within the partner's organization and behave fairly. For example, unexpected external political decisions or governmental restrictions may influence the delivery time. While an unfair client will force the provider to keep the SLA, a fair client will show understanding.

The second layer – forbearance – describes the reaction to (minor) underperformance or other variations from the fixed agreements in the contract and SLAs. Forbearing behavior depends on the project maturity. One expert stated that forbearance is more probable during the early stages of a sourcing arrangement (G). This is mostly due to the fact that almost every sourcing project is confronted with teething troubles. Forbearance helps to gain more stability and establish a fair relationship. However, in any phase of a relationship, forbearance depends on the frequency of issues that appear. The experts agreed that it is important to learn from mistakes but also concluded that a problem should not appear twice.

The goal to create a win-win situation builds the third layer of fairness. Since there exist usually some conflicting objectives in an outsourcing relationship – for example concerning the price vs. quality of the service delivery – the partners need to create a situation which is profitable for both of them.

4.2   Setting the Configurational Framework

To develop the configurational framework we adopted ideas of previous studies on configurational analysis in ITO and IT project research [e.g. 7, 8, 10] and adjusted these to the context of our research. The overall framework consists of three contextual factors which mainly influence the formation of relationship quality in a partnership. These are: type of partnership, geographical distance and type of service. The factors are further attributed by specific characteristics which are described in the following (see Table 2).

Type of Partnership. To specify the type of partnership we draw on the gestalts of IT outsourcing strategies proposed by Lee, Miranda and Kim [9]: Independent, Arm's-length, and Embedded. The authors labeled the three types of partnership as gestalts which they proved to be more likely to succeed in a specific outsourcing outcome. The three forms are described by four characteristics: governance form, decision scope, contract type, and contract duration (see Table 3).

Table 2. Contextual factors in ITO relationships

Type of partnership	Embedded partnership
	Independent partnership
Geographical distance	Farshore
	Onshore/nearshore
Type of service	Information systems development
	IT operations

Table 3. Outsourcing Gestalts [8], adapted from Lee, Miranda and Kim [9].

Gestalt	Governance form	Decision scope	Contract type	Contract duration	Anticipated Outcome
Independent	Hierarchy	Minimal	Buy-in	Short-term	Strategic competence
Arm's-length	Market	Selective	Fee-for-service	Medium-term	Cost efficiency
Embedded	Network	Comprehensive	Partnership	Long-term	Technology catalysis

In the interviews we noticed difficulties in the separation of (1) arm-length and embedded partnership and (2) arm-length and independent partnership. Because arm-length partnership is a mix of independent and embedded partnership we straitened our focus on embedded vs. independent partnerships.

Geographical Distance. Because many outsourcing partnerships pass national borders we extend the framework by the contextual factor of geographical distance [18]. In the interviews, we noticed that distance plays a crucial role in the management of IT projects not only because of cultural dissimilarities but also because of communicational difficulties due to fewer personal meetings and different time zones. We distinguish between farshore outsourcing and nearshore/onshore outsourcing. While farshore outsourcing goes beyond the borders of the outsourcer's continent (e.g., India, China, from a Western European perspective), nearshore outsourcing remains within a continent to a country close to the outsourcer (e.g., Poland, Slovakia).

Type of Service. The configurational factor 'type of service' has been considered by several previous studies in related research domains [e.g. 8, 18, 19]. The type of service describes the main object (i.e. service) that is provided by the vendor. Leimeister and Krcmar [7] differ between IT infrastructure, IT applications and IT-supported business processes. A more holistic classification has been presented by Zelt, Wulf, Neff, Übernickel and Brenner [8] who differ between standardization, technical condition and complexity of the application portfolio. Thus, they categorize the objects (or services) into standardized vs. complex applications. However, in practice a sharp differentiation between standard project partnerships and complex project partnerships can be problematic because in several interviews we found partnership patterns with more standardized *and* more complex projects or project stages. For that reason we found the classification based on Leimeister and Krcmar [7] to be more suitable. Based on the background of our interviewees, we can differ between Information System Development (ISD) and management of IT operations (IT Ops.) like application or IT infrastructure management.

4.3   Contextual Relationship Quality

The findings of the contextual RQ dimensions are presented in the following. The framework provides an overview of the most critical characteristics of the RQ dimensions (see Fig. 1). It is important to notice that the characteristics that we *did not* include in the tables are still important for the relationship but do not represent the most critical characteristics in the respective dimension.

An important finding relates to the mutual understanding about the values from the perspective of the type of partnership and the geographical distance. Even though the mutual understanding about the respective values has been mentioned in all interviews, the understanding of the respective (cultural) value system becomes essentially important in farshore outsourcing projects. Considering the geographical distance we found an important distinction of personal value systems and country-related value systems (O). Because in nearshore projects the outsourcer is more or less familiar with the country-related value systems, the discussions focused on the personal value systems influenced by individual experiences and preferences (e.g. E). Farshore projects on the other hand are more complex; in many cases the interviewees mentioned dissimilarities of the country-related value systems in addition to the personal value systems (e.g. F, N). Thus, the partners need to understand the respective country-related values and the personal values (Table 4).

Table 4. Configuration of mutual understanding (most critical aspects)

Type of partnership	Geographical distance	Type of service	RQ Dimension: Mutual Understanding of …
Embedded partnership	Farshore	ISD	Personal and country-related values; Agreement on values should be achieved
		IT Ops.	Vision; Country-related values
	Nearshore/Onshore	ISD	Personal values; Agreement on values should be achieved
		IT Ops.	Vision; Personal values
Independent partnership	Farshore	ISD	Country-related values
		IT Ops.	Market; Objectives
	Nearshore/Onshore	ISD	Market; Processes
		IT Ops.	Market; Processes

In the context of values and geographical distance we found another important aspect which has been mentioned by three managers (F, I, L). When analyzing the understanding of values as a critical success factor one needs to consider the experience of the company with outsourcing projects. The managers distinguished between "global player" and "local firm". If at least one partner of the collaboration is a global player the handling of the different value systems becomes easier than in cases in which both parties do not have much experience in working with other cultures.

Another important finding in this context relates to the type of partnership. We found several statements of managers responsible for embedded partnerships who declared the understanding of values as the most critical factor in managing an embedded relationship (e.g. O, F, J). On the other hand a manager responsible for the IT infrastructure managing mainly nearshore and onshore projects mentioned that he is not interested in the values of the provider and the provider does not need to know the values of the client (N). To manage the client's infrastructure the provider 'just' needs to understand the internal processes of the client which relate to the IT infrastructure. Another manager who is responsible for a nearshore application management project declared the understanding of values as not important and stated that "we are all professional". He mentioned that in his project there exists just one cultural value system – "the business culture" (N). Thus, while values have been stated as the most important characteristic in a high performing network, the relevance in independent collaborations is much lower than, for example, the mutual understanding about processes and objectives. A possible explanation for this crucial alteration of this characteristic could be the IT outsourcing object which is usually much more standardized in independent collaborations than in networks.

Focusing on embedded partnerships we found a distinction of the level of understanding of the values. Four managers (C, F, J, O) stated that the pure understanding of the respective values is an essential step in a work relationship. Especially in ISD projects this pure understanding should ideally result in a mutual agreement of the value systems. We found such statements especially in ISD projects because of the very high frequency of interaction and communication, which is important to 'get along' with the partner's values than in more formalized projects (comprehensive evidence in interview O) like management of IT infrastructure.

Besides the understanding of values, we found, in some configuration patterns, the mutual understanding about the objectives to be an important success factor. As expected the understanding of the projects objectives should be shared in all types of partnerships regardless of the geographical distance. Nevertheless, especially in embedded application and infrastructure management partnerships we found a higher importance for the understanding of the respective vision, which goes beyond the understanding of the projects objectives. While managers of independent partnerships and ISD projects joked about the belief in a shared vision (e.g. K, L), managers of highly embedded partnerships emphasized the importance of a shared vision in which direction both partners want to jointly develop (e.g. C, G). Obviously, the value of a shared vision is perceived to be more important in IT operations than ISD projects. One possible argument could be that the outcome of the discussed ISD projects is more concrete and gets finalized at a specific date compared to IT operations arrangements.

Thus, in independent partnerships the understanding for values und long-term objectives or visions takes a subordinate role in the mutual understanding dimension. Instead, factors like understanding of market behavior or understanding the skills and competencies of the partner become more important. In an example, manager N described a scenario in which the service could not be delivered in time because the provider did not have the necessary documents and identification cards which are necessary to enter the client's facilities. Another manager (M) pointed out the necessity of reading the national newspapers to be informed about political or governmental changes that can influence the partnerships to that specific country.

Similar to the academic research on relationship quality the dimension of trust has been frequently mentioned as an important aspect of a harmonized relationship. Most interviewees described trust as trust in the reliability of the client/provider in keeping promises and agreements, e.g., that the provider will perform as specified in the contract. The sustainability of trust in reliability depends on the successful achievement of milestones or service delivery – thus the level of actual previous reliability. Thereby, two managers (G, M) differed, with regard to trust, between reliability and competence. They mentioned competence-based trust as an initial trust type of every relationship which will become trust in the reliability if the agreements are fulfilled. One manager (G) noticed the importance of the awareness of both types of trust by describing his following experience: A relationship between an outsoucer and insourcer has been established and maintained over several years in one specific service type. Because of the high level of trust (here reliability) the partners agreed on expanding the portfolio of service delivery without noticing that the insourcer was not able to adequately deliver the service because of missing competence. This example shows that any relationship constellation should begin with trust in the competence, which can later transform into trust in the reliability (Table 5).

Table 5. Configuration of trust

Type of partnership	Geographical distance	Type of service	RQ dimension: trust
Embedded partnership	Farshore	ISD	Reliability
		IT Ops.	Reliability
	Nearshore/Onshore	ISD	Reliability
		IT Ops.	Reliability
Independent partnership	Farshore	ISD	Reliability
		IT Ops.	Predictability
	Nearshore/Onshore	ISD	Reliability
		IT Ops.	Predictability

While we did not find any conspicuousness in the descriptions of trust in embedded partnerships, there are two interesting arguments provided by managers responsible for independent partnerships. The first one, responsible for the management of infrastructure services, mentioned that he does not only want a reliable partner but a predictable one (N). Instead of only relying on the partner, the concept of predictability includes the possibility of assessing the partner's reaction in different situations. The interviews indicate that the demand for this type of trust is more common in standardized service delivery in independent partnerships while in other configurational patterns the volatile environment confirms reliability as a major characteristic of sustainable trust. Competence-related trust on the other hand has been mentioned as being important in all configurational patterns.

In the second argument, one senior manager (H), who is responsible for independent partnerships, even stated the dimension of trust as not being as important as other factors in a successful partnership: "I found this factor a little bit too romantic. It is all about business. The major part of the discussion is: where have you done this previously? Show me that you are able to deliver adequately." This statement could be interpreted as a characteristic of an independent or distant partnership. Nevertheless, it can be questioned if this interpretation of trust results in a more successful relationship than independent but fully trusting relationships.

Section 4.1 describes commitment as a dimension which includes identification, sense of obligation, and can be expressed by going the "extra mile" (i.e. performing better/more than contractually specified). The major content of the discussion during the interviews provided the characteristics of identification. The practitioners partly disagreed about what needs to be identified. While all interviewees agreed that there needs to be identification with the task, especially the managers responsible for embedded partnerships additionally highlighted the importance of identification with the client (e.g. C, F, J). In this context we found two competing statements. One manager, being responsible for a highly embedded and long-term partnership, stated that "if an employee who works for us receives his paycheck from the provider, s/he should still feel like one of our employees" (D). Another manager, being responsible for a large number of independent sourcing partners, argued that "everybody gets his/her paycheck every month and consequently knows for whom s/he is working for." (G). The latter manager also stated that the belief in identification with the client is a "misconception". Another manager (M) considered that identification does not play a crucial role in their organizational partnerships but also mentioned that he can imagine great importance in close sourcing arrangements like joint ventures. This notion was confirmed by several other interviewees: The closer the relationship is the more important identification with the client gets. This argument does not change when involving the geographical distance. The importance for identification still remains the same if the embedded partner is located in Poland or in India. The difference between farshore and nearshore in this context is that in farshore outsourcing providers identification with the client is much more difficult to achieve and influence than in nearshore or onshore partnerships (F). Nevertheless high identification with the client's organization or brand supports an embedded partnership in farshore, nearshore and onshore projects. An interviewee (F) in this context mentioned that in an ideal relationship the provider identifies with the client's brand while the client identifies with the collaborative task (Table 6).

Another aspect addresses the question if a partner is committed to perform more/better than specified in the contract – is he/she going the extra mile? Statements which confirm this question have been found mainly in the interviews with mangers that are involved in embedded partnerships managing applications and infrastructure. Managers from other configurational patterns commonly mentioned that this aspect is either not expected or that in practice this "overfulfillment" will never happen. In contrast two managers of the embedded partnership pattern even stated that the request for the extra mile is postulated from the client and that a fully committed provider always tries to deliver some extras and more than expected (D, I).

Table 6. Configuration of commitment

Type of partnership	Geographical distance	Type of service	RQ dimension: Commitment
Embedded partnership	Farshore	ISD	Client/Task Identification
		IT Ops.	Client/Task Identification; Extra Mile
	Nearshore/Onshore	ISD	Client/Task Identification
		IT Ops.	Client/Task Identification; Extra Mile
Independent partnership	Farshore	ISD	Task Identification
		IT Ops.	Task Identification
	Nearshore/Onshore	ISD	Task Identification
		IT Ops.	Task Identification

The last characteristic is the sense of obligation. The practitioners that raised the importance for that aspect are located in different configurational patterns for which reason we could not find a contextual change in this characteristic. Thus we assume that this characteristic is an equally important feature for any harmonized relationship.

Configuration of Communication. Similar to the previous three dimensions, the communication dimension has been raised as one of the most important aspects in RQ. Considering communication quality factors like open communication and effective problem solving processes, we could not find specific or reliable differences related to the different configurations.

Nevertheless, especially when focussing on farshore projects we determined some specificities in which there should be a greater awareness than in onshore or nearshore cases. Due to the geographical distance, workgroups that work in different time zones have more problems in the communication than closely located teams. One interviewee mentioned that in some cases the partners or workgroups "could not even say 'Hello' to each other because of the time differences" (O). Thus, farshore projects need higher attention in the implementation of a sufficient level of communication frequency. Another interviewee stated that the most important aspects in project (here embedded farshore ISD projects) is to be on site where the project happens. He proclaimed emails as the worst invention of our modern time due to the high number of misunderstanding caused by email communication.

Second, the language skills can differ between several countries. A project manager (J) stated that one important aspect in the selection of project members is "that I can basically understand the person on the other end of the telephone", which is often an issue in farshore countries like India or China.

Even though we found some aspects that differ between farshore vs. nearshore and ISD vs. IT operations when focusing on communication intensity and channels we could not find reliable differences in the importance of different characteristics in the various configurational patterns.

Configuration of Fairness. Fairness is especially formed by the collective ambition of a joint win-win situation. If one partner tries to maximize the own outcome by minimizing the partners outcome there will not be a harmonized and balanced partnership in any configurational pattern. Thus, the presence of a win-win situation is important in any partnership constellation. Similar findings have been exposed in the characteristic of consideration of the situation of the partner. There exists agreement that a fair partner has to consider changes of the partners market or political environment in the negotiations and decision making which affects the partners.

Another characteristic is the provision of forbearance. The interviewees commonly agreed that forbearance only can exist if there is a truthful relationship and problems have been previously addressed in an open manner. Only one interviewee stated that this characteristic is not relevant in a relationship because "you learn from mistakes and if there are no consequences you do not learn" (N). In another interview a global sourcing manager (C) argued that it depends on the type of mistakes and the preferences for the project. If the project is really important for the client there will be less forbearance than in projects of lower importance. Because the results on this characteristic have been very mixed, we argue that the provision of forbearance depends first of all on the preferences of the client and second on the level of trust and efforts of the provider to find a quick solution for the problem. These findings are independent to the configurational partnership patterns.

5   Contributions and Limitations

Our results show that the role of some of the RQ dimensions strongly depends on the respective contextual situation. The most crucial differences were identified for the dimensions of mutual understanding and commitment. This study highlights the importance for the consideration of context factors when developing research studies on relationship quality. For example, when focusing on commitment it could be an insufficient question to ask representatives of embedded partnerships for their level of task identification. On the other hand, if independent partners mention a low level of client identification it does not necessarily mean that the partners are not committed to the relationship.

In the following, we summarize and discuss the key results which showed up from our configurational analysis

Understanding the partner's values is more important in embedded teams than in independent teams. In embedded partnerships, the focus on understanding the partner's values is generally higher than in independent partnerships. One reason is that the partners in such relationships have informally agreed on working closely together for a longer period of time in more complex or in multiple projects. Especially the type of projects (long duration, high complexity, and high importance for both partners) requires a highly aligned team that understands each other's preferences, strategies and values. Cannon-Bowers and Salas [20] described this requirement as a perfectly aligned basketball team in which every player knows exactly where their team members will stand in any situation. The importance of understanding the values in embedded teams has been proven by Chua, Lim, Soh and Sia [21] who analyzed the influence of teams' social capital on the effectiveness of clan control. The authors showed that in a highly embedded team there is a need for a high level of social capital – i.e. sharing the same values etc. Our findings now show that there is a concrete linkage between team embeddedness and importance of understanding and sharing the team's values.

The types of values differ when changing from nearshore/onshore to farshore projects. When considering geographical distance, we can differ between country-related values and personal values developed from individual experiences. While in nearshore projects the country-related value differences are a minor issue but only the personal values stand in focus, farshore projects imply the complexity of personal *and* country-related values.

Commitment to the project tasks is necessary in any partnership; commitment to the partner should be present in embedded teams but not necessarily in independent partnerships. Besides the understanding of the values and preferences of the team members, every worker should be committed to the partnership and not only to the project goals. Based on the statements of one manager with experience of more than 22 years in outsourcing projects, this commitment to the team is more difficult to manage and achieve in farshore than in nearshore projects.

Willingness to go the 'extra mile' is postulated in some partnerships but not even expected in other partnerships. When including the type of service in embedded partnerships, we found higher presence of the clients' request *and* the providers' commitment to 'go the extra mile' (perform better than contractually specified) when focusing on IT operations. Clients responsible for farshore projects or independent partnerships consequently experienced that this kind of commitment does not happen in practice and thus they do not request and expect the 'extra mile'. These are just some examples for the importance of contextual inclusion in research projects on outsourcing relationship quality.

Limitations. The following limitations need to be considered when interpreting our results. First, referring to the configurational dimensions (type of partnership, geographical distance and type of service) we cannot limit the set of reasonable dimensions to those three. We selected these three dimensions as the critical dimensions based on a literature review, mainly based on six papers [7–10, 18, 19]. Second, in some interviews we had the problem to differ between the current state and the ideal state. We realized this limitation when an interviewee responsible for independent partnerships mentioned that he simply is not interested in the values of his partner and that he does not want the partner to know his personal values. Even in a case of a very independent and anonymous partnership we do not want to exclude the possibility that the understanding or sharing of values can further sustain the partnership and should be understood as an ideal status. On the other hand, several managers have been aware that for example aspects like sharing a vision can be important in some partnership types but clearly explained why this is not the case in their forms of partnerships. Nevertheless, further research should more explicitly focus on the differentiation between as-is and to-be situation. Third, due to the explorative nature of this study the results could be attached with subjective statements. To overcome this limitation we suggest richer case studies that involve multiple stakeholders and perspectives during the data collection.

6 Conclusion

In this study, we analyzed the context-dependent role of relationship quality in outsourcing arrangements. We zoomed into the RQ dimensions and analyzed the meaning and importance of the dimensions' characteristics with different contextual partnership configuration. The results are based on 16 explorative interviews with leading outsourcing managers from different industries. First, we provided a general, practitioner-related conceptualization of relationship quality. Then, we established a configurational framework which facilitates the categorization of different forms of relationships. The categories are (1) type of partnership, (2) geographical distance, and (3) type of service. In a last step, we merged the generic conceptualization of RQ with the configurational framework patterns. Thus, we could highlight different key aspects when varying the configurational partnership pattern.

Due to the explorative nature of this study the findings provide only a first insight into the change of key aspects in the different partnership patterns. To further validate these findings, a more structured and theory-driven approach is needed. Methodologically, we suggest either several case studies in which different project-related partnerships are observed or a structured survey across multiple types of outsourcing arrangements and other contextual aspects.

Overall, our study helps to gain more detailed insights into the configuration of the relationship quality dimensions. We could show that the detailed conceptualization of the RQ dimensions highly depends on the contextual situation within the specific outsourcing arrangement. We developed a generic framework (Sect. 4.2) which can be applied to analyze and compare relationship quality in the most common types of outsourcing arrangements. This generic framework can be applied to different scenarios and in turn enables researchers to understand and explain diverging results of different studies. Moreover, it will allow practitioners to gain comparable insights into all different outsourcing efforts of their organization.

Appendix

See Table 7

Table 7. Dimensions of Relationship Quality (extension based on Goles and Chin 2005)

RQ dimension	Ring and Van den Ven 1994	Kern 1997	Klepper 1995	Lee and Kim 1999	Willcocks and Kern 1998	Henderson 1990	Mohr and Spekman 1994	Anderson and Narus 1990	Dywer et al. 1987	Morgan and Hunt 1994	Heide and John 1992	Kanter 1994	Goles and Chin 2005	Blumenberg et al. 2008	Winkler et al. 2008	Goo et al. 2009	Beimborn 2012
Trust	X	X	X	X	X	X	X	X	X	X	X	X	X	X		X	X
Commitment	X	X		X	X	X	X		X	X	X	X	X	X		X	X
Communication		X		X	X		X	X	X		X	X	X	X			X
Mutual understanding				X		X							X				X
Conflict resolution	X		X	X			X	X				X	X	X		X	X
Consensus	X											X	X	X			X
Cooperation		X	X					X					X				
Coordination				X			X						X				
Flexibility / adaption	X				X						X		X	X			
Integration / participation				X													
Culture / Norm				X										X		X	
Benefit + risk sharing				X													
Interdependence				X										X		X	
Forbearance																	X
Reputation															X		
Joint action				X													
Information sharing				X													

References

1. Goles, T., Chin, W.W.: Information systems outsourcing relationship factors: detailed conceptualization and initial evidence. DATA BASE Adv. Inf. Syst. **36**, 47–67 (2005)
2. Lee, J.-N., Kim, Y.-G.: Effect of partnership quality on IS outsourcing success: conceptual framework and empirical validation. J. Manag. Inf. Syst. **15**, 29–61 (1999)
3. Lacity, M.C., Khan, S.A., Willcocks, L.P.: A review of the IT outsourcing literature: insights for practice. J. Strateg. Inf. Syst. **18**, 130–146 (2009)
4. Lacity, M., Khan, S., Yan, A., Willcocks, L.P.: A review of the IT outsourcing empirical literature and future research directions. J. Inf. Technol. **25**, 395–433 (2010)
5. Grover, V., Cheon, M.J., Teng, J.T.C.: The effect of service quality and partnership on the outsourcing of information systems functions. J. Manag. Inf. Syst. **12**, 89–166 (1996)
6. Beimborn, D.: Considering the relative relevance of outsourcing relationship quality. In: 20th European Conference on Information Systems (2012)
7. Leimeister, S., Krcmar, H.: Identifying different IS outsourcing client types. In: 15th Americas Conference on Information Systems (2009)
8. Zelt, S., Wulf, J., Neff, A.A., Übernickel, F., Brenner, W.: Succeeding in application service outsourcing strategies - A contingency perspective. In: 22th European Conference on Information Systems (2012)
9. Lee, J.-N., Miranda, S.M., Kim, Y.-M.: IT outsourcing strategies: universalistic, contingency, and configurational explanations of success. Inf. Syst. Res. **15**, 110–131 (2004)
10. Frey, T., Buxmann, P.: IT project portfolio managment - A structred literature review. In: 18th European Conference on Information Systems (2012)
11. Reich, B.H., Benbasat, I.: Factors that influence the social dimension of alignment between business and information technology objectives. MIS Q. **24**, 81–113 (2000)
12. Hart, P., Saunders, C.S.: Power and trust: critical factors in the adoption and use of electronic data interchange. Organ. Sci. **8**, 23–42 (1997)
13. Das, T.K., Teng, B.-S.: Trust, control, and risk in strategic alliances: an integrated framework. Organ. Stud. **22**, 251–283 (2001)
14. Anderson, J., Narus, J.: A model of distributor firm and manufacturer firm working partnerships. J. Mark. **54**, 42–58 (1990)
15. Blumenberg, S.: IT outsourcing relationship quality dimensions and drivers: empirical evidence from the financial industry. In: 14th Americas Conference on Information Systems (2008)
16. Fehr, E., Schmidt, K.M.: A theory of fairness, competition, and cooperation. Q. J. Econ. **114**, 817–868 (1999)
17. Rabin, M.: Incorporating fairness into game theory and economics. Am. Econ. Rev. **83**, 1281–1302 (1993)
18. Müller, R., Martinsuo, M., Blomquist, T.: Project portfolio control and portfolio management performance in different contexts. Proj. Manag. J. **39**, 28–42 (2008)
19. Blomquist, T., Müller, R.: Practices, roles, and responsibilities of middle managers in program and portfolio management. Proj. Manag. J. **37**, 52–66 (2006)
20. Cannon-Bowers, J.A., Salas, E.: Reflection on shared cognition. J. Organ. Behav. **22**, 195–202 (2001)
21. Chua, C.E.H., Lim, W.-K., Soh, C., Sia, S.K.: Enacting clan control in complex IT projects: a social capital perspective. MIS Q. **36**, 577–600 (2012)
22. Dwyer, R., Schurr, P., Oh, S.: Developing buyer-seller relationships. J. Mark. **51**, 11–27 (1987)

23. Goo, J., Kishore, R., Rao, H., Nam, K.: The role of service level agreements in relational management of information technology outsourcing: an empirical study. MIS Q. **33**, 119–145 (2009)
24. Heide, J., John, G.: Do norms matter in marketing relationships? J. Mark. **56**, 32–44 (1992)
25. Henderson, J.: Plugging into strategic partnerships: the critical IS connection. Sloan Manag. Rev. **31**, 7–18 (1990)
26. Kanter, R.M.: Collaborative advantage: the art of alliances. Harvard Bus. Rev. **72**, 96–108 (1994)
27. Kern, T.: The gestalt of an information technology outsourcing relationship: an exploratory analysis. In: ICIS 1997 Proceedings, Atlanta, Georgia, pp. 37–58 (1997)
28. Klepper, R.: The management of partnering development in I/S outsourcing. J. Inf. Technol. **10**, 249–258 (1995)
29. Mohr, J., Spekman, R.: Characteristics of partnership success: partnership attributes, communication behavior, and conflict resolution techniques. Strateg. Manag. J. **15**, 135–152 (1994)
30. Morgan, R.M., Hunt, S.D.: The commitment-trust theory of relationship marketing. J. Mark. **59**, 20–38 (1994)
31. Ring, P., Van de Ven, A.: Developmental processes of cooperative interorganizational relationships. Acad. Manag. Rev. **19**, 90–118 (1994)
32. Willcocks, L.P., Kern, T.: IT outsourcing as strategic partnering: the case of the UK inland revenue. Eur. J. Inf. Syst. **7**, 29–45 (1998)
33. Winkler, J.K., Dibbern, J., Heinzl, A.: The impact of cultural differences in offshore outsourcing - Case study results from German-Indian application development projects. Inf. Syst. Front. **10**, 243–258 (2008)

The Role of Social Capital as Antecedent in Clan Formation in Information Systems Outsourcing Project

Riitta Hekkala[1(✉)], Ari Heiskanen[2], and Matti Rossi[1]

[1] Department of Information and Service Economy, School of Business,
Aalto University, Chydenia, P.O. Box 21220, 00076 Aalto, Finland
{riitta.hekkala,matti.rossi}@aalto.fi
[2] Department of Information Processing Science, University of Oulu,
Silkkitie 1 C 46, 01300 Vantaa, Finland
ari.heiskanen@oulu.fi

Abstract. This paper focuses on how different aspects of social capital facilitate or prevent clan control in two related inter-organizational system (IOS) projects during the projects' four years life span. We observed the building of social ties in the projects and tried to understand how trust is build or destroyed in large teams, which are organizationally and physically separated, but need to work together for an extended period of time. The data for this qualitative study was collected from two large IOS projects. We analyzed how the social capital helps us to interpret the process of building clan control in an IOS project. We found out that clan control is difficult to achieve and the organizations need to be aware of ways of building social capital and be able to build and maintain social capital across organizational borders to succeed in such projects.

Keywords: Clan control · Social capital · Information system development project

1 Introduction

As outsourced projects, with rapidly assembled teams from several organizations and often from different cultural backgrounds, seem to be the current norm in information systems (IS) sourcing, it is important to identify possibilities and challenges of controlling such projects. The challenges come from the different backgrounds (e.g. clients with low understanding of the development work and consultants/developers with low domain knowledge), tight time pressures and the limited time windows for team building - just to name a few. Rustagi et al. [1] have highlighted that only few studies have systematically investigated the exercise of control in an outsourcing arrangement.

The prior IS studies have focused on the different types of control mechanisms (behavior, outcome, or clan controls) (e.g. [2, 3]), and the factors such as project size, outcome measurability, behavior observability and their influence on the choice of control modes [4]. Kirsch et al. [5] have argued that clan control is used in cases where the client's knowledge of the software process is low. Long et al. [6] have suggested

© Springer International Publishing Switzerland 2015
I. Oshri et al. (Eds.): Global Sourcing 2015, LNBIP 236, pp. 83–99, 2015.
DOI: 10.1007/978-3-319-26739-5_5

that clan control is also used in organizations where reward distributions are not the most valid indicators of professional success and relational status. It has been assumed that clan control is harder to exercise in outsourced project for example because of the differences in norms and beliefs between client and vendor organizations [2].

There is a paucity of knowledge about the antecedents of clan control. However, recent research has focused on how social capital attributes are antecedents of team-based clan control [5, 7]. This is an important issue for complex project teams, as they come from heterogeneous backgrounds and cultures and need to form an effective clan in a short period of time. A further limitation of clan control based explanations of project control is that they do not explain sufficiently factors that facilitate clan control [5, 7, 8]. It has been argued by O'Dwyer et al. [8] that how clan control develops and how clan control can be achieved are neglected topics in previous research.

We studied two related IS outsourcing projects over a period of four years during 2002–2006. We were interested in the formation of groups and internal controls in outsourced information system development (ISD) projects and how different clusters of social capital attributes: (1) the structural cluster, (2) the relational cluster and (3) the cognitive cluster (c.f. [5, 9]), are antecedents of clan control in outsourcing IS project. The social capital is understood as a process of social interaction leading to constructive outcomes (c.f. [5, 10]) in this study.

The specific research question addressed by this research paper is: *How different attributes of social capital facilitate or prevent clan control in inter-organizational system (IOS) projects?*

The paper is organized as follows: In the next section we present the relevant literature for the study. The third section outlines research methods we employed. The fourth section gives two project cases. The fifth section presents the findings of our study. The sixth section discusses the implications of our findings, and presents a theoretical integration of our findings. We then conclude our study with a brief summary of our contributions, implications and limitations.

2 Theoretical Background

In this section we discuss the relevant literature on the paper topic including control in IS outsourcing, control modes and mechanisms, factors that facilitate clan control, and different aspects of social capital as a predictor for team-based clan control.

2.1 Control in IS Outsourcing

Control is a multidimensional concept, with many definitions, interpretations and theories [5, 11, 12]. Control has long been central to both management and organizational theory and practice. A very common view of control is an attempt by an individual or organization to influence the actions and behaviors of other individuals or organizations by using certain mechanisms in order to achieve organizational objectives better [1, 12, 13]. Vlaar et al. [14] state that the degrees to which managers trust or distrust their partners during the initial stages of cooperation have a strong impact on the development of these relationships in later stages of collaboration. In their study, Vlaar et al. [14] discuss the evolution of trust, distrust, and formal coordination and control in inter-organizational (IO) relationships. Das and Teng [11] posit that neither trust nor control alone is sufficient for explaining confidence, but even with minimum trust the partners can develop a fairly high level of confidence if the power bases and control mechanisms are adequate. Some researchers have maintained that trust and control are 'the different sides of the same coin' and if it is possible to fully trust a partner, there is no need for control activities [15].

IS outsourcing has been long seen to be one of the major issues facing organizations [16–18]. Lacity et al. [19] reviewed 191 information technology-outsourcing papers to get an understanding of the outsourcing practices. They have listed five key success factors for IT outsourcing such as (1) client readiness, (2) good strategy, (3) good processes, (4) sound contracts, and (5) good relationships management. Choudhury and Sabherwal [2] have identified factors that influence the choice of control modes such as task characteristics, project-related knowledge of the participants, and role expectations. In the following subsections we look at the aspects of formal and informal control in outsourced IS projects.

2.2 Control Modes and Mechanisms, and Factors that Facilitate Clan Control

Formal control includes both outcome control and behavior control [2, 5]. Outcome control mechanisms specify outcomes to be realized by the IO relationship and by its partners, and monitor the achievement of these performance targets. Behavior control mechanisms specify how IO partners should act, and monitor whether actual behaviors comply with this pre-specified behavior [3].

Informal controls are defined as modes that use social or people strategies to reduce goal differences between controller and controllee [2]. Several researchers have defined self-control and clan control as forms of informal control [2, 20]. Kirsch and Sambamurthy [20] define self-control in a way that the individual institutes the rewards because she/he is independent of organizational or group norms. Chua et al. [7] have highlighted that clan control is a direct opposite to behavior and outcome control, and instead of relying on formal power, clan control draws on interactions and creation of common values and norms among clan members in order to achieve project goals. They have highlighted that religious groups are examples of strong communities of social capital [7]. Generalising – in a clan we have control that people do not feel as a control.

Kirsch et al. [5] explain clan control as group phenomenon and 'soft' form of control. In addition, using clan control ensures that individuals have appropriate values and beliefs, and they are willing to behave in a manner that is consistent with clan values, norms, and goals [8]. Choudhury and Sabherwal [2] believe that behavior control and clan control are not used extensively in outsourced ISD projects because they might be difficult to achieve. Previous studies [2, 3, 19] have identified socialization process, shared experiences, shared beliefs, and common goals as difficult to achieve across the border of a client firm and a vendor firm.

2.3   Team-Based Clan Control

Clan control has its roots in the organizational literature [8, 12]. O'Dwyer et al. [8] identified and categorized certain conditions for the development of clans (such as stable membership, lack of exposure to other organizations, and absence of interaction with other groups of employees) and conditions for the implementation of clan control: (1) careful selection and socialisation of members, (2) a culture of shared norms, values and beliefs must develop within the clan, (3) the existence of traditions, ceremonies and rituals, (4) provision of necessary resources for members to complete their work, (5) a lack of prescribed behaviors and outcomes for tasks, and (6) a high level of interaction and communication. These conditions must be present in order for clan control to develop. It takes time for a clan to develop naturally [8].

Organizational control theory [12] has frequently been utilized in outsourced ISD project studies [1, 2, 5], but recent evidence suggests that there is a lack of empirical work that assesses Ouchi's [12] propositions about clan control [5]. Kirch et al. [5] have highlighted that Ouchi's model supports the view that when managers' knowledge of the transformation process is imperfect and when it is difficult to measure individual outputs, they utilize clan control to control the behavior of subordinates'. This is clarified in Fig. 1.

		Knowledge of the transformation process	
		Perfect	**Imperfect**
Ability to measure outputs	**High**	Behavior control OR Output Control	Output Control
	Low	Behavior Control	Clan Control

Fig. 1. Antecedents of control (adapted from [12]) (see [5], p. 473)

2.4   Different Aspects of Social Capital as Predictors for Team-Based Clan Control

The concept "social capital" has been widely used in recent years and it has become common for many researchers to observe that the term is applied in so many different ways. It is even argued that it is used in so many different situations that it is often difficult to say precisely what this term means [21]. Social scientists have had challenges not only to define the concept of social capital theoretically, but they have also engaged in debates over how to measure it. Level of analysis has also posed a particular problem. Social capital has been located at the level of the individual, the informal social group, the formal organization, the community, the ethnic group, and even the nation [10]. In social sciences, Putnam [22] draws on Coleman's [23] idea of social capital as networks of relationships based on trust, norms of reciprocity, mutual obligation, cooperation, and so on that lead to productive outcomes for individuals and groups. In addition to this, Putnam [22] talks about horizontal and vertical networks. The nature of horizontal networks is that there is equality for team members, and power is divided equally. The nature of vertical network in turn is that there is hierarchy, and power asymmetry. According to Putnam [22] horizontal networks are better ones, because they create more trust and reciprocity.

In the field of IS, different aspects of social capital have been explained by Kirsch et al. [5] as follows: **The structural cluster** reflects connections among individuals and how openly and freely they share information. **The relational cluster** refers to relationships that have developed over time, such as the extent to which trust exists among individuals. **The cognitive cluster** refers to a shared system of meaning in which a collective understanding can develop. Attributes of this cluster include shared language, codes, and narratives. These attributes reflect shared cognition, as well as different individual expertise and opinions, all of which facilitate knowledge expansion, combination, and innovation ([5], p. 476). We focus on these three different elements of social capital defined by [5, 9] in this study because we believe that they can explain how control can be achieved in outsourcing and there is a dearth of previous research on them [5, 8].

Kirsch et al. [5] have presented a research model which explains how different aspects of social capital, outcome measurability and behavior observability - together with project manager's knowledge of the transformation process and different control variables – have an effect on team-based clan control. Chua et al. [7] point out that the enactment of clan control is a dual process of building the clan by developing its social capital dimensions or re-appropriating social capital from elsewhere. Social capital is understood as a process of social interaction leading to constructive outcomes [10] in this study. The authors also stress that it is crucial to apply social capital lens as it helps to understand challenges in complex projects.

3   Methodology

We collected the data from two IS projects: one year long (2002–2003) outsourcing project (called PreViWo in this article) and a three year long (2004–2006) outsourcing project (called ViWo in this article). One year long project consisted of seven organizational teams and two consortias. The data from this project consist, for example, of personal project documentation, contracts, memos of meetings and emails.

The three year long outsourcing project (ViWo) consisted of nine organizational project teams and two inter-organizational project teams. Data was collected by in-depth interviews (250 pages of transcripts), to observations of project meetings (20), diaries (80 pages of notes), 48 memoranda of project and steering group meetings, and e-mails (738) containing messages that IS project members sent to each other during these three years. We interviewed fourteen members of the project: there were managers from the steering group, representatives of suppliers, members of the research organization associated with the project, and users active in the project. The interviews lasted from 45 min to two-and-a-half hours. In this study project members' experience was explored through narratives: interviewees were asked to tell their own story about the project and its progress. All quotations presented in this article are gained from this ViWo project.

The original nature of this study was interpretative grounded theory study that described and analyzed the actual lived experiences of project members who worked in this three year long IS project [24]. The earlier study indicated that it is important to understand the processes of social interaction leading to specific outcomes in the project i.e. to understand "a dense set of associations" [23] within this specific group. To gain an understanding about the factors that prevented or promoted cooperative behavior that is advantageous to project group members, we analyzed the data using the 'frames' of social capital attributes identified by Kirsch et al. [5].

4   The Outsourcing Projects

This section presents the very complex background of the IS project we studied. This history provides some necessary context and helps to understand the findings.

4.1   History of the Project

The ViWo project was preceded by a pilot project called PreViWo, which had the aim of building and implementing a specialized record management system for four public sector organizations. PreViWo was implemented in three steps (specification, interface pilot and planning) in the years 2002–2003. Table 1 contains the actors in the pilot project. The pilot project was influential in framing the organization of the larger project we studied (ViWo), and it also contained many of the same actors. Alpha was the leading organization for the pilot project, as the organization who applied for and received funding for the pilot project.

Table 1. Organizations involved in PreViWo.

Organization	Role of organization
Ministry	Ministry responsible for funding the pilot project
Nofco	Consortium of user organizations in charge of the project (a virtual organization)
Lambda	Consortium of user organizations (an of cooperation) that used a similar IOIS
Theta, Iota	Suppliers of the software
Eta	Expert consultants
Alpha	User organization that was a member of Nofco and Lambda and initiated the project

The project faced its main challenge late in 2002. To manage not only two consortias but also two software houses in a same project proved to be very difficult (for example the two consortia had a different view of the project goals). Some project members also felt that the project manager did not have enough experience of running a project of this size and complexity. After these experiences two organizers from user organizations, Matthew (Epsilon, c.f. Table 2) and Lucy (Alpha) thought that the new project ViWo needs re-organizing in many ways. First, Matthew and Lucy thought that it would be sensible to do a pilot project in three user organizations (Alpha, Beta and Gamma) before establishing the system at the national level.

Table 2. Organizations involved in ViWo.

Actors	Role of organization	Previous role in PreViwo
Ministry	• Ministry responsible for funding the IOIS project. • A part the Steering Group.	Yes, it was a funder
Nofco	• Consortium of 21 user organizations (Virtual organization) • The basic function of Nofco was to promote and develop locally, regionally, and nationally the utilisation of IT and to enhance inter-organizational collaboration in multiple research-related issues and administrative practices. Oversees technical system and human resource coordination between all organizations. • A part of both the Steering Group and the Project Group.	Yes, Nofco was in charge of PreViwo project.
Alpha, Beta, Gamma, Delta	• Lead user organizations in the project. Alpha was also the fund holder for the project. • A part of both the Steering Group and the Project Group.	Yes, Alpha initiated PreViwo
Epsilon	• Organization responsible for project management and research objectives • A part of both the Steering Group and the Project Group. The Quality Assurance group came from Epsilon.	No. Epsilon was a new player for ViWo.
Zeta	• Software company that supplies the software solutions for the project	No. Zeta was a new player for the new project as well
Eta	• Part of the national research network that develop research and IT based services for the needs of research and education, and the supporting IT administration. • Acted as an expert advisor. Withdrew from the project before it ended.	Yes, Eta had a role of advisor on PreViwo

4.2   From PreViWo to ViWo

ViWo built substantially on the pilot project PreViWo, and contained some of the same actors. The development of ViWo involved the computerisation of work processes to facilitate office work, the consolidation of information across organizations, and the management of key activities. Table 2 below sums up the actors and their previous role, if any, in PreViwo.

In the ViWo project, Nofco was no longer in charge of the project management organization. Epsilon was brought in to perform and manage the project management and some academic research objectives around the project. The basic function of Nofco was to promote and develop both locally, regionally, and nationally the utilisation of information and communication technology and to enhance inter-organizational cooperation in multiple research-related issues and administrative practices. Furthermore, Nofco aimed to accomplish flexible interchange of people and information between the member organizations (21 organizations altogether including Alpha, Beta, Gamma and Delta). The key user organizations now consisted of Alpha, the original lead user organization, plus user organizations Beta, Gamma and Delta. There were 21 user organizations altogether, and the aim was that it would be these 21 organizations that would eventually use ViWo. The organizations collaborated with the relevant Ministry, suppliers and consultants. At the end of the ViWo project, the leading group of the project considered that the process was a success, after all.

5   Findings

The aim of this study is to understand the role of social capital for team-based clan control in information systems outsourcing project. The essence of social capital approach is that a "dense set of associations" [23] within an IS project groups can promote cooperative behavior. Thus, our interest is to analyze in more detail, what are the factors of social capital that may facilitate or prevent clan control. Following the research model of Nahapiet and Ghoshal and Kirsch et al. [5, 9], we analyze the three aspects of social capital (the structural cluster, the relational cluster and the cognitive cluster) in this section.

5.1   The Structural Cluster

From the point of view of structural cluster the situation was interesting: The work of PreViWo project was defined as a starting point for the ViWo project. The project manager (Ruth) of ViWo project felt that the materials from PreViWo were a stumbling block to the ViWo project. Because the steering group accepted the material of Pre-ViWo project as a starting point, the project manager (Ruth) thought that she needed to follow them (steering group): *'Of course, I can't say that your project was a dud...If someone who is more valued [the steering group] than me says that it is very well done, I have to believe and accept it.'*

Many other members of the project, like Matthew (Organizer, Epsilon), Jack and John (Suppliers, Eta) questioned the suitability of the material for the ViWo project. Several representatives of the user organizations met at the first stage of the project (in March 2004) and the researcher's diary notes indicate that they did not want to continue using the previous specifications. Matthew pointed out that there was some kind of blundering in the PreViWo project: *"Afterwards it turned out that the quality of the specifications was not such that further work could have been based on them...."*

Sheila (PreViWo's project manager) reminded that the work of PreViWo project should be a starting point for the ViWo project. Ruth (Epsilon) the project manager for ViWo project felt that the previous project caused challenges in many ways: *"Naturally the previous project has caused pressures especially because the former people are there. I have sometimes sensed an air of competition concerning who is in charge…"* (Ruth).

The project manager (Ruth) of ViWo organized issues so that the project manager of PreViWo was not present at the project meetings of ViWo. This led to the situation that the knowledge sharing between these two projects was minimal during ViWo. Some project members thought that in this way competition between Ruth and Sheila was avoided. Ruth wrote to Sheila: *"I ask this because I don't intend to invite the whole steering group. At the moment there are already 19 people invited. Do you think that your presence is also necessary?"*.

Sheila was not the only person whose presence Ruth wanted to prevent from the project meetings. Ruth and Simon (project member) were colleagues, they came from the same organization (Epsilon) and for some reason did not work well together. Ruth informed Simon that it is not necessary to come to the project meeting. Simon was very astounded about the behavior of Ruth and was wondering if some other project members presence was necessary if his presence was not. Some other project members saw that Ruth was able to keep control of issues better by excluding them.

Thomas (Epsilon) thought that because legitimate power was not clearly defined in the project, project members 'took' power but did not always manage it. Supplier Eta claimed that disagreements were continual and they 'tattled' about them to the project manager. Supplier Eta sought a boost for their work from other project members on the basis of their expert power. At that time in the project, Eta had a pretty good status, probably because they were seen as experts in this project as well. Even project management people discussed that it was not easy to disagree with Eta because of the know-how possessed by the company. However, the status of Eta started to wane later in the project.

Sophie (User, Delta) criticized that Ruth did not look or discuss for alternative solutions for problems with other project members but made decisions based on position or time, and she often chose the 'fastest' way to get something done but this was not necessarily the best one: *"Project members were at the mercy of the project manager and were not able to interfere or say that why we didn't pay attention to… or ask if we could do this a different way…"* (Sophie, User, Delta).

At the end stage of the project, Nofco took merit from the ViWo work. Other project members (Supplier, Zeta and Project management people, Epsilon) judged that Nofco did not do it alone. Thus, the representative of the supplier, Walter, posed the question: '…what was it that Eta had planned and Nofco implemented? And noted that Zeta's name had not been mentioned at all in that connection … '(Walter, supplier Zeta, email sent 30th June 2005).

Status and its effect on knowledge sharing and knowledge building: There were situations where project members wanted to control decision making in the project like 'Who decides, and on what? It would be good to know, so that the matters do not need to be hashed over unnecessarily at meetings.' (Walter, Project meeting). Both Suppliers and Project Management felt that the representatives of Nofco (Consortium of User Organizations) inhibited decision-making. Sheila (Nofco), for her part, saw that the problem was that suppliers had the power to decide on matters in the project group.

John (Supplier Eta) thought that users did not take enough part in decision-making. Lisa (User Representative, Alpha) defended herself that she did not understand what was discussed [technical matters]: 'Let's speak about matter without technology...' (Lisa). Tensions between PreViWo members and ViWo members were evident. Ruth felt that she was an 'outsider' whereas Sarah and Sheila (Members of Nofco) felt that maintaining a separation between the two projects caused problems for organizational memory. Sarah and Sheila were longing for their earlier partner companies and felt that they were reinventing the wheel: *"We assumed then that since Eta was chosen as the second supplier, it would ensure the continuance...but the old information had not been passed on, that gatekeeper's task did not continue..."* (Sheila). Sheila noted that Zeta had begun to design a user interface even though one had been produced for PreViWo.

5.2   The Relational Cluster

Unclear situation and plans, responsibilities and time pressure brought distrust among the project members. The members of Nofco demanded that some kind of long term plans should be made for project because they felt that it was difficult to plan schedules and estimate coming workloads because there were no clear plans: 'In other words, matters have occured kind of unexpectedly, or is that typical in IT projects and IS projects that it is so...' (Sheila).

It was a challenge for the ViWo project that the members of the previous project (PreViWo) and the new actors (Ruth, project manager, Epsilon; the representatives of the other supplier, Zeta and academic researchers, Epsilon) had different kinds of positions and expectations with regard to the background work that was carried out before the ViWo project was established. Matthew (Organizer, Epsilon), for example, pointed out that the new organization was chosen because of negative experiences in the PreViWo project. The project manager of ViWo considered it unnecessary to employ two people from the background project (PreViWo). The representative of the supplier (John, Eta) claimed that they were engaged in the project because of small-scale 'blackmailing'. There were contradictory views among others about the organization pattern: Jack (Eta) thought that the organization pattern of the project was strange: *"I have never seen such a loose project as this"*.

It became evident through analysis that the perceptions about the presence and workload in the project team differed quite a bit. Nofco people cultivated an image according to which they did something that they did not in fact do and thus took credit for work that they had neither planned nor implemented alone. Zeta's representative criticized Eta for wanting to emphasize their expertise although it was not clear what Eta actually did or planned to do in the project. Furthermore, according to Lisa, the considerable turnover of Eta's representatives and Eta's unclear role in the project significantly hindered the progress of the project.

There were also a number of situations where project members analyzed probable reasons why the collaboration did not work, why people were not able to work together. According to Jack, collaboration did not function at all in the project, because there was no common language and no readiness for communication. Jack also thought that his company, as a supplier, was given an interpreter's role for users in the project. Eta's other representative, John, felt that collaboration with Zeta was close. Despite that, he felt that disagreements were frequent and faults were dealt with by 'tattling' to the project manager. The bond of belonging was found through positive emotions, when project members were able to joke with each other.

According to Sheila (Nofco), Eta should have made sure they kept Alpha (the user organization) up to date on what their areas of operation were. According to Eta's representative (Peter), they acted according to instructions received from Nofco. Nofco's representative, Sheila, thought that not even Alpha (the user organization) had a picture of how the two projects related to each other: According to Sheila, 'we had to reinvent the wheel' in the ViWo project. Lisa (User, Alpha) felt that collaboration was very challenging and required patience due to the variety of actors and the physical distance between them. She felt that collaboration became easier as she got to know the people better but her adaptation to the project took a very long time. Another user representative, Sophie (Delta), also felt that collaboration did not materialize in the project, despite numerous meetings.

There was criticism that people who had high power trusted people who had high status: Jack (Zeta) criticized the project manager for trusting Eta's expertise too much. According to Jack 'We can just see Eta as merely a tool for the project, but there has to be someone who has a leadership role, so that it is not possible to shift responsibility to the supplier.' Some project members also stated that the project manager tried to show by fast decisions that the project was progressing well. It seemed evident that those who have high power should try to work towards a collective view: Thomas (Epsilon) suspected that 'The steering group's understandings resulted from how the project manager presents the matter to them…'. Many of the project members' comments highlighted the significance of the communication in achieving a common viewpoint.

5.3   The Cognitive Cluster

The cognitive cluster of social capital refers to a shared system of meaning in which a collective understanding can develop. The baggage of history on opinions in ViWo project was evident. Project members from Nofco organization were longing for their earlier partner companies. They felt disempowered even though the aim was to ensure that the project produced what the Ministry wanted. Historical issues had a big role in narratives. There were conflicts between the different organizations and it did not facilitate collaboration. Not only collaboration between Epsilon and Nofco was challenging but also collaboration between the two suppliers (Eta and Zeta) was challenging. Furthermore, one of the suppliers (Zeta) felt that decisions that had already been made by the network organization (Nofco) in the previous project influenced heavily this project.

According to John (Supplier, Eta), the change in the project organization affected the manageability of the project. The point of the criticism was that the applicant for financing (Alpha) did not eventually assume responsibility for the financing but 'outsourced it' (John, Supplier, Eta) to the persons in charge of the project (Epsilon, the Research Organization). What made the governance very challenging was the fact that the authority of Nofco, the user consortium, and its relationship to the lead organizations were not defined. The fact that the background of the project was ambiguous to many participants made issues more complicated.

Frustration was evident from many members of the project: Thomas (Epsilon) was not convinced of the significance of his role within the project. Lisa (User representative, Alpha) felt frustration in many phases during the project. Jack (Eta) felt lack of communication, especially between the project manager, the other supplier (Zeta) and the users in the project. Thomas (Epsilon) also highlighted in a project group (1st November 2004) that 'it is worrying that the project manager is talking about the resource problems of Eta... The bigger concern to her seems to be that the project is some weeks late...'. Thomas also criticized the way in which some things, which were presented to the steering group by the project manager, were wide off the mark: *"Documents are meaningless if things are embellished."* It became evident that people in the ViWo project had very different starting points, because some people had been involved in the previous PreViWo project, while others had not. It did not help knowledge combination either that there were conflicting visions about the project between project members. Ruth the Project Manager (Epsilon) said: *"I have tried to have an attitude that this project will end...but the operation will continue, and I can't manage it after that..."*

According to Ruth the biggest challenge was clarifying what the previous vision had been, not only for the previous project but even further back into the past. Ruth took the view that knowledge sharing between organizations occurred in a collegial and efficient manner, despite the hierarchical nature of those organizations. However, Daniel (Eta) felt that his role as an expert was not easy: *"I felt that I was supposed to be a telepathic database link, and have the talent of a clairvoyant if I was to know all the information they wanted us to know...".*

Lisa (User representative, Alpha), and previous member of PreViWo, for her part, trusted in the supplier's expertise. Sophie (User, Delta) felt that project management had become more important to the project manager than the content of the project. Jack (Supplier, Eta) felt that the project was more of a 'technology project' for the project manager and the other supplier, Zeta. Sheila (Steering Group, Nofco) for her part felt that the main problem was the integration of PreViWo and ViWo. It was hindered by the fact that Eta did not convey information about the previous project (PreViWo). Lucy (Project Leader, Alpha) felt that she was making a lot of decisions relying on others' expertise, because she herself did not have skills and background in ISD. For example, when Ruth (Project manager Epsilon) pointed out something in a plausible way, Lucy gave the necessary final authority.

6   Discussion

In this chapter we sought to understand clan control, especially the role of social capital attributes: (1) the structural cluster, (2) the relational cluster and (3) the cognitive cluster [5, 9], as it is at the same time difficult to achieve [8] and critical for complex outsourcing arrangements [7]. This paper focuses on how these aspects facilitate or prevent clan control in inter-organizational system (IOS) projects. The main findings are summed up in Table 3 according to the clusters of social capital.

Table 3. Main social capital issues that prevented clan control.

Social capital attributes	Main findings in our case
The structural cluster (reflects connections among individuals and how openly and freely they share information)	The main issues were that connections were not strong and the starting point was not clear to all participants. Especially the role of previous work and the previous participants was opaque and caused uncertainty. Some people felt that they reinvented the wheel whereas some people felt that the previous work was 'rubbish'. Project members failed to convey to Nofco organization that they did not value previous specifications. Project manager did not invite all project members to the meetings.
The relational cluster (refers to relationships that have developed over time)	The level of trust was not strong between organizations. Some members questioned others presence and their knowhow. Many people did not trust that the project manager could cope with the task at the beginning of the project. There were fights between different organizations and teams about how the issues should be solved.
The cognitive cluster (refers to a shared system of meaning in which collective understanding can develop)	It was hard to find a common language between stakeholders – some people felt they needed to be interpreters in the project and that this role was perceived as very hard. The "drag" of the history on current activities caused that there was no clear understanding of what was known and by whom.

Our case demonstrates how people from different organizations had very different views on information. When the PreViWo project started the structure and personnel of the project were not clear for project members. This led to situations where authority and power were fought for severely. One project member highlighted that because legitimate power was not clearly defined in the project it led to project members 'grabbing' the power but not always managing it.

We claim that in order to understand the structural cluster in team-based clan control better we need to be aware of 'social hierarchies', history, and their influence on knowledge sharing issues and outcomes. We could identify at least two critical issues that prevented clan control: first, the real reasons behind the reorganization were not told to Nofco, which was leading the PreViWo project. Second, the project manager of ViWo prevented some members from participating in project meetings and it can be argued that this is because the project manager wanted to present an image that the project progressed better from her point of view than what was the real status of the project. The complicated structures seen in this project show that when individuals lose status or power, the dynamics of power come much more complicated.

The relational cluster issues refer to relationships that have developed over time, such as the extent to which trust exists among individuals or expectations that each team member will perform his or her tasks completely [5]. The reorganization revealed that there were unclear roles and expectations among the stakeholders in the project. Collaboration between two suppliers (Eta and Zeta) was not easygoing, and collaboration between respective project managers for PreViWo and ViWo was not easygoing either. There were critical challenges in responsibilities, trust and scheduling. Furthermore, the supplier (Zeta) felt that some decisions had already been made by the network organization (Nofco) and influenced this project. While Eta tried to get more power and status, Zeta tried to keep its' status and power over Eta. It is important to note that positive emotions were experienced in situations where project members were capable of joking with each other. However, the fact is that those members who had power mostly experienced positive emotions, for example the project manager of ViWo thought that knowledge sharing between organizations occurred in a collegial manner, despite the hierarchies between these organizations. The cognitive issues refer to a shared system of meaning in which a collective understanding can develop [5]. Our study highlights that actors who have more power and status, and who use their power and status in more socialized ways play crucial roles in stimulating for example collective understanding and organizational learning behavior.

The structural and relational issues led to a situation where Nofco took the merit from the PreViWo project at the end stage of the project. Other project members felt that it was unfair. What was interesting was that the project manager of PreViWo thought that the project has been successful and everything went as planned and the output was great. Thus, our case shows that those with power may experience issues much more positively, especially when being fed with limited information. Someone could also argue that they might also present things more positively to researchers and to their management because they are responsible. Talking negatively would shed a dark light on their own work. One possibility might be also that the project manager did not listen well to the problems or did not take them seriously enough.

Formal authority can help avoid a confusion of responsibility. We identified difficulties in establishing clan control because there was no clear decision making authority and employees were able to make different choices, and act independently, for example by manipulating the project manager. This finding contradicts with previous findings [7]. Kirsch et al. [5] emphasized that clan control works in cases where the client's knowledge of the software development is low. This was a starting point of our case: Matthew (Organizer, Epsilon) stressed that "We chose Zeta as supplier because it will deliver the system that the client needs, even though the client is not able to express what it needs". This was an ideal situation for using clan control, but we could identify several issues that prevented knowledge sharing and had a negative effect on social relationships and collective understanding, thus hampering control.

Organizers (Matthew and Lucy) aimed at increasing the controllability of the process via strengthening the social capital attributes when they did the changeover from PreViWo to ViWo. This was tried by reducing the number of participants from the user side from two large consortia to three single units of PreViWo and one unit proposed by the Ministry. Moreover, as the convenience choice of vendors in PreViWo appeared problematic, these vendors were replaced for ViWo with new ones that were according to Matthew's experiences more responsive towards the "difficult to define" requirements of the client community. In this way the stage was tried to set as manageable as possible for the new project manager Ruth who replaced Sheila. An additional motive of Matthew for this change was that now the project manager was from his organization (Epsilon). An additional reason to Matthew for this change was that both Ruth and Matthew had also research interests towards ViWo.

Unlike Chua et al. [7], who argue that it is possible to enact clan control within a few months in a complex IT project, we argue that in such a project it may be difficult to utilize clan control based on the findings on social capital attributes in this study. Our case study confirms findings of other researchers [2, 3, 25] that clan control might be harder to exercise in outsourced projects and we even question if it is even possible in very complex cases. We think that outsourcing projects are easily 'the combination of multiple clans' and that 'different clans' compete with each other without necessarily sharing the same goals and this leads into often-unmanageable conflicts. Chua et al. [7] highlighted that many social capital building mechanisms required organizational support and would not have worked without controller involvement. We can also confirm that social capital is important to clan control and the social capital perspective helps to understand distinction between controllers and controllees [5, 7]. Based on our study it is evident that project managers face challenge to get controllees from diverse groups to work together to deliver the project.

To sum the issues who are controlling whom by which means and when: Leaders and managers (like Lucy, Matthew, Ruth) are controlling the vendors, user organizations representatives are trying to control each other. It seems also that client organizations have only few means to control each other, clan control may be the most dominant (or only) option. Moments of control towards the vendors (control is a dynamic phenomenon): from PreViWo to ViWo Matthew controlled the vendors by changing (or suggesting to change of) vendors. During ViWo, Ruth had a key role to control the vendors. We can also identify control within the user community (from PreViWo to ViWo). We can interpret the history as a conscious movement to a smaller and more coherent set of user organization in ViWo.

Limitations and further research: As the lifespan of the projects lasted for several years, the interviews were settled mostly in the middle of the ViWo project. The perceptions might be different if the interviews were repeated or scheduled later in the project lifespan. Paths for future research include for example the analysis of outcome control, behavior control and project manager's knowledge of the transformation process and their affect on clan control.

7 Conclusion

This qualitative study studied clan control issues in two related outsourcing IS projects over a period of four years. This paper focused on how different attributes of social capital facilitate or prevent clan control. We have analyzed how the social capital attributes defined by [5, 9] help us to understand the process of building clan control in an IOS project. This four years longitudinal study of information systems development demonstrates that clan control demands very strong social capital. Our study provides a case that shows how in a very complicated organizational setting the leading actors could structure the process in such a way that the successful outcome could be reached. None of the main actors had direct power over the others, so it was not possible to rely on hierarchical methods to guide the development process. The ultimate power was with the Ministry, because it funded the ViWo development work via Alpha. However, the Ministry could not compel the actors to co-operate. The gradual establishment of clan control made the success possible, although many actors expressed that the process was chaotic.

Acknowledgments. This study was funded by the Academy of Finland (grant number 259454).

References

1. Rustagi, S., King, W.R., Kirsch, L.J.: Predictors of formal control usage in IT outsourcing partnerships. Inf. Syst. Res. **19**(2), 126–143 (2008)
2. Choudhury, V., Sabherwal, R.: Portfolios of control in outsourced software development projects. Inf. Syst. Res. **14**(3), 291–314 (2003)
3. Kirsch, L.S.: Portfolios of control modes and IS project management. Inf. Syst. Res. **8**(3), 215–239 (1997)
4. Beath, C.M.: Managing the user relationship in information systems development projects: a transaction governance approach. In: Proceedings of the Eighth International Conference on Information Systems, Pittsburgh, PA, pp 415–427 (1987)
5. Kirsch, L.J., Ko, D.-G., Haney, M.H.: Investigating the antecedents of team-based clan control: adding social capital as a predictor. Organ. Sci. **21**(2), 469–489 (2010)
6. Long, C.P., Bendersky, C., Morrill, C.: Fairness monitoring: linking managerial controls and fairness judgments in organizations. Acad. Manag. J. **54**(5), 1045–1068 (2011)
7. Chua, C., Lim, W.-K., Soh, C., Sia, S.K.: Enacting clan control in complex IT projects: a social capital perspective. MIS Q. **36**(2), 577–600 (2012)
8. O'Dwyer, O., Conboy, K., Lang, M.: A conceptual framework for understanding clan control in ISD project teams (2013)
9. Nahapiet, J., Ghoshal, S.: Social capital, intellectual capital, and the organizational advantage. Acad. Manag. Rev. **23**(2), 242–266 (1998)
10. Bankston, C.L., Zhou, M.: Social capital as process: the meanings and problems of a theoretical metaphor. Sociol. Inq. **72**(2), 285–317 (2002)
11. Das, T.K., Teng, B.-S.: Trust, control, and risk in strategic alliances: an integrated framework. Organ. Stud. **22**(2), 251–283 (2001)
12. Ouchi, W.G.: A conceptual framework for the design of organizational control mechanisms. In: Emmanuel, C., Otley, D., Merchant, K. (eds.) Readings in Accounting for Management Control, pp. 63–82. Springer, US (1992)
13. Eisenhardt, K.M.: Control: organizational and economic approaches. Manag. Sci. **31**(2), 134–149 (1985)
14. Vlaar, P.W., Van den Bosch, F.A., Volberda, H.W.: On the evolution of trust, distrust, and formal coordination and control in interorganizational relationships toward an integrative framework. Group Organ. Manag. **32**(4), 407–428 (2007)

15. Gallivan, M.J., Depledge, G.: Trust, control and the role of interorganizational systems in electronic partnerships. Inf. Syst. J. **13**(2), 159–190 (2003)
16. Pannirselvam, G.P., Love, M.S., Madupalli, R.K.: IT outsourcing: culture/cohesion's impact on vendor performance. Int. J. Bus. Humanit. Technol. **1**(3), 266–278 (2011)
17. Lacity, M.C., Khan, S., Yan, A., Willcocks, L.P.: A review of the IT outsourcing empirical literature and future research directions. J. Inf. Technol. **25**(4), 395–433 (2010)
18. Feeny, D.F., Willcocks, L.P.: Core IS capabilities for exploiting information technology. Sloan Manag. Rev. **39**(3), 9–21 (1998)
19. Lacity, M.C., Khan, S.A., Willcocks, L.P.: A review of the IT outsourcing literature: insights for practice. J. Strateg. Inf. Syst. **18**(3), 130–146 (2009)
20. Kirsch, L.J., Sambamurthy, V., Ko, D.-G., Purvis, R.L.: Controlling information systems development projects: the view from the client. Manag. Sci. **48**(4), 484–498 (2002)
21. Sandefur, R.L., Laumann, E.O.: A paradigm for social capital. Rationality Soc. **10**(4), 481–501 (1998)
22. Putnam, R.D.: Bowling Alone: The Collapse and Revival of American Community. Simon and Schuster, New York (2001)
23. Coleman, J.S.: Foundations of Social Theory. Harvard University Press, Cambridge (1994)
24. Hekkala, R.: The Many Facets of an Inter-organizational Information System Project as Perceived by the Actors. University of Oulu, Oulu (2011)
25. Lacity, M.C., Willcocks, L.P., Khan, S.: Beyond transaction cost economics: towards an endogenous theory of information technology outsourcing. J. Strateg. Inf. Syst. **20**(2), 139–157 (2011)

Information Technology Outsourcing
and the Bottom Line

Paul Alpar[(⊠)] and Patrick Noll

School of Business Administration and Economics,
Philipps University at Marburg, Universitätsstr. 24, 35032 Marburg, Germany
alpar@wiwi.uni-marburg.de, patrick.noll@gmail.com

Abstract. Outsourcing of information technology has substantially increased in
the last two decades but doubts about the business success of such arrangements
persist. This paper examines whether a difference in business performance can be
determined between firms that outsourced information technology in a given
period and those that did not. We compare four performance key figures before
and after outsourcing. The data cover deals executed in Germany from 2000 to
2006 and key figures from 1997 to 2008. The results show that a significant
difference can be observed for only two out of four key measures. However, while
the cost savings of firms that outsourced information technology are not impressive compared to other firms on average, they often show a superior financial
performance indicating that they seem to enjoy strategic benefits from the move.

Keywords: Information technology · Outsourcing · IT outsourcing ·
Outsourcing success · Firm performance

1 Introduction

The value contribution of information technology (IT) has been extensively studied
since the late 1980s (see, e.g., the reviews in [1, 2]). This is, however, much less so in
the case of IT outsourcing (ITO) although ITO has become a common practice since
the beginning of the 1990s [3]. In the USA and Canada about 10.6 % of the total IT
budget was spent on ITO in 2013 [4], up from 5 % to 6 % in 2009 [5]. Despite this rise,
doubts about the business value of ITO persist and in- or backsourcing of previously
outsourced IT functions takes place [6]. Recent examples are General Motors in USA
[4] and Daimler in Germany [7] which were both reported to plan major IT backsourcing projects. Still, empirical studies on the success of outsourcing at the firm level
are relatively rare [8]. From 147 analyzed ITO papers in the time period 1992-2000 22
papers were dealing with outsourcing success but only 9 were identified as quantitative
positivist [9]. Outcome success was measured with different constructs in these papers
but their quantification was subjective in all cases. Another survey on ITO identified
only 8 out of 205 studies that concentrated on success factors [10]. The most recent
comprehensive review of ITO literature applying empirical research studied 164 papers
which contained 741 relationships between an independent and a dependent variable
[11]. Client's business performance occurred only 31 times in these relationships (less
than 5 %) and it was only one of 25 variables used to represent ITO outcome.

© Springer International Publishing Switzerland 2015
I. Oshri et al. (Eds.): Global Sourcing 2015, LNBIP 236, pp. 100–123, 2015.
DOI: 10.1007/978-3-319-26739-5_6

We define ITO following the literature as a long-term contractual relationship between one or more independent service providers and a client to provide the client with all or part of the needed information systems services including the necessary infrastructure (e.g., [12]). When IT services are being outsourced their costs become more transparent. Service levels for contracted services are usually agreed upon, but it is not known how the provider will be reacting to a changing environment. For an optimal value contribution, it is necessary that the provider be responsive to new developments in technology and business requirements. To determine the value contribution of outsourced services remains difficult. First, additional costs occur that are not contained in the service price and that may not be easy to calculate, e.g., costs of governing ITO contracts or costs of coordinating vendors of different services. Second, the benefit side may be difficult to determine because ITO is not only undertaken to reduce costs. Some of the other important reasons to outsource IT are the wish to concentrate on core competencies, assuming that IT is not one of them, or the desire to use new technologies for which no internal knowledge is available. It is very difficult, for example, to directly and objectively measure the difference in the capability of top managers to concentrate on core competencies before and after ITO. Therefore, we attempt in this paper to identify whether a differential performance can be observed at all and, if so, what the patterns of differential performance are.

IT-related studies on differential performance have been conducted for specific applications, e.g., ERP systems [13–15], or for the general usage of IT [16, 17]. In analogy to the referenced literature, we are not attempting to prove that ITO by itself is causing the differential performance or to determine the exact value added by ITO. A superior performance of firms that outsourced IT could indicate that ITO was one of the success factors or that it is a correlate of other organizational choices that positively influence firm performance. It is often the early observable part of general company changes, e.g., restructuring of infrastructure services or start of new strategies enabled by selected partnerships. So even if the budgetary value of outsourced activities may be small compared to the total firm costs, the impact can be over proportional if ITO supports transformation [18]. Finally, our interest in potential differential performance of ITO firms is supported by a number of event studies on ITO that show that investors react to ITO announcements although ITO costs constitute a relatively small percentage of total costs (e.g., [19] and [20]).

We measure firm performance based on published and audited accounting data. This study, therefore, first reviews papers on ITO and firm performance based on accounting data. Then, we define hypotheses based on economic theories and literature findings. This is followed by the description of the applied method and the data studied. The presentation of results is followed by their discussion and conclusions.

2   Literature Review

We classify the quantitative positivist studies that analyze ITO and firm success as follows:

- Success as perceived by outsourcing participants (clients, vendors, consultants),
- Success as expected by investors and represented by market value, and
- Success as exhibited in audited accounting data.

Some of the characteristics of the three approaches are shown in Table 1.

Table 1. Characteristics of research on IT outsourcing and firm success

Type of success measure	Observation time	Information source	Data collection	Data usage
As perceived	Ex post	Survey respondents	Questionnaire, interview	Primary
Market value	Ex ante	Stock market	Data base retrieval	Secondary
Financial key figures	Ex post	Balance sheet data	Data base retrieval	Secondary

The first stream of quantitative studies employs perceived ITO success as the dependent variable. This is being assessed like most of the other variables through multi-item survey instruments (e.g., [21, 22]). While such analyses are still being carried out (e.g., [23, 24]), a number of studies where ITO success is measured by objective figures has appeared after the period surveyed in [9] and [10].

The second group of papers analyzes the effect of ITO announcement on the outsourcing firms' valuation in the capital market (e.g., [19, 25, 26, 20]). They employ the established econometric approach of an event study with cumulative abnormal returns (CAR) after the announcement of outsourcing as the success indicator. In this review, we concentrate on the third group of studies which employs accounting figures to reflect ITO success. Some of these studies compare ITO firms with non-ITO firms analyzing their comparative success.

Probably the first study that measured the relation between ITO and financial key figures was [27]. It observed the association of ITO on one side with the return on equity (ROE) and the ratio of market to book value on the other side assuming that the relationship is moderated by total costs. The relationship was positive for both success measures and moderated by costs as hypothesized. Otherwise, the research on the ITO decision dominated at that time, a situation that started changing after 2000 [11].

The use of accounting data was resumed by [28] who combined the market evaluation approach with the analysis of accounting data. The study used sales per employee (SPE) and operating income (OpInc) per employee as success measures. The positive changes in industry-adjusted medians from the year before ITO up to three years after ITO were all significant. The same was true for firms with Tobin's Q above 1. The study also identified a significant relationship between changes in accounting figures and long-run abnormal returns after three years.

A study on the performance of Korean ITO firms compared those with a fit between business and outsourcing strategy with ITO firms where these strategies did not fit [29]. Firm performance was measured by sales growth and return on assets (ROA). The firms with a fit performed significantly better than the "misfits."

Researchers at IBM analyzed the changes in key financial ratios after ITO in two studies. In the first study, they observed 56 firms that outsourced some or all IT between 1998 and 2002 and which are publicly traded on a U.S. stock exchange for up to three years after ITO began [30]. Performance was measured by earnings before interest and taxes (EBIT), selling, general, and administrative expenses (SG&A), and ROA. ITO companies exhibited a superior performance compared with companies that did not report an ITO deal in that time period. The difference in performance was statistically significant at the level of $p = 0.1$ based on the sign test. SG&A of ITO firms was already growing slower before ITO but it further improved after ITO. The highest improvement compared to non-ITO firms occurred in EBIT. In the second study, the sample contained 244 publicly traded companies which initiated ITO between 2001 and June, 2006 [31]. This time, earning performance was measured by earnings before taxes (EBT) and OpInc while SG&A and ROA were retained. Companies were observed up to three years after ITO but results are only reported for some individual years in the post-ITO period for each variable. Again, outsourcing firms performed significantly better after ITO than the comparison group. The highest difference in growth rates between the two groups occurred with respect to EBT two years after the start of the outsourcing relationship. This time, the results are significant at $p <=0.05$.

The effect of ITO on total non-interest operating costs in credit unions in the USA was studied for the period 1992–2005 in [32]. The study is very interesting from the methodological point of view but the results cannot be compared with other studies discussed in this overview because the authors use another definition of outsourcing. They consider the use of purchased software also as outsourcing: "In a VIH [vendor-supplied in-house] arrangement the credit union purchases a software program and installs it on its own computers; all data reside in-house, and the credit union typically bears responsibility for maintaining the system...".

The key figures can be assigned to two levels [33]: the process level as an intermediate level (five key figures) and the firm level (three key figures). The study compared 120 ITO firms with those that did not outsource their IT in the observed period. Each company was observed one year prior to ITO and for three years after the event. The authors found some evidence for superior performance at the process level but not at the firm level. However, some of their process level key figures (e.g., SPE, SG&A, and OpInc) were considered as firm level figures in other studies. The researchers further considered a firm's IT capability as a moderating variable assuming that benefits from ITO can only be realized with complementary IT capabilities. Companies listed in Information Week's list of 500 most innovative companies in the USA with respect to IT use were considered to possess a high core IT capability. 22 of the 120 ITO firms were on that list. Their performance was significantly better at both levels for some key figures and some years than the performance of ITO firms that were not on the Information Week list.

Another study analyzed the effect of outsourcing of two IT services with a low level of specificity, network and telecommunication services, on the ratio of total annual revenue divided by total annual operating cost in hospitals [34]. It determined that each outsourced function was associated with an average increase in profit of 25 %. Increased IT expenses were also associated with better financial performance.

The study in [33] was extended in [35] by assigning ITO initiatives to specific value chain processes. Superior performance was identified in inbound logistics (represented by raw materials inventory turnover, cost of goods sold (COGS), and gross profit margin) and supporting activities (represented by SG&A) but no or marginally significant changes in return on sales and ROA respectively were identified relative to non-ITO firms at the firm level. Here again, the assignment of key figures to levels (process or firm) contradicts some of the other studies referred to in this section.

The impact of ITO on productivity gains was analyzed in [36]. The study compares firms that outsourced IT with firms that did not but exhibit the same propensity for outsourcing. The first group achieved significantly higher productivity. The authors show that this is due to their use of IT service providers' knowledge, esp. with respect to software. Higher gains were associated with higher propensity by clients to outsource. The authors utilize data from the time period 1987 to 1999 but productivity gains are calculated only on the basis of two consecutive years (year of ITO and one year after). The authors of [37] also identify productivity gains from ITO but their analysis was carried out at the industry level (60 industries in the USA) while we concentrate on studies that analyze the success of individual firms.

The association between ITO, investments in internal IT and non-IT operating costs was analyzed in [38]. The research determines that ITO is associated with lower non-IT operating costs, esp. when accompanied by higher investments in internal IT-labor. ITO firms are not compared with non-ITO firms in that study.

There are also two papers that do not fit the classification in Table 1. They analyze financial key figures that are not drawn from balance sheets but they rely on survey respondents (perceived accounting data). The effect of outsourcing of three specific IT services on labor productivity in German firms (measured by SPE) was studied with data collected in telephone interviews [39]. The impact of strategic control on firm performance was analyzed applying resource dependency theory [40]. The respondents of the questionnaire were asked to fill in accounting data. In both cases, two difficulties exist with the approach: First, it is not clear how accurate the figures are because it is not known on what basis the respondents reply and, second, the key figures may have been calculated differently by different respondents. Therefore, these two studies are disregarded from further comparisons.

The reported findings are summarized in Table 2.

As it can be seen, the studies come to conclusions on some issues, like on the association between success and low asset specificity of outsourced services. This was predicted in early theory-based decision models for selecting IT activities for outsourcing (e.g., [41, 42]). But there is not one key figure on which all studies agree. One of the often used figures, SPE, rises with ITO according to [28] but not in the analysis in [33]. ROA, also often observed, improves according to [35] but it gets worse following [33]. Significant improvements in SG&A after ITO occur in individual years but not in the whole after-period and not with the same pattern [33, 35, 31]. It can hardly be seen as a big success of ITO and possible relating strategic changes if benefits already disappear after a year.

Our study differs from the reported ones in several ways. First, all reported papers except one [29] analyze data from the USA; our study analyzes another important market, Germany, one of the biggest economies in the world. Second, all studies

Table 2. Research findings on IT outsourcing and firm success expressed by accounting figures

Paper	Year	Firm performance	Years obs.	N	Comp.[1]	Outcome	Comments
Loh, Venkatraman [27]	1995	ROE	1	114	No	Positive	Cost structure moderates the relationship between ITO and performance
Gao [28]	2005	SPE;	5	341	Yes	Positive	
		OpInc per employee				Positive	
Lee [29]	2006	Sales growth	-	136	No		ITO firms with fit between business & outs. strategy outperform "misfits"
		ROA					
Mojsilovic et al. [30]	2007	SG&A;	4	56	Yes	Positive	Only in years t+1 and t+2
						Positive	Only in year t+3
		EBIT;				Positive	Only in years t+3
		ROA					
Wang et al. [33]	2008	**Process level:**	5	120	Yes		High core IT-capability
		Sales;				No[2]	supports ITO success
		SPE;				No	Only in years t+1 and t+2
		SG&A/Sales (SGAS);				Marg.	Only in year t+1
		Depr. exp./Sales;				pos.	
		OpInc before depr./ Sales				Marg. pos.	
		Firm level:				No	
		ROA;				Negative	
		ROE;				No	

(Continued)

Table 2. (*Continued*)

Paper	Year	Firm performance	Years obs.	N	Comp.[1]	Outcome	Comments
Thouin et al. [34]	2009	ROI				No	
		Revenue/Operating cost	1	1110	No	Positive	Holds for IT functions with low asset specificity (only hospitals)
IBM [31]	2010	SG&A;	Max. 4.5	244	Yes	Positive	Only in t+1
		EBT;				Positive	Only in t+2
		OpInc;				Positive	Only in t+2
		ROA				Positive	Only in t+2
Gwebu et al. [35]	2010	**Process level:**	5	90	Yes		
		Inbound logistics;				Positive	Significant in some years
		Operation;				No	Significant in most years
		Outbound logistics;				No	
		Supporting activities				Positive	
		Firm level:				Marg. pos.	
		ROA;					
		Return on sales				No	
Chang, Gurbaxani [36]	2012	Productivity	2	97	Yes	Positive	IT knowledge of service providers enables productivity gains
Han, Mithas [38]	2013	Non-IT OpEx/revenues	5	281	No	Positive	ITO and IT labor investments are complementary

[1] means that ITO firms are compared with non-ITO firms;
[2] means no significant difference

observe ITO firms for only up to 5 years in total. Here, we observe the firms for up to 12 years in total, as will be described below. Our results are, therefore, less sensitive to fluctuations that may occur in an individual year before or after ITO. Also, short-term impacts which, for example, may stem from the sale of IT assets in the year of the deal carry less weight. Third, we analyze the different patterns of outcomes with respect to various performance measures for each individual ITO firm. This way, we can better judge the overall impact of the move.

3   Research Hypotheses

Perception-based metrics are important as perceptions often represent the basis on which decision-makers in companies decide about future actions. This is especially true if the dependent variable represents an intention (e.g., to employ ITO). However, if audited accounting data are available then such data are a more objective representation of what has happened in the past. Therefore, we base the research reported in this paper on audited balance sheet data. The potential changes in the key figures are observed over several consecutive outsourcing contract years. We do not attempt to model a causal relationship between ITO and firm performance. This would require much more detailed data from each company. Given the limited availability of data and the high aggregation level of available data (see the section on data) we try to answer the question:

Did firms that outsourced IT in the observed time period perform better after ITO than firms that did not?

We, further, examine based on the industry membership of companies which outsourced IT activities:

Do firms in different industry sectors perform differently after ITO?

As stated in the introduction, we assume that ITO is often part of wider strategic moves and expect that benefits will accrue beyond (or instead of) relative cost savings. Financial performance of business decisions manifests itself in different dimensions. Therefore, we examine four key figures that reflect different perspectives of financial success. The specific key figures are chosen later; here, we discuss the four perspectives and our expectations on how ITO may relate to them. The information content of absolute performance measures is limited. Success in terms of a superior performance needs to be assessed by comparing performance with the market or an appropriate subgroup. Therefore, all hypotheses are formulated with respect to a control group.

First, a key figure should reflect the cost perspective since IT-cost containment has been a driver for ITO from its beginning (e.g., [43]). This is still the case: an analysis of 55 IT outsourcing contracts revealed that "reducing IT costs" was the highest ranked objective [44]. Following transaction cost economics (TCE), firms should consider outsourcing as the governance structure for recurring activities of medium asset specificity at a medium level of uncertainty to reduce transaction costs [45]. This does not mean that firms should always opt for ITO because internal provision of IT services may turn out to be more economic [46]. It was also shown in [26, 20] that investors appreciate the intent of cost reductions in ITO announcements. ITO may lead to improvements in all business processes so cost savings should also occur outside of IT. This block of costs is usually much bigger than the IT block [38]. Therefore, the observed cost figure should include the IT budget, costs related to ITO (e.g., coordination with the vendor) that are often not contained in it [47, 48] and all other operating expenses. As customary, we disregard production costs because they are usually dominated by raw materials and other purchased goods. Accordingly, we formulate the first hypothesis with respect to costs:

Hypothesis 1. Operating expenses in firms that outsourced IT will decrease more than in the control group.

Strategic aspects such as the desire to concentrate on activities that create more value for the firm, e.g., on the development of new products or the improvement of customer relations, are another important reason for ITO [49]. The theoretical backing for positive expectations from such a move stems from the resource-based view (RBV) of the firm [50]. Firms should be able to perform better after ITO because they can reallocate their resources (not just the financial ones) to activities with a higher value. Whether the firm succeeded to better use their resources or to successfully implement new strategies can be observed from different perspectives. We take the profit, the personnel, and the asset perspective. The hypothesis relating to the profit perspective which has also been analyzed in [30, 31] is stated as:

Hypothesis 2. Profit will increase in firms that outsourced IT more than in the control group.

Many ITO deals include a transfer of employees. On one hand, if the sales and other costs positions are kept, the decrease in headcount leads directly to an increase in profits per employee. On the other hand, the skills of remaining employees should better fit with the core competencies of the company. It was determined that both, sales and income per employee, increased after ITO [28]. Differences in the performance of employees have also been investigated in other studies of IT deployment. For example, income per employee was used as a performance measure in a study of effects of successful implementation of strategic information systems (SIS) [51]. To reflect the personnel perspective we examine:

Hypothesis 3. Employee performance will increase in firms that outsourced IT more than in the control group.

ITO deals that include the transfer of data centers, hardware, or other assets often generate cash that can be used to reduce debt (or for other investments). Usually, this also leads to a decrease in assets. If the company can keep its returns at the previous level or even increase them, then we expect ROA to improve. Note that computer assets continue to be in use in the case of ITO, they are just taken off the balance sheet. But even in the case of application outsourcing or BPO, less investment in infrastructure will be needed in the future than in firms that keep the functions in-house since growth of data and IT applications usually necessitate a growth in computers and peripheral and network facilities. Therefore, we assume based on the asset perspective:

Hypothesis 4. The asset performance in firms that outsourced IT will increase more than in the control group.

We refer above to TCE and RBV to formulate reasonable hypotheses. However, the hypotheses are not designed to test these theories with empirical data because they are formulated with respect to relative performance following our goal to observe differential performance, if it occurs. It is possible, for example, that firms achieve cost savings through ITO by minimizing the sum of production and transaction costs as suggested by TCE but that the control group achieves even higher cost savings with other actions. Then, hypothesis one will not hold although TCE cannot be refuted.

The four hypotheses are graphically shown in Fig. 1.

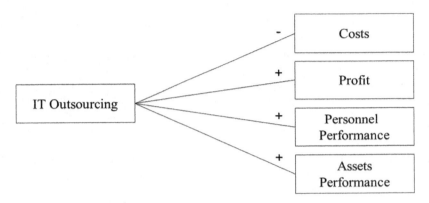

Fig. 1. Hypotheses on the correlation of IT outsourcing and relative performance

The observed effects could vary by industry sectors given that the role of IT differs by sectors. Service provisioning is often strongly supported by IT (e.g., in the financial industry). IT costs usually represent a higher share of operating expenses in the service than in the industry sector. Changes in the provision of IT services may, therefore, have a higher impact on firms in this sector. Literature reports that ITO announcements of service sector firms were valued higher than those of industry sector firms [19, 20]. Based on these arguments and observations, we assume:

Hypothesis 5. Service sector firms will gain from ITO relatively more than firms from the industry sector.

Ideally, all performance measures improve when ITO and other corresponding strategic measures are taken. However, other patterns may also be desirable. This is, for example, the case when relative costs go up but other financial figures still improve. On the opposite side, a decrease in relative costs accompanied by decreases in other financial figures is of little value.

4 Method

The applied method is guided by following ideas: Whatever tangible and intangible effects are envisioned by an ITO move, over time, they should show up in the key success figures used in a company. Therefore, rather than introducing new metrics, we concentrate our analyses on established financial key figures. Another important aspect is a suitable comparison. It is possible that a company reduced its IT costs through outsourcing but that overall savings achieved by other companies that did not outsource IT are even higher because they are using more efficient supply chains, cheaper selling channels, or simpler organizational structures. Therefore, the measurement should be such that success is measured with respect to other companies (see, for example, [8]). Finally, just as it often takes time for large IT investments to show positive impacts [1], the same is true for ITO. It always entails organizational changes, learning, and, adjusting to new relationships. The impact should be, therefore, observed for at least a few years after the deal.

To determine whether differential performance occurred, we compare firms that outsourced their complete IT or parts of it with firms that did not undertake such a move in the observed time period. Since the observed firms have different sizes, we do not consider absolute figures but the growth of key figures over time. More precisely, we compare whether there is a difference in growth between the two groups before and after ITO. Similar approaches were also applied in [30, 31] but they did not disclose all details. The exact procedure used in this research is described below. The idea of industry- or peer-adjusted comparisons itself is not new and has also been applied in non-IT contexts, for example, in the analysis of post-merger performance [52]. In the context of ITO, it had been also applied in [28, 33, 35, 36].

ITO could have occurred in different years within the observed timeframe (1977-2008). For each company that outsourced IT, we appropriately define the "before" and "after" time periods. For example, if an outsourcing contract was started in 2003 then the pre-outsourcing period for this company is from 1997 to 2002 and the post-outsourcing period is from 2004 to 2008. If a contract was started in 2005 the pre-outsourcing period for this company is from 1997 to 2004 and the post-outsourcing period is from 2006 to 2008. The key figures of the comparison group are always looked up for the same periods as for ITO firms. This way, it is guaranteed that the compared companies operated under same economic conditions as the ITO firms no matter when ITO occurred. This also allows us to consolidate "before" ("after") differences although ITO occurred at different times.

Some outsourcing deals include significant transfers of assets which can lead to an immediate impact on the bottom line but in most cases benefits only accrue over (contract) time. Therefore, for an ITO deal to be included into our calculations, performance figures are required for at least one year prior to the year in which ITO started and for at least two years after the year in which it started, i.e., we need at least figures of four consecutive years. In most cases, more consecutive years than the required minimum were available. The post-outsourcing figures were followed at most till the expiration of the outsourcing contract.

The procedure to determine whether a differential performance occurred is as follows:

1. Calculate yearly growth rates for each key figure for each company that outsourced IT and for each company from the control group.
2. Calculate geometric means of growth rates for the periods before and after ITO depending on the year in which it started.
3. Calculate average growth rates of the control group for each year and key Fig.
4. For each company that outsourced IT, calculate the difference between the mean growth rate "before" (and "after") and the average growth rate of the control group for the same time period.
5. Examine whether the difference of medians before and after ITO is statistically significant using t-tests for paired samples.

The approach is referred to as "double differencing" in [35] since it considers time and company differences. Following the arguments of [17], we compare ITO firms with the average of all other firms rather than making paired comparisons between each ITO firm and a "most similar" firm that did not outsource ITO because this constitutes a more robust analysis, esp. for relatively low sample sizes. In [36], firms are matched by their general propensity to outsource. This propensity is calculated on the basis of several figures with IT intensity being one of them. We do not possess such detailed data of each company to follow the approach. This means that if we identify significant differences in goal achievement of ITO versus non-ITO firms, differences in propensity to outsource could be one reason since we are not controlling for it. This can lead to an overestimate of benefits of 5–15 % according to [36].

For the analysis of industry sector differences, we vary the procedure in steps 3 and 4 by calculating average growth rates separately for the two sectors, industry and service. In this way, the potentially different states in the business cycles of the two sectors are accounted for. In summary, our procedures control for firm size, economic conditions, and industry sector.

The group of ITO companies can be considered a sample of all companies. It could be that other samples would lead to the same results, i.e., that statistically significant differences between "before" and "after" time periods, if there are any, occur only by chance. Therefore, a Monte Carlo analysis is conducted to determine how reliable the results are. It is conducted here by drawing 100 times a random sample of companies with a sample size that equals the number of ITO companies. Since these companies did not experience an ITO "event" in the observed time period, a "before-after" structure is created that follows the structures in the ITO sample. That is, if five companies outsourced IT in 2002, then in the random sample for five companies 2002 is used to split the whole time frame into a "before" and "after" part. The distribution between companies from the industrial and service sector is also controlled to equal the one of ITO companies. The differences of the growth rates of companies in the sample and the rest of the companies are again calculated for the "before" and "after" time periods. Paired t-tests are run to determine whether the average differences "before" and "after" are significantly different. The number of samples is recorded for which the relative difference in growth rates was significant.

As already mentioned, the approach cannot show the causality of differential performance. However, this is also true for the perception-based method and event studies. The former approach can only prove that some variables as perceived by some informants influence their perception of ITO success. This is no proof of the influence of actual variables on actual success. The existence of a relationship between ITO announcements and CAR, on one side, also does not necessarily prove causality. For example, an ITO announcement of the observed firm may coincide with a positive announcement of a customer firm which actually leads to the CAR of the observed firm. On the other side, the lack of CAR after a public ITO announcement may be due to the fact that the move was already expected and priced in well ahead of the announcement. This behavior was proven even for most clandestine non-IT operations [53].

5 Data

Details of outsourcing contracts are generally kept secret but unlike with some other business contracts, general information about the arrangement is communicated to the public. The reason is that usually both sides have an interest in announcing the deal. Outsourcing vendors wish to let the market know that they gained a new customer or retained an existing one. Growing business supports their image in the market and trust into their stability. Outsourcing companies wish that the move be perceived as a positive sign by financial analysts and other observers of the company. They want to impose their view of the deal on the market. They do not want that the market considers it as an emergency action. Therefore, they either communicate the deal by themselves or they coordinate the announcement with the outsourcing vendor. The following contract information was usually available: partners, begin, length, total contract volume (TCV), scope (with the values: total outsourcing, application outsourcing, business process outsourcing (BPO), or infrastructure outsourcing), regional scope in case of internationally operating companies, type (with the values: new, renewal, or extension). Statistical use of some of these attributes was limited for the following reasons:

(a) Total contract value (TCV) needs to be spread over the full contract length but the payments are often not spread evenly. The exact contract starting dates were also sometimes not given, so altogether we cannot know how to correctly discount the TCVs to make them comparable.

(b) Number of vendors per deal. There was too little variation in this variable, most deals were serviced by one vendor. Of course, the outsourcing companies often close different deals with different vendors. This is partly reflected in the data but not enough to undertake specific evaluations.

(c) The content of the outsourcing deal was often specified more exactly than by the outsourcing scope as defined above. However, this finer classification, e.g., about the exact application that has been outsourced, leads to many different values with low frequency which does not allow any statistical evaluation.

In most studies of ITO deals in the USA, the researchers retrieved the announcements from media archives. We did not need to peruse media archives but received data on ITO deals for our research from an outsourcing vendor for deals closed in Germany in the time period from 2000 to 2006. They also let us access purchased data collected by Pierre Audoin Consultants (PAC), a specialized market research firm. We used this data to verify the vendor's database or add missing information. We consulted media archives only in cases in which the information in the database was ambiguous, e.g., to determine the exact client firm.

It cannot be proven that no important ITO deal is missing in this data collection but this is very unlikely. In addition to the above mentioned interests of the contracting parties to publicize the deal, there is a third party in Germany that has an interest in making the outsourcing contract public. These are the trade unions that are represented in works councils. In general, each German company with more than 20 workers has to have a works council. These councils need to agree to any outsourcing arrangement that impacts workers. Being concerned that an outsourcing contract may lead to a loss of jobs, the trade unions often try to raise public attention early on in the negotiation process. Finally, listed companies may in some cases be obliged by the law to report outsourcing arrangements if they can be relevant for stock movements.

Performance data at the aggregated company level can be found in balance sheets. Some large public companies offer highly aggregated balance sheet data on their websites. However, many do not offer enough details or it is not exactly clear how they calculate some of the key figures or ratios. Therefore, we decided to use performance data from a leading commercial provider of such data, Creditreform e. V. These data are checked for quality and all ratios are calculated in the same way. Creditreform is an association of over 170 individual agencies and offices in Europe, the majority in Germany, which exists since 1879. Their products are used by companies to manage functions like marketing, credit and risk, and receivables. Most of Creditform's customers become members of the association and use the firm's debt collection services. Over 165,000 companies are members of Credireform. We were granted access to Creditreform's database called DAFNE and retrieved performance data for about 8000 companies for the period of 1997 to 2008. First, we looked for companies that outsourced their IT (or parts of it) according to the above mentioned file of outsourcing deals. Then, we recorded data for other companies if they had a yearly return of over five million Euro and if data for at least four consecutive years were available.

Based on previous research, our research goals, and data availability, we chose to record the following key figures for the four above mentioned aspects of financial performance and business activity:

1. The *cost perspective* is reflected by other operating expenses (OOE). It corresponds to SG&A used in other studies. They are defined as all costs that do not directly relate to production. No figure for IT costs is found in the data set. The use of all operating expenses is appropriate and backed by literature as pointed above.

2. Earnings before interest and taxes (EBIT) is a key figure observed by all financial analysts. It reflects the *profit performance* of a company. Creditreform calculates EBIT as:

Net sales (i.e., sales without value added tax)
minus production costs of goods sold
minus other operating expenses.

3. To reflect the *personnel perspective* we observe the profit per employee (PPE). Some studies use sales per employee but PPE better reflects the ultimate business success. PPE is calculated as:

   Operating and financial profit divided by the number of employees.

4. Finally, the *asset perspective* is represented by the established key ratio return on assets (ROA). ROA is calculated as

   *Operating and financial profit divided by total assets * 100.*

We started with 600 outsourcing deals but had to exclude the majority of them because they did not qualify for the research for reasons explained below:

- Outsourcing vendor resides in Germany but the customer is based in another country where it complies with different accounting rules. Their statements are usually also not found in DAFNE.
- The unit that has chosen ITO does not publish earnings and other statements because it is just a subsidiary of a company, not a legal entity by itself.
- The outsourcing organization is a governmental organization at federal, state, or communal level or another not-for-profit organization that does not generate sales or follow accounting rules for private sector companies.
- Outsourcing company merged or was taken over after ITO.
- Sufficient consecutive financial figures could not be found in DAFNE either for the period before or the period after ITO.
- Few contracts covered specific system integration tasks. They were already characterized as "non-outsourcing" contracts in the original data and were excluded from our analyses.

Data for analysis could be found in 102 cases but not necessarily for all four key figures. Several of the studies listed in Table 2 had a similar sample size [30, 35, 36]. Especially OOE was often missing. The dataset contains big world-known companies but also medium-size and non-listed firms.

6 Results

The German outsourcing market resembled the USA in the analyzed period with respect to ownership relations between clients and vendors. They were usually independent of each other unlike in Korea where ITO takes place within a conglomerate [29]. The average contract carried a TCV of more than 40 million € or US $ (currency was not converted since we have no information about the payment structure and, therefore, cannot know which exchange rates to apply to which amounts) and was signed for almost five years. Table 3 shows the results of comparison tests. Columns 3 and 4 show the average difference in medians of growth rates between ITO firms and the control group in percentage points (ppt).

It is interesting that the situation before outsourcing resembles the situation of companies in the USA in the time period between 1988 and 1993 as analyzed in a pre-event study [54]: Companies which embarked on the outsourcing journey were not

Table 3. Comparison of relative performance before and after IT outsourcing

Key figure	N	Difference in growth rates between ITO firms and the control group *before* outsourcing in ppt	Difference in growth rates between ITO firms and the control group *after* outsourcing in ppt	Difference in ppt ("after" – "before")
OOE	37	++−14.95	1.26	16.21
EBIT	90	−0.44	++12.59	*13.03
PPE	73	−0.62	++10.06	**10.68
ROA	89	1.87	4.65	2.77

Significance in t-tests for paired samples: ** $p \leq 0.01$, * $p \leq 0.05$
Significance in Mann-Whitney-tests: ++ $p \leq 0.01$
Reading example: ITO firms were growing with respect to EBIT 0.44 ppt slower than the control group before ITO, but this difference was not statistically significant. After ITO, they were growing significantly faster (by 12.59 ppt). The change of 13.03 ppt (from −0.44 to 12.59) was significant.

more or less productive or profitable than other companies but they were already more cost conscious. Their OOE were growing almost 15 percent points slower than in the control group before ITO. They lost their cost advantage as measured by OOE and slightly increased their advantage with respect to ROA. However, these changes are statistically not significant. It can only be stated that ITO did not correlate with better cost or asset performance. The calculations show that ITO firms achieved a significantly higher growth after ITO than other firms with respect to EBIT and PPE.

We also created separate control groups for the two industry sectors. The growth rates of ITO firms were then compared with growth rates of firms in the same sector but the differences are still averaged for the whole sample. The results of this somewhat finer procedure are basically the same as before: ITO firms grew significantly stronger than other companies with respect to EBIT and PPE. Differences in the other two key figures remain non-significant.

To test hypothesis 5, we separate firms by sector. Firms in the industry sector "beat" their control group with respect to EBIT ($p \leq 0.05$) and PPE (marginally significant at $p \leq 0.10$) but the loss of cost advantage is significant ($p \leq 0.05$). The ROA advantage remained almost the same (Fig. 2, left). Firms in the service sector improved their position in all aspects except the assets perspective (Fig. 2, right). However, this change in growth is only significant with respect to PPE ($p \leq 0.01$) and marginally significant with respect to EBIT ($p \leq 0.10$). The ITO firms from this sector were lagging the control group before ITO. After ITO, they managed to grow with respect to PPE on average 15.4 ppt faster than the control group. Since the number of observations of OOE and PPE is relatively small in this subgroup, we also performed the non-parametric Wilcoxon test for dependent samples. The results were the same as with the t-test.

The performance of ITO firms from the two sectors after ITO can also be compared directly with each other. T-tests for independent samples and Mann-Whitney tests (if one of the groups had less than 30 members) were performed for each key figure for both time periods. A significant difference occurred only with respect to PPE before

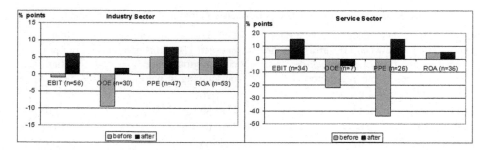

Fig. 2. Growth rates differences between ITO firms and other firms in the industry and in the service sector

outsourcing. In that period, firms from the industry sector had a higher PPE (mean rank 43.16 (n = 43) vs. 17.58 (n = 24)). No performance differences could be identified after ITO. In other words, service sector firms performed poorer than industry sector firms before ITO but were on par with them after ITO.

All results for the full sample and the sector subgroups were checked with a Monte Carlo simulation for randomness as described in the Methods section. The difference in growth rates of key figures between the random sample and the rest of the companies before and after a given time cut was significant in less than (or equal) 10 % of the cases. This can be considered as a proof that the above results are not random at the level of $p \leq 0.10$. Table 4 summarizes the results of the tests of the five hypotheses.

Table 4. Summary of hypotheses tests

Hypothesis	Finding
ITO associated with relative cost decrease	Not supported
ITO associated with relative profit increase	Supported
ITO associated with relative increase in personnel performance	Supported
ITO associated with relative increase in asset performance	Not supported
ITO firms in the service sector increased their performance more than ITO firms in the industry sector when compared with non-ITO peers	Partly supported

7   Discussion

7.1   Differences Between ITO and Non-ITO Firms

While some of the results can be characterized as "as expected," other results are rather surprising. A higher PPE can be expected because ITO usually leads to a transfer of IT employees from the outsourcing firm to the vendor. Profits of the ITO firms, represented by EBIT, grow faster than those of their peers which further supports the effect on PPE. A positive effect on PPE was also determined in [40, 28]. Superior PPE after ITO could be observed for companies in both sectors (although it is only marginally significant in firms from the industry sector). The improvement in EBIT could also be identified in both sectors. The finding on EBIT is congruent with [34] although these authors use a somewhat different key figure and with [31] where EBT has been analyzed.

The perhaps surprising result is that no superior cost performance can be observed although cost reduction is often the declared goal of an ITO announcement [26, 20, 44]. This does not mean that absolute operating costs were not reduced after ITO. In fact, the average costs decreased by 15.5 ppt but the control group also managed to reduce costs in other ways. When reducing costs is "in fashion," there seem to be various ways to achieve this goal, ITO being just one of them. For example, many big firms are meanwhile taking advantage of lower wages in off- or near-shore developing countries (Eastern Europe in the case of Germany) by setting up subsidiaries for development and operation of information systems in those countries. This practice is referred to as captive sourcing (e.g., [55]) or quasi-outsourcing [56]. The exact details of such moves are usually not widely reported as they are not based on a contract between independent parties. In the above mentioned intention of Daimler to backsource some of their IT, part of the plan is to build up an internal IT work force in India and Turkey [7].

Another important issue with respect to costs is the fact that outsourcing of infrastructure (e.g., data centers) will also affect IT costs attributed to production which are not reflected in the key figure OOE. This means that overall cost savings from ITO in the industry sector may be higher than represented by OOE. This could be an explanation for the seemingly poor performance in this sector with respect to costs (see Fig. 2) and in the full sample (see Table 3) since it contains much more companies from the industry than the service sector (30 and 7 observations of OOE respectively). This assumption is backed up by the fact that 60 % of those 30 contracts relate to IT infrastructure or total ITO. This means that some cost reductions may have occurred in production but they remain unaccounted for in OOE.

The results in [31] differ from ours where a comparative improvement in SG&A was determined. However, the development in that study was only observed for one year after ITO which makes the observation less reliable. A similar point holds for [33, 35]. Greater improvement in SG&A expenses per sales dollar (SGAS) in ITO companies was identified for years $t + 1$ and $t + 2$ over $t - 1$ in [33]. However, when we calculate the mean growth rate of SGAS over the complete post event time period (t to $t + 3$) based on the reported yearly means, we obtain a growth rate of 25 % for ITO companies and 20 % for the control group. The cost containment advantage of ITO companies seems to have disappeared after three years. In [35], the advantage in SGAS after ITO becomes smaller and only marginally significant after two years.

A study that concentrated on ITO and IT spending determined that ITO was associated with higher IT spending [57]. It assumes that this represents a move by the sampled firms to enhance their IT capabilities. Higher IT spending obviously diminishes effects of cost savings from ITO. ITO was associated with lower non-IT expenses in the sample of firms in [38] but this was often complemented by higher internal IT investments. Again, these investments offset some of the savings of non-IT expenses. Thus, the results on absolute cost savings may not differ much. No peer comparison was undertaken in that study, i.e., it is not known whether relative cost advantage was achieved.

Small non-significant changes in ROA are not surprising since IT assets often represent a relatively small share of total assets, especially in the industry sector that prevails in our sample. If only deals of 50 or more million dollars (or euro) in TCV are considered, since big contracts are more likely to include high asset transfers, the improvement rises to above 14 percent points but it is still not statistically significant. A lack of superior performance in ROA after ITO was also found in [33].

Our finding that no significant difference in performance between firms in the service and the industry sector occurs after ITO seems to contradict [19, 20]. This could be due to methodological differences since they analyze *capital market expectations* while we examine *actual performance*. However, the comparison of the situation before ITO shows that firms in the industry sector enjoyed a significant advantage with respect to PPE which disappeared after ITO. ITO may not have a very big impact on PPE in the industry sector because PPE is already at a high level. The results suggest that ITO supported firms from the service sector to catch up on their counterparts in the industry sector relating to PPE. This is in line with the moves of many service firms to lower their vertical integration. It has been shown for Germany that the industry sector still uses a much higher share of intermediate products and services of its total output than the service sector but that the latter increased this share much faster in the last decades [58]. For example, in car manufacturing this figure rose from 57 % in 1970 to 75 % in 2006 (31.6 % increase) while in banking and insurance it rose from 38 % to 57 % in the same time period (50 % increase). The gap decreased from 19 to 18 % points.

The results reported and discussed above mainly compare average performance between ITO and non-ITO firms. It is important to identify whether performance differences among ITO firms can also be observed (in addition to their sector membership).

7.2 Differences Among ITO Firms

When distinguishing ITO deals by contract type, renewals and extensions of an ITO contract were associated with relative cost decreases while new contracts were associated with relative cost increases compared with the control group. The finding is congruent with [28] who determined that contract renewals are associated with CAR in the stock market. This may help to explain the overall result. Starting a new ITO relationship seems to create costs that strongly diminish the savings from pure IT operations. These could be costs from learning effects, e.g., how to govern the relationship, or one-time costs like severance payments for released employees. Such costs are usually much lower when an existing contract gets renewed or extended if they occur at all.

The analysis by contract scope reveals that most cost advantage relative to peers was lost in cases of total outsourcing (18 cases). Application outsourcing and BPO (six cases) were associated with small cost disadvantages while in cases of infrastructure outsourcing superior performance was observed after ITO (13 cases). The latter differences are not statistically significant due to small group sizes but they complement the findings in the non-comparative study of [40]: Selective outsourcing was preferable to complete outsourcing. Also, defining "clean" interfaces with the vendor is easier for infrastructure than for applications.

We did not find any differences in performance among ITO firms with respect to firm size expressed in either sales or number of employees. It seems that the chance to improve the financial performance with ITO does not depend on firm size.

Finally, a look at individual patterns of change in all four key figures can help to judge the overall impact of ITO for the firms. Less than 30 % of ITO firms decreased their costs more than their peers. This means that the averaged result (Table 3) is not based on some extreme values but that the majority of ITO firms did not decrease their total non-production costs more than other firms. Further, three of the nine firms with a superior cost performance could not improve their EBIT performance (which includes costs) rendering the cost performance almost useless. They are falling behind the market just as almost 25 % of ITO firms that did poor, both with respect to costs and EBIT. However, the biggest share of ITO firms (almost 50 %) managed to grow their EBIT and PPE figures more than the non-ITO firms despite their inferior performance with respect to cost containment. This is a strong indication that strategic moves beyond savings from ITO were successful.

7.3   Qualitative Analysis

While establishing the facts is important, the question remains how ITO supports superior performance and complements broader strategies. We did not attempt to answer this question quantitatively because we did not have access to the individual cases and other important data on the companies. However, we tried to get more insight by examining media reports on the cases and press releases on the web sites of ITO companies in the sample. Unfortunately, the smaller companies in the sample were not covered by media and did not provide much archived reports. Just a few reports from or about the big companies touched strategic issues in sourcing and went beyond the facts of the deal.

A big manufacturer of engines reported in an annual report that standardization and modernization of IT-infrastructure were continuously taking place with a help of external providers. This means that ITO supports their goals by reducing complexity (standardization) and making up to-date technology available to the company (modernization).

An automotive supplier negotiated on-demand pricing with its provider in order to increase its agility. While the firm also seeks to decrease costs of IT through increased cost transparency, it feels that it can only remain competitive if it can quickly adjust to fluctuating demands by its customers. ITO helps the company to scale IT services according to business needs. It demands less IT services when business is slow and quickly takes advantage of opportunities when demand rises. Here, ITO supports their goals by providing corporate agility.

A major construction and property management company outsourced IT to a vendor for whose holding company they managed buildings and facilities. The stated purpose of the contract was not only to save costs but to strengthen the partnership.

A manufacturer of printing machines used ITO to consolidate business applications from three data centers into one run by the ITO provider. While the consolidation helps to reduce operating IT costs, it also supports reduction of complexity and standardization.

The same was true for a car manufacturer who used ITO to standardize its desktop environment.

These cases indicate how ITO supports more general strategies and superior business performance that often go beyond cost savings.

8 Limitations

Our analyses are subject to some limitations and inaccuracies.

We did not control for the propensity of firms to outsource in general. This may have led to an overestimation of benefits from ITO [36] but based on the calculations in that paper, this would amount to an overestimate of between 0.5 and less than 2 ppts for EBIT and PPE in our case. The performance advantage of ITO firms, measured by these key figures, still remains impressive.

For some of the outsourcing deals only the beginning year but not the exact date was known. It could be that in some of these cases the outsourcing relationship started at the end of the year but that we could not adjust for it because of a lack of information. The consequence in such cases could be that we do not observe the company long enough after outsourcing.

Each contract is treated equally in our analyses. However, they probably have a different quantitative importance for the outsourcing firms. The available total contract value is not sufficient to represent the quantitative importance of the contract (aside from the mentioned difficulties of proper discounting and currency conversion). A contract of €10 million per year may represent just 1 % of the IT budget of a big company but 100 % of the IT budget of a small or medium-sized company. The yearly IT budget or a similar figure that could be used to calculate the yearly contract value as a percentage of IT expenses as an indicator of contract importance was not available in either of the two data sources we used. One could use industry estimates, e.g., for IT expenses as a percentage of sales, but these are just rough industry averages. A reliable figure for the majority of observed companies could be only obtained from the companies themselves.

The stratification of firms by industry branch (instead of industry sector) was not possible because the number of companies per industry branch was too small. When a single representative control firm is chosen, industry membership often constitutes a matching criterion.

Although all companies had to follow the same legal accounting rules, they still have certain degrees of freedom, which can reflect on the key figures. For example, certain "special effects" may or may not be reflected in EBIT. Changes in exchange rates constitute such a special effect. Companies are allowed in Germany to position resulting costs (or gains) in their balance sheets in such a way that they do not enter the calculation of EBIT. The same issues apply to other key figures. Therefore, there could be still variations in the information content of the key figures.

9 Conclusions

Our research adds to the evidence that firms that outsourced IT show a superior performance with respect to certain key figures a few years after ITO start. The results are not restricted to specific industries (e.g., [34]) or selected business functions (e.g., [39, 34]). Superior growth compared to the control group occurred with respect to EBIT and PPE but no relative advantage in ROA and in costs, as measured by OOE, could be identified. We gave possible explanations for the latter observations. There is, however, qualitative and quantitative evidence that in many cases despite unimpressive performance in cutting costs strategic benefits must have been realized since the profit performance clearly improved.

There are at least two implications of our research for practice. First, companies should be very cautious about the results that can be expected from a new ITO contract. This should probably be considered as a learning experience that is necessary to achieve superior performance in the future. Cost savings can be achieved but better cost performance than peers is most likely to occur with contract renewals and selective outsourcing. Second, companies should immediately plan accompanying organizational measures and initiatives that will let them take full advantage of ITO, beyond possible cost savings. These could be process standardization, access to new technology, more flexible service offerings or a shift of attention to other activities that can lead to earning improvements.

References

1. Brynjolfsson, E.: The productivity paradox of information technology. Commun. ACM **36**(12), 66–77 (1993)
2. Dedrick, J., Gurbaxani, V., Kraemer, K.L.: Information technology and economic performance: a critical review of the empirical evidence. ACM Comput. Surv. **35**(1), 1–28 (2003)
3. Lacity, M., Hirschheim, R.: The information systems outsourcing bandwagon. Sloan Manag. Rev. **35**(1), 73–86 (1993)
4. Computer Economics: IT Outsourcing Statistics: 2013/2014, Irvine CA, USA (2013)
5. Computer Economics: IT Outsourcing Statistics: 2009/2010, Irvine CA, USA (2009)
6. Hirschheim, R., Lacity, M.: The myths and realities of information technology insourcing. Commun. ACM **43**(2), 99–107 (2000)
7. Krust, M.: Daimler will 150 Millionen Euro an IT-Kosten sparen. In: Automobilwoche 2013, 9 June 2013
8. Jiang, B., Frazier, G.V., Prater, E.L.: Outsourcing effects on firms' operational performance: an empirical study. Int. J. Oper. Prod. Manage. **26**(12), 1280–1300 (2006)
9. Dibbern, J., Goles, T., Hirschheim, R., Jayatilaka, B.: Information systems outsourcing: a survey and analysis of the literature. Database Adv. Inf. Syst. **35**(4), 6–102 (2005)
10. Gonzales, R., Gasco, J., Llopis, J.: Information systems outsourcing: a literature analysis. Inf. Manag. **43**, 821–834 (2006)
11. Lacity, M.C., Khan, Sh, Yan, A., Willcocks, L.P.: A review of the IT outsourcing empirical literature and future research directions. J. Inf. Technol. **25**, 395–433 (2010)

12. Gurbaxani, V.: IT outsourcing contracts: theory and evidence. In: Apte, U., Karmarkar, U. (eds.) Managing in the Information Economy. Springer, New York (2007)

13. Poston, R., Grabski, S.: Financial impacts of enterprise resource planning implementations. Int. J. Account. Inf. Syst. **2**, 271–294 (2001)

14. Nicolau, A.: Firm performance effects in relation to the implementation and use of ERP systems. J. Inf. Syst. **18**(2), 79–105 (2004)

15. Nicolau, A., Bhattacharya, S.: Organizational performance effects of ERP systems usage: the impact of post-implementation changes. Int. J. Acc. Inf. Syst. **7**, 18–35 (2006)

16. Bharadwaj, A.S.: A resource-based perspective on information technology capability and firm performance: an empirical investigation. MIS Q. **24**(1), 169–196 (2000)

17. Santhanam, R., Hartono, E.: Issues in linking information technology capability to firm performance. MIS Q. **27**(1), 125–153 (2003)

18. Linder, J.C.: Tansformational outsourcing. MIT Sloan Manage. Rev. **45**(2), 52–58 (2004)

19. Hayes, D.C., Hunton, J.E., Reck, J.L.: Information systems outsourcing announcements: investigating the impact on the market value of contract-granting firms. J. Inf. Syst. **14**(2), 109–125 (2000)

20. Beasley, M., Bradford, M., Dehning, B.: The value impact of strategic intent on firms engaged in information systems outsourcing. Int. J. Acc. Inf. Syst. **10**, 79–96 (2009)

21. Lee, J.-N., Kim, Y.-G.: Effect of partnership quality on IS outsourcing success: conceptual framework and empirical validation. J. Manag. Inf. Syst. **15**(4), 29–61 (1999)

22. Lee, J.-N., Miranda, S.M., Kim, Y.-M.: IT outsourcing strategies: universalistic, contingency, and configurational explanations of success. Inf. Syst. Res. **15**(2), 110–131 (2004)

23. Han, H.-S., Lee, J.-N., Seo, Y.-W.: Analyzing the impact of a firm's capability on outsourcing success: a process perspective. Inf. Manag. **45**, 31–42 (2008)

24. Mani, D., Barua, A., Whinston, A.: An empirical analysis of the impact of information capabilities design on business process outsourcing performance. MIS Q. **34**(1), 39–62 (2010)

25. Agrawal, M., Kishore, R., Rao, R.R.: Market reactions to E-Business outsourcing announcements: an event study. Inf. Manag. **43**, 861–873 (2006)

26. Oh, W., Gallivan, M.J., Kim, J.W.: The market's perception of the transactional risks of information technology outsourcing announcements. J. Manag. Inf. Syst. **22**(4), 271–303 (2006)

27. Loh, L., Venkatraman, N.: An empirical study of information technology outsourcing: benefits, risks, and performance implications. In: ICIS Proceedings 1995, Paper 25 (1995)

28. Gao, N.: What does Stock and Accounting Performance tell us about Outsourcing? Katz Graduate School of Business, University of Pittsburgh 2005. http://ssrn.com/abstract= 681321. Accessed 15 December 2009

29. Lee, J.-N.: Outsourcing alignment with business strategy and firm performance. Commun. AIS 2006, **17**, 1, Article 49 (2006). http://aisel.aisnet.org/cais/vol17/iss1/49

30. Mojsilovic, A., Ray, B., Lawrence, R., Takriti, S.: A logistic regression framework for information technology outsourcing lifecycle management. Comput. Oper. Res. **34**(12), 3609–3627 (2007)

31. IBM Corporation: Business impact of outsourcing – a fact-based analysis (2010)

32. Knittel, C. R., Stango, V.: The Productivity Benefits of IT Outsourcing. Working Paper, University of California, Davis (2007)

33. Wang, L., Kholekile, L., Gwebu, K.L., Wang, J., Zhu, D.X.: The aftermath of information technology outsourcing: an empirical study of firm performance following outsourcing decisions. J. Inf. Syst. **22**(1), 125–159 (2008)

34. Thouin, M.F., Hoffman, J.J., Ford, E.W.: IT outsourcing and firm-level performance: a transaction cost perspective. Inf. Manag. **46**, 463–469 (2009)
35. Gwebu, K.L., Wang, L., Wang, J.: Does IT outsourcing deliver economic value to firms? J. Strateg. Inf. Syst. **19**, 109–123 (2010)
36. Chang, Y.B., Gurbaxani, V.: Information technology outsourcing, knowledge transfer, and firm productivity: an empirical analysis. MIS Q. **36**(4), 1043–1063 (2012)
37. Han, K., Kauffman, R.J., Nault, B.R.: Returns to information technology outsourcing. Inf. Syst. Res. **22**(4), 824–840 (2011)
38. Han, K., Mithas, S.: Information technology outsourcing and Non-IT operating costs: an empirical investigation. MIS Q. **37**(1), 315–331 (2013)
39. Ohnemus, J.: Does IT outsourcing increase firm success? An empirical assessment using firm-level data. Centre for European Economic Research (ZEW) Discussion Paper 07-087, 2007
40. Straub, D., Weill, P., Schwaig, K.S.: Strategic dependence on the IT resource and outsourcing: a test of the strategic control model. Inf. Syst. Frontiers **10**, 195–210 (2008)
41. Cronk, J., Sharp, J.: A framework for deciding what to outsource in information technology. J. Inf. Technol. **10**, 259–267 (1995)
42. Alpar, P., Saharia, A.: Outsourcing information systems functions: an organization economics perspective. J. Organ. Comput. **5**(3), 197–217 (1995)
43. Altinkemer, K., Chaturvedi, A., Gulati, R.: Information systems outsourcing: issues and evidence. Int. J. Inf. Manage. **14**(4), 252–268 (1994)
44. Fitoussi, D., Gurbaxani, V.: IT outsourcing contracts and performance measurement. Inf. Syst. Res. **23**(1), 129–143 (2012)
45. Williamson, O.E.: The Economic Institutions of Capitalism. The Free Press, New York (1985)
46. Gurbaxani, V., Whang, W.: The impact of information systems on organizations and markets. Commun. ACM **34**, 59–73 (1991)
47. Barthélemy, J.: The Hidden Costs of IT Outsourcing. MIT Sloan Manag. Rev. **42**(3), 60–69 (2001)
48. Overby, S.: The hidden costs of offshore outsourcing. CIO Mag. 1 September 2003, p. 13 (2003) http://www.cio.com/archive/090103/money.html. Accessed on 15 December 2009
49. Grover, V., Cheon, M.J., Teng, J.T.C.: A descriptive study on the outsourcing of information systems functions. Inf. Manag. **27**(1), 33–44 (1994)
50. Wernerfelt, B.: A resource-based view of the firm. Strateg. Manag. J. **5**, 171–180 (1984)
51. Brown, R.M., Gatian, A.W., Hicks Jr., J.O.: Strategic information systems and financial performance. J. Manag. Inf. Syst. **11**(4), 215–258 (1995)
52. Pilloff, S.J.: Performance changes and shareholder wealth creation associated with mergers of publicly traded banking institutions. J. Money Credit Bank. **28**(3), 294–310 (2006)
53. Dube, A., Kaplan, E., Naidu, S.: Coups, Corporations, and Classified Information. NBER Working Paper No. 16952 (2011)
54. Smith, M.A., Mitra, S., Narasimhan, S.: Information systems outsourcing: a study of pre-event firm characteristics. J. Manag. Inf. Syst. **15**(2), 61–93 (1998)
55. Oshri, I.: Offshoring Strategies: Evolving Captive Center Models. MIT Press, MA (2011)
56. Barthélemy, J., Geyer, D.: An empirical investigation of IT outsourcing vs. quasi-outsourcing in France and Germany. Inf. Manag. **42**, 533–542 (2005)
57. Kobelsky, K.W., Robinson, M.A.: The impact of outsourcing on information technology spending. Int. J. Account. Inf. Syst. **11**(2), 105—119 (2010)(in press). doi:10.1016/j.accinf. 2009.12.002
58. Grömling, M.: Makroökonomische Daten zur Messung von Outsourcing. AStA Wirtschafts- und Sozialstatistische Archiv **4**(3), 185–199 (2010)

Riding for a Fall in Outsourced ISD: Knowledge Transfer Challenges Between the Onshore Vendor and the Offshored Unit

Aki Alanne and Samuli Pekkola[✉]

Department of Information Management and Logistics, Tampere University of Technology,
PO Box 541, 33101 Tampere, Finland
{Aki.Alanne,Samuli.Pekkola}@tut.fi

Abstract. Contemporary information systems development (ISD) is often conducted in a multi-stakeholder network where parts of the development are offshored. This entails several risks and challenges as inter-organizational boundaries get blurred and relationships become complex. Knowledge transfer (KT) is especially difficult; however, it has not been thoroughly studied from the network's perspective. This interpretive case study investigated why KT between onshore vendor and offshored unit is difficult in the ISD network. Numerous KT challenges were found and organized into four categories. In addition, some root causes were identified, including the nature of knowledge to be transferred, inappropriate systems development methods, the number of middlemen, and political issues. The study contributes to research by confirming insights from the literature on KT and also providing novel issues unique to a networked perspective. For practitioners, this study shows some potential issues to be considered when planning how to organize the outsourcing or offshoring of their systems development.

Keywords: Knowledge transfer · Offshore outsourcing · Information system development · Challenges

1 Introduction

Information systems development (ISD) is often conducted in the networks of organizations. Those networks include the customer organization, i.e., the organization that requires a new system; its business unit or units, i.e., the future user groups; its IT department, i.e., the unit with adequate IT expertise; and, of course, the system provider or developer organizations. This means that there are several stakeholders from different parts of participating organizations involved [1, 2]. Development may also be partly sourced to low-cost offshore locations [3] where skilled employees may be available or to bridge the capacity constraints [4]. This obviously adds new partners and relationships to the network.

Developing IS in this manner entails several risks and challenges [5, 6]. Inter-organizational boundaries get blurred and relationships become complex. This makes collaboration and knowledge transfer (KT) between the parties difficult [3, 5, 7]. For example,

© Springer International Publishing Switzerland 2015
I. Oshri et al. (Eds.): Global Sourcing 2015, LNBIP 236, pp. 124–141, 2015.
DOI: 10.1007/978-3-319-26739-5_7

traditional solutions to overcome KT barriers, such as master-apprentice learning or personnel movement, may not be available for transferring tacit knowledge because of the physical distance [4]. Even though the literature coverage on different issues of KT is broad, there are some limitations. For example, such studies are often limited to local settings [8] or do not investigate both the client/customer and vendor-side KT challenges [9]. IS offshore outsourcing studies on KT usually focus on the customer-vendor relationship or the vendor's capabilities (c.f., [10–12]), not the entire development network and the interactions therein [1, 13]. This motivates our paper.

We study KT within an IS development network by focusing especially on the boundary between onshore and offshore units. However, focusing solely on the issues between onshore and offshore sites is not sufficient as issues and challenges may stem from the customer's processes, issues, and understandings as well [12]. Consequently, we will incorporate the insights of the operations of the whole network to study KT at this particular boundary. We formulate our research question as follows: *Why is knowledge transfer between onshore vendor and offshored unit difficult in ISD networks?* To answer this, we conducted an interpretive case study with 30 semi-structured interviews in two separate rounds.

The paper is structured as follows. First, related research about KT challenges in general, and from an IS offshoring perspective in particular, is presented. Then the case and research methods are introduced. The findings include the description of an overall workflow and knowledge transfer within the IS development network, as well as the KT challenges the parties face therein. Identified challenges are organized into four categories knowledge characteristics and difficulties in articulation, vendor-related issues, offshoring-related, and communication channels and tools. In the discussion, the findings are synthesized and their implications in relation to the literature are drawn. Finally, the conclusions summarize the paper and cover limitations and future research directions.

2   Knowledge Transfer Between Onshore and Offshore Units

Although the advantages of outsourcing and offshoring software development [14–16] are promising, a number of challenges have been identified [5]. For example, compared to traditional in-house or onsite projects, globally distributed projects are more complex [17] as coordination and integration of multiple knowledge sources is needed [18]. Project participants may be separated by multiple and overlapping organizational, cultural, national, and professional boundaries [3]. Consequently, cultural differences, separate time zones, varying working and development methods, and the incongruent levels of common understanding of the end-user environment are evident [17, 19]. These issues may potentially hinder the development, for example, by delaying the development that is often considered vital in contemporary projects. Bearing these issues in mind, much stronger efforts in communication and knowledge transfer are required [17].

KT entails both sharing and using the transferred knowledge [20]. It is thus a prerequisite for successful ISD, since effective KT may reduce the time to solve problems.

This is because knowledge accumulates and the level of common understanding increases [5, 21]. Systems development is clearly knowledge-intensive work where both technical and business domain knowledge needs to be transferred [4, 22], and hence both explicit and tacit knowledge are important to consider [19, 23]. However, KT is often difficult and laborious because the organizations and individuals have dissimilar experiences, backgrounds, expertise, and cultures. Articulating knowledge across organizational boundaries is particularly problematic as it is sticky and resides in practice [24].

Language barriers are rather obvious challenges for effective KT as the native language of the offshore personnel is usually not the same as the onshore personnel's language. Language barriers are related to difficulties in translation, e.g., different interpretations of the meanings, or dissimilar business terminology and acronyms [5, 25]. Different dialects and cultural norms and habits may also play a role in hampering the understanding of the message [26].

Spatial difference refers to the lack of face-to-face communication. This makes KT more difficult as alternatives, such as video conferencing, either do not provide similar possibilities for negotiations and/or do not help the offshore personnel to grasp what is really happening in the end-user environment [7, 17, 27]. The work to overcome physical distance takes time, leaving fewer resources for the development work [12]. Temporal distance, e.g., working in different time zones, makes synchronous communication difficult. This affects, for example, decision making by delaying negotiations, handshake arrangements, and problem solving [5, 17].

The distance issues may privilege the onshore vendor over the offshore provider and thus accentuate status inequity. This makes it harder for the offshore developers to form interpersonal bonds or engage in joint discourse [3]. The distance between participants also emphasizes the selection of tools and their capacity. Proper infrastructure for knowledge sharing helps to capture implicit knowledge and to make it explicit [5, 26].

The relationships between organizations and individuals cause certain distinct challenges. The social dimension of the collaborative work needs to be acknowledged [7]. As the relationship between onshore and offshore organizations is often strictly bound by formal contracts and agreements, individual-level social ties and personal connections promoting KT are difficult to establish and maintain [19]. Furthermore, onshore and offshore cooperation generally lasts for a relatively short period of time and thus little shared capital is accumulated [3]. For effective KT, some level of shared understanding is nonetheless needed [28]. To gain such understanding, more effort is required compared to onshore projects.

These issues are just some of the challenges identified in the literature. The list is not exhaustive but still provides an overview regarding which kinds of issues are problematic in KT in offshored ISD. It seems that the KT challenges vary greatly between different projects and environments. This is plausible, as Nidhra et al. [5] found 60 different factors hindering KT in global software development, while Clarke and O'Connor [29] identified 44 contextual factors and 170 sub-factors that are significant in software development. Thus, instead of creating just another list of KT challenges, we try to go deeper by explaining how these challenges appear and what their root causes are.

3   Research Approach

We have conducted an interpretive qualitative case study [30] of an IS development network. The customer organization of 2,000 employees is a global service provider in the retail business with over one thousand sales outlets and operations in 26 countries. The customer's operations are divided into three primary business areas (consumer, B2B, and wholesale) and several support functions (HR, finance, logistics, IT, and marketing). A customized Enterprise resource planning (ERP) system has been used for more than ten years to satisfy their unique business process needs, including, for example, storage of clients' property and extremely seasonal business logic.

The initial push for the ERP system renewal project came from the vendor. They wanted to update their current software platform by building a completely new system. The vendor also delivered the customer's previous customized ERP solution that is used as a basis for the forthcoming system. The vendor also planned to offer and sell the new system to the vendor's other customers. This added pressure to the development as the vendor had to constantly balance between customer-specific features and generally useful ones. However, in practice, the customer needs were stronger and thus they were prioritized over others. The vendor offshored the majority of the coding to another country (India) in order to acquire both additional resources and technological expertise. The original onshore vendor remained responsible for the overall management and design.

The ISD touches multiple organizations and individuals, each having their own roles and interests. In this case, the following four relevant stakeholder groups are identified: the customer's business, the customer's IT department, the onshore vendor, and the offshored unit. There are also other external parties involved, for example, for visual design, but their role in the development activities and decision making were minimal. In principle, communication and management models were straightforward, meaning that there are fixed routes and responsibilities. In practice, however, these strict, well-defined practices were bypassed.

3.1   Data Collection

Data collection relied on semi-structured interviews. In total, 30 interviews were conducted in two rounds of interviews. In the first round in February–April 2013, the informants were selected via a snowball sample [31] so that all relevant stakeholder groups are identified and covered. In the second round in January–March 2014, the informants were hand-picked based on the insights gained from the first-round interviews. We also shifted our focus toward the offshoring part. Table 1 lists the interviewees and their organizations.

In the first round, the interview guide can be described as loose. It only contained open-ended questions, such as who are the most important stakeholders in the development process for each informant; which methods and practices are considered effective/ successful; and what could have been done better in terms of systems development. The second-round interviews had more specific questions, which were informed by the first round. The focus in the second-round interviews was on what kind of changes had happened; what are the processes and practices for the system development; what kind of knowledge is relevant for each informant and how is it obtained; and what tools and objects are used in communication with the stakeholders. The duration of the interviews varied between 11 and 98 min, the average being 55 min. All interviews were recorded and transcribed.

Table 1. The interviewees and their organizational positions

Organization	Role in organization	ROUND 1	ROUND 2
Customer IT	Corporate CIO	x	x
Customer IT	ICT Manager	x	x
Customer IT	IT support	x	x
Customer IT	Technical support	x	
Customer IT	Former project manager	x	
Customer IT	System specialist		x
Customer Business	Sales office manager	x	x
Customer Business	Sales person	x	x
Customer Business	CEO	x	x
Customer Business	Operative Business Manager	x	
Customer Business	Controller	x	
Customer Business	Concept Manager	x	
Customer Business	Business Area Manager	x	
Customer Business	Finance department rep		x
Vendor	Vendor CEO	x	x
Vendor	Customer Liaison	x	x
Vendor	Lead Designer	x	x
Vendor	Product Development Leader	x	x
Vendor	Product Manager		x
Vendor	Technology leader		x
Offshore	Team leader		x
Offshore	Developer		x

Some secondary material was also utilized in the data analysis. These included, for example, excerpts from the communication system between onshore and offshore, requirement specification documents, a version of the project plan, meeting minutes (where the decisions were made), priority and rollout lists of errors and needs, original evaluation criteria for the system acquisition, and the original request for information document. Although the impact of secondary material on the case analysis was not very significant, it helped the researchers understand the organizations and their structures.

3.2 Data Analysis

Similar to the data collection, the first author conducted the analysis in two separate rounds. The first round consisted of qualitative data-driven analysis and coding of the themes that emerged from the data. The ISD challenges were searched from the data, and then the first version of coding categories was created. The focus was on knowledge attributes and on challenges in transferring and distributing the knowledge. The findings were further categorized. In the first-round analysis, an overall picture of the development network and its operation was formed.

The second round continued where the first round ended, i.e., the analysis of a new set of data was informed by the previous round. This time the goal was to evaluate the earlier knowledge transfer-related issues, and to gain new insights especially about the offshoring part of the development. Nevertheless, the second-round coding was still done with an open mind for novel issues (c.f., [32]), and thus new issues were found. Coding examples are shown in Table 2.

Table 2. Extracts from the interview data and related codes

Extract from the data	Used codes
"She is not a project manager, or it does not say that in her card. But in practice, she is the one who has always dealt with the customer and then forwarded the issues to the product development [team]" (Vendor CEO).	"informality", "gate-keeper"
"There are certain cultural differences. And thus, for example, in the case of the electronic purchase invoice system, there is no one knowledgeable in India. This may cause some issues if the offshored team members do not know how these things are done in Finland" (Product Manager).	"domain knowledge", "organizing the development"
"The advantage with this vendor is that over the years, domain knowledge has been accumulated to a certain level within them. So they really understand immediately what we are talking about" (Customer IT department).	"domain knowledge", "common language", "expectations"

Even though in practice most of the identified issues are intertwined and have an impact on each other, it is possible to divide the challenges into four categories: knowledge, vendor, offshoring, and relationship-related. This categorization (simplification) was done both for analytical and presentation purposes, i.e., to make reading the findings easier.

In both rounds, the data was revisited iteratively to gather more detailed information and to confirm earlier identified issues. Initial findings were also discussed with the main contact persons in the case organizations and further revised according to their feedback.

4   Findings

We will begin by explaining the IS development practices and processes in our case network. This provides an overview of the environment, and its particular limitations and impacts on the KT between the onshore vendor and the offshored development team. In the case, certain KT challenges stem from the customer's business domain and from their relationship with the vendor. These must be taken into account when addressing the "end-part KT."

Within each organization, there is a dedicated person or a group in charge of the inter-organizational relationship and communication. The official guidelines for cooperation are rather straightforward. As the customer has various business areas that the system will serve, different needs and requirements are gathered and synthetized by the customer IT department. The IT department is further responsible (and is expected) to handle the communication with the vendor.

From the vendor's side, there is a dedicated customer liaison person responsible for communication with that particular customer. The customer's needs and requirements are further discussed and negotiated within the vendor. Only the lead designers are supposed to forward these needs and requirements to the offshored unit.

> ...we have received a requirements definition document from the customer, or a list of features that they would like to have. I examine the specifications regarding what we are actually going to do, and I describe to India how it should be coded (Lead Designer).

At the offshore site, a team leader is appointed to manage the vendor relationship and to communicate with the onshore designer. The team leader forwards information to the appropriate developers. Similarly, when information is transferred to another direction, i.e., from the developers to the customer, the team leader discusses with the lead designers. The development network and the flow of the work are depicted in Fig. 1, which is nevertheless a simplified situation.

The main "line" of both requirement management and solutions development thus consists of intra-organizational negotiation and inter-organizational gatekeepers. In practice, communication practices are not as mechanistic.

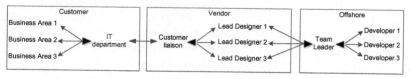

Fig. 1. The development network and the flow of work

4.1   Knowledge Characteristics and Difficulties in Articulation

The customer organization obviously holds the most in-depth knowledge about its business domain and about its processes and functional aspects of the work where the system will be implemented. However, most of the knowledge related to the customer's business processes is tacit and embedded in practices (as a way of doing things is a part of culture, for instance). This knowledge is not well documented. Although the customer has its own process handbook describing the processes, it is not updated or used in cooperation with the vendor. The vendor has to make extra effort to understand why certain functionalities need to be designed as the business needs are not always accurate. The vendor's product manager commented as follows:

> After getting a request from the customer, we have to unwind it backwards in order to identify what is the actual need behind it, why a certain button must be there, and so forth.

The complexity and stickiness of domain knowledge was also acknowledged among the parties. Particular methods to achieve the transfer of domain knowledge were utilized. These included, for example, the observation of work practices and how the current system was used, and bringing the offshore developers onto the customer premises.

Situatedness and difficulties in articulating the business domain knowledge were evident as well:

> After releasing a feature, it became apparent how the users are actually using it, what issues they are facing, and what are the exact requirements for more efficient use. So only then will I be able to work and fine-tune those features according to the customer's needs (Offshore Developer).

Despite these difficulties in the vendor's understanding of the business domain and processes, the customer still had strong confidence in the vendor's competences. However, this led to poor documentation of issues and had unfortunate consequences for the offshored unit as we will demonstrate later.

On the other hand, the offshored personnel are experts in the technology. They thus possess the most detailed knowledge about how to utilize the technology and implement it. This knowledge is crucial to make the best out of the system, for example, in terms of developing functionalities that may provide competitive advantages. However, some informants argued this potential was not redeemed:

> They would like to be more involved. How to take advantage of their expertise and insights is a challenge for which we have no solution now, and thus is an area where we have not achieved much progress (Technology Leader).

Despite the previously mentioned activities, the developers still had limited knowledge of the customer's business environment, which makes it more difficult for developers to suggest new ideas or alternative solutions. This further hinders the development, at least from the customer's perspective, as the technology behind the system is not exploited to its full potential. Quality and performance issues are also evident. For example, in the piloting phase the customer ordered an outside consultant to do capacity/stress tests on the system. For some reason, when running the system as designed, power consumption at the terminal end and the server load increased. Consequently, scaling the system to all the customer's office sites would not have been possible. Because of these results, the planned rollout was postponed.

Understanding the requirements and communicating them to the right people is a matter of each team member's individual skillset. A certain degree of flexibility is required since different people are involved in the development network. The individuals' skills are tested in such situations:

> Every team member is not the same. If I want to talk to A, if I want to talk to B, both are giving me the requirements, and then there will be a change in the communication methodology between the two of us (Offshore Team Leader).

4.2 Vendor-Related Issues

KT challenges related to poor documentation were not only a result of the customer-side. The vendor's internal documentation practices seemed to be equally lacking rigor, or at least they were not done thoroughly: "The requirement specification done with the vendor can just be a set of email conversations" (Customer IT support).

Requirements from the customer were not explicitly written down as official documents; requirements and changes were just added as complements to the issue management system's tickets. Detailed descriptions were indeed missing, making the systems development very difficult as the bigger picture was not seen. The customer understood that the system under development included at least all the same functionalities and features as the former system, which was also provided by the vendor. This was problematic because:

> The old version has many features that are not documented anywhere. So digging them up and finding out what is there has been quite a big part of the work (Lead Designer).

Although this level of documentation might be sufficient for the vendor's internal work, it was certainly not adequate for the offshored unit. The vendor's employees work in two locations in Finland. They did not perceive any problems because of their continuous collaboration with a small team of developers. In other words, current documentation practices were adequate as their weaknesses were compensated by communication and tacit knowledge. Yet, at the same time, these practices did not allow the offshored personnel to grasp the necessary information. New, more specific documentation was required. The Lead Designer made the following suggestion:

> …currently the best way would be to have some kind of wiki-based instructions for the end-user. This should be kept as up-to-date as possible. Customer support, lead designers, product managers, and developers could then use that to see how a particular function works (Lead Designer).

This would assist the offshored developers not only to gain important insights about the customer's business domain but could also bring them into the same discourse with the onshore personnel. This would be even more important as the offshore unit had no access to the old system, which was constantly referred to as a "requirement specification" in the onshore cooperation.

The fixed organizational routines and rigid structure caused, to a certain extent, an unwillingness to share the vital knowledge. This appeared, for example, in terms of allocating the project responsibilities. Everyone in the project had their own duties. They were thus reluctant to share their knowledge or potential problems and solutions. The Technological Leader sees this as problematic: "…there are some silos so that I do this part and you then do yours." Such an approach was not sufficient as excessive work arises when different parts of the system are integrated and the code is harmonized. This was particularly difficult for the offshore developers. They were not aware of the other modules or of the general functionalities developed by the others. They were then either doing duplicate work or rework. The offshored developer explained this as follows:

> We are not getting the latest updates about what are the new features and what modules are done elsewhere. We could actually use those, reuse them in our code and modules, and even enhance that use (Offshore Developer).

The offshored unit's only contact point was the lead designers. This was not, however, considered sufficient. Developers felt they were left without important information, especially related to the end-user environment and overall scope of the system:

> I'm getting a technical specification that needs to be implemented in a certain way. But how the customer is going to use the system, it's not exactly clear to me (Offshore developer).

Being a gatekeeper between the organizations and trying to understand the whole system and its requirements requires tremendous effort from the lead designers. In other words, the success of transferring knowledge between these organizations is largely on the shoulders of a few individuals. For example, the Product Manager, who is responsible for the overall product design and for prioritizing and integrating the modules, was not in direct contact with the developers or even with the team leader. This practice hindered the vendor's ability to take full advantage of the developers' knowledge and competence. This can be seen as a matter of attitudes among the onshore personnel: "It is about how much freedom we are willing to give these Indian guys. It seems a little bit like people would not like to give it up" (Technological Leader).

This is again linked to the fixed routines and habits. Earlier system development and maintenance involved only personnel from within the vendor organization. The offshored unit acknowledged this, and stated that they were only independent to a certain degree. That is, they can divide the given task within the team as they please, but any kind of long-term planning is difficult due to the small scope of given tasks.

> If you know in advance where to go and what to reach, then it is easier to plan, to achieve that thing… But, I am working on just some particular module. I should know how that is related to the bigger picture, what I need to do, or as a team what we need to reach (Offshore team leader).

4.3 Offshoring-Related

The offshore team conceptualized all problems related to communication, and its exiguousness:

> This is not about the technical incapability. Rather, this is about communication (Offshore Team Leader).

The vendor's personnel shared this feeling. They felt the offshoring scheme has been successful even though certain challenges have occurred and needed to be taken into account.

> It brings certain inconvenience on the work, there are language barriers and other barriers as well. One must describe things more accurately than to someone sitting next to one, to whom it can be explained in Finnish or you can draw a picture for and so on (Vendor CEO)

Further on, the Lead Designer complained of extra work, caused by the offshoring scheme:

> It brings an additional layer, in the sense that I have to transform and translate the knowledge. And when translating that to English, I have to open up the terms and different needs more precisely. It is much easier if I can do it myself directly (Lead Designer)

One evident issue affecting the KT between the teams was the technology-oriented mindset of the offshore personnel. For them, the customer's business environment consisted basically of just production data. They were not concerned with real manual work, such as using a cash machine at the sales offices. Certainly this is related to restrictions in terms of how often they are in contact with customers. Yet, even when asked several times, the offshored personnel kept referring to the testing environment, its deficiencies, and the integration between the modules. The vendor perceived this as the offshored developers were not motivated to accumulate the customer-specific knowledge, perhaps due to the nature of the onshore-offshore relationship.

Another issue impeding KT was the type of relationship between onshore and offshore staff. Onshore staff had the contractual power to decide how the development is going to happen. This left no room for negotiation:

> We have to follow such processes that have been followed by the on-site team... Whenever something is happening, changes in the task descriptions or anything, then they just sent us an email telling that somebody has changed the values of description, remaining work hours, or the type of a task, or assignment, whatever (Offshore Team Leader).

Due to the hierarchical relationship with predefined contracts, the offshore personnel were reluctant to tell whether certain things or processes were not working well:

> In Finland, there is an on-site team that is a technical team, but that is our client. We don't know the end-client [i.e., the customer]. My first job is to make my client happy. I'm not here to raise the concern (Offshore Team Leader).

Another challenge related to the offshore team was their expectations, and their lack of independent decision-making power and desire to make innovations. The vendor considered this as their own fault since they had become accustomed to their partners' work as being only "according to the specifications." There has never even been a thought to offer them a possibility to gain an overview of the whole system.

The cultural and language barriers were also evident. Almost all information had to be translated by the onshore lead designer. This obviously left room for errors as often only one person was responsible for this translation. However, the document translations were not sufficient. The offshored unit could not fully comprehend the situation. A developer commented as follows:

...the testing environment is not in my local environment. It is in Finland. They have a different database, different culture, and different languages. In my development environment, I'm testing the test cases in the English language, as I only know the English language (Offshore developer).

4.4   Communication Channels and Tools

The vendor set the tools and practices for communication. Yet collaboration following a rigid process and certain tools did not always support knowledge exchange sufficiently, or at all. This was particularly the case when dealing with more abstract concepts or novel issues. The offshore team leader explained the shortcomings of their current methods:

> Sometimes the tool makes the [collaboration] process somewhat complex and even time consuming. If there is a tool and I want to draw a diagram and design something, to suggest something, I should have the bigger picture and an understanding about the context. Let's consider you are building your house in the summertime. If you are in Finland, you also think about winter and temperature differences. If you forget them, and just consider the current environmental condition, then you will face problems later for sure (Offshore Team Leader).

The level of formality of the methods used by the customer and the vendor, and by the onshore unit and the offshore, differed significantly. In the former case, communication took place via multiple channels and the documentation was vague, while in the latter case the situation was very different, as discussed earlier. Nevertheless, knowledge that needed to be transferred was somehow the same: business domain knowledge, process information, and technical constraints and possibilities, among others. This further highlights the difficulty in explicitly articulating domain knowledge from the end-user environment. Sticking with rigid tools did not enable technical knowledge to be transferred from the offshore team to the vendor.

> Currently we are not involved as production team members, and we are not talking to the end-client [customer] directly. So, whatever is happening at the end-client side, they are transferring that to the [onshore team]. And they are creating those bugs or tasks or features, whatever they want, or whatever they're creating, into the [product development tool] (Offshore Team Leader).

Furthermore, the structure of the development network did not nurture KT. The physical distance between the developers and the designers hindered the development. More negotiation and discourse was preferred and more explicit tools needed to be utilized:

> In cooperative work, it is nice to have all the video conferencing tools, etc. But it is still not the same (Customer ICT Manager).

The offshored team leader continues:

> It is not a question of how much some team member is communicating with his/her counterpart, or how the goal is achieved with 99 % accuracy. It's more about the level and intensity of communication when the two teams are sitting very far across the globe (Offshore Team Leader).

Furthermore, the lack of formality was also evident in the use of different communication channels. Often email and telephone calls were preferred instead of filling out standard forms, or using the issue management system. This obviously caused misunderstandings:

> There are individuals calling each other over the phone and everyone is uncertain what the current state of the system is (System Specialist).

This hindered, or at least slowed down, KT as all necessary bits and pieces of information had to be "fished" from various stakeholders. This fishing became even more problematic when it became clear that the customer's project manager, who had already resigned from the project, was actually the one coordinating the activities within the vendor organization. Avoiding strict standard forms and guidelines also offered flexibility and speed for collaboration between the customer and the onshore vendor. This flexibility was considered necessary for responding to the business ideas and needs quickly.

5   Discussion

Identified KT challenges can be categorized as knowledge, vendor, offshore, or communication-related. The challenges from the vendor's and offshored unit's perspectives are rather similar – yet their causes are not. For example, the vendor's unwillingness to articulate or share the vital knowledge is caused by fixed routines and rigid structure, while at the offshored unit it is caused by the hierarchical position, e.g., not having the desire to accumulate the business knowledge. The challenges are summarized in Table 3.

Table 3.   A summary of the findings: the KT challenges in the ISD network

Category	KT challenges
Knowledge-related	– difficulties in articulating different requirements
	– complexity and stickiness of knowledge
	poor documentation different levels of communication skills
Vendor-related	– inadequate understanding of the customer's business
	– unwillingness to communicate
Offshoring-related	– rigid and routine operating models
	– lack of competence in the ISD process
Communication channels and tools	– lack of appropriate tools
	– different ways of working
	– extensive use of informal communication methods
	– structure of the development network does not nurture KT

Some of the identified challenges are, of course, idiosyncratic to our case; however, general implications can also be drawn. Even though KT is a major issue in offshored ISD networks, and may lead to serious problems or failures [17, 26], most challenges are not only caused by *the nature of the knowledge* itself. Besides that, in relation to our research question, the KT challenges also stem from *unsuitable development practices*, from *too many middlemen*, and from *political issues*. We thus argue these are the four root causes generating KT challenges between onshore vendors and offshored units in offshored ISD. Their relation to current literature and implications are discussed below.

The nature of the knowledge. As expected, the tacitness and stickiness of knowledge was causing problems for KT. From this perspective, our findings are in line with the literature. Explicitly articulating the business domain knowledge is difficult and does not allow the necessary building of shared understanding [28, 33]. This was evident as certain issues and requirements emerged only after the system was in use. Relying only on explicit documentation is not sufficient as, for instance, contextual issues and logic are difficult to articulate in a universally understandable form [34]. This parallels with the earlier studies' implications by showing how personal and informal ways of communication are preferable to more rigid methods when dealing with more complex knowledge (c.f., [5, 19]). In fact, focusing narrowly on the codification of knowledge may even be counterproductive [25, 33]. Whether informality is chosen because of practicality, habit, or simply because of communication speed, it introduces additional troubles, especially for the onshore-offshore collaboration. Due to the poor level of documentation or not being allowed to utilize similar methods, the offshore unit was not really grasping the meaning as they were supposed to. This further troubled the development activities.

Unsuitable development practices. The current development practices, which are largely controlled and dictated by the onshore vendor, also do not allow knowledge to be transferred effectively. Sometimes inappropriate inter-organizational processes, management styles, and development practices determined by the onshore vendor hinder KT [4, 12, 26, 35]. This was particularly evident when the vendor assigned only very small tasks to the offshored team. As a result, real debate of issues was missing, diminishing the utilization of the offshored developers' expertize. Another issue related to the development practices is the unsuitable tools. The current tools may serve the customer and onshore vendor reasonably well. However, although they are not suitable for KT between the onshore and offshore units, no one mentioned whether different, more descriptive communication tools would have been available or discussed their limitations. Other tools were not employed even though the offshored unit had clearly stated this concern. This gives us a reason to believe that the reason for selecting certain tools and practices had more to do with politics and attitudes than the lack of competence. On the other hand, these tools could have been "chosen" since they were already there as they were used in earlier occasions when doing in-house development. These shortcomings in development practices and routines could be due to a higher level management problem. The Customer ICT Manager explicitly speculated in this regard as follows:

> The project was not managed as a software project should be managed. This was maybe the biggest mistake in the first place. There were no clear responsibilities, plans, or milestones in place…A real attitude for working was missing. It was already suggested that someone should "cast the CEO aside and get a real manager in." I think it is completely a matter of leadership. They do have good people at the [Vendor].

Too many middlemen. Communication practices and strict flow of development needs was also a source of KT challenges. As the customer needs and requirements were difficult to articulate, the developers would have needed to be closer to the actual users. Currently there were too many middlemen and nodes between them. Not only does the number of middlemen influence the virtual distance of these ends of the development, but it also makes the whole chain likely to suffer from the "broken telephone" syndrome. In other words, having multiple gatekeepers disturbs the message, and blurs its nuances and details. Consequently, the final outcome, i.e., the shared understanding, may not reflect the original needs. The long chain of actors is definitely not supporting the utilization of the offshore personnel's competences, which, ultimately, was one of the prime reasons for engaging them in offshoring.

Political issues. Finally, different political tensions between the organizations add complexity. Regardless of whether it is the vendor not willing to give up its power or the offshored unit not interested in accumulating the customer-related knowledge, the situation is detrimental. This affects the motivation and attitudes of the people involved (see also [36]). Furthermore, political issues were also causing rigidness in the operating model. For example, rigid practices do not support KT as requirements are difficult to articulate. To understand them, the developers and designers need to often take a different stance (e.g., more abstract viewpoint, directive debate, or managerial approach), or communicate directly with other people, not just with the gatekeepers. Consequently, both personal preferences and attitudes and organizational obstacles and practice prevent such dynamicity. This, in turn, made KT difficult.

Besides political issues and client-supplier mentality, another reason for low motivation to transfer knowledge might be the job switching. For example, almost one fifth of the offshore outsourcing company's staff left the company within a year[1]. The low level of retention of the offshored employees or organizations influences KT and knowledge accumulation [9, 37]. This eventually leads to additional efforts to bridge the knowledge gap [5]. As KT is a time-consuming activity, this issue necessitates special attention. Thus, considering the enormous efforts needed for KT, the companies must really take this possibility into account and come up with a suitable solution. Nevertheless, if the team members are expected to leave, they are lacking motivation to study and understand this particular customer's business. However, the turnover of the offshore personnel is not the only dynamic element in the ISD network; other employees, such as the project manager in this case, and organizations may also change. In fact, the whole network evolves during a project (c.f. [38]).

---

[1] http://www.itnews.com.au/News/385123,indian-outsourcing-giant-hits-trouble.aspx

Furthermore, addressing the development network introduces additional insights. Offshore outsourcing literature has often focused on the vendor's absorptive and retentive capacities [12]. Our findings highlight that the customer organization and its knowledge, along with knowledge processes between the customer and the vendor, have a significant impact on the KT between onshore and offshore parts of the vendor. Thus, focusing solely on tools for transferring knowledge over that boundary is not sufficient. The whole network needs to be taken into account. Additionally, communication tools and practices developed and used between some parties may not be adequate for all the other parties in the network because they do not provide an adequate level of abstraction or allow detailed discourse regarding different, emerging issues [28].

The difficulty of using and deploying different development methods and practices also has an impact on KT. The practices were not alike in both dyadic relationships: between the customer and the vendor, and between the vendor and the offshored unit. Harmonizing and developing development practices have proven to be difficult, as discussed by Fitzgerald et al. [39] and Larsen et al. [40]. This implies that KT practices and tools, possibly integrated with systems development practices and tools, need to cope with similar rational, political, organizational, contextual, and individual issues as ISD methods and their organizational deployment. How this can be accomplished remains to be seen, although its importance of succeeding in offshored development work is evident.

6   Conclusions

In this paper, we have studied knowledge transfer and its challenges in a situation where the customer organization has outsourced the systems development to a vendor, which, in turn, has offshored the development to a cheap-labor country. Although the findings mostly parallel the previous literature, especially the nature of the knowledge to be transferred, systems development methods that are inappropriate and unsuitable for the networked collaboration, the number of middlemen in the network, and all kinds of political issues seem to be major challenges. They seem to be root causes for traditional KT challenges – at least in this case. Whether they are root causes elsewhere and in other contexts requires future research.

The study contributes to research by providing a rare snapshot of KT in a networked situation. This snapshot highlights that some challenges and their impact multiplies when there are several parties involved. The paper thus opens up new research avenues to focus on the relationships between the organizations and individuals, and on their different issues. For example, ISD method researchers and developers could utilize these findings when designing development practices and tools for offshored systems development. The study contributes to practice by showing some potential points of problems so that they can be tackled when one organization plans whether and how to outsource or offshore their systems development.

The IS development network we have studied has not been successful. The customer organization has not received what they expected. On the other hand, the vendor has struggled to produce both a customized system for the customer and to develop a generic software product. We argue that some of these problems can be explained by an inexperienced development practices and KT: the customer and the vendor have had no experiences on offshoring the development. Consequently, they have not been able to proactively prepare for different challenges that are ahead. It seems that they are riding for a fall.

Acknowledgement. This study was funded by the Academy of Finland grant #259831. We also thank the reviewers and discussants at Global Sourcing Workshop 2015 for their constructive comments and feedback.

References

1. Dittrich, Y., Vaucouleur, S., Giff, S.: ERP customization as software engineering: knowledge sharing and cooperation. Softw. IEEE **26**, 41–47 (2009)
2. Sammon, D., Adam, F.: Decision Making In The ERP Community (2002)
3. Levina, N., Vaast, E.: Innovating or doing as told? status differences and overlapping boundaries in offshore collaboration. MIS Q. **32**, 307–332 (2008)
4. Chua, A.L., Pan, S.L.: Knowledge transfer and organizational learning in IS offshore sourcing. Omega **36**, 267–281 (2008)
5. Nidhra, S., Yanamadala, M., Afzal, W., Torkar, R.: Knowledge transfer challenges and mitigation strategies in global software development—A systematic literature review and industrial validation. Int. J. Inf. Manag. **33**, 333–355 (2013)
6. Sakthivel, S.: Managing risk in offshore systems development. Commun. ACM **50**, 69–75 (2007)
7. Kotlarsky, J., Oshri, I.: Social ties, knowledge sharing and successful collaboration in globally distributed system development projects. Eur. J. Inf. Syst. **14**, 37–48 (2005)
8. Sarker, S., Nicholson, D., Joshi, K.: Knowledge transfer in virtual systems development teams: an exploratory study of four key enablers. IEEE Trans. Prof. Commun. **48**, 201–218 (2005)
9. Gregory, R., Beck, R., Prifling, M.: Breaching the knowledge transfer blockade in IT offshore outsourcing projects—A case from the financial services industry (2009)
10. Blumenberg, S., Wagner, H., Beimborn, D.: Knowledge transfer processes in IT outsourcing relationships and their impact on shared knowledge and outsourcing performance. Int. J. Inf. Manag. **29**, 342–352 (2009)
11. Teo, T.S., Bhattacherjee, A.: Knowledge transfer and utilization in IT outsourcing partnerships: a preliminary model of antecedents and outcomes. Inf. Manag. **51**, 177–186 (2014)
12. Madsen, S., Bødker, K., Tøth, T.: Knowledge transfer planning and execution in offshore outsourcing: an applied approach. Inf. Syst. Front., 1–11 (2014)
13. Hackney, R., Desouza, K.C., Irani, Z.: Constructing and sustaining competitive interorganizational knowledge networks: an analysis of managerial web-based facilitation. Inf. Syst. Manage. **25**, 356–363 (2008)
14. Gupta, K.S.: A comparative analysis of knowledge sharing climate. Knowl. Process Manag. **15**, 186–195 (2008)
15. Lee, Z., Lee, J.: An ERP implementation case study from a knowledge transfer perspective. J. Inf. Technol. **15**, 281–288 (2000)
16. Lacity, M.C., Khan, S., Yan, A., Willcocks, L.P.: A review of the IT outsourcing empirical literature and future research directions. J. Inf. Technol. **25**, 395–433 (2010)

17. Betz, S., Oberweis, A., Stephan, R.: Knowledge transfer in IT offshore outsourcing projects: An analysis of the current state and best practices (2010)
18. Desouza, K.C., Awazu, Y., Baloh, P.: Managing knowledge in global software development efforts: issues and practices. IEEE Softw. **23**, 30–37 (2006)
19. Al-Salti, Z., Hackney, R.: Factors impacting knowledge transfer success in information systems outsourcing. J. Enterp. Inf. Manag. **24**, 455–468 (2011)
20. Argote, L., Ingram, P.: Knowledge transfer: a basis for competitive advantage in firms. Organ. Behav. Hum. Decis. Process. **82**, 150–169 (2000)
21. Park, J., Lee, J.: Knowledge sharing in information systems development projects: explicating the role of dependence and trust. Int. J. Proj. Manag. **32**, 153–165 (2014)
22. Pee, L.G., Kankanhalli, A., Hee-Woong, K.: Knowledge sharing in information systems development: a social interdependence perspective. J. Assoc. Inf. Syst. **11**, 550–575 (2010)
23. Nonaka, I.: A dynamic theory of organizational knowledge creation. Organ. Sci. **5**, 14–37 (1994)
24. Volkoff, O., Elmes, M.B., Strong, D.M.: Enterprise systems, knowledge transfer and power users. J. Strateg. Inf. Syst. **13**, 279–304 (2004)
25. Levina, N., Vaast, E.: Turning a community into a market: a practice perspective on information technology use in boundary spanning. J. Manag. Inf. Syst. **22**, 13–37 (2006)
26. Noll, J., Beecham, S., Richardson, I.: Global software development and collaboration: barriers and solutions. ACM Inroads **1**, 66–78 (2010)
27. Pekkola, S.: Multiple media in group work: Emphasising individual users in distributed and real-time CSCW systems. University of Jyväskylä, Jyväskylä (2003)
28. Rosenkranz, C., Vranešić, H., Holten, R.: Boundary interactions and motors of change in requirements elicitation: a dynamic perspective on knowledge sharing. J. Inf. Syst. **15**, 306–345 (2014)
29. Clarke, P., O'Connor, R.V.: The situational factors that affect the software development process: towards a comprehensive reference framework. Inf. Softw. Technol. **54**, 433–447 (2012)
30. Walsham, G.: Doing interpretive research. Eur. J. Inf. Syst. **15**, 320–330 (2006)
31. Myers, M.D., Newman, M.: The qualitative interview in IS research: examining the craft. Inf. Organ. **17**, 2–26 (2007)
32. Urquhart, C., Fernández, W.: Using grounded theory method in information systems: the researcher as blank slate and other myths. J. Inf. Technol. **28**, 224–236 (2013)
33. Kotlarsky, J., Scarbrough, H., Oshri, I.: Coordinating expertise across knowledge boundaries in offshore-outsourcing Projects: the role of codification. MIS Q. **38**, 607–627 (2014)
34. Bechky, B.A.: Sharing meaning across occupational communities: the transformation of understanding on a production floor. Organ. Sci. **14**, 312–330 (2003)
35. Heeager, L., Nielsen, P.A.: Agile software development and the barriers to transfer of knowledge: an interpretive case study. In: Aanestad, M., Bratteteig, T. (eds.) SCIS 2013. LNBIP, vol. 156, pp. 18–39. Springer, Heidelberg (2013)
36. Szulanski, G.: Exploring internal stickiness: impediments to the transfer of best practice within the firm. Strateg. Manag. J. **17**, 27–43 (1996)
37. Dibbern, J., Winkler, J., Heinzl, A.: Explaining variations in client extra costs between software projects offshored to India. MIS Q. **32**, 333–366 (2008)
38. Alanne, A., Kähkönen, T., Niemi, E.: Networks of pain in ERP development. In: Proceedings of the 16th International Conference on Enterprise Information Systems (ICEIS) (2014)
39. Fitzgerald, B., Russo, N.L., Stolterman, E.: Information Systems Development: Methods in Action. McGraw-Hill Education, New York (2002)
40. Larsen, E.Å., Päivärinta, T., Smolander, K.: A model for analyzing changes in systems development practices. J. Inf. Technol. Theor. Appl. **13**, 21–48 (2012)

How to Drive Innovation Within Outsourcing Relations: The Role of Performance Evaluation and Management Control Systems

Giovanni Vaia[1(✉)], Marco Bisogno[2], and Giancarlo Bizzarri[3]

[1] Department of Management, Ca' Foscari University of Venice,
Cannaregio 873, 30121 Venice, Italy
g.vaia@unive.it
[2] Department of Management and Information Technology,
University of Salerno, Giovanni Paolo II, 84084 Fisciano, SA, Italy
mbisogno@unisa.it
[3] ULSS 9 Treviso, Sant'Ambrogio Di Fiera, 37, 31100 Treviso, Italy
gbizzarri@ulss.tv.it

Abstract. The themes of performance and outsourcing have been the subjects of extensive studies in academic literature for a long time. Literature has explored a variety of control structures and practices, as archetypes of management control within and between organizations, with the aim of identifying the optimal control design. The design of management control in ITO becomes part of a general problem of effective governance structures and the role of accounting information. However, many accounting related aspects remain unexplored.

We explore in this paper the "lateral processing of information" [1], trying to move beyond the static concept of control, adopting a dynamic view, with the aim of better taking into account both the evolution and change of the outsourcing relationship as well as the factors that have influenced this process. Our empirical study focuses on the outsourcing relationship between a public healthcare organization, in Italy, and its supplier. This case highlights how a management control system acts as a mechanism that facilitates to mediate, shape and construct outsourcing relations through self-regulating and orchestration mechanisms.

Keywords: Outsourcing governance · Outsourcing performance evaluation · Return on investment · Open book accounting

1 Introduction

During the last decades, empirical studies on outsourcing have showed how several sourcing models have evolved enhancing firms' efficiency, effectiveness as well as their competitiveness.

Customers find themselves facing new challenges in managing and innovating outsourced services, due to a high technological dynamism and a continuous evolution of the markets, determining a situation of growing uncertainty. Providers become a strategic resource for companies thanks to an effective support to strategic changes,

© Springer International Publishing Switzerland 2015
I. Oshri et al. (Eds.): Global Sourcing 2015, LNBIP 236, pp. 142–155, 2015.
DOI: 10.1007/978-3-319-26739-5_8

innovation and improvement of performances [2]. Providers are called upon to improve critical aspects of the business performance of the client with levels of complexity, uncertainty and integration, which are often very high.

The themes of performance and outsourcing have been the subjects of extensive studies in academic literature for a long time [3]. Principally, we have learned how mechanisms of performance evaluation, that are based not on blaming one of the parties but on the pursuing of the advancement of the relationship outcomes, are able to generate a positive cycle of continuous improvements [3, 4]. Choudhury and Sabherwal [5] underlined how effective governance assumes a portfolio of controls that evolves over the relationship. However, many accounting related aspects still remain unexplored. Numerous studies emphasize cost savings rather than strategic partnership when dealing with performance, focusing on the definition and evaluation of outputs and outcomes. Conversely, according to Blaskovich and Mintchik [6] ITO research in accounting has studied in greater details topics that include the optimal ITO contracting [7], alternative models for evaluation of the ITO decision [8], stock reaction to ITO [9, 10], the role of accounting information in ITO governance [11], and the organizational consequences of ITO. Scholars [11–15] have debated about accounting as trust-building mechanism, useful for long-term success in transactional relationships. For example, open-book accounting provides data for savings as well as mutual trust. Other techniques, such as Total Cost of Ownership, increase the effectiveness of sourcing. This stream of literature has also explored a variety of control structures and practices, such as archetypes of management control within and between organizations, with the aim of identifying the optimal control design. The design of management control in ITO becomes part of a general problem of effective governance structures and the role of accounting information [6].

Recent studies in accounting [11, 14, 15], that explore the use of control as a driver for setting up strategic alliances, highlight how information-sharing practices build trust among the parties. We explore in this paper the "lateral processing of information" [1], trying to move beyond the static concept of control, adopting a dynamic view, with the aim of better taking into account both the evolution and change of outsourcing relationship as well as the factors that have influenced this process.

Our empirical study focuses on the outsourcing relationship between a public healthcare organization, in Italy, and its supplier. This case highlights how a management control system (MCS) acts as a mechanism that facilitates to mediate, shape and construct outsourcing relations through self-regulating and orchestration mechanisms.

This longitudinal analysis also shows how the client and supplier, using the means of MCS, decomposed the process of value creation for a better understanding about the benefits arising from particular organizational processes, tasks, and projects. This inquiry about the value creation allowed them to integrate, build and reconfigure the internal and external competencies toward innovation.

2 Literature Background

The concept of management control has been widely debated over the last decade. The emerging themes discussed, on ontological and epistemological perspectives, are related to [16]: decision making for strategic control, performance management of strategic control, control models for performance measurement and management, management control and new forms of organization, control and risk, culture and information technology. The concept of performance is linked to management control systems (MCS) through an integrated view that includes objectives, strategy, measures, incentives, information flows and contextual issues like organizational culture and social control [17]. Developed under a more financial view, rather than a social one, MCS includes traditional operational tools such as budgeting procedures, financial control, regular feedback, performance evaluation linked at an individuals and company level. Simons [18] broadened the role of MCS debating the effect of MCS in managing behaviors and supporting the strategic change [19], introducing more informal controls (belief, culture, social norms). Dekker [20], combining both management control theory and organization theory, also agreed that inter-organizational relationships require both formal and informal control mechanisms. Formal control consists of contractual obligations, service level agreements, structural arrangements, planning procedures, performance monitoring and reward systems. Informal control, also referred to as social control and relational governance, includes informal cultures and systems influencing members, with it essentially relating to mechanisms encouraging self-regulation [16].

The shift toward cooperation and the subsequent collaboration into horizontal organizations has called for the development of concepts and management control systems to orchestrate horizontal and vertical relationships [21, 22].

Following the seminal paper of Hopwood [1], many management accounting studies explored both the forms and features of controls in inter-organizational settings. Management accounting researchers have recognized that the inter-organizational field represents a new and stimulating environment [23, 24]. According to Coad and Cullen (2006) [25], the central concept of inter-organisational cost management studies is information sharing, through which network members can identify cost reduction and value creating opportunities [26]. Scholars [27, 28] have argued that the resulting hybrid forms of governance are expected to require management accounting and control systems that extend beyond the organisational boundaries of the involved organizations.

The management control issues differ under the different types of inter-firm relationships as well as the theoretical approaches that have been adopted to analyse the empirical settings.

Caglio and Ditillo [29] identified three different breadths of analysis of inter-organizational control solutions:

- Control archetypes in inter-firm settings;
- Management control mechanisms of inter-firm relationships;
- Cost and accounting controls in inter-organizational relationships.

The *first stream* is largely based on transaction cost economics, organizational theory and trust-based literature; therefore, management control studies concerning this stream have proposed several control patterns [12, 27, 30, 31], such as: (*i*) market-based patterns, considered appropriate in the context of high to low level of uncertainty, low asset specificity and high task programmability, output measurability; (*ii*) hierarchical/bureaucratic patterns, whose adoption is suggested in environments characterized by medium uncertainty, moderate asset specificity, high task programmability and output measurability, as well as low to medium repetitiveness of transactions; (*iii*) other alternative patterns. The main limitations of these studies concern both the contradictions of the conclusions achieved and the lack of explicit recognition of accounting in controlling inter-organizational relationships.

The *second stream* has focused either on a specific type or on a subset of management control mechanisms used in inter-firm relationships [20, 32–35]. These studies neither investigate the impact of uncertainty nor clarify the effects of trust on inter-firm control mechanisms, and do not to link these mechanisms to other forms of control (such as contracts or price of competitive biddings).

Finally, the *third stream* of analysis has focused on forms as well as functions of cost and accounting controls in inter-firms relationships, investigating the role played by cost accounting mechanisms between these relationships. These studies have also analysed several accounting techniques such as the total cost of ownership in supply chain relationships [15], value chain analysis in supply networks [26], target costing, inter-organizational cost management [36] and the open book accounting, whose essential requisite is the transparency of cost structures [14].

While some scholars [34, 37, 38] are quite cautious and dubious about the roles of accounting information flows in inter-organizational relationships, others [32, 36, 39–42] have pointed to the fact that accounting information exchanges may support cross-border collaboration.

Earlier contributors focused on the opportunities for cost reduction that arise through open accounting exchanges, compared to traditional cost management in single companies. Carr [43] observed the sharing of accounting information as a prerequisite for implementing target costing at an inter-organizational level. Evidence from his study showed how firms are able to achieve total cost control through the whole supply chain by means of peculiar target costing techniques, and how firms use open book accounting to control the discrepancies of the different suppliers from the negotiated target cost. In addition, Seal et al. [44] described the possibility of a cost decrease, related to the use of open book practices in a network. The authors proposed the use of an activity-based costing system and a balanced scorecard to support the collaborative relationship.

An interesting perspective has drawn on actor network theories to analyze inter-organizational relationships. In this perspective, accounting and control systems are conceptualized as "actants", helping to build, shape and mediate inter-organizational relationships through both self-regulation and orchestration [46]. The self-regulating mechanisms facilitate interaction and exchange, while orchestration mechanisms involve structuring these interactions.

Berry et al. [16] underline how "techniques such as activity-based cost management [46] and the balanced scorecard [47, 48] can provide ways of thinking about cost, value and performance that connect parts of the value chain between suppliers and customers. However, they are not without their critics, given that major expectations of horizontal organisation are to encourage flexibility and learning, both of which often require effective co-ordination across the internal (functional) boundaries of organisations".

Elsewhere, Håkansson and Lind [24] demonstrated how management control creates contradictions, which required actors to continuously find provisional solutions to problems. This perspective would abandon a static concept of control, adopting a dynamic view that takes into account both the evolution and change of an inter-organizational relationship as well as the factors that have influenced this process.

This is in line with the empirical evidence of Mouritsen et al. [40]. The authors found that inter-organizational management controls such as open book accounting and target cost management/functional analysis create continuously new possibilities for management intervention. When such controls were introduced into the two firms they took part in re-presenting corporate phenomena such as technology, organization and strategy and re-translating the 'identity' or 'core competence' of the firms. Inter-organizational management controls shaped a new space for management, which had not only inter- but also intra-organizational effects.

In the next section, through a case study, we analyze how the introduction of a new management control system influenced not only the inter-organizational relations, but also the intra-organizational activities (supplier).

3   Method

In this paper, we present a longitudinal explanatory case study, carried out from 2011 to 2014. We studied the development and implementation of a system of performance evaluation and a MCS between the *Ulss 9* in Treviso (Italy) and its service centre *Noveservizi*.

Ulss 9 is a public healthcare unit that provides healthcare services to 37 cities and 418.459 citizens in the area of Treviso (roughly 30 miles from the city of Venice).

In 2009, *Ulss 9* created *Noveservizi*, a wholly owned service centre, with the goal of designing and supporting high added-value services and innovation, supporting the improvement of the processes in terms of effectiveness and efficiency, and ensuring adequate standards of satisfaction to the end users (citizens).

Noveservizi was created to support the modernization process of public organizations with the ambition of improving medical and care activities, while also changing the internal processes and competences. This service centre was organized around four main stream projects and services:

1. Design and implementation of a new system for the management control and the organization of a new Data Warehouse (DW), aiming to improve the quality of the data for decision-making. This area dealt with the revision and development of operational, economic and financial reporting;

2. Design and implementation of an internal system control, identifying the enterprise risk through a wide risk analysis and executing internal audit activities;

3. Design and implementation of a monitoring system for external suppliers. They developed a new method for monitoring the outsourcing of contracts and revised the

outsourcing lifecycle from planning, to execution and reporting, and coordinated the implementation of actions to improve outsourced services and the relations with suppliers;

4. Design and implementation of IT projects from definitions of requirements to project implementation. They supported the implementation of the Electronic Health Record (EHR) as a complex innovation that involved many actors in the Veneto Region.

During 2011 and 2014, we interviewed administrators from both organizations (the managing director of the *Ulss 9* and the *Noveservizi* President) and senior managers in each functional area. We took part as participating observers in some 1 day meetings where managers, professionals and physicians described their experiences using the tool and we studied full secondary material.

During the end of 2013 and the first semester of 2014, we conducted group interviews with employees at *Noveservizi*, with the goal of understanding how the tool was used in their context and what effects it had brought.

Table 1. Interviewees

	Role of interviewee	Number of interviews		
		2012	2013	2014
Client (*Ulss 9*)	Managing director	1	1	1
	CIO	4	5	5
	Planning and control manager	2	3	3
	Financial manager	2	2	1
	HR manager	1	2	4
	Purchasing manager	1	3	4
	Administrative manager	2	2	1
	Healthcare service manager	1	2	2
	Professionals in different functional area	4	4	6
	Doctors in different areas	3	2	3
Supplier (*Noveservizi*)	President	2	5	6
	Managing director	5	7	8
	Manager for management control services	6	6	7
	Manager for internal control	7	5	8
	Manager for outsourcing services	5	5	6
	Manager for IT services	7	10	
	Administrative staff	3	2	4
	Professionals from different functional areas	6	6	3

The interviews had an average duration of 1 h. Semi-structured interviews were carried out and the analysis was sent out to the respondents as feedback. Comments were then received. We participated in meetings and interviews and tried to engage in conversations about the design and use of the MCS, and how it changed over time. We gathered data freely, letting the respondents present what they considered to be of importance in their own way in connection to the use of the MCS in relation to *Ulss 9)* (Table 1).

All the interviews were transcribed and coded in accordance with the approach presented by Yin [49] (2003). Any inconsistencies have been specifically confronted and resolved through triangulation with archival data, and in some cases, given the units of analysis, they have been considered indicative of different perspectives and used to better explain the role of the MCS within the client-supplier relationship.

4 Analysis

4.1 Design and Use of the Performance Evaluation and MCS Tool

In 2012, the *Ulss 9* managers during interviews attributed to *Noveservizi* the following general benefits: innovation; contribution to the internal professional growth; contribution to organizational change; improvement of the quality of services; reduction of waste and better process efficiency; greater control and risk reduction.

After 3 years from *Noveservizi* start up, *Ulss 9* would understand the contribution of the service centre in creating value for the end users.

During interviews, the managing directors reported that for the public company the concept of value creation has two levels of analysis: the value in use and the value in the exchange. The value in use refers to the specific qualities of a new product or service, as perceived by the users in relation to their needs, such as the speed or quality of the performance of a new healthcare service or the performance characteristics of new products or services. The value in the exchange is defined as the monetary amount realized at some point in time, for instance the amount paid by the user for using products or services. In this process, *Noveservizi* creates value through the development of new activities, services, products, and processes. Even in this case, the focus is on how the target user benefits from the new product or service. This approach takes into

Benefits	*Category*: Financial benefits *Reduction of the expenses related to medicines*	*Category*: Non financial benefits *Improvement of ULSS 9 employees skills on internal auditing*
Costs	*Category*: Financial costs *Noveservizi's costs for services*	*Category*: Non-financial costs *Learning Costs*
	Financial	**Non financial**

Fig. 1. Categories of financial and non-financial benefits/costs

account the importance of end users, their perceptions, desires, alternatives and the context in which the users are included.

Ulss 9 referred to a broader concept of Return On Investment (ROI) as a proxy for the value creation. They designed a general framework to analyse *Noveservizi*'s performance, and their contribution to the creation of value. This framework included financial outcomes as well as intangible benefits, expected and realized, like changes in organizational behaviour (Fig. 1).

Ulss 9 organized focus groups and interviews to isolate data and values that had no direct or indirect correlation with the goals of the evaluation process. The results were crossed between the different working groups and different levels of responsibility. The participants estimated the amount and type of improvements and output generated. They then converted the data into financial values.

The ROI was measured as

$$\text{ROI} = [(\text{Net benefits} - \text{Net investments})/\text{Net investments}]$$

Net investments are determined by subtracting the cost of outsourcing to Ulss 9 internal running costs (internal costs incurred before outsourcing). The cost of outsourcing includes the costs for services contracted out, the start-up costs, relationship management. The internal costs are primarily determined by the cost of employees per hour and infrastructure costs (computers, printers).

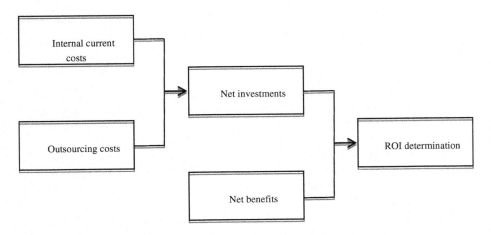

Fig. 2. Process of ROI determination

In order to calculate the ROI, it was necessary to convert the impact data (qualitative and quantitative) into financial values (i.e. new services delivered by Noveservizi are converted into cost savings; the time saved for Ulss 9' employees was considered as more capacity or lower costs of wages; saving physical space was calculated as direct savings). The framework also included indirect and organizational variables related to the change enabled, such as changes in attitudes, improvement of skills and knowledge.

Project Name	Expressed needs	Outputs	Receiver	Expected change in behavior	Actual change in behavior
E-PRESCR	• To achieve the 90% of the organization's goal concerning MMG and PLS • To follow tests of Arsenal.it	• Reports • Process indicators	ICT Dep..	• Physicians prescribe with RNE receiving a notification of medical report availability in 60% of cases	
SATPPIP-SATVA-SATAMB-SATADI	• To achieve the organization's goal concerning electronic transmission of PPIP and ADI requests in 90% of cases	• Reports • Process indicators	ICT Dep.	Physicians send electronically PPPs achieving a reduction in: • Moving times (MMG) • Authorization times • Supply costs	• Reduction in moving times • Reduction in authorization times • Reduction in supply costs • Reduction in control costs
SAIA-SAIN	• To achieve the organization's goal concerning personal data alignment of MMG/PLS	• Reports • Process indicators • Meeting minutes	ICT Dep.	MMG aligns correctly patients' personal data	• Reduction of errors concerning personal data

Outputs				
Value per unit (•)	Financial statements value		Ratios (%)	KPI
	Direct savings	Indirect savings	No. MMG/PLS sent *via* NRE/No. of total MMG	98%
			No. of provided notifications of medical reports/No. of total medical reports	45%
		• 60,000	MMG/PLS sending PPIP and ADP	96%
0,25 •/min.		• 32,500	No. of doctors making coding mistakes/No. of total MMG	1%
550 •/day	• 16,500			
6,16 •/Vacc.	• 10,550		No. of MMG with aligned personal data/No. of total MMG	6%

Fig. 3. Example of the collection and representation of data based on *Noveservizi* internal documents

Productivity gains and improvements in quality were taken into account as well as goals for each service stream managed by Noveservizi, output realized, target users, delivery time, activities delivered, changes in behaviours expected, changes in behaviors realized, performance on processes (KPI) (Fig. 2).

The creation of the framework represented a learning process in itself for *Noveservizi* employees, whom shared and standardized modes of data collection and representation (Fig. 3). The staff was also encouraged to develop appropriate representations of the results and benefits achieved.

From 2011 to 2013, *Noveservizi* estimated a direct net benefit, i.e. with an impact on the financial statement, about 9 M of euros with a ROI of about 6 euros against each 1 euro invested in the service centre (Fig. 4).

4.2   MCS and Inter/Intra Company Coordination

The tool demonstrated a good performance of the supplier over the last 3 years and it was used to renew the client's commitment to support the relationship.

However, this MCS had as major impact reorganization within *Noveservizi* and then at *Ulss 9*.

Created value (Extended ROI) 2013		Created value (Extended ROI) 2012		Created value (Extended ROI) 2011	
A Outsourcing costs (·)		**Outsourcing costs (·)**		**Outsourcing costs (·)**	
Costs of services	1,563,446	Costs of services	1,482,856	Costs of services	1,313,319
Start up	0	Start up	0	Start up	38,508
Governance costs	3,780	Governance costs	3,780	Governance costs	3,780
Risks	0	Risks	0	Risks	0
Tot. A	*1,567,226*	*Tot. A*	*1,486,636*	*Tot. A*	*1,355,607*
B Current costs (·)		**Current costs (·)**		**Current costs (·)**	
Wages	982,920	Wages	947,156	Wages	796,360
Infrastructure costs	147,438	Infrastructure costs	142,073	Infrastructure costs	119,454
Tot. B	*1,130,358*	*Tot. B*	*1,089,229*	*Tot. B*	*915,814*
C Net Investment (A-B)	**436,868**	**Net Investment (A-B)**	**397,407**	**Net Investment (A-B)**	**439,793**
D Net direct benefits	**2,145,386**	**Net direct benefits**	**2,187,643**	**Net direct benefits**	**4,662,014**
ROI = (D – C)/C	4	ROI = (D – C)/C	5	ROI = (D – C)/C	10

Fig. 4. ROI 2011–2013 generated by Noveservizi based on internal documents

Noveservizi used the tool as a budget planning to analyze the impact of each project at the beginning of the year. The projects were discussed in the light of the impact on behaviors, changes into routines, and the final financial value for the client. This analysis was carried out two/three times per year and increased the customer adaptation of *Noveservizi*.

However, in 2013, *Noveservizi* realized that the ROI decreased from 10 euro for every euro (2011) invested in the company to 4 euro (2013). The cause was related to a refocus on daily operational activities rather than a support to innovation. They were

Area	Avoidable activities/projects	Reduction of HR per area	Cost savings (·)	ULSS's cost equivalents (·)	ULSS net year saving (·)
Control	6	1.6	120,120.00	77,898.08	42,221.92
PM Extra SIO	6	2.5	187,687.50	121,715.75	65,971.75
PM SIO	1	1.5	112,612.50	73,029.45	39,583.05
Outsourcing	1	1	75,075.00	48,686.30	26,388.70
Internal audit	2	1.1	82,582.50	53,554.93	29,027.57
Noveservizi	16	7.7	578,077.50	374,884.51	203,192.99
			1,156,155.00	**749,769.51**	**406,385.98**

Fig. 5. 2014 - The back sourcing project based on *Noveservizi* internal documents

now engaged in roughly 50 % of the management of the internal processes and doing routine activities and 50 % developing new projects, new processes and supporting innovation.

This analysis led a discussion between *Ulss 9* and *Noveservizi* about the redesigning of the boundaries of the relationship. They agreed to start with a new project called "Release". Release was a back sourcing project. They decided to organize the transition of 16 projects and about 8 resources (in terms of Full-Time Equivalent) with a saving about 406.000 euros (Fig. 5).

Noveservizi maintained a primary role on the activities with a focus on innovation and an impact on the quality of primary healthcare services, while any standardized processes were transferred back to the client. *Ulss 9* preserved an increase in productivity and internal efficiency, containing a loss of internal skills. In fact, *Noveservizi* is still supporting the client to internalize activities, with training and coaching, raising the skill of people and trying to keep a high level of efficiency.

5   Discussion and Conclusions

According to Henry [50], in this study we found that performance evaluation and a system of MC have been used in an interactive, diagnostic fashion and contributed positively to the development of the capabilities of client orientation, innovativeness, and organizational learning.

In this case, accounting information allowed to regulate horizontal relationships, leaving room for the parties to act flexibly, share information, and create opportunities for learning. In this manner, management control was implicated in orchestrating a dynamic inter-organizational relationship that could develop and change. A reorganization of the internal roles and competences was motivated by financial opportunities. The access and sharing of financial information increased the "production" on both sides.

The client internalized standardized processes, thus obtaining more savings from an increased productivity (an internal employee is less costly when compared to a *Noveservizi* employee at the same level of productivity), and the supplier continued to bear high levels of ROI focusing on innovative activities. This would support and change the core development competence of the firms over time.

After accounting information sharing, both companies experienced a 'knowledge-gap' about the outsourced activities. For almost 3 years, the activities had been performed by the service company, the client felt it had lost touch with the outsourced activities. Accounting information sharing allowed for intra-functional discussions and facilitated an economic and financial translation of a strategy, focusing on efficiency and strategy.

These findings support Henry's [50] findings that, "by focusing organizational attention on strategic priorities and stimulating dialogue, MCS contribute to the process of knowledge generation and dissemination, and foster collaboration throughout the organization... viewing control systems as more than mechanistic tools used to support strategy implementation, but also powerful devices to stimulate and manage the emergence of strategies throughout the organization".

	Inter-organizational effects	Intra-organizational effects: Client	Intra-organizational effects: Supplier
Strategy	Increased focus on innovation	Increased focus on strategic partnerships	Refocus on core business
Organization	Increased coordination on knowledge transition	Increased focus on project management and absorption capacity	Increased communication among areas and inter-functional teams
Control	MCS enabled managers to control the production of value, financial and non financial, at a distance	MCS enabled the control of internal productivity against the supplier	MCS enabled to control the variance between innovative and routine activities

Fig. 6. The inter-organizational effects

Outsourcing often brings a new idea of aspects of company identity present in translations of strategy, technology and organization. Control also played a role in new re-presentations of organizational life in the two firms. It not only affects the inter-organizational relations (Fig. 6).

Concluding, the results support the view of the control system not only as a tool that is critical for the implementation of intended strategies, but also as one pushing the emergence of new strategies in the inter-organizational relationship, developing new organizational models, support trial-and-error processes and coordinating new initiatives. Evidence, described in the previous section, suggests how a MCS can support situations of reciprocal interdependence among parties. Accounting information transcends authority-based coordination, where it is not only essential for checking the state of the relationship but also for deciding how to revise the joint plans as well as manage the future of the relationships accordingly.

References

1. Hopwood, A.G.: Looking across rather than up and down: on the need to explore the lateral processing of information. Acc. Organ. Soc. **21**, 589–590 (1996)
2. Weill, P., Subramani, M., Broadbent, M.: Building IT infrastructure for strategic agility. MIT Sloan Manag. Rev. **44**(1), 1–11 (2002)
3. Poppo, L., Zenger, T.: Do formal contracts and relational governance functions as substitutes or complements? Strateg. Manag. J. **23**(8), 707–725 (2002)
4. Vaia, G., Zirpoli, F.: Le relazioni informali nella governance dei processi di IT outsourcing. Econ. Manag. **2**, 67–84 (2011)
5. Choudhury, V., Sabherwal, R.: Portfolios of control in outsourced software development projects. Inf. Syst. Res. **14**(3), 291–314 (2003)
6. Blaskovich, J., Mintchik, N.: Accounting executives and IT outsourcing recommendations: an experimental study of the effect of CIO skills and institutional isomorphism. J. Inf. Technol. **26**(2), 139–152 (2011)

7. Yost, J.A., Harmon, W.: Contracting for information system outsourcing with multiple bidders. J. Inf. Syst. **14**(2), 109–125 (2002)
8. Lee, C., Miranda, S., Kim, Y.: IT outsourcing strategies: universalistic, contingency, and configurational explanations of success. Inf. Syst. Res. **15**(2), 110–131 (2004)
9. Baldwin, L., Irani, Z., Love, P.E.D.: Outsourcing information systems: drawing lessons from a banking case study. Eur. J. Inf. Syst. **10**(1), 15–24 (2001)
10. Agrawal, M., Kishore, R., Rao, H.R.: Market reactions to e-business outsourcing announcements: an event study. Inf. Manag. **43**(7), 861–873 (2006)
11. Vosselman, E., van der Meer-Kooistra, J.: Accounting for control and trust building in interfirm transactional relationships. Acc. Organ. Soc. **34**(2), 267–283 (2009)
12. Langfield-Smith, K., Smith, D.: Management control systems and trust in outsourcing relationships. Manag. Account. Res. **14**, 281–307 (2003)
13. Smedley, G.A., Sutton, S.G.: Explanation provision in knowledge-based systems: a theory-driven approach for knowledge transfer designs. J. Emerg. Technol. Account. **1**(1), 41–61 (2004)
14. Kajüter, P., Kulmala, H.I.: Open-book accounting in networks. Potential achievement and reasons for failures. Manag. Account. Res. **16**, 179–204 (2005)
15. Wouters, M., Anderson, J.C., Wynstra, F.: The adoption of total cost of ownership for sourcing decisions—a structural equations analysis. Acc. Organ. Soc. **30**, 167–191 (2005)
16. Berry, A., Coad, A., Harris, E., Otley, D., Stringer, C.: Emerging themes in management control: a review of recent literature. Br. Account. Rev. **41**(1), 2–20 (2009)
17. Otley, D.: Management control in contemporary organizations: towards a wider framework. Manag. Account. Res. **5**(3/4), 289–299 (1994)
18. Simons, R.: Levers of Control, How Managers Use Innovative Control Systems to Drive Strategic Renewal. Harvard Business School Press, Boston (1995)
19. Langfield-Smith, K.: A review of quantitative research in management control systems and strategy. In: Chapman, C.S., Hopwood, A., Shields, M.D. (eds.) Handbook of Management Accounting Research, pp. 753–784. Elsevier, Oxford (2007)
20. Dekker, H.C.: Control of inter-organizational relationships: evidence on appropriation concerns and coordination requirements. Acc. Organ. Soc. **29**, 27–49 (2004)
21. Cooper, R., Yoshikawa, T.: Inter-organizational cost management systems: the case of the Tokyo-Yokohama-Kamakura supplier chain. Int. J. Prod. Econ. **37**(1), 51–62 (1994)
22. Kulmala, H.I., Paranko, J., Uusi-Rauva, E.: The role of cost management in network relationships. Int. J. Prod. Econ. **79**, 33–43 (2002)
23. van der Meer-Kooistra, J., Vosselman, E.: Research on management control of interfirm transactional relationships: whence and whither. Manag. Account. Res. **17**(3), 227–237 (2006)
24. Håkansson, H., Lind, J.: Accounting in an interorganizational setting. In: Chapman, C.S., Hopwood, A.J., Shields, M.D. (eds.) Handbook of Management Accounting Research, vol. 2, pp. 885–902. Elsevier, Oxford (2007)
25. Coad, A., Cullen, J.: Inter-organizational cost management: towards an evolutionary perspective. Manag. Account. Res. **17**(4), 342–369 (2006)
26. Dekker, H.C.: Value chain analysis in interfirm relationships: a field study. Manag. Account. Res. **14**, 1–23 (2003)
27. Spekle, R.: Explaining management control structure variety: a transaction cost economics perspective. Acc. Organ. Soc. **26**, 419–441 (2001)
28. van den Bogaard, M.A., Speklé, R.F.: Reinventing the hierarchy: strategy and control in the shell chemicals carve-out. Manag. Account. Res. **14**(2), 79–93 (2003)
29. Caglio, A., Ditillo, A.: A review and discussion of management control in inter-firm relationships: achievements and future directions. Acc. Organ. Soc. **33**, 865–898 (2008)

30. Sartorius, K., Kirsten, J.: The boundaries of the firm: why do sugar producers outsource sugarcane production? Manag. Account. Res. **16**, 81–99 (2005)
31. van der Meer-Kooistra, J., Vosselman, E.G.: Management control of interfirm transactional relationships: the case of industrial renovation and maintenance. Acc. Organ. Soc. **25**, 51–77 (2000)
32. Tomkins, C.: Interdependencies, trust and information in relationships, alliances and networks. Acc. Organ. Soc. **26**, 161–191 (2001)
33. Coletti, A.L., Sedatole, K.L., Towry, K.L.: The effect of control systems on trust and cooperation in collaborative environments. Account. Rev. **80**, 477–500 (2005)
34. Baiman, S., Rajan, M.V.: Incentive issues in inter-firm relationships. Acc. Organ. Soc. **27**, 213–238 (2002)
35. Mahama, H.: Management control systems, cooperation and performance in strategic supply relationships: a survey in the mines. Manag. Account. Res. **17**, 315–339 (2006)
36. Cooper, R., Slagmulder, R.: Interorganizational cost management and relational context. Acc. Organ. Soc. **29**, 1–26 (2004)
37. Gietzmann, A.: Incomplete contracts and the make of buy decisions: governance design and attainable flexibility. Acc. Organ. Soc. **21**(6), 611–626 (1996)
38. Gietzmann, M.B., Larsen, J.G.: Motivating subcontractors to perform development and design tasks. Manag. Account. Res. **9**, 3 (1998)
39. Munday, M.: Accounting cost data disclosure and buyer-supplier partnerships—a research note. Manag. Account. Res. **3**, 245–250 (1992)
40. Mouritsen, J., Hansen, A., Hansen, C.Ø.: Interorganizational controls and organizational competencies: episodes around target cost management/functional analysis and open book accounting. Manag. Account. Res. **12**, 221–244 (2001)
41. Seal, W.: Towards an enabling research agenda for the accounting/contracting nexus. Account. Forum **28**, 329–348 (2004)
42. Thrane, S., Hald, K.S.: The emergence of boundaries and accounting in supply fields: the dynamics of integration and fragmentation. Manag. Account. Res. **17**, 288–314 (2006)
43. Carr, N.: The end of corporate computing. Sloan Manag. Rev. **46**(3), 67–73 (2005)
44. Seal, W.B., Cullen, J., Dunlop, A., Berry, A., Mirghani, A.: Enacting a European supply chain: the role of management accounting. Manag. Account. Res. **10**, 303–322 (1999)
45. Mouritsen, J., Thrane, S.: Accounting, network complementarities and the development of inter-organisational relations. Acc. Organ. Soc. **31**, 241–275 (2006)
46. Kaplan, R.S., Cooper, R.: Cost and Effect: Using Integrated Cost Systems to Drive Profitability and Performance. Harvard University Press, Boston (1998)
47. Kaplan, R.S., Norton, D.P.: Translating Strategy into Action (The Balanced Scorecard). Harvard Business School Press, Boston (1996)
48. Kaplan, R.S., Norton, D.P.: The Strategy Focused Organization: How Balanced Scorecard Companies Thrive in the New Business Environment. Harvard Business School Press, Boston (2001)
49. Yin, R.K.: Case Study Research. Design and Methods. Sage Publications, London (2009)
50. Henri, J.F.: Management control systems and strategy: a resource-based view. Acc. Organ. Soc. **31**, 529–558 (2006)

Innovation Offshoring by Small and Medium-Sized Enterprises – Establishing the Research Gap

Michael Gusenbauer[1]([⊠]), Silvia Massini[2], and Matthias Fink[1,3]

[1] Institute for Innovation Management, Johannes Kepler University Linz,
Altenberger Straße 69, 4040 Linz, Austria
michael.gusenbauer@jku.at

[2] Manchester Institute of Innovation Research, The University of Manchester Business School,
Booth Street West, Manchester M15 6PB, UK

[3] Institute for International Management Practice, Anglia Ruskin University,
East Road, Cambridge CB1 1PT, UK

Abstract. Research on innovation offshoring (IO) has increased substantially over the last decade. IO is (still) widely regarded as the domain of multinational enterprises. Even though more and more researchers are claiming that small and medium-sized enterprises (SMEs) also practise IO, so far, the particularities of SMEs have been widely neglected. This is unfortunate, since a small business is not a little big business and thus most of the IO research lacks generalizability to SMEs. This study uncovers the gap and extends the empirical evidence available from scientific publications, obtaining a more current and accurate picture of IO research on SMEs. We directly approached academic experts through an online survey to collect information regarding the specific characteristics of SMEs relevant for IO, managerial needs arising from those characteristics and theoretical approaches appropriate to framing SME-specific IO research. This study provides a toolkit and roadmap for subsequent IO research aimed at SMEs.

Keywords: Offshoring · Outsourcing · Innovation · Small and medium-sized enterprises · Author survey

1 Setting the Stage

Offshoring of innovation (IO) is a phenomenon that has steadily gained importance over the last decades, in both practice and academic research. Over time, researchers have looked at the phenomenon from different angles. Compared to the a priori sourcing situation of a firm, IO itself is a management innovation, geographically and organizationally reconfiguring the innovation value chain (i.e. the innovation of the innovation process). Offshoring is a socio-technical business innovation that provides a rich new source of competitive advantage. To succeed, offshoring requires skillful management of both people and technology [1]. The reasoning behind and concrete layout of the IO operation is unique in each case. For some, it provides an enhancement of capabilities and resources, increased flexibility or reduced costs. All these potential opportunities that can be gained from IO depend greatly on the set of goals of the planned operation and the concrete sourcing arrangement (i.e. mode, governance, organization).

© Springer International Publishing Switzerland 2015
I. Oshri et al. (Eds.): Global Sourcing 2015, LNBIP 236, pp. 156–170, 2015.
DOI: 10.1007/978-3-319-26739-5_9

The authors of this study have started the Innovation Offshoring (IO) Initiative (see ifi.jku.at), which aims to (1) track and systematize the body of knowledge of IO research and (2) revaluate the underlying definition of the phenomenon of IO. This study presents the second step in the initiative and follows up on findings from a systematic review of IO literature, in which the authors systematized the fragmented picture of the field of IO. They identified a great lack of evidence-based insights into IO, a view that is shared by many scholars in the field [2–7]. Lewin and Volberda [8] even note that research on IO is still in its infancy.

The IO Initiative has had to put up with the problem that academia does not know collectively what has already been researched by individual academics regarding IO. This is because contributions to scientific journals and conferences, as a process of sharing and transferring evidence-based knowledge between different fields of research, and even between different networks of researchers, are not effective. The fragmentation of the scientific community and the specialization of the individual researchers hamper the diffusion of new insights. This is even exacerbated by the incommensurability of the technical languages. The very same term often has different meanings in different fields of research. This is especially true for key concepts of IO and, most importantly, the phenomenon itself. To overcome this hurdle, the IO Initiative started from a generic understanding of offshoring and innovation and set out to conduct a systematic literature review (SLR) of the empirical evidence base on IO. After elaborately categorizing the existing body of knowledge and reviewing 331 academic publications in the field of IO (starting from a total set of 14,119 hits), the researchers defined the phenomenon as the *foreign sourcing of activities, which are critical for implementing significantly improved or new-to-organization goods, services, processes, or methods in marketing or the organization – a definition that tries to delineate the field of IO sharply and clearly.*

Furthermore, the IO Initiative engaged in mapping the themes driving the discourses in empirical IO research and linking them to each other. This activity led to a map of IO research (see Fig. 1). With this map, it was possible to track the elements of the discussion and the links between these research topics, formed by empirical IO research: e.g. the level of autonomy of foreign R&D units in an emerging market *(sourcing procedure: bubble E)* is negatively associated with the regulatory influence they face *(sourcing location: bubble D)*. The diameters of the circles show the significance of each of the categories, while the thickness of the lines reflects the amount of studies investigating relations between multiple topical areas.

The IO Initiative found IO to be a strategy regarded as the domain of multinational enterprises (MNEs). IO research has so far mainly taken the perspective of the large corporations. Indeed, IO is not a new phenomenon for MNEs, at least not for those from industrialized countries, evidence of whose R&D offshoring dates back to the 1930s [9, 10]. Recently, however, IO has become a reality for business practice in SMEs too. This new type of internationally active company has discovered the opportunities of IO as, empowered by advances in IT, the growing availability of specialized foreign service providers and standardized services, SMEs have started to discover that IO can enhance their limited innovation capabilities [8, 9, 11–13]. Zedtwitz et al. [14] note that, in the current business environment, even SMEs can afford IO.

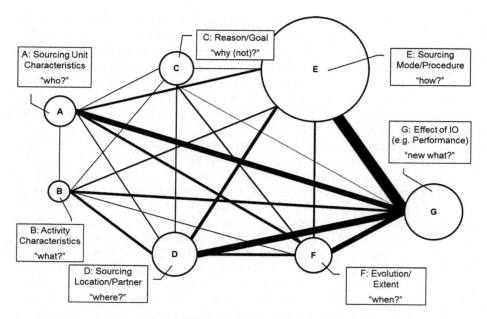

Fig. 1. Thematic map of IO research

We think that management knowledge that is developed with regard to large companies cannot be transferred to SMEs directly without examination. Against the backdrop of the insight that a small business is not a little big business [15], we assume that this size difference manifests in management practices that also influence IO. Therefore, in the context of IO research too, a specific investigation regarding SMEs seems to be necessary. However, the specific needs of SMEs have not been the focus of IO research so far.

We have identified two fundamental shortcomings of IO research regarding SMEs. First, research greatly neglects the particularities of SMEs by considering MNEs as the natural research subjects. Therefore, most of the existing studies lack generalizability to the case of SMEs. The topic of SMEs engaging in IO is largely unexamined. This void represents a significant research gap. In fact, investigations of the IO of SMEs are almost non-existent. Among the 331 studies covered in the IO Initiative's research, only a few consider SME-specific characteristics such as size or revenue thresholds as variables. In total, only 19 studies explicitly focus on SMEs in their research (sampling SMEs alone or as part of a larger sample) (Fig. 2).

In it is clearly visible that research into SMEs' IO only very fractionally covers the fundamental questions. Some possible connections between the thematic questions (i.e. bubbles) are missing entirely. Besides the quantitative evidence from the systematic literature review, other IO authors also point out the research gap: Massini and Miozzo [2, p. 1224] find that *"[...] small and medium-sized companies, in general neglected by the mainstream international business literature, seem to be adopting innovation offshoring strategies in order to augment their limited innovation capabilities."*

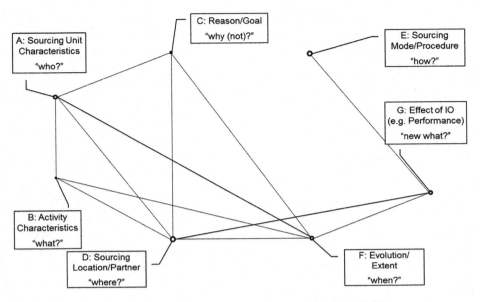

Fig. 2. Thematic map of IO research with a focus on SMEs

This lack of knowledge is extremely unfortunate, as SMEs are by far the dominant size-class and, thus, practice needs to be informed about the potential benefits and risks of IO conducted by SMEs. Empirical data are urgently needed to address these blind spots in the academic research.

Second, there are contradictory claims concerning SMEs' IO. It has not been fully accepted among scholars, as some still deny such firms possess the capabilities, resources and managerial skills to pursue this strategy. Carmel and Nicholson [16], for example, note that for SMEs offshoring proves to be a major undertaking due to their limited resources. On the contrary, others (e.g., Dossani and Kenney [13]) point out that SMEs (as well as larger firms) apply IO, clearly refuting the notion of missing offshoring capabilities. In fact, Di Gregorio et al. [12] and Lewin et al. [9] note that SMEs indeed have limited home-based innovation capabilities and therefore predominantly use IO to counteract these short-comings. Contrary to large companies, they *enrich* their innovation process by offshoring innovation rather than replacing domestic innovation activities with foreign ones [12, 13, 17, 18]. Prater and Ghosh [19] note that SMEs are typically more innovative and innovate faster due to their greater vulnerability compared to large MNEs. SMEs seem to benefit relatively more from advancements of IT as they enhance their limited capabilities and allow them to do business abroad, beyond simple exporting. SMEs are more and more realizing the opportunities of outsourcing and offshoring. These claims are strongly supported by the research of Di Gregorio et al. [12], who find that the offshore outsourcing of services enhances the international competitiveness of SMEs. They find that SMEs are generally keener on enhancing their limited capabilities or getting improved market access than on reducing costs. Offshoring is seen as extending the possibilities for expansion for smaller firms, letting them focus on their core capabilities.

In order to gain a current picture that is not blurred by the various forces present in review procedures as part of the publication process in academic outlets, we investigated whether IO topics are indeed size-contingent, by directly approaching academic authors with expertise in the fields of IO and SME internationalization. We presumed that these groups of researchers would have the greatest expertise on the subject of IO by SMEs, and therefore sought to gain their knowledge in order to establish and explore the research gap on SMEs' IO. The resulting sample consists of 1,066 authors who have contributed a total of 549 publications to renowned academic journals. Via an author survey, we asked fundamental questions concerning IO in SMEs that should prepare the field for further investigation. We found out whether SMEs were a specific group of firms that have specific managerial needs and whether special theories were needed to research IO in SMEs.

Contentwise, the study serves mutually reinforcing objectives: We contribute to the scientific discourse and practice in several ways: first we establish the gap in IO research that takes into consideration the specific characteristics and managerial needs of SMEs. We advance the IO Initiative, which has identified the lack of empirical research in this specific field, by demonstrating that such research would in fact be needed. Second, our findings provide rich insights regarding which facets of research into IO are especially relevant in the context of SMEs. This fine-grained list of aspects provides an elaborate roadmap for fruitful further research. Third, we provide a first insight into the appropriate theoretical approaches that are perceived as feasible for such research efforts.

On the practical level, we take a first step towards SME-specific recommendations for action in IO. The managerial recommendations developed based on our findings will better meet the specific requirements of SMEs. At the same time, based on such SME-specific IO research it is easier to draw tailored implications for practice. Furthermore, we inform those responsible for the creation of the regulative framework conditions regarding the specific needs of SMEs, in their endeavour to peruse IO operations.

In sum, this investigation provides the groundwork for a large-scale quantitative investigation into SMEs' IO. Only with the augmented knowledge obtained from the examination conducted through this step, can the following investigation be assured of its relevance, target the right research objects and ask the right questions, well-grounded in the theoretical discussion.

The remainder of this article develops as follows: after setting the stage by defining the key constructs and presenting a brief overview of the systematic review of IO literature, we develop a set of research questions that are the focus of the author survey. Finally, we discuss the empirical findings and draw implications for research and practice.

2 Empirical Study

This study builds on the findings of the first step of the IO Initiative, especially its newly developed definition, thematic map and the literature base of IO publications. The establishment of the gap in the research on SMEs' IO was achieved through an author survey targeting academic experts in the research fields closest to SMEs' IO. We collected expert knowledge from IO and SME internationalization scholars regarding (1) the specific characteristics of SMEs that are relevant for IO, (2) the specific managerial needs arising from those characteristics and (3) the specific theoretical approaches appropriate to framing SME-specific IO research.

We directly approached authors, as experts in their fields with ample theoretical and empirical knowledge to tap the socialized knowledge-base of the community. The aim was to collect the insights on IO (and especially on the IO of SMEs) that the individual researchers had gained in their scientific work, directly from them. We argue that there are more insights available at the level of the individual researcher than can be extracted from publications at the level of the research community. One reason for that is the unpublished work that never finds its way into the public arena. A second reason is the long delay prior to publication, due to complex review processes and huge backlogs in editorial offices. Moreover, tapping knowledge directly from the source also helps one to collect information that has not been blurred by the interventions of reviewers and editors during the publication process. At the same time, however, this approach is not feasible when the quality control of peer-review regimes is needed. As there is no wrong opinion on the topics covered by this survey, the filter of review procedures is not needed and would only be harmful, as described above.

Asking SMEs about their IO directly requires this preceding step to be taken first, in order to render the research questions more precise and to specify the phenomenon in the first place. The common body of knowledge of the IO and SME internationalization researcher community has a high level of aggregation and stems from a number of sources and data points, notions etc., that have been collected over time. The overall assessment of the current state of SMEs' IO gives a picture of the spectrum and variance of the researchers' opinions. As has already been noted, the opinions on SMEs' IO differ greatly among scholars. It will be of special interest to examine whether there are systematic differences in the perceptions of SMEs' IO between different groups of scholars. All in all, we believe that, by providing the toolkit and roadmap, the preceding empirical investigation into the IO of SMEs will (1) be more efficient in terms of sampling, (2) be more precise in terms of the questions asked and (3) subsequently more successfully advance the discussion of IO in SMEs. Furthermore, (4) the question of the size-dependence of IO impacts on many other related management fields.

The empirical data were collected via a standardized web-based online survey asking authors to give their assessments, so that we could track the notions of the individual researchers. The email linking to the online survey at Unipark.com contained customized information obtained through the preceding systematic literature review, to facilitate connection to the IO debate.

Before distribution, we were able to pre-test our survey on participants at the 2015 Global Sourcing Workshop, with whose help we improved the design of the questions. In a focus group that was held during the 2015 AIB-UKI conference, the preliminary interpretations of the findings of the author survey were discussed with experts in the field.

The sample consists of 1,066 academic authors who have been published in peer-reviewed academic journals of above-average quality, in the fields of IO and SME internationalization. The sample of *IO researchers* was based on the research of the IO

Initiative, which identified 633 authors who published IO research between 2003 and 2012. The sample of *SME internationalization researchers* was identified through a keyword search of the most relevant SME and entrepreneurship journals (according to the Association of Business Schools ranking), which resulted in a sample of 433 authors. In total, we sent out 1,041 emails. Even though we used up-to-date email information gathered using a web search of all authors, we could not find email addresses for 25 authors. We then received notification of 142 undeliverable emails. Therefore, we were able to reach the inboxes of 527 IO authors and 374 SME internationalization authors. Due to spam filters and outdated email addresses, the number of individuals actually reached is presumably lower than this. Therefore, we reached a maximum of 901 authors with the invitation email and two follow-up reminders.

We received a total of 134 usable responses (overall response rate = 14.7 %). The response rate of 13.4 % (50 usable responses) from the SME internationalization authors was only slightly lower than the response rate of 15.9 % (84 usable responses) achieved among the IO authors. For data analysis, we used the software package SPSS 22 to calculate descriptive statistics and mean comparisons between subsamples of the dataset. In the following, we first unfold our guiding research questions and then present and discuss the findings.

3   Results

3.1   SMEs a Specific Group Regarding IO

It is widely accepted that "a small business is not a little big business", indicating that SMEs have different qualities, needs and capabilities that cannot be associated directly to their size but are linked to their specific attributes [15]. It is not enough to investigate SMEs as part of a sample involving all size groups, as SMEs have to be examined in their own context. Roza et al. [20] point out the gap in IO research on SMEs, stating that "firms of different sizes use offshoring in a different way". Although they suggest some differences between small and large firms, including that SMEs overcome their resource constraints to also (along with large firms) engage in IO, these findings need further validation and exploration. Therefore, we formulate our first research question as follows: *Are SMEs a specific group regarding IO?*

We asked the authors about the relevance of IO for the international business activities of both small and large firms. IO was rated relevant for large and small firms by both author groups (see Fig. 3).

However, the relevance for large firms was, on average, rated higher than that for SMEs. In fact, only every fourth researcher thinks that IO has the same relevance for both SMEs and large companies, indicating the specificity of SMEs. This finding is not surprising given the fact that MNEs' IO has received much more attention in research and among the public. It is also very clear that researchers who are more interested in IO research perceive the importance to be higher for both company size groups. Interestingly, the IO authors rated the relevance of IO for international business activities higher for both small and large firms than SME authors, arguably due to the fact that they are more familiar with IO in general. However, the identified differences between

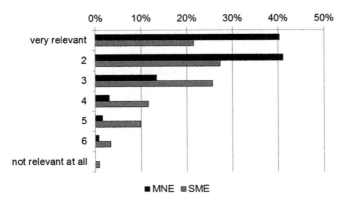

Fig. 3. Relevance of IO for MNEs and SMEs

the perceptions of IO and SME researchers are not statistically significant. Building on the first finding – namely, that researchers believe in certain differences between size groups impacting on the relevance of IO for international business activities – in the next step we investigate which firm characteristics are especially important for the decision to engage in IO. We based the selection of the firm characteristics on a recent critical review of the literature on SME management by Frank and Roessl [21], who identify a number of SME characteristics that go beyond the quantitative indicators. They argue that, for management science, definitions of SMEs that only take into account quantitative indicators of firm size – and ignore the firm characteristics that are antecedents or consequences of firm size – miss those dimensions of what SMEs are about that account for their particular managerial needs. From their study, we extracted 18 dimensions that have been used to define SMEs in existing studies.

From the author survey we learned that the most commonly used criteria for defining SMEs are not the ones that have the greatest impact on IO. Among the commonly used criteria are headcount, turnover, company age, number of hierarchical levels and legal form, which are all relatively easy to track and easily accessible (from secondary data providers). Therefore, using the common notion of SMEs, it is less likely that one will find significant offshoring within this group of companies. Interestingly, other criteria that are not so commonly found in the literature, such as the degree of formalization and transparency, are not seen to have an impact on IO either.

What, however, seem to substantially influence any firm's decision to offshore innovation, are primarily so-called "soft" managerial factors such as the managerial skills, instruments and capacity of the top management, the firm's planning and strategic thinking, its entrepreneurial orientation/mindset, its organizational learning competencies and its management of innovation and change (see Fig. 4). Besides the question of how a company manages its affairs, internal knowledge (i.e. number of specialists, knowledge concentration) and the industry within which it operates are factors with a significant impact on a firm's decision to offshore innovation. All these "soft" characteristics do indeed correlate with size, age and other quantitative measures. For example, the management of innovation and change (i.e. organizational implementation competencies) is assumed to be more structured and advanced in larger or more senior firms with more established procedures and skilled management.

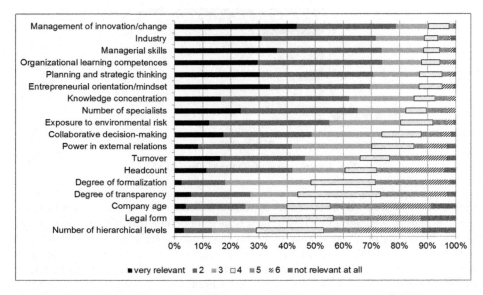

Fig. 4. Importance of SME characteristics for the decision to engage in IO

Interestingly, the experiences and notions of both the IO researchers and the SME internationalization researchers point in the same direction. There are only marginal differences in their answers concerning the relevant characteristics that impact on the IO decision. This indicates that these findings are grounded in a common understanding of the phenomenon of IO, stemming from experience and interaction with practice. By asking two distinct groups of academic authors, we have found that both groups have similar notions of the field of IO. Both see differences between types of companies (large firms and SMEs).

As a result, we have found that IO is not specifically different for SMEs, but rather for the "mature firm" that has pronounced managerial skills and capacities, a supportive hierarchical layout and high absorptive capacity. This profile matches basically any vital company with a good track record. Of course, these characteristics only present dimensions, along which endless typologies are possible. It remains for empirical firm-level research to uncover existent typologies and their IO-related particularities.

3.2   The Specific Managerial Needs of SMEs Engaging in IO

The particularities of SMEs might also bring about specific managerial needs when it comes to IO. Managing and organizing IO in SMEs presents specific challenges, and the lessons learned from IO in large firms cannot be transferred to the context of SMEs. Consequently, there is a need to further explore some of the unique management complexities surrounding IO and SMEs in order to further the debate.

The very fundamental SME-related questions, such as the extent, mode and evolution of IO, the motivation for it, and obstacles to it, have not yet been fully investigated. Therefore, we formulate our second research question as follows: *Do SMEs have specific managerial needs regarding their IO operations?*

SMEs have specific managerial needs, which are attributable to their specific characteristics. As we have already learned, the relevant IO characteristics for SMEs (and firms of all size groups) are "soft factors" rather than "hard factors". Indeed, these soft factors (i.e. managerial skills, learning capacity, experience, etc.) heavily influence the business behaviour of SMEs.

We asked the authors questions about the specific managerial challenges for SMEs and found strong support for the claim that IO in SMEs requires a different management practice. We identified seven topical clusters that were mentioned at least five times; the remaining seven clusters were less frequently mentioned. By far the most serious obstacles to IO are found in the "management at home". SMEs often lack both the managerial skillset, due to limited experience and capabilities, and the managerial resources needed. Compared to more established companies, it is relatively more expensive to retain staff that can be assigned exclusively to managing IO. Along these lines, the internal organization and the management of IO at the operational level pose significant challenges for SMEs. For example, the coordination of teams across nations does not seem to be a task for which SMEs tend to have a special skillset. These managerial drawbacks are especially true for captive operations, which not only need more financial funds, but are also a constant commitment and need permanent managerial attention. Furthermore, we found that "relationship work with the foreign IO partner" was considered the second most important challenge for SMEs by the authors we surveyed. Drawing up reliable contractual agreements between partners and managing relationships with partners do not seem to be easy tasks for SMEs. This hinders the creation of lasting relationships, in which the full potential of IO can unfold over time. Another major managerial difficulty for SMEs is the "identification and selection of suitable IO partners". This shortcoming mostly depends on how internationally experienced an SME is. Better connections to relevant offshoring destinations and a good network of foreign partners help SMEs to find adequate IO partners.

Other significant challenges mentioned by the surveyed authors were the "limited learning capabilities" of SMEs and their "limited resources", especially financial resources. Limited resources also have a negative effect on learning capabilities as SMEs cannot afford trial-and-error testing. Additionally, SMEs often do not have sufficient "capacities for knowledge management and transfer" that would enable them to engage in IO. Their absorptive capacities are assumed to be inferior to those of large companies.

In order to dig deeper into the particularities of SMEs engaging in IO, we asked the authors about the relevance of IO topics to SMEs compared to large companies. These topics are the same as those used to classify the IO research publications in the SLR guided by broad questions (i.e. who, what, why, how, when, where, new what). It seems evident that topical areas are in fact not always relevant for SMEs, even when they are for large companies. Along the same lines, what is interesting for small companies can be relatively uninteresting for large companies. Figure 5 presents the findings from the author survey.

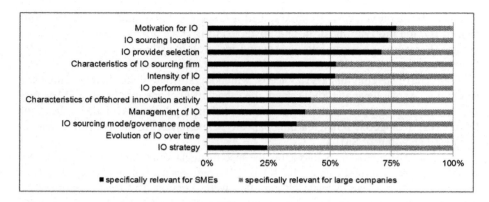

Fig. 5. Relevance of topics for SMEs or large companies

From the results, three groups of topical areas emerge, showing different levels of importance for firms of different sizes. (1) The topics of IO provider and location selection seem to be relatively much more important for SMEs. With smaller networks and less international know-how and experience, it seems harder for SMEs to connect with foreign partners and locations. The authors also expressed the belief that IO motivation was more relevant for SMEs than for large companies. An explanation could be that, because these firms are rather founder-centric, decision making is fast and hierarchies are flat, the justification for and risk-benefit assessment of IO is in the hands of a few and more prone to gut feeling. (2) The second group of topics neither seem to be specifically relevant for SMEs nor for large companies. The characteristics of the sourcing firm, the intensity of IO and IO performance are seen as equally relevant for both groups of firms. (3) Finally, for large companies, topics like IO strategy and evolution of IO over time (i.e. the development or advancement of IO operations) seem to be very important topics. It is not surprising that larger, more structured companies tend to have strategies at hand and have the capability to think of IO in the long term as a practice that evolves over time. Furthermore, the management of IO and the IO sourcing or governance mode, questions related to the "how" of IO relations, seem not to be the focus of SMEs.

3.3   A Toolkit for Research into the IO of SMEs

There is a broad range of theories used by IO research that originate from fields such as international business, supply chain management, organizational studies, innovation management, knowledge management and general management. None of these, explaining phenomena within the field of IO, looked at specifics of SMEs. However, there is a rich set of theories that examine the characteristics of SMEs or that can be used to explain the differences between certain groups of companies. Small business research, for example, typically highlights two disadvantages that SMEs are likely to face in the innovation process. First, the liability of smallness denotes the lack of a critical mass of resources needed for innovation projects [22]. Second, the liability of outsidership refers to the dearth of SMEs engaging in new management approaches such as IO [23]. Looking at the limited capabilities of SMEs, the necessity of SME-specific parameters becomes evident and frames the third question that guides our research: *Does research into the IO of SMEs require specific theories?*

A majority of the authors surveyed stated that SMEs present a special case of IO and their study requires distinct theoretical approaches. Nearly two thirds (61.5 %) of the respondents believed that, for research on IO in SMEs, specific theories were required. Compared to the IO researchers, the SME researchers significantly (p = .010) more often indicated a need for specific theories. This is not surprising as this group of researchers knows more about the specific needs of SMEs and the distinct theories that come along with these needs.

Researchers agreeing to the notion that SMEs need specific theoretical approaches also rated SME-specific theoretical approaches as highly relevant for IO research. Even though universal constructs were also deemed suitable for explaining SMEs' IO, the concepts of the liability of newness and smallness were rated as most relevant. These two concepts are traditionally used to explain SME-related issues. Figure 6 summarizes the perceived relevance of various theoretical approaches, according to the surveyed authors.

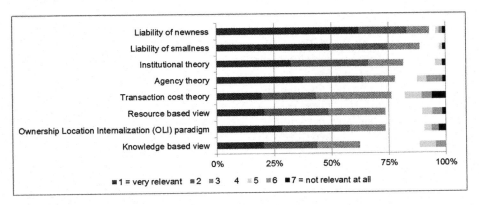

Fig. 6. Relevance of theoretical approaches to research on SMEs' IO

In addition to the theories and theoretical concepts that are frequently used in IO research, the authors supplemented these with concepts suitable for explaining SMEs' offshoring: network theory and organizational learning theory were the most cited ones not covered in the list provided in Fig. 6. Other significant theories mentioned for explaining SMEs' IO were entrepreneurship theory, evolutionary theory, growth theory and dynamic capabilities.

These concepts either explain the necessity of IO for SMEs or specific subquestions related to the IO activity of SMEs. As noted before, these subquestions can be classified using the framework as visualized in Fig. 1 and thus connected with the corresponding theoretical concepts.

The authors who indicated that there was no need for a distinct theoretical approach for explaining SMEs' IO argued their point in various ways. The majority of these authors believed that there was one theory that could explain IO for both SMEs and large companies. Basically, they had two lines of argument:

First, theory is universally true for both small and large firms as they are inherently the same, functioning according to the same universal principles of management. In other words, the reasons why companies offshore their innovation are fundamentally the same, regardless of firm size.

Second, even though SMEs and large companies are in fact different in some dimensions, the fundamental principles still apply for both. A holistic approach is needed for all firms, in which the characteristics of small or large firms present distinct types. The theory should then hold for all situations.

A third view was that, while sticking to existing theories and keeping them as general as possible, these concepts should be adapted to the context of smaller firms. Like in a car workshop where the technician adjusts his torque wrench to the bolt, in our case existing theories ought to be adapted to fit SMEs while still staying as general as possible.

4   Discussion and Conclusion

Motivated by the findings of the Innovation Offshoring Initiative that uncovered voids in the current empirical body of knowledge on IO regarding research focused on SMEs, we set out to (1) uncover, describe and assess this gap, and (2) extend and update the empirical evidence by conducting a survey directly among IO and SME researchers. In a nutshell, the expert survey highlighted the relevance of SME-specific IO research and revealed a catalogue of specific characteristics of SMEs that have to be taken into account in IO research, because they give rise to specific managerial needs and call for specific theoretical approaches. With our findings we offer a toolkit for the work on filling the voids that have been found relevant (research gaps) in the thematic map developed by the IO Initiative (roadmap).

While most of the results have already been discussed directly in the respective sections of this paper, we would like to draw specific attention to the findings on the need for SME-specific theories. In the survey, some respondents claimed that theory is universal and thus there is no need for a specific theory when it comes to researching a specific type of firm, such as SMEs. However, in order to gain generalizability across a large number of different types of research settings, theories need to be independent of the characteristics of the specific setting. This, of course, is the strength of theory. At the same time, it is a threat to the relevance of the findings of theory-guided empirical studies. More specifically, this threat unfolds its harmful power if the theory ignores the very characteristics that are causally linked to the phenomenon researched. In that case, the findings, conclusions and implications drawn based on the theory would be practically useless.

For research on IO, in this study, we found that the specificity of SMEs regarding their IO is not so much linked to the firm size as such, but rather to the antecedents and consequences of this size. These size-linked characteristics make SMEs a distinct group, with specific IO-related topics relevant to them, and specific managerial needs. Thus, theory that is employed as the basis of empirical research focusing on these topics and needs must cover the dimensions of the SME-specific context that are relevant to IO. Therefore, we argue that putting together a customized toolkit for research on IO in SMEs is necessary in order to tap the full potential of such research activities.

Also, sampling needs to account for this insight. While future samples for empirical IO-specific studies will, for practical reasons, still be drawn using quantitative indicators of firm size, the characteristics of SMEs that have been found to be causally linked to IO need to be included in the research design. Alternatively, the strength of the openness of qualitative research methods could be used to advance our knowledge on SMEs' IO activities without suffering the limitations of sampling.

Additionally, this study will help researchers to test and potentially transfer the great pool of MNE-based research findings on IO to the context of SMEs, gradually filling the void in SME-specific IO research. The results from the author survey presented here also provide rich insights into the current understanding of IO as a phenomenon and thus offer a first indication of the direction in which future research will go in this field. We hope that SME-specific research will constitute a significant part of future IO research. We argue that SME-specific research will result in theoretical insights and practical implications that will advance the relevance of IO in research and practice.

Acknowledgement. The authors would like to thank the participants in the 2015 Global Sourcing Workshop for pretesting our survey and the participants in the 2015 AIB-UKI Conference for their valuable feedback.

References

1. Saxena, K.B.C., Bharadwaj, S.S.: Managing business processes through outsourcing: a strategic partnering perspective. Bus. Process Manag. J. **15**(5), 687–715 (2009)
2. Massini, S., Miozzo, M.: Outsourcing and Offshoring of business services: challenges to theory, management and geography of innovation. Reg. Stud. **46**(9), 1219–1242 (2012)
3. Blomkvist, K., Kappen, P., Zander, I.: Quo vadis? the entry into new technologies in advanced foreign subsidiaries of the multinational enterprise. JIBS **41**(9), 1525–1549 (2010)
4. Bunyaratavej, K., Doh, J., Hahn, E.D., Lewin, A.Y., Massini, S.: Conceptual issues in services offshoring research: a multidisciplinary review. Group Organ. Manage. **36**(1), 70–102 (2011)
5. Rilla, N., Squicciarini, M.: R&D (Re)location and offshore outsourcing: a management perspective. IJMR **13**(4), 393–413 (2011)
6. Carayannopoulos, S., Auster, E.R.: External knowledge sourcing in biotechnology through acquisition versus alliance: A KBV approach. Res. Policy **39**(2), 254–267 (2010)
7. Lewin, A.Y., Peeters, C.: Offshoring work: business hype or the onset of fundamental transformation? Long Range Plann. **39**(3), 221–239 (2006)
8. Lewin, A.Y., Volberda, H.W.: Co-evolution of global sourcing: The need to understand the underlying mechanisms of firm-decisions to offshore. Int. Bus. Rev. **20**(3), 241–251 (2011)
9. Lewin, A.Y., Massini, S., Peeters, C.: Why are companies offshoring innovation? The emerging global race for talent. JIBS **40**(6), 901–925 (2009)
10. Cantwell, J.: The globalisation of technology: What remains of the product cycle model? Cambridge J. Econ. **19**(1), 155–174 (1995)
11. Kenney, M., Massini, S., Murtha, T.P.: Offshoring administrative and technical work: New fields for understanding the global enterprise. JIBS **40**(6), 887–900 (2009)
12. Di Gregorio, D., Musteen, M., Thomas, D.E.: Offshore outsourcing as a source of international competitiveness for SMEs. JIBS **40**(6), 969–988 (2009)
13. Dossani, R., Kenney, M.: The next wave of globalization: relocating service provision to India. World Dev. **35**(5), 772–791 (2007)

14. von Zedtwitz, M., Gassmann, O., Boutellier, R.: Organizing global R&D: challenges and dilemmas. J. Int. Manag. **10**(1), 21–49 (2004)
15. Welsh, J.A., White, J.F.: A small business is not a little big business. Harvard Bus. Rev. **59**(4), 18–32 (1981)
16. Carmel, E., Nicholson, B.: Small firms and offshore software outsourcing: high transaction costs and their mitigation. J. Glob. Inf. Manage. **13**(3), 33–54 (2005)
17. Murtha, T.P., Lenway, S.A., Hart, J.A.: Managing New Industry Creation: Global Knowledge Formation and Entrepreneurship in High Technology. Stanford Business Books. Stanford University Press, Stanford (2001)
18. Rangan, U.S., Schumacher, P.: Entrepreneurial Globalization: Lessons from the Experiences of European Small and Medium Enterprises. IIM-B Conference, Paper 105-15 (2006)
19. Prater, E., Ghosh, S.: A comparative model of firm size and the global operational dynamics of U.S. firms in Europe. J. Oper. Manage. **24**(5), 511–529 (2006)
20. Roza, M., van den Bosch, F.A.J., Volberda, H.W.: Offshoring strategy: motives, functions, locations, and governance modes of small, medium-sized and large firms. Int. Bus. Rev. **20**(3), 314–323 (2011)
21. Frank, H., Roessl, D.: Problematization and conceptualization of "entrepreneurial SME Management" as a field of research: overcoming the size-based approach. Rev. Manage. Sci. **9**(2), 225–240 (2015)
22. Brüderl, J., Schüssler, R.: Organizational mortality: the liabilities of newness and adolescence. Admin. Sci. Q. **35**(3), 530–547 (1990)
23. Johanson, J., Vahlne, J.-E.: The Uppsala internationalization process model revisited: From liability of foreignness to liability of outsidership. JIBS **40**(9), 1411–1431 (2009)

Understanding Collaboration in Multisourcing Arrangements: A Social Exchange Theory Perspective

Albert Plugge[(✉)] and Harry Bouwman

Faculty of Technology, Policy and Management, Delft University of Technology, Delft, The Netherlands
a.g.plugge@tudelft.nl

Abstract. As IT functions of clients are often outsourced to multiple vendors, all partners have to take the multisourcing arrangement into account when providing services. This paper examines how a client establishes strategic collaboration within a multisourcing arrangement. Due to heterogeneous, but also overlapping resources and heterogeneous strategic interests, collaboration between partners is challenging as they have to develop and manage IT services on an operational level at the same time. Social Exchange Theory is used to understand the complexity of collaboration within a multisourcing arrangement. Dependent on the client's multisourcing objectives for its vendors collaboration tensions become apparent. Our research reveals that when client and vendors pay more attention to creating common goals, mutual collaboration between the partners' employees is increased. This results in an improvement of the operational performance of the IT services. On an individual level, it was found that the behaviour of individuals may compensate for the lack of collaboration and the lack of exchange of information between partners. Furthermore the research suggests that partners within a multisourcing arrangement have to anticipate exogenous developments and adapt in order to be resilient.

Keywords: Collaboration · Multisourcing · Social Exchange Theory · Case study

1 Introduction

As the market for outsourcing services increased significantly over time, IT vendors specialized to distinguish themselves to remain competitive [1]. With the maturing of the market single vendor arrangements have declined and are replaced by smaller, selective contracts provided to multiple vendors [see for example 2, 3]. Currently, a multisourcing strategy is said to be *the* dominant modus operandi of firms [4]. Multisourcing is defined as 'a sourcing arrangement which entails a one-to-many relationship, in which one client uses multiple vendors, and where division of labour is jointly negotiated and understood by all included partners' [adaptation based on 5]. This implies that, as a part of a multisourcing arrangement, clients and vendors need to cooperate. Although each party in a multisourcing arrangement aims to create business value, the conditions for each stakeholder with regard to their position in the arrangement might be different. As vendors' objectives might be conflicting and as they also compete, this may result in tensions between partners [6].

© Springer International Publishing Switzerland 2015
I. Oshri et al. (Eds.): Global Sourcing 2015, LNBIP 236, pp. 171–186, 2015.
DOI: 10.1007/978-3-319-26739-5_10

Multisourcing is studied from various perspectives such as strategic decision-making [7], understanding and managing risks [8], expertise [9], and forced coopetition [6]. However, empirical insights in the field of multisourcing are still limited [10]. As an effect of a client's multisourcing strategy, IT services, such as workplace automation and application maintenance, are decomposed and divided amongst multiple vendors. Subsequently, some IT tasks as provided by various vendors need to be aligned in order to create an end-to-end IT service towards the client. Vendors' provisioning of services requires intensive collaboration, which may be difficult to achieve due to the complex technical, operational and organizational interdependencies [11]. Moreover, managing the interdependencies between vendors is challenging as each involved party may have conflicting strategic goals and different and/or comparable competencies and resources. Literature reveals that indistinct ties between vendors create tensions regarding mutual responsibilities [12]. A lack of collaboration may result in failures, which might have a negative impact on service performance. Establishing collaboration with a focus on improving individual and joint business performance and value creation is a prerequisite. Building and strengthening relationships between multiple vendors encourage vendors to work together to achieve the described results.

Despite its significance, multisourcing has been given scant attention in outsourcing literature [11]. Given the importance of multisourcing, we need to understand the nature of collaboration and how to strengthen collaboration, and to meet challenges within the context of a multisourcing arrangement. This research examines collaboration between partners – the client and its vendors - within a multisourcing arrangement with a view to their heterogeneous as well as overlapping resources and heterogeneous strategic interests, while at the same time developing and managing IT services on an operational level. To create a better understanding on collaboration within a multisourcing arrangement, we aim to answer the following research question: *How does a client establish strategic collaboration between multiple vendors who offer IT services to the client?*

While organizational and external factors influence collaboration at a firm level, this study focuses on collaboration on an inter-organizational level. So this paper wants to contribute to deeper insights in the dynamics of collaboration arrangements in a multisourcing environment. As collaboration is related to the exchange of value, information and knowledge between organizations, we opted for the Social Exchange Theory to study how collaboration is established. This paper is organized as follows. Section 2 presents a review of collaboration literature based on Social Exchange Theory. Section 3 explains the research approach. Next, the findings of a case study are presented in Sect. 4. In Sect. 5 we discuss the findings and finally we present our conclusions as well as limitations and ideas for future research in Sect. 6.

2   Literature Background

2.1   Multisourcing and Collaboration

Literature on supply chain management indicates that multiple vendors form a part of a 'supply network that is actively managed by the focal company' [13, p. 638]. Such supply networks can be perceived as a value network [14] in which a focal firm is able to switch between vendors to increase flexibility. [15] argue that IS literature contains extensive discussions of trade-offs that result from using one or many vendors per function [see for example: 8, 16, 17]. An important issue for focal firms is to decrease transaction costs as focal firms have to manage multiple vendors instead of a single vendor. As a result, the degree of uncertainty and coordination cost will increase. Compared to dyadic outsourcing arrangements, a multisourcing arrangement becomes more complex with every additional vendor that participates. Determinants that affect the degree of complexity are related to a client's geographical reach [18], a client's and vendor's organizational complexity [4], the range of a vendor's portfolio [15], and the degree of competition between vendors [6]. Consequently, governing multisourcing arrangements becomes a challenge as a focal firm and its vendors need to align their strategic objectives, as well as day-to-day operations, more regularly.

Specifically from an operational perspective specifying long-term sourcing contracts is complex and inherently incomplete because firms have to deal with uncertainty and unanticipated obligations and incidents. Hence, firms should govern a multisourcing arrangement beyond traditional contractual agreements and also built mutual relationships to support the exchange of information [19, 20]. [16] argue that 'decreased mutual commitment reduces incentives for vendors to invest in client relationships, which potentially weakens the value of each relationship (p. 545)'. In contrast, [21] found that clients might underinvest in developing vendor relationships, which results in a decline of service quality or in increased costs. Building relationships is a way to address some of the deficiencies in contract governance, e.g. the failure to account for social structures within which the inter-firm exchanges are embedded, and the overestimation of hazardous elements in the exchange [22]. [23] found that strengthening collaborative relationships was realized most frequently by knowledge sharing, communication, trust, and framing the vendor as a partner. So collaboration between partners in a multisourcing arrangement opens new ways of value creation as information and knowledge can be shared, enabling partners to respond to market dynamics more effectively.

Collaborative relationships in multisourcing become increasingly important as IT services provided by various vendors are often interrelated. For example, application maintenance services managed by Vendor A are making use of a data centre managed by Vendor B. As a result, changes in applications may affect data centre services, too, for instance by moving parts of the applications to the cloud. To deal with interdependencies vendors rely on intense collaboration, and sharing of mutual knowledge and expertise. A collaborative multisourcing arrangement represents 'an association of autonomous, geographically distributed, and heterogeneous organizations related to their service environment, culture, social capital and goals that mutually collaborate to achieve common goals and whose interactions form a part of a coherent sourcing environment' [adaptation based on 24, 25]. As collaboration is related to the exchange of value, information and knowledge between organizations, we opt for the Social Exchange Theory to frame this study on how collaboration is established.

2.2 Social Exchange Theory

Social Exchange Theory (SET) received attention in social sciences [26–28] as well as in management studies [29]. One of the strands of SET is that firms engage in social exchange due to the need to receive an economic reward that they are unable to obtain themselves. [27] perspective on socio-economic motivations, therefore, is applicable to collaboration in multisourcing. A general assumption of social exchange theorists is that there are differences in actors involved in the relationships [30]. Firms' employees can form various relationships, ranging from co-workers [31] up to competing vendors [32]. Differences in foci will lead to different implications. As individuals return received benefits, they are likely to be helpful to partners with whom they have positive social exchange relationships [33]. Therefore, rules of exchange are based on 'normative definition of the situation that is formed among or is adapted by the participants in an exchange relation, p. 351' [34]. Thus, norms of exchange form guidelines to facilitate the exchange process between firms. Key exchange rules or control mechanisms are used to govern people's social behaviour [35, 36]. We discuss the three most common exchange rules.

First, generalized reciprocity is recognized as a norm for collaboration between firms [36]. As multiple actors are involved in social exchanges between firms, obligations of one actor may be transferred to one or multiple other actors. [35] describe generalized reciprocity as 'a group-based exchange relationship in which actors expect quid pro quo exchanges within the group, but not necessarily with any specific actor'. An important tenet of SET is that relationships between firms change over time, influencing the degree of trust, which results in mutual commitments [30]. Related to generalized reciprocity, trust is developed through indirect reciprocal processes, as actors in a group receive benefits from a specific actor and subsequently pay back the favour to another actor. Therefore, actors of a multisourcing arrangement have to demonstrate that they contribute, assuming that other actors will reciprocate at some moment in time. So, generalized reciprocity may be more productive in building trust when compared to a restricted form of reciprocity. Thus, we formulate the next proposition:

P1. In multisourcing arrangements generalized reciprocity positively contributes to building trust, which, in turn, may support collaboration between actors (in the long run).

In contrast, as social exchanges rely on incomplete and informal contracts [27], tensions and disputes may arise between actors in a multisourcing arrangement. Social sanctions, which are related to mutual monitoring between the actors of a multisourcing arrangement, can be seen as a behavioural control mechanism to facilitate conflict resolution. Due to the interdependencies between the actors in a multisourcing arrangement it is important to observe and monitor the contribution of all other actors. Continuous monitoring of behaviour is essential as an actor can be affected negatively by the behaviour of another member of the multisourcing arrangement, which, in turn, may influence the reputation of other actors involved. Sanctions may result in excluding an actor from interactions within a multisourcing arrangement [37]. As actors in a multisourcing arrangement are more aware of their position and reputation related to other actors, they are expected to contribute to collaboration. The actors in a multisourcing arrangement relay on social sanctions to resolve conflicts while punishing norm violations. So we formulate the next proposition:

P2. Social sanctions, which are actually norm violations punishments, affect the concerned actor of a multisourcing arrangement negatively.

Third, actors' objectives as part of a multisourcing arrangement may be contradictory. This might hinder the exchange of information and services and increase the need for coordination. Literature revealed that creating a common culture is an effective mechanism to decrease coordination needs. A common - or macro - culture is described as 'a system of widely shared assumptions and values, comprising industry-specific, occupational, or professional knowledge, that guide action and create typical behaviour patterns among independent entities, p. 929' [38]. [35] argue that a common culture forms a prerequisite for behavioural control in an inter-firm relationship. The basic assumption of a common culture is that it is less complex to coordinate social exchange relationships if actors have common values and beliefs. Research of [39] illustrates that in generalized social exchanges shared values and beliefs are important to build stable exchange relationships. Moreover, [28] argue that a cooperative form of a common culture is valuable as it facilitates both generalized reciprocity and social sanction. So we suggest the next proposition:

P3. A common culture encourages actors in a multisourcing arrangement to share information and services as it contribute to the collective interest of the actors involved.

3   Research Approach

The unit of analysis in this research is collaboration, while the unit of observation is a multisourcing arrangement. Our research question and propositions require a qualitative research method, as we aim to create an in-depth understanding of collaboration within multisourcing arrangements. We have chosen a qualitative and interpretive IS case study research strategy, based on a single case study [40]. Hence, we opt for an interpretive approach to understand the deeper structure of the phenomenon, which is collaboration, as we try to understand the meanings of behavior of the subject [41]. Qualitative research method is useful in answering 'how' and 'why' questions, as they focus on understanding the nature and complexity of the processes that are taking place. Our qualitative method thus yielded an exploratory, case-study-based research [40], which is one of the most common qualitative methods used in the field of Information Systems [42]. We made use of a semi-structured interview method, besides document research, including sourcing contracts, as the data-collection method [43].

We used two main criteria to select a single multisourcing case study. First, we identified the broadness of type of IT services. Depending on the client's outsourced scope of IT services, e.g. IT infrastructure, application maintenance, or application development, collaboration in delivering services may vary. Due to mutual dependencies, for instance, in case of application development, we may assume that the client and vendors have to collaborate in the delivery of end-to-end IT services. Second, the role of each vendor in a multisourcing arrangement can be different. Some vendors are only responsible for the delivery of their own services, while others are assigned with the responsibility to integrate IT services delivered by various vendors. Therefore, service integration can be considered to be the second criterion. We selected a case study in which a client outsourced their entire IT function to the market and multiple vendors are jointly involved in the provisioning of IT services. As such, a large variety of IT services was outsourced (selection criterion one). Three global IT vendors were contracted, one operating as the IT infrastructure vendor and the other two as IT service integrators (selection criterion two). All vendors are acting in the field of IT outsourcing specifically.

Data Collection and Analysis. Data was gathered over a 11-month period from February 2013 up to December 2013, and drew on various sources. These ranged from desk research, and field notes to a series of interviews, both formal face-to-face and informal telephone interviews. Regarding desk research, information was gathered from three contracts, governance schedules, and satisfaction reports. In addition, field notes were recorded during informal meetings as well as during the in-depth interviews. These field notes provided relevant background information to the way client and vendors act in real life. The in-depth interviews with both the client's and the vendors' staff representatives, included IT executives, transition managers, service delivery managers, contract manages and experts positioned across the firm. In this way we have a cross-section of insights within the organizations, which enables us to establish a holistic view. The interviews were semi-structured and based on a protocol that included open questions on collaboration. In total we conducted 19 interviews and all interviewed participants had been engaged in the multisourcing arrangement. As the interviews were confidential, we anonymised the company names as listed in Table 1 and the participant's roles as listed in Appendix A. The varying hierarchical levels of the interviewed staff actors prevent potential limitations of group thinking. The interviewees were asked to describe their role in the multisourcing arrangement and specifically how they experienced collaboration. Interviews varied from 60 min to 90 min. All interviews were transcribed, and the transcripts were sent to the participants to be validated.

Table 1. Case study characteristics

Party	Focus	Geographical position	Type of services	Start of the contract	Length of the contract	Generation	Number of FTE transferred
Client		Europe	Complete IT function is outsourced			Second generation	800
Vendor A	Focus on infrastructure	Top 3 Global vendor	IT infrastructure,service desk,workplace automation	2009	7 years	Extended contract (1st time)	350
Vendor B	Service integrator (old world)	Top3 European vendor	Application development, Applciation maintenance	2010	5 years	Extended contract (1st time)	450
Vendor C	Service integrator (new world)	Top 5 Indian vendor	Application development, Applciation maintenance	2008	5 years	First contract	N.A

Interview data of the staff actors was stored in a case study database. Coding and clustering techniques were used to meet internal validity requirements [40]. Our first attempt at the theorization of the collected data involved coding of the interviews, using development categories and data displays [44]. Atlas.ti was used for coding and combing the interview data. When executing our qualitative research, concept maps were used to guide us through the process of data analysis. As a result of the coding process we are able to identify links between concepts, so that we can fathom the data [42]. Patterns were gradually identified that resulted in direct and indirect links between the concepts. Next, we were able to draw conclusions on how actors experience collaboration in the multisourcing arrangement.

4   Case Study Findings

4.1   Context of the Multisourcing Arrangement

The case study is positioned in the retail market, and concerns a company, the client, that sells products in Europe. Importantly, the client's business processes are highly dependent on IT to fulfil their customers' needs in time, e.g. ordering systems, logistic function, replenishment, retail payments. Today, the client is expanding their portfolio as online business is growing while new store formats are developed to extend the range of products. In order to retain their competitive position in the market the client had to decrease the cost level of their IT. Currently, the client is in the midst of a business application transformation. This involves transitioning from various legacy applications to a new application landscape developed to support new business strategies (e.g. online shopping). The client perceives the current application landscape as critical as it enables the day-to-day business operations. The empirical setting for this case study focuses on the outsourcing relationships between the client and three key IT vendors. Importantly, the client has direct contractual relationships to its three outsourcing vendors. Vendor A is responsible for IT infrastructure services that are geographically dispersed amongst various data centers. Vendor B, who acts as a service integrator, provides services related to various legacy applications. Next, Vendor C also acts as service integrator, however,

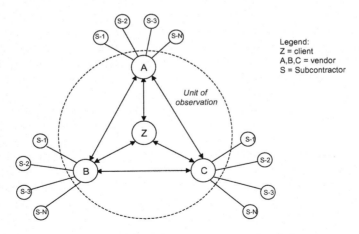

Fig. 1. Multisourcing arrangement under study

with regard to cloud services enabling applications that support the new business strategy. In addition, the client extended the multisourcing arrangement by contracting 60 smaller IT vendors, all acting as subcontractors providing services to the three key vendors (see Fig. 1).

4.2   Collaboration Between the Client and Its Vendors

Due to the client's strategy to establish direct contractual relationships with its vendors as well as with third parties, there are interdependencies between partners, leading to increased complexity of the multisourcing arrangement. Based on the interviews we find that multiple service interdependencies were identified between vendors that affected the integration of IT services by Vendor B and Vendor C negatively. As various partners were reluctant to collaborate, both vendors experienced performance issues when integrating IT services.

> 'We have to become much more mature to encourage collaboration with partners in our arrangement. For instance, we have to improve our internal forecasting process and share the information with the vendors that may prevent technical discussions towards and between vendors'. (Source: Client CIO).
> 'Regarding conflicts we often stick our head in the sand and try to neglect issues between vendors. Actually, in case of performance issues we try to mitigate these issues, however, we are not the experts. We just expect that vendors will work together and if they are not: we have a problem.' (Source: Client sourcing director).

Studying the multisourcing arrangement, two phases can be identified: the period of building the arrangement (period 2008–2010) and the exploitation of the arrangement (period 2011–2013). With regard to the first phase, interviews revealed that the client focus was on utilizing resources at the lowest costs and, in doing so, the client paid insufficient attention to mutual collaboration. Studying the contractual documentation between client and its vendors we find no evidence that collaborative agreements or mechanisms between partners were described and implemented. This immaturity is further reflected by a lack of a coherent strategy as well as a lack of plans related to the collaboration between partners. Importantly, client interviewees explained that meeting structures to discuss the service performance on a regular basis were neglected. Consequently, multiple ad hoc meetings were initiated to discuss operational performance issues and the lack of collaboration between partners. For example, the execution of IT infrastructure related tasks can be allocated to Vendor A or Vendor B, depending on the knowledge and experience of the client employees. This resulted in fierce discussions between the client and vendors regarding the boundaries of IT services and IT infrastructure. Our analysis of the documentation revealed that at the start of the arrangement the client did not describe the position and responsibilities of each vendor and their mutual relationships in detail. Interviews revealed that the lack of behavioural controls resulted in vendors' unwillingness to share technical information on firm level with regard to applications and infrastructure. Moreover, the absence of unambiguous behavioural controls increased the competition between vendors as they wanted to protect their Intellectual Property Rights. The client experienced that the lack of collaboration between vendors caused a decrease of service performance and an extension of the project lead times.

'Vendors have difficulties with mutual collaboration. For example, last year Vendor C acted as service integrator for a large software change program. However, Vendor A was not willing to report financial information of their services to Vendor C as they are also competitors in the market. For this reason, Vendor A was only willing to send their commercial information to the client directly.' (Source: Client sourcing manager).

'Collaboration is not high on the agenda. We try to scope it per project basis. There are IP issues amongst vendors, even for simple things like sharing information on Unit Testing and end-to-end testing. Due to the degree of competition vendors do not want to share technical information. Moreover, Vendor B and Vendor C provide similar type of services in the same market and both act as strong competitors.' (Source: Client sourcing manager).

During the period 2010–2013 we find that the client changed their strategy towards vendors and refocused from competition to collaboration between vendors to improve operational service performance. The client initiated a program to improve collaboration between all partners and overcome the challenges as experienced previously. Interestingly, the vendors funded the collaboration sessions as organized by an external firm. Senior vendor representatives were invited to discuss the competition between vendors and their interdependencies regarding service provisioning. Based on the outcome of these sessions areas of improvement were defined. The client's collaboration initiative increased the degree of commitment between the vendors on an operational level. More specifically, collaborative agreements were tested on a project level first and extended to regular services later.

'We want to increase the commitment in our relationship with and between the vendors – so that they do not compete but work together. Moving forward, we will have collaboration ambassadors who will implement collaboration on a project level.' (Source: Client program manager).

In addition to collaboration meetings the client decided to change their ad hoc meeting approach. Regular meetings were scheduled on an operational and tactical level to discuss the tension between the responsibilities of the client, e.g. contract management, and those of the vendor, e.g. service management.

4.3   Collaboration Between the Vendors

In the first phase of the arrangement (period 2008–2010) the absence of a coherent interorganizational structure of the multisourcing arrangement resulted in fierce discussions about service provisioning between the vendors over time. Relevant issues were related to the description of the position, role, and mandate of each vendor in the arrangement. For example, we found that Vendor B and Vendor C are responsible for the deployment of software and the relationship with technology partners (e.g. Oracle, Microsoft). As formal agreements on collaboration are neglected, the collaboration between vendors and third parties is based on the need and willingness of each party. Our analysis shows that multiple misunderstandings and debates between vendors and technology partners arose with regard to technical and financial issues. Importantly, technology partners were unwilling to share technical details that were needed to develop software technology projects, which influenced the implementation of the software project negatively.

'Since we (Vendor C) are responsible for the overall implementation of a new software package, our competitor (Vendor B) is responsible for part of the solution (testing). These interweaving

activities result in financial disputes as their intellectual property rights forbid to exchange information with other partners for free. Then, we have another conflict.' (Source: Vendor C - Service delivery manager).

Within the multisourcing arrangement both Vendor B and Vendor C are responsible for providing end-to-end IT services towards the client. We observed that the service boundaries of both vendors overlapped, resulting in various operational disputes. This resulted in a reluctant behaviour of the vendors and decreased willingness to collaborate with each other. Addressing the development and implementation of end-to-end services, which concerned all vendors, we did not find any collaboration agreements or mechanisms applied and implemented to deal with these issues.

'As disputes with our competitors regarding overlapping contracts resulted in constant financial fights, we mutually decided to set up a non-aggression pact. In practice we experienced that collaboration would benefit for all of us as the client was threwing financial penalties due to our non-performance.' (Source: Vendor B - Account executive).

Importantly, our analysis shows that as Vendor C is dependent on Vendor A to provide end-to-end IT services, Vendor A kept relevant financial information internally to prevent that their competitor became successful. Next, Vendor A sent their financial information to the client directly. As a result, Vendor C was challenged by the client to decrease their cost level. In doing so, Vendor A's behaviour was based on self-interest, trying to 'game' the perception of the client at the cost of their competitor. This impacted the degree of collaboration between the actors resulting in financial disputes and loss of value creation. The opportunistic behaviour of Vendor A can partially be explained by the desire to maximize their own utility as the client encouraged strong competition between the vendors to achieve cost reduction. We argue that by consciously applying a more balanced multisourcing strategy between the actors the vendors are more willing to collaborate.

In the second phase (period 2011–2013) the collaboration between vendors increased, which was partially influenced by the client's collaboration initiative. We observed that all vendors in the multisourcing arrangement experienced mutual dependencies in providing services to the client. Interviews revealed that the service delivery of multiple vendors and third-parties is stressed regularly as various service levels are breached, resulting in a decrease of the performance to the client. This insight changed the vendors' behaviour over time into a more collaborative approach based on the need to act positively. Establishing regular meetings further encouraged collaboration between vendors on an operational level. For example, vendor representatives exchanged technical information on applications and IT infrastructure, and collaboratively developed workarounds. Consequently, this approach was beneficial for all vendors, which increased the degree of trust between the client and its vendors. We observed that during the arrangement Vendor B and Vendor C set up Operational Level Agreements (OLAs) with Vendor A as a behavioural control mechanism to improve the end-to-end service performance. After implementing these behavioural control mechanisms the satisfaction reports showed an increase of service performance.

'Based on an agreement with the other vendors we started to collaborate on an operational level. This initiative was strictly our idea, not the client's. Importantly, all partners experienced

their value as the service performance increased significantly and less incidents occur.' (Source: Vendor C - Contract and delivery lead).

5   Findings and Discussion

The client's change of their vendor competition strategy and initiative to establish collaboration sessions was perceived by the vendors as a landmark. Our analyses revealed that the client's change created stability in the multisourcing arrangement and decreased the pressure of vendors from a financial point of view. We found that the actors experienced that other actors were willing to exchange technical information that could be beneficial at a certain moment in time. However, based on the analyses of all contracts we did not find any contractual agreements that supported the exchange of technical information between vendors. The absence of such supporting contractual agreements underpin the importance of behavioural controls. This case study shows that the absence of behavioural controls resulted in both operational and financial conflicts between vendor representatives. The lack of mutual agreements can partially be explained as the contracts reflect existing dyadic relationships between client and vendors. Thus, the contracts as studied were incomplete as external factors, including the dependencies between vendors, were not perfectly foreseeable at the start [45, 46]. Therefore, it can be argued that multisourcing related contracts need to comprise agreements between all actors and thus reflect mutual interdependencies.

Interviews indicated that during the second phase (period 2011–2013) the behaviour of all vendors changed as they were convinced that collaboration with other actors in the multisourcing arrangement would be reciprocal and create joint value. The client's initiative to actually support vendors in achieving their service related goals improved the relationship between vendors. In particular, interviews revealed that the degree of trust between individual employees of the vendors in the arrangement increased. This finding confirms group-based exchange relationship as described by [35] and is consistent with research of [30] who argue that trust between actors will result in mutual commitments. This finding supports the *first proposition* arguing that generalized reciprocity positively contributes to building trust, which, in turn, may support collaboration between actors.

Discussing the second proposition, interviews shows that the complexity within the multisourcing arrangement increased as the responsibilities with regard to contractual relationships and operational relationships are dispersed between client and its vendors. Consequently, tensions arose between actors in the multisourcing arrangement on an operational level. For example, Vendor B and Vendor C breached end-to-end SLAs with the client regularly, as they are dependent on information of other actors in the arrangement. As a result, the client punished Vendor B and Vendor C with financial penalties, which decreased both vendors' degree of commitment. The absence of monitoring mechanisms by the actors in the arrangement could partially explain the lack of conflict resolutions measurements. We identified that both Vendor B and Vendor C mitigated their risk by means of decreasing their resource planning related to future client projects. At a later stage, when the client initiated new projects, the vendors could not start immediately, resulting in a delay for the client. This supports the *second proposition* that social sanctions affect the concerned actor of a multisourcing arrangement negatively.

As the second phase of the arrangement can be described as collaborative-oriented we identified an increase of trust amongst the actors. During this second phase the client's management paid more attention to creating common goals with the vendors' management to improve the operational performance of service provisioning, as is reflected in the example of the initiation of collaboration sessions. Consequently, this resulted in an increase of their willingness to contribute to collective value creation and work in the interest of all actors. Due to internal discussions with business departments the client's retained IT organization failed to provide timely information with regard to application requirements to vendors. This may hinder the vendors' obligation to provide project deliverables based on agreed and scheduled deadlines. Interestingly, we find that former client employees, now working at Vendor B and located on the client's premises, show compensation behaviour by discussing the requirements with the client's business departments directly. Although it is not their primary responsibility Vendor B individuals repaired the lack of information by which Vendor B was able to meet service requirements as planned. These findings are consistent with [28] who argues that shared values and beliefs of a group is valuable as it facilitates both generalized reciprocity and social sanction. This finding supports the *third proposition* stating that a common culture encourages actors in a multisourcing arrangement to share information and services as it contribute to the collective interest of the actors involved.

6   Conclusions and Limitations

This research examines collaboration between partners within a multisourcing arrangement with a view to their heterogeneous as well as overlapping resources and heterogeneous strategic interests, while at the same time developing and managing IT services on an operational level. We investigated a multisourcing arrangement by focusing on how actors collaborate and on which resources the actors are dependent. Our findings contribute to the Social Exchange Theory applied within a multisourcing arrangement, and in particular the way in which actors attempt to achieve balance in their exchange relationships. This finding is consistent with literature as according to [27], social elements of the exchange may involve benefits to either party which are either extrinsic (e.g. information) or intrinsic (e.g. support or friendship). There are two important findings that contribute to practice. The first contribution of our study shows a tension in collaboration as the client and vendors under study focus on competition rather than on collaboration. The lack of a common culture hinders the degree of collaboration between the actors. As a result, the actors were unwilling to share information and services as it contribute to the collective interest of the actors involved. From the perspective of individuals we find compensation behaviour with regard to exchanging information. Driven by reciprocal processes individuals are willing to collaborate to achieve agreed goals in favour of the collective interest of actors in the multisourcing arrangement to create and capture value. We argue that actors within a multisourcing arrangement have to anticipate exogenous developments and adapt in order to be resilient. Consequently senior management involved must be capable of anticipating unexpected developments and be willing to change. The second contribution of our research suggests that when the client opts for a multisourcing strategy, the type of contracts need to be changed. Dyadic oriented contracts have to be extended and include multisourcing agreements and clear control mechanisms. It can be argued that contracts based on a multisourcing strategy need to contain agreements between all actors and thus reflect all interdependencies in a multisourcing arrangement. Moreover, analyses of multisourcing arrangements may profit by including theories with regard to control mechanisms, such as input and output control versus behavioural as proposed by [47] and later expanded by [48]. Importantly, collaboration in multisourcing arrangements is difficult as a result of endogenous and exogenous developments. Hence, it can be argued that the degree of collaboration may vary depending on external and internal dynamics, as well as the actors' goals and experiences. However, we also see avenues to explore multisourcing arrangements by paying attention to control mechanisms and concepts based on business ecosystem thinking. Research into roles like dominators and keystones may shed some light on the effect of mutual collaboration.

Our research has some limitations. We only studied one multisourcing arrangement including three vendors. However, it is possible that third-parties, which were excluded in our research, influence the multisourcing arrangement as a whole and thus our findings. Hence, future empirical research is necessary to test the relationships between the constructs. Another limitation is that collaboration is only studied on a generic level. More detailed distinctions between the nature and type of collaboration are not made. Additional aspects that can be considered include senior management capacity to anticipate change within the multisourcing arrangement and the degree of resilience.

Appendix A: Overview Interview Participants

Party	Job description	Date	Interview duration
Client	CIO	13 February 2013	1 hour
Client	Sourcing director	13 February 2013	1 hour
Client	Sourcing manager	13 February 2013	2 hours
Client	Sourcing manager	13 February 2013	2 hours
Client	Program manager large IT projects	14 February 2013	1 hour
Client	IT manager (domain infrastructure, applications)	14 February 2013	1 hour
Client	Service manager	14 February 2013	1 hour
Vendor A	Account executive	9 October 2013	1 hour
Vendor A	Account manager	16 October 2013	1 hour
Vendor A	Delivery manager	23 October 2013	1 hour
Vendor B	Account executive	17 May 2013	1 hour
Vendor B	Contract manager	23 may 2013	1 hour
Vendor B	Manager Service Integration	24 May 2013	1 hour
Vendor B	Delivery manager	31 May 2013	1 hour
Vendor C	Relationship manager	6 September 2013	1 hour
Vendor C	Contract and delivery lead	17 September 2013	1 hour
Vendor C	Delivery program manager	25 June 2013	1 hour
Vendor C	Head of Oracle retail competency services	5 September 2013	1 hour
Vendor C	Service delivery manager	1 October 2013	1 hour

References

1. Lacity, M.C., Khan, S.A., Willcocks, L.P.: A review of the IT outsourcing literature: insights for practice. J. Strateg. Inf. Syst. **18**(3), 130–146 (2009)
2. Oshri, I., Kotlarski, J., Willcocks, L.P.: The Handbook of Global Outsourcing and Offshoring. Palgrave Macmillan, London (2009)
3. Beulen, E., Ribbers, P., Roos, J.: Managing IT Outsourcing. Governance in Global Partnerships, 2nd edn. Routledge, London (2011)
4. Palvia, P.C., King, R.C., Xia, W., Palvia, S.C.J.: Capability, quality, and performance of offshore is vendors: a theoretical framework and empirical investigation. Decis. Sci. **41**(2), 231–270 (2010)
5. Dibbern, J., Goles, T., Hirschheim, R., Jayatilaka, B.: Information systems outsourcing: a survey and analysis of the literature. DB Adv. Inf. Syst. **34**(4), 6–102 (2004)
6. Wiener, M., Saunders, C.: Force coopetition in IT multi-sourcing. J. Strateg. Inf. Syst. **23**, 210–225 (2014)
7. Currie, W.L., Willcocks, L.P.: Analysing four types of IT sourcing decisions in the context of scale, client/supplier interdependency and risk mitigation. Inf. Syst. J. **8**(2), 119–143 (1998)
8. Aron, R., Clemons, E.K., Reddi, S.: Just right outsourcing: understanding and managing risk. J. Manag. Inf. Syst. **22**(2), 37–55 (2005)
9. Oshri, I., Kotlarski, J., Willcocks, L.P.: Managing dispersed expertise in IT offshore outsourcing: lessons from Tata Consulting Services. MIS Q. Exec. **6**, 53–65 (2007)
10. Su, N., Levina, N.: Global multisourcing strategy: integrating learning from manufacturing into IT service outsourcing. IRR Trans. Eng. Manag. **58**(4), 717–729 (2011)
11. Bapna, R., Barua, A., Mani, D., Mehra, A.: Cooperation, coordination, and governance in multisourcing: an agenda for analytical and empirical research. Inf. Syst. Res. **21**(4), 785–795 (2010)
12. Chua, C.E.H., Lim, W.K., Soh, C., Sia, S.K.: Client strategies in vendor transition: a treat balancing perspective. J. Strateg. Inf. Syst. **21**(1), 72–83 (2012)
13. Choi, T.Y., Krause, D.R.: The supply base and its complexity: implications for transaction costs, risks, responsiveness, and innovation. J. Oper. Manag. **24**(5), 637–652 (2006)
14. Adner, R., Kapoor, R.: Value creation in innovation multisourcings: how the structure of technological interdependence affects firm performance in new technology generations. Strateg. Manag. J. **31**, 306–333 (2010)
15. Levina, N., Su, N.: Global multisourcing strategy: the emergence of a supplier portfolio in services offshoring. Decis. Sci. **39**(3), 541–570 (2008)
16. Rottman, J.W., Lacity, M.C.: Proven practices for efficiently offshoring IT work. MIT Sl. Manag. Rev. **47**(3), 56–64 (2006)
17. Burke, G.J., Carrillo, J.E., Vakharia, A.J.: Single versus multiple supplier sourcing strategies. Eur. J. Oper. Res. **182**(1), 95–112 (2007)
18. King, W.R., Torkzadeh, G.: Information systems offshoring: research status and issues. MIS Q. **32**(2), 205–225 (2008)
19. Lee, Y., Cavusgil, S.T.: Enhancing alliance performance: the effects of contractual-based versus relational-based governance. J. Bus. Res. **59**(8), 896–905 (2006)
20. Rai, A., Keil, M., Hornyak, R., Wüllenweber, K.: Hybrid relational-contractual governance for business process outsourcing. J. Manag. Inf. Syst. **29**(2), 213–256 (2012)
21. Deming, W.E.: Out of the Crisis. MIT Centre for Advanced Engineering Study, Cambridge (1996)
22. Xiao, J., Xie, K., Hu, Q.: Inter-firm IT governance in power-imbalanced buyer–supplier dyads: exploring how it works and why it lasts. Eur. J. Inf. Syst. **21**, 1–17 (2012)

23. Lacity, M.C., Willcocks, L.P.: Advanced Outsourcing Practice: Rethinking ITO, BPO and Cloud Services. Palgrave Macmillan, London (2012)

24. Camarinha-Matos, L.M., Afsarmanesh, H.: Collaborative networks: a new scientific discipline. J. Int. Manuf. **16**(4–5), 439–452 (2005)

25. Camarinha-Matos, L.M., Afsarmanesh, H.: Collaborative networks: value creation in a knowledge society. In: Wang, K., Kovács, G.L., Wozny, M.J., Fang, M. (eds.) Knowledge Enterprise: Intelligent Strategies in Product Design, Manufacturing and Management. International Federation for Information Processing (IFEP), vol. 207, pp. 26–40. Springer, New York (2006)

26. Homans, G.C.: Social Behavior: Its Elementary Forms. Hartcourt Brace, New York (1961)

27. Blau, P.M.: Exchange and Power in Social Life. Wiley, New York (1964)

28. Ekeh, P.P.: Social Exchange Theory: Two Traditions. Princeton University Press, Princeton (1974)

29. Muthusamy, S.K., White, M.A.: Learning and knowledge transfer in strategic alliances: a social exchange view. Organ. Stud. **26**(3), 415–441 (2005)

30. Cropanzano, R., Michell, M.S.: Social exchange theory: an interdisciplinary review. J. Manag. **31**(6), 874–900 (2005)

31. Flynn, F.J.: How much should I give and how often? the effects of generosity and frequency of favor exchange on social status and productivity. Acad. Manag. J. **46**, 539–553 (2003)

32. Perrone, V., Zaheer, A., McEvity, B.: Free to be trusted? organizational constraints on trust in boundary spanners. Organ. Sci. **14**, 422–439 (2003)

33. Masterson, S.S., Lewis, K., Goldman, B.M., Taylor, M.S.: Integrating justice and social exchange: the differing effects of fair procedures and treatment on work relationships. Acad. Manag. J. **43**(4), 738–748 (2000)

34. Emerson, R.M.: Power-dependence relations. Am. Sociol. Rev. **27**, 31–41 (1962)

35. Das, T.K., Teng, B.S.: Alliance constellations: a social exchange perspective. Acad. Manag. Rev. **27**(3), 445–456 (2002)

36. DiDomenico, K., Tracey, P., Haugh, H.: The dialectic of social exchange: theorizing corporate social enterprise collaboration. Organ. Stud. **30**(8), 887–907 (2010)

37. Coleman, J.S.: The Foundations of Social Theory. Harvard University Press, Cambridge (1990)

38. Jones, C., Hesterly, W.S., et al.: A general theory of network governance: exchange conditions and social mechanisms. Acad. Manag. Rev. **22**(4), 911–945 (1997)

39. Nord, W.R.: An integrative approach to social conformity. Psychol. Bull. **71**, 174–208 (1969)

40. Yin, R.K.: Case Study Research. Design and Methods. Sage Publications, Thousand Oaks (2009)

41. Lee, A.S.: Integrating positivist and interpretive approaches to organizational research. Organ. Sci. **2**(4), 342–365 (1991)

42. Orlikowski, W.J., Iacono, C.S.: Research commentary: desperately seeking the "IT" in IT research-a call to theorizing the IT artifact. Inf. Syst. Res. **12**(2), 121–134 (2001)

43. Denzin, N.K.: The Research Act: A Theoretical Introduction to Sociological Methods. McGraw-Hill, New York (1978)

44. Miles, M.B., Huberman, A.M.: Qualitative Data Analysis: An Expanded Sourcebook, 2nd edn. Sage Publications, Thousand Oaks (1994)

45. Williamson, O.E.: Markets and Hierarchies. Free Press, New York (1975)

46. Hendry, J.: The principal's other problems: honest incompetence and the specification of objectives. Acad. Manag. Rev. **27**(1), 98–113 (2002)

47. Ouchi, W.G.: The relationship between organizational structure and organizational control. Adm. Sci. Q. **22**(1), 95–113 (1977)
48. Eisenhardt, K.M.: Control: organizational and economic approaches. Manag. Sci. **31**(2), 134–149 (1985)

Multi-sourcing Governance: In Perception and in Practice

Tingting Lin[(⊠)]

TUCS – Turku Centre for Computer Science, Turku School of Economics,
University of Turku, Turku, Finland
tingting.lin@utu.fi

Abstract. Multi-sourcing has emerged as an important pushing force on the global growth of ITO contracts. However, most of our understanding in various aspects of ITO still derives from dyadic client-vendor relationships. With a single case study on the ITO governance among a client and its two suppliers, I strive to increase the understanding on governance in the specific context of multi-sourcing. Departing from the theoretical framework aligning governance mechanism and governance structures, the case analysis reveals the diverging perception and practice of governance, which have caused the tension and conflicts among the multi-sourcing participants. With implications on both theory and practice, the findings shed lights on the understanding of conflicts and restructuring of supplier relationships in multi-sourcing situation.

Keywords: IT outsourcing · Governance · Multi-sourcing

1 Introduction

The phenomenon of multi-sourcing, defined as outsourcing arrangements with multiple vendors, is not novel in the research and practices of IT Outsourcing (ITO). As a widely considered landmark, the influential outsourcing decision of Kodak already involves multiple vendors led by IBM but also with Digital Equipment Corporation (DEC) and Businessland [1, 2]. In this classic case, different IT operations are outsourced to different vendors; IBM was in charge of the data centre, Businessland managed the microcomputer operations, and DEC took over the telecommunications and data networks together with IBM. Since then, the interest on ITO has been widespread all over the world, and different strategies are attempted on the arrangement of multiple vendors. For example, British Petroleum (BP) adopted a different strategy in their outsourcing decision, in which they hired three vendors who are required to deliver an integrated operational service together. The cornerstone of this strategy is identified as "multiple IT suppliers that act as one" [3] (p. 95). In contrast to BP's strategy, selective outsourcing was favoured by South Australian Water (SA Water), a public owned corporation, in their strategic broker model for outsourcing [4]. Their strategy positions the CIO as broker of services pooling both external service providers and internal IS department with different task focuses; it also shifts the organization of IS from a centralized form to a role-based model associating multiple organizational styles to carry out various IS roles. Different benefits of diverse multi-sourcing

© Springer International Publishing Switzerland 2015
I. Oshri et al. (Eds.): Global Sourcing 2015, LNBIP 236, pp. 187–205, 2015.
DOI: 10.1007/978-3-319-26739-5_11

strategies are also recognized in prior literature, such as creating vendor competition, retaining strategic control [5] and mitigating ITO risks [6, 7]. In recent years, the significant growth of multi-sourcing is perceptible in the IT outsourcing (ITO) practice. According to the outsourcing index by Information Services Group (ISG) for the third quarter of 2014 [8], the trend on the global level towards increased multi-sourcing is a powerful pushing force for a high number of ITO contracts in the past nine months of 2014.

While prior studies have shed light on our understanding in various aspects of ITO, most of them derive from a dyadic relationship between the client and a single vendor. Besides the extensive research on such dyadic relationship in ITO, the management of multiple vendors has posed new challenges to IT outsourcing scholars and practitioners [9]. On one hand, despite being competitors, different vendors have to work in synergy for a common business objective of the client. On the other hand, more often than not, these vendors are dispersed in different geographical locations. Hence, our under-standing of ITO management based on dyadic client-vendor relationship is insufficient to address the nuances and complexity in this new context. Recognizing this research opportunity in a new era of ITO, studies have emerged on different aspects of multi-sourcing, such as the rationale to opt for multi-sourcing [10, 11], the selection of vendor portfolio [12], knowledge transfer between vendors [13], and effective practices for management [14]. As in Bapna et al.'s [9] call, the complexities derived from interdependencies between client and multiple vendors require more management and research attention on multi-sourcing governance. In response to this call, a few recent studies have explored this phenomenon in different ways. For instance, Plugge and Janssen [15] investigated the governance of multiple vendors through the lenses of coordination theory and resource dependency view. While the study of multi-sourcing governance can be informed by reference theories, it can also contribute in the development of existing theories. With a longitudinal case study on IT multi-sourcing, Wiener and Saunders [16] extended the theory of coopetition into forced coopetition, and classified different multi-sourcing models in practice. While these studies signifi-cantly enhanced our understanding on multi-sourcing governance, they mostly focus on the coordination aspect, thus more studies are still needed to expand the scope with alternative views and in different contexts.

This study is motivated by a real-life case on the multi-sourcing of IT infrastructure. In this particular case, all involved parties have experienced some extent of conflict within the multi-sourcing governance, which was derived from the discrepancies between perception and practice among various parties. As identified by Miranda and Kavan [17], during the execution of ITO governance, the process of conflict resolution effects, hand-in-hand with the process of coordination, the alignment across client and vendor. Thus in addition to the routinized coordination, non-routinized conflict is also an important aspect of governance that needs to be addressed both in theory and in practice. This paper addresses conflict from the aspect of governance in perception and in practice. Hence the focus of this paper is not to theorize conflict, but rather to explore emerging discrepancies between perception and practice in multi-sourcing governance, which can lead to different conflicts. Correspondingly, this following research question is asked: How do multi-sourcing governance unfold in perception and in practice? To answer this research question, I will first synthesize prior literature on ITO governance into an integrated theoretical framework for a holistic understanding of this concept. Then, governance is examined again in the light of specific literature on multi-sourcing. Following theoretical discussion is my empirical study on a single case, which is analysed with interpretive approach to reveal the conflicting interpretations among different parties. Then, the findings are presented with the empirical results on three aspects of governance mechanisms: contract, control, and information system. Finally, I conclude the paper with both theoretical and practical implications.

2 Theoretical Background

In this section, we will discuss the theoretical background of ITO governance, and a theoretical framework aligning governance structure and governance mechanisms. Then I will explain how the framework can be used to examine governance in multi-sourcing context.

2.1 ITO Governance

Governance has been recognized as an important topic of ITO, both in theory [18] and in practice [19]. A widely adopted definition of ITO governance as "the framework for decision rights and accountabilities to encourage desirable behaviour in the use of IT" [20] (p. 3) is actually derived from the concept of IT governance. In one of the earliest research papers on ITO, Loh and Venkatraman [21] views ITO as an alternative governance option extending the traditional IT governance from the internal hierarchy to the external market. With the maturity of ITO practice, the research perspective of governance also expands towards a more holistic view to understand ITO relationship as an entity instead of the internal-external dichotomy. Hence, the definition of ITO governance structure starts to depart from the traditional view from IT governance, focusing more on the integrated relationship. Such holistic approach and relational focus is shown in recent definitions of ITO governance structure, for example, as "the ownership and control structure used to formalize the relationship, and distinguish among these structures by the level of hierarchical control, length, and extent of formalization" [22] (pp. 44–45). Three types of governance structure have been addressed [17, 23, 24]: market, hierarchy, and network. Although different scholars and research fields have contrasting interpretations and definitions on these three structures, this paper follows Miranda and Kavan's [17] synthesis that "the market is an institutionally derived and transaction- or contract-based governance form; the hierarchy is an institutionally derived authority-based form; the network is a socially-derived informal form" (p. 153), because this definition is particularly tailored for ITO governance.

Besides governance structure, which resembles different options to shape the governance, the aspect of governance mechanisms is also essential in both decision and implementation phases of ITO. Indeed, ITO governance is realized and embodied through various mechanisms involving synergic processes and practices, which are categorized into the two interrelated types of contractual and relational governance [25–27]. Lacity et al. [18] address both contractual and relational governance as important constructs for theory building in ITO; according to their definition, contractual mechanisms are "the formal contractual controls used to govern ITO", and relational mechanisms are "the informal controls and relationship attributes between client and supplier firms" (p. 150). This definition focuses on the control aspect of governance mechanisms, manifesting the dichotomy of formal and informal controls [28, 29]. Besides, contract is also a key aspect of governance mechanisms, including both formal [30–32] and psychological contracts [26, 33, 34]. In addition to contract and control, the information system supporting governance is also an essential mechanism in the process and coordination of ITO. The design of such information system should be aligned with the overall governance structure and other governance mechanisms [35]. With different configurations of contracts, controls and supporting information systems, the boundary between contractual and relational governance is blurred and the interrelation between them becomes salient [25–27].

As suggested in prior literature, contractual and relational governance tightly relate to each other, as complementarities and/or substitutions [25, 26, 36]. Miranda and Kavan [17] have synthesized the alignment of different governance structure and contract mechanisms with the "Moments of Governance" (MoG) model, including two sequential stages: promissory contract and psychological contract. Besides psychological contract which is already mentioned above, the term promissory contract resembles formal type of contract, as a specified promise to establish the commitments. The three governance structures of market, hierarchy, and network are also circumscribed into each stage pertaining to the outsourcing context. According to the authors, promissory contract can be established under market and hierarchy governance; whereas only hierarchy and network governance are viable during psychological contract. Besides the contract mechanism in MoG model, governance mechanisms also involve control mechanism and the supporting information system [37]. On the basis of the MoG model, the alignment of governance mechanisms and governance structure is illustrated in Table 1, where promissory contract and psychological contract are respectively categorized into contractual and relational governance, together with related control and information system. It is worth mentioning that the divide between contractual and relational governance is marked as discontinuous line in Table 1 due to the close inter-relations between the two categories. In addition, the structure of hierarchy governance can also accommodate both contractual and relational mechanisms [17].

Table 1. The alignment of governance structure and governance mechanisms

	Governance structure		
	Market	Hierarchy	Network
Governance mechanisms	*Contractual Governance*		*Relational Governance*
Contract	*Promissory contract*		*Psychological contract*
Control	*Formal control*		*Informal control*
Information system	*Process-oriented design*		*Agility-oriented design*

2.2   Governance in the Context of Multi-sourcing

In the context of IT multi-sourcing, the complexity of governance is raised by the increased number of participants, especially vendors [9]. Therefore, the holistic approach needs to be combined with the externalized view when assessing the governance structure; in other words, while the ITO relationship should be perceived as an entity, each firm's internal characteristics have to be taken back into consideration [38]. Moreover, the establishment of client-vendor relationship is not necessarily synchronous for all; the clients' relationship with some vendors might have started long before the multi-sourcing contracts are signed with additional vendors. Thus, the governance mechanisms can be different between the client and different vendors, and both contractual and relational governance need to be considered in a multi-sourcing context. In addition to client-vendor governance, the governance mechanisms between vendors also need extra attention, especially under some particular structures such as the guardian vendor model [9, 10].

Multi-sourcing, as an emerging phenomenon of ITO, has indeed attracted much research attention on different aspects, including the rationale to opt for multi-sourcing [10, 11], the selection of vendor portfolio [12], knowledge transfer between vendors [13], and effective practices for management [14]. However, research focusing on the governance aspect of multi-sourcing is still scant. In a recent study, Plugge and Janssen [15] investigated the governance of multiple vendors through the lenses of coordination theory and resource dependency view. Their findings confirm the high interdependency of IT services among multiple parties, and emphasize the importance of a clear governance structure with rationalized governance mechanisms including appropriate contractual and relational elements. In the multi-sourcing context, Wiener and Saunders [16] extended the theory of coopetition into "forced coopetition", and classified different multi-sourcing models, respectively as mediated, direct, and direct-overlapping. Here the "coopetition" specifically describes the vendor-vendor relationships in multi-sourcing, which is "forced" by the client.

While these new contributions have shed light to the literature on multi-sourcing governance, they mostly focus on the aspect of coordination in governance. According to Miranda and Kavan [17], both routinized process of coordination and non-routinized process of conflict resolution contribute to the client-vendor alignment during the execution of ITO governance. Being non-routinized, conflict often emerges as unexpected in practice. As conflict resolution is an integral content of governance, discrepancies in the perception and practice of governance can indeed derive conflicts, especially in novel contexts like multi-sourcing where complexity is increased with the additional number of vendors. Lin [39] has contrasted Governance-in-Contract and Governance-in-Practice within an outsourcing dyad, and argued that these two concepts are inter-related during the stage of psychological contract in governance. In the context of multi-sourcing, such discrepancy between perception and practice of governance need to be re-examined for further conflict resolution. Based on the synthesis of Table 1 incorporating both governance structure and governance mechanisms, this study investigate each mechanism in perception and in practice, and thus unfold governance in the multi-sourcing scenario. The theoretical framework is presented in Table 2.

Table 2. Theoretical framework

	Governance structure		
	Market	Hierarchy	Network
Governance mechanisms			
Contract		In perception	
Control		In Practice	
Information system			

3 Methodology

Given the limited knowledge on the governance of multi-sourcing in prior literature, this study is positioned as exploratory in nature, which is manifested in my research questions focusing on "how". To address these research questions, I choose qualitative approach [40], specifically an interpretive case study [41], to dive deeper into this contemporary phenomena of multi-sourcing. The empirical work follows a long term multi-sourcing relationship for IT infrastructure maintenance among an insurance company (CL) and its two service suppliers (SP1 and SP2). Since the start of this new sourcing arrangement in 2010, various issues emerged as unexpected, causing confusion and conflicts among the client and both suppliers. Thus one of the managers in CL invited the researcher as an external observer to investigate the case. Therefore, from the initiation, this case study is aimed for both theoretical and practical implications. Besides the granted access, another reason to opt for this single case study is that its problematic nature makes it a unique setting with unexpected complexity and nuances. A close look at such deviant issues can potentially generate new understanding on the subject matter [42], i.e. governance of multi-sourcing. I choose to conduct the data collection and analysis with interpretive stance, as an important objective of the empirical work is to making sense of the perception and practice of participants in their working context [41, 43].

3.1 Data Collection

Empirical data was collected from April to November 2012, consisting of 23 in-depth interviews, four meeting observations, and various company documents. Before the data collection started, I signed a Non-Disclosure Agreement (NDA) with each of the three companies to guarantee anonymousness of all participants. The NDA helped to foster mutual trust between the researcher and the interviewees; then information was shared more openly in the interviews, and the researcher's access to governance meetings was granted with no further constraints. Among the interviewees, there are 15 from CL, six from SP1, and three from SP2. With the support of key managers from all three companies, interviewees were selected based on their role in the multi-sourcing governance – I attempted to cover all the important governance roles on all levels in the hierarchy (see Table 3).

Table 3. Roles of interviewees

Firm	Role	Number of interviewee(s)
CL	Head of IT	1
	Middle manager[a]	6
	Operational manager	7
SP1	Customer manager	1
	Financial controller	1
	Service delivery	4
SP2	Customer manager	1
	Service delivery	2

[a]Interviewed middle management group of CL involves managers on business liaison, IT operations, procurement services, application infrastructure, end-user services and sourcing contract.

The interviews are all conducted face-to-face as unstructured interviews without pre-designed question list [44]. However, the themes for discussion, as well as seed questions are planned in advance, in order to avoid irrelevant conversations or embarrassment of silence. During the process of the interview, I strive to achieve a balance between over-passivity and over-direction [41]. First, the researcher started the conversation with self-introduction to clarify the purpose and theme of this interview. Then, some seed questions are asked to the interviewee on his/her role in the multi-sourced work, inspiring him/her to recall the unique challenges in this new setting of two suppliers with his/her personal experience. Following the conversation, the researcher then encouraged the interviewee to describe different examples that he/she had encountered during the work related to governance. Due to the rich context and increased complexity in this case, this approach is appropriate to enable vivid social interaction during the interview, thus generate deeper insights from the interviewees and enable the researcher to capture more situated nuances [45]. Each interview last between one hour to two hours, and was tape-recorded and transcribed. Moreover, the researcher observed four of the regular governance meetings in a non-participative way [44]; in other words, the researcher was sitting on the same meeting site for observation, but not interacting with others during the meeting. Due to the confidentiality, meetings were not tape-recorded, but observation notes were generated during and after each meeting. In addition, the researcher was granted access to various documents and presentation materials regarding governance, including organization charts, documents on formal processes, the ITO contract, reports in form of meeting presentations, meeting minutes, etc. Although the researcher did not gain full access to the key information system supporting governance, the interface as well as basic functions and processes were shown by an expert in CL. In addition, during the empirical study, field notes were also generated in different occasions outside the formal encounters.

3.2 Data Analysis

Due to my interpretive stance, I strive to preserve the openness not only in data collection, but also in data analysis [41]. On one hand, prior literature is reviewed and recorded throughout the whole process of research, which means that the modification of initial theoretical framework did not stop at the start of empirical work [40]. During the data collection and analysis, the initial theoretical framework was being revised; in turn, the development of theoretical framework affected the fine-tuning of subsequent empirical study. This process is iterative with the constant interaction between theory and data [41]. On the other hand, the timing for data analysis was not delayed until the end of data collection. Instead, the analysis was continuous since the first bit of data has been obtained; because insights are generated from the analysed data, and the subsequent data collection can be adjusted based on this new understanding [40]. Specifically, the analysis of data incorporates the interpretation of interview transcripts, meeting notes and documents as soon as they are obtained. Using such multiplicity of sources, I am able to unfold contrasting interpretation of participants' perception and practice on each mechanism of governance.

4   Findings

Findings are presented in this section. First, the case background is described to show the company profiles of all the three parties, as well as an illustration of the multi-sourcing arrangement. Then, the perception and practices of governance are introduced for each mechanism, i.e. contract, control, and information system. Due to confidentiality requirement and the sensitive nature of the information, original transcripts of interviews are not presented; instead, the information generated from interviews is aggregated to the company level, so that the context would not be lost while individual informants are kept unexposed.

4.1   Case Description

CL is a leading Nordic insurance company, with operations also encompassing Russia and the Baltic countries. At the time of my empirical work in 2012, CL has approximately 7000 employees and 3.1 million customers. In CL's daily business, a new claim is reported every 10th second, 30 customers call occur in every minute, a customer visit is made every 18th second, 20 insurance renewals are registered every minute, and new sales are accomplished every 30th second. Therefore, no process development can be achieved without stable IT infrastructure. The case study is initiated in the department of IT services in CL which has 61 employees. The main task of this department is to manage outsourced IT services with various external suppliers, and to serve their internal customers in CL.

One of their most important outsourcing vendors is an IT service supplier SP1, who is a leading IT service company with approximately 18000 employees worldwide. The contract between CL and SP1 was signed in 2005, initially concerning all the services on delivery and development of IT infrastructure, including server and storage, mainframe services, end-user services, and other ad-hoc IT projects. SP1 has assigned a team of 24 people to work exclusively for CL. In 2010, CL demanded SP1 to sub-contract part of the services to a second supplier SP2. In this new arrangement, SP1 is still responsible to deliver most IT infrastructure service directly to CL; whereas the majority of end-user services (i.e. services for client terminals) are provided by SP2 instead, except for the Service Desk tasks which are still carried out by SP1 (see Fig. 1). As shown in Fig. 1, this study focus on the end-user services which is handled by the two different suppliers. SP2 is a smaller (with ca. 6500 employees) but fast-growing company providing IT infrastructure services in the Nordic and Baltic regions. SP2 has been working for CL as a computer hardware provider since 2006, but they have only been involved in the infrastructure services since this new sourcing contract in 2010. Five people from SP2 are devoted to providing this exclusive service. As all the three parties are international companies with branches in different countries, the partici-pating employees in this multi-sourcing work are geographically distributed. Although both suppliers' primary tasks are mainly carried out with the client branch in the same country, some of the participants are also responsible for many collaborative tasks for other client branches abroad. Although the new sourcing contract is not direct between CL and SP2, all the three parties consider the relationship as multi-sourcing, because the IT infrastructure service is indeed being handled by two different vendors. This multi-sourcing arrangement was contracted for five years from 2010 until the end of 2015, with wide scope and high volumes involving 8400 end-users in CL.

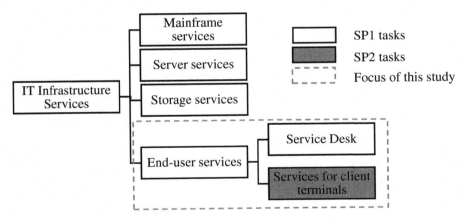

Fig. 1. Task allocation

4.2 Governance Mechanisms

Contract. As mentioned in the case description, there is not a single contract in place to involve all three parties, but two separate ones between CL and SP1, and between SP1 and SP2. These two formal contractual relations are illustrated with the continuous arrow lines in Fig. 2. Such contractual arrangement is actually on the purpose of CL, who wants to minimize the management effort on multiple vendors. As a result, the guardian vendor model is adopted, where SP2 is SP1's subcontractor, and SP1 is fully responsible of SP2's delivery, without the supervision of CL. In the contract between CL and SP1, the ITO governance model is defined as a "strong vision of the relationship development", which is expected to acts as reference to the daily governance works defining agendas and processes. In this governance model, three levels of hierarchy are designed: strategic, tactical and operational, involving both CL and SP1 but not SP2. Furthermore, the linkages across various governance forums in different hierarchical levels are also strictly defined.

The structure of formal contract shows the perception on "who you should reach and how you should reach them", whereas the related practices show "who you actually reach and how you actually reach them". As shown by the dotted arrow lines in Fig. 1, direct interactions do occur between CL and SP2 in the practices of the contract. Moreover, the frequency of such direct interactions is as high as daily, despite the stipulations in the contract. In fact, CL directly participates in the requirement design for SP2's work, and people from the SP2 team also attend several joint meetings together with the other two parties. According to SP2's point of view, on one hand, CL has a strong role on defining the contract, where the guardian vendor model is clear; SP2 also wants to follow the structure in the contract. On the other hand, in practice, CL tends to seek direct interaction with SP2, which causes SP2 to assume that it has been intended alongside the contract from the very beginning. It is a common consideration by CL people that the direct contact to SP2 is a progress to ease the work, as they can track directly to the person who is actually responsible in the operation. In their perspective, this "workaround" to the original contract using "shortcut" in practice also enhances the efficiency and saves time in their work. Though the SP2 customer manager expressed her perception that aligns with the contract, in fact, SP2 recruited one former operational manager from CL into their own service delivery team, to facilitate such direct interaction. According to this new service delivery manager in SP2, 70 % of his work time is devoted on the communication with his previous CL colleagues. Moreover, SP2 actually participates in various governance meetings together with CL and SP1, on all of strategic, tactical and operational levels. Concerns from SP1 are shown towards such issues, as the extra participant from SP2 prolongs the meeting time, and brings them the risk of increasing cost and exposing confidential information. Moreover, being in between an important client and the other supplier and competitor, such work-around between the other two parties is the least desirable for SP1.

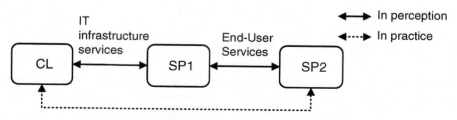

Fig. 2. Contractual structure in perception and in practice

Control. Before we look into the control mechanisms for this multi-sourcing governance, it is necessary to first clarify the perception of trust among all parties, as trust is identified as an important premise to determine the choice of control mechanisms [29, 46, 47]. During the field work in 2012, most interviewees, from all three parties, perceive this new ITO arrangement as "forced marriage". In CL's consideration, the reason for involving SP2 as an additional supplier is twofold. On one hand, during the previous contract period from 2005 to 2010, CL was not fully satisfied with the deliveries of SP1. For instance, many projects suffered long delays. On the other hand, CL believes SP2 is the "best-of-breed" supplier in the area of end-user services; as mentioned in the case description, they also had collaborated with SP2 in other areas before, and the service quality was satisfactory. Therefore, at the beginning of the new arrangement, the trust of CL towards SP1 and SP2 depended on whether the suppliers had met the obligations and expectations in the history of collaboration. Nevertheless, CL also acknowledge that such trust is hard to compare, as SP1 had worked for CL in much wider areas than SP2 had (see Fig. 1), and the possibility of unsatisfactory results is naturally much higher in SP1's work. Between the two suppliers, trust is also implied in each party's perception of potential conflicts and benefits. Between SP1 and SP2, they see each other as direct competitors, as the market of end-user services is of strategic importance for both. Moreover, the contrasting company identities and values between the two suppliers are commonly recognized by all three parties. SP1 is an incumbent multinational IT supplier, who has developed their own "best practices" and formal processes during the long experience to serve clients as large as CL; while this profile is valuable for the client, it also causes the high negotiation power and higher cost towards the client, as well as the lack of flexibility in their services. Whereas SP2, though also fairly large in size, is still a growing company through ongoing merges and acquisitions of smaller firms, which pushes them to aggressively expand in the market; while the customer-oriented quality and flexibility of their work is remarkable, they still lack the experience to deal with such a large client. However, despite the opposition and differences, for both SP1 and SP2, CL is a client of equal importance. This is the main reason why both suppliers have accepted the "forced marriage" arranged by CL. Meanwhile, both suppliers also realized the potential benefits and opportunities from the collaboration with each other; both of them would gain experience to work with a competitor into a stronger partnership, thus improve their competitiveness in the market.

Having perceived the potential risks and conflicts between SP1 and SP2, CL emphasized formal control in the practice, starting with the rigid stipulations in the contract with SP1, which affirms "strong control of the service, through a well-structured governance framework, [...]. As such, the governance framework shall touch all parts of the services." Moreover, very detailed service level description is stipulated for SP1's deliveries. Nevertheless, it is pointed out that "these service levels will be under continuous change thus regular follow-up is needed", which renders the possibility for modifying the formal contract with emerging informal acts. However, as shown in multiple aspect of this case, such formal and informal controls are hard to balance. During the operation, control is mainly realized by written reports and regular governance meetings. As mentioned in the last section, formally these governance meetings should involve only CL and SP1, but SP2 was also invited by CL to facilitate direct information sharing. In contrary to CL's optimist intention, this practice has caused further tension between the suppliers; especially, the boundary of their respective obligations became blurred. Due to the unclear responsibilities, arguments and disagreement occurred frequently in the governance meetings. SP1 tended to avoid explaining about incidents in the area of end-user services, though the contract requires them to be responsible to manage SP2 as a subcontractor and deliver final solutions to CL. Instead, SP2 was asked to reply to questions directly and take responsibilities in end-user services directly for CL. Due to the increasing tension and conflicts, almost only minimum contacts were carried out in daily operations between SP1 and SP2 when absolutely necessary, although CL expected them to work closely with each other under the same governance framework. Hence in practice, the suppliers' mutually "wished" benefits out of this collaboration failed to realize, and CL's expectation of strong control through both formal and informal channels is also impaired.

Information System. As shown in Fig. 1, although the major part of end-user services is handled by SP2 as a subcontractor of SP1, the part of Service Desk is still kept within SP1. This is due to CL's desire for a single point of contact to manage information from all external suppliers. Hence, SP1's Service Desk is in charge of coordination with other suppliers including SP2[1] to ensure a smooth information flow and shared understanding with unified codes and jargons. The work of Service Desk, as a mediating link of the ITO governance, is supported by an information system called Service Management Technology (a pseudonym, hereafter addressed as SMT), which is owned by SP1. The process supported by SMT is highly standardized. Whenever an end-user calls Service Desk for an incident, problem, or change request, a ticket will be created in the SMT system. As a subcontractor, SP2 receives these tickets from SP1's Service Desk through SMT, and solves the tickets according to the assigned responsibilities. In turn, SP2 is supposed to give status reports to Service Desk through SMT to record the fulfilled assignments and resolution in the ticket logs. Before a ticket is closed, its ticket log has to be reported by SP1's service delivery manager to the related operation manager in CL who then checks and approves the ticket closing. Therefore, SMT is perceived as central in the coordination between different parties throughout the entire lifecycle of a certain service, by assigning tasks to subcontractors' support, following up the resolution, recording problems, and being assessed by relevant party.

In practice, the coordinative function of SMT is impaired. First, the integration between SMT and SP2's own handling systems is difficult. As mentioned before, SP2 has grown through mergers and acquisitions, so in the first place, they have different internal systems within different branches. The Norwegian and Swedish branches of SP2 are both involved in the delivery of end-user services; however, only the integration between the systems of SP2 Sweden and SMT was successful, and the integration work of SMT with SP2 Norway system suffered problems and delays at the time of my field work. Specifically, it is hard to match the tickets in the Norwegian system to those in SMT, which causes difficulty for Service Desk in both the follow-up of non-closed tickets and the confirmation of already closed tickets. Then, SP1 found it

---

[1] CL also has several other suppliers, whose work is also through the coordination of Service Desk. However, these suppliers work in other areas outside infrastructure services, thus are not concerned in the scope of this case study.

difficult to identify and track the tickets created for SP2; a new function is needed in SMT to filter the SP2 tickets which are otherwise mixed with other tickets addressed to SP1. Although this is not a difficult task, it generates additional cost for SP1, and also delays the resolution time for end-users in CL. Last but most importantly, the use of the system reflects the contrasting working style accommodated by the two suppliers. For SP1, handling this type of work through SMT is natural and easy, especially because their internal processes are mostly standardized and are accustomed to this system. In contrary, SP2 suffers from using this system, as they are used to a more flexible working style, in which they strive to directly find the root cause and solve it without starting any formal process. This divergence caused frustration for both suppliers, thus their enacted use of the system became completely different. SP2 perceived the strict use of the system as an obstacle to efficiency, as going through the system will cost them longer resolution time and lower satisfaction by the end-users. Hence they started to skip the system and do workarounds in their own way, i.e. contacting end-users in CL directly. The end-users in CL are actually accommodating towards such work-arounds, as the direct contact by SP2 practically facilitated the "shortcut" procedure that they prefer (See "Contract" section). However, for SP1, such workarounds are troublesome, because they lose control and recording of the whole process. The most common consequence is that many open tickets in the system are actually resolved, which increases the difficulty in both operational follow-ups and reporting. Further-more, if the ticket is solved without the formal process through the system, SP1 might not even be aware of the existence of the incident or problem. Therefore, SP1 escalated the resistance of SP2 in using SMT as a critical problem in several governance meetings, and attempted to enforce their conformance to the formal process.

5   Discussion

Based on the elaborated governance mechanisms of this multi-sourcing relationship, here I will discuss the findings through the theoretical framework. As this multi-sourcing relationship is already at the post-adoption stage, the structure of market governance is not applicable here [17]. Therefore, here the governance mechanisms used in this multi-sourcing case, both in perception and in practice, are mapped into the two structures of hierarchy and network, as presented in Table 4.

Different contract mechanisms, i.e. promissory contract and psychological contract, are inscribed into corresponding governance structures in the original MoG model by Miranda and Kavan [17]. Referencing to Rousseau and Parks [48], they define promissory contract as formally stipulated in form of "paid for promises", which is mostly under hierarchy structure in the post-adoption stage; whereas psychological contract relates to people's beliefs regarding their reciprocal exchange, which can either be hierarchy or network in structure. In my case, the perception of contract is mani-fested as the stipulation of "who you should reach and how you should reach them", as well as the clear specification of "what is expected to be done". The original percep-tions of the three parties are also aligned with the structural configuration in the contract, which considers SP2 as a guardian vendor with no direct link between CL and SP2, manifesting an authority relationship with clear hierarchy. However, in practice

Table 4. Governance in perception and in practice

Governance mechanisms \ Governance structure		Hierarchy	Network
Contract	Perception	– *Promissory contract.* – *Guardian vendor model with SP1 as the middle link.*	
	Practice	– *SP1 attempted to keep practice aligned with perception.*	– *Psychological contract* – *Direct links between CL and SP2.*
Control	Perception	– *Different level of trust among all parties, and distinct company identities and values between SP1 and SP2.* – *Formal control expected by CL.*	– *CL expected SP1 and SP2 to work closely with each other.* – *Some expectation for potential partnership between SP1 and SP2.*
	Practice	– *Trust, identities and values in perception influence the practice.* – *Strong formal control by CL on both SP1 and SP2, conducted through reports and regular governance meetings.* – *Minimal interactions are practiced between SP1 and SP2.* – *Expectation for potential partnership between SP1 and SP2 is failed.*	– *Informal control as workaround to the formal control.*
Information system	Perception	– *Formal design as efficient tool for coordination.*	
	Practice	– *For SP1, system-in-practice conforms to the perception.*	– *For SP2, system-in-practice diverges from the perception with flexible ways to use the system.* – *SP2's workarounds are accommodated by CL's practices.*

employees of CL initiated direct contact with SP2, due to the emerging needs for interaction. At the other end, SP2 would like to stick to the contract, but has to conform to CL's practices and facilitate the shortcut in practice. Therefore, both CL and SP2 have mutually adjusted their practices from the perception. As the guardian vendor in contract, the perception and practice of SP1 are the most unified; however, they are not able to eliminate the workarounds by the other two given SP1's position in the relationship, as CL is positioned as the highest authority in the hierarchy. Thus, the perception of contract here is dominated by hierarchy structure of governance, while the practices show a hybrid structure of hierarchy and network which is divergent among different parties.

Besides contract, my study adds to the MoG model by incorporating control and information systems in the alignment of governance structure and mechanisms. As premises of the chosen control mechanisms, the perceptions of the suppliers on relational trust are manifested by the contrasting and competitive identities towards each other, resulting in the lack of trust and increased conflicts in their practices. CL's trust on each supplier depends on the experience from prior collaboration. Although recognizing such tension between suppliers, CL still practiced strong control on both SP1 and SP2, which in fact further aggravated their conflicts. In parallel, as mentioned in the last paragraph, informal control as workaround to the formal control is also initiated by CL. Therefore, the two suppliers minimized mutual interactions, and failed CL's expectation on their obligation to work closely in the same governance framework. In the end, the "forced marriage" also failed to grow into a beneficial partnership. Thus regarding control mechanism, perception and practice are intertwined with mutual influence, and with the presence of both hierarchy and network structure. It is worth noticing that here we can observe several contradictions between perception and practice. Regarding interaction and partnership between the two vendors, practice failed to realize perception; while informal control emerges in CL's practices, which diverges from the perceived formal control mechanism. In the end of the day, the practices in this multi-sourcing relation manifests more characteristics of hierarchy governance than what is perceived.

Information system represents a type of resources that facilitate coordination in governance, thus is also identified as an essential mechanism here. Concerning this multi-sourcing relationship, the system SMT is perceived as an efficient tool to coordinate among different parties through the intended hierarchy structure, supporting the strict formal processes. However, the enacted practices in using the system become very different by the two suppliers, which can be attributed to the contrasting working style fostered in each of them. Due to such difference in practices, the intended coordinating value failed to establish with the support of SMT, and the tension between SP1 and SP2 was further exacerbated. Regarding this mechanism, the practice of SP1 people, as experienced users of SMT, is in line with the perceived functionality of the system under hierarchy structure; whereas the enacted practice of SP2 people, who are new users and whose working style is contradictive with the system design, is severely conflicting with the perceived usage. Similar to the prior two mechanisms, workarounds are practiced by SP2 in the use of SMT with the structure of network governance, which is then accommodated by CL. Therefore, the practices of this mechanism is also featured by the mix of both hierarchy and network structured among different parties.

According to Orlikowski's [49] distinction on the mode of incorporating practice in research, practice is regarded as a 'phenomenon' in my study. I focus on what happens 'in practice', and explicate the divergence and interactions between 'practice' and 'perception'. On one hand, perception and practice diverge for the same object, such as CL and SP2 in the mechanism of contract; on the other hand, the relational trust discussed in the mechanism of control shows evidence about the influence of perception on practice. Additionally, as in the discussion about SMT, practices are enacted in contrasting ways among different parties, even though the perceptions are similar. The findings also suggest that the three governance mechanisms are interrelated in practice. For instance, the informal control and flexible use of the system are both related with the "workaround" from the formal contractual structure. However, as the findings derive from a single case, this relationship among the governance mechanisms still needs further confirmation.

In general, the perceived governance mechanisms in this case are featured with promissory contract based on formal documents, dominated by formal control with regulated communication, and supported by an information system with process-oriented design. Therefore, hierarchy is the most appropriate to label the governance structure in perception, although the perception of control has shown some feature of network governance. As shown in Table 4, characteristics of the network governance structure mainly emerged in the practices among different parties, such as psychological contract, informal control, and the flexible way to use the information system. Actually, the conflicts and tension within this multi-sourcing relationship lie on the divergence between the governance structure in perception and in practice, which ultimately derives from the differences of internal practices in each supplier company. Therefore, the multi-sourcing governance needs to be restructured. The guardian vendor model, in this case, has aggravated the conflicts and hindered the harmonization of the relationships. Instead of the current hierarchical structure, the client needs to enhance their own capabilities with an insourced service desk to manage different vendors directly in a networked structure.

6   Conclusion

In this study, I have demonstrated how governance unfolds in perception and in practice in a multi-sourcing context. As the divergence of governance structure and mechanisms in perception and practice has raised various conflicts in the relationships, especially between the two vendors, the governance of this multi-sourcing relationship will need to be restructured. When the involved suppliers manifest different organizational identities and values, the guardian vendor model (i.e. using one main supplier to manage other suppliers) will aggravate the conflicts in the outsourcing relationships. In this case, the client needs to enhance their own capabilities to manage different vendors directly. Extrapolating to the contrary situation, if the involved suppliers are similar in practice styles, it is more cost and management efficient to apply the guardian vendor model.

My findings contribute to the understandings of IT multi-sourcing relationships with both theoretical and practical implications. The theoretical framework aligns governance mechanisms with governance structures on the basis of Miranda and Kavan's [17] MoG model. According to a comprehensive literature review [37], two more mechanisms, i.e. control and information systems, are added to the mechanism of contract in the original model to provide a more comprehensive theoretical understanding. The framework serves as a starting point for the analysis of the empirical work, and the data analysis further reveals more nuances on multi-sourcing governance by detangling perception from practice, which in turn enriches the theoretical framework. As shown in the case analysis, such distinction of perception and practice has explanation power for different conflicts, which otherwise would appear as complex and contradictory. The understanding of conflicts can serve as a starting point for the research on conflict resolution, extending our knowledge on coordination [15, 16] in multi-sourcing governance. For practitioners, on one hand, my findings can raise their awareness of the conflicts caused by potential disparity of perception and practice; on the other hand, the finding on structuring and restructuring the multi-sourcing governance also enhances their mindfulness on the decision of vendor structure.

While the findings can contribute to multi-sourcing governance both in theory and in practice, I am also aware of the limitations of this study. The main limitation lies in the single case design. Although significant depth was achieved by contextualizing this study only on one specific case, the generalizability of this study is limited and uncertain in other contexts, such as different sized contracts, geographical locations, and number of clients and suppliers. Meanwhile, as mentioned in the discussions, the findings on the interrelationship among the three governance mechanisms also need to be further confirmed in future studies within different empirical sites.

References

1. Dibbern, J., Goles, T., Hirschheim, R., Jayatilaka, B.: Information systems outsourcing: a survey and analysis of the literature. DATA BASE Adv. Inf. Syst. 35(4), 6–102 (2004)
2. Loh, L., Venkatraman, N.: Determinants of information technology outsourcing: a cross-sectional analysis. J. Manag. Inf. Syst. 9(1), 7–24 (1992)
3. Cross, J.: IT outsourcing: British Petroleum's competitive approach. Harv. Bus. Rev. 73(3), 94–102 (1995)
4. Thorogood, A., Yetton, P., Vlasic, A., Spiller, J.: Raise your glasses – the water's magic! Strategic IT at SA Water: a case study in alignment, outsourcing and governance. J. Inf. Technol. 19(2), 130–139 (2004)
5. Currie, W.L., Willcocks, L.P.: Analysing four types of IT sourcing decisions in the context of scale, client/supplier interdependency and risk mitigation. Inf. Syst. J. 8(2), 119–143 (1998)
6. Currie, W.L.: Using multiple suppliers to mitigate the risk of IT outsourcing at ICI and Wessex Water. J. Inf. Technol. 13(3), 169–180 (1998)
7. Huang, R., Miranda, S., Lee, J.: How many vendors does it take to change a light bulb? Mitigating the risks of resource dependence in information technology outsourcing. In: ICIS 2004 Proceedings (2004)
8. ISG, "ISG Index: Global Outsourcing Industry on Track for Strong 2014, Despite 3Q Softness," Information Service Group (ISG) Press Release (2014). http://www.isg-one.com/web/media-center/press/141014-US.asp

9. Bapna, R., Barua, A., Mani, D., Mehra, A.: Research commentary —cooperation, coordination, and governance in multisourcing: an agenda for analytical and empirical research. Inf. Syst. Res. **21**(4), 785–795 (2010)
10. Bapna, R., Gupta, A., Ray, G., Singh, S.: Specialization, integration, and multi-sourcing: a study of large IT outsourcing projects. In: ICIS 2013 Proceedings (2013)
11. Cullen, S., Seddon, P.B., Willcocks, L.P.: IT outsourcing configuration: Research into defining and designing outsourcing arrangements. J. Strateg. Inf. Syst. **14**(4), 357–387 (2005)
12. Fridgen, G., Mueller, H.: An approach for portfolio selection in multi-vendor IT outsourcing. In: ICIS 2011 Proceedings (2011)
13. Schott, K.: Vendor-Vendor knowledge transfer in global ISD outsourcing projects: Insights from a German case study. In: PACIS 2011 Proceedings (2011)
14. Beck, R., Schott, K., Gregory, R.W.: Mindful management practices in global multivendor ISD outsourcing projects. Scand. J. Inf. Syst. **23**(2), 5–28 (2011)
15. Plugge, A., Janssen, M.: Governance of multivendor outsourcing arrangements: a coordination and resource dependency view. In: Kotlarsky, J., Oshri, I., Willcocks, L.P. (eds.) Global Sourcing 2014. LNBIP, vol. 195, pp. 78–97. Springer, Heidelberg (2014)
16. Wiener, M., Saunders, C.: Forced coopetition in IT multi-sourcing. J. Strateg. Inf. Syst. **23**(3), 210–225 (2014)
17. Miranda, S.M., Kavan, C.B.: Moments of governance in IS outsourcing: conceptualizing effects of contracts on value capture and creation. J. Inf. Technol. **20**(3), 152–169 (2005)
18. Lacity, M.C., Willcocks, L.P., Khan, S.: Beyond transaction cost economics: towards an endogenous theory of information technology outsourcing. J. Strateg. Inf. Syst. **20**(2), 139–157 (2011)
19. Lacity, M.C., Khan, S., Willcocks, L.P.: A review of the IT outsourcing literature: Insights for practice. J. Strateg. Inf. Syst. **18**(3), 130–146 (2009)
20. Weill, P.: Don't just lead, govern: How top-performing firms govern IT. MIS Q. Exec. **3**(1), 1–17 (2004)
21. Loh, L., Venkatraman, N.: Diffusion of information technology outsourcing: influence sources and the kodak effect. Inf. Syst. Res. **3**(4), 334–358 (1992)
22. Mani, D., Barua, A., Whinston, A.B.: An empirical analysis of the impact of information capabilities design on business process outsourcing performance. MIS Q. **34**(1), 39–62 (2010)
23. Powell, W.W.: Neither market nor hierarchy: network forms of organization. Res. Organ. Behav. **12**, 295–336 (1990)
24. Adler, P.S.: Market, hierarchy, and trust: the knowledge economy and the future of capitalism. Organ. Sci. **12**(2), 215–234 (2001)
25. Huber, T.L., Fischer, T.A., Dibbern, J., Hirschheim, R.: A process model of complementarity and substitution of contractual and relational governance in IS outsourcing. J. Manage. Inf. Syst. **30**(3), 81–114 (2013)
26. Lioliou, E., Zimmermann, A., Willcocks, L., Gao, L.: Formal and relational governance in IT outsourcing: substitution, complementarity and the role of the psychological contract. Inf. Syst. J. **24**(6), 503–535 (2014)
27. Poppo, L., Zenger, T.: Do formal contracts and relational governance function as substitutes or complements? Strateg. Manage. J. **23**(8), 707–725 (2002)
28. Choudhury, V., Sabherwal, R.: Portfolios of control in outsourced software development projects. Inf. Syst. Res. **13**(3), 291–314 (2003)
29. Tiwana, A.: Systems development ambidexterity: explaining the complementary and substitutive roles of formal and informal controls. J. Manage. Inf. Syst. **27**(2), 87–126 (2010)

30. Chen, Y., Bharadwaj, A.: An empirical analysis of contract structures in IT outsourcing. Inf. Syst. Res. **20**(4), 484–506 (2009)
31. Bhattacharya, S., Gupta, A., Hasija, S.: Joint product improvement by client and customer support center: the role of gain-share contracts in coordination. Inf. Syst. Res. **25**(1), 137–151 (2014)
32. Mani, D., Barua, A., Whinston, A.B.: An empirical analysis of the contractual and information structures of business process outsourcing relationships. Inf. Syst. Res. **23**(3), 618–634 (2012)
33. Kim, H.J., Shin, B., Lee, H.: The mediating role of psychological contract breach in IS outsourcing: inter-firm governance perspective. Eur. J. Inf. Syst. **22**(5), 529–547 (2013)
34. Koh, C., Ang, S., Straub, D.W.: IT outsourcing success: a psychological contract perspective. Inf. Syst. Res. **15**(4), 356–373 (2004)
35. Mani, D., Barua, A., Whinston, A.B.: Successfully governing business process outsourcing relationships. MIS Q. Exec. **5**(1), 15–29 (2006)
36. Goo, J., Kishore, R., Rao, H., Nam, K.: The role of service level agreements in relational management of information technology outsourcing: An empirical study. MIS Q. **33**(1), 119–145 (2009)
37. Lin, T., Vaia, G.: The concept of governance in IT outsourcing: a literature review. In: ECIS 2015 Proceedings (2015)
38. Lin, T., Hekkala, R.: Exploring IT outsourcing governance with vendor's interpersonal networks: a case study. In: Kotlarsky, Julia, Oshri, Ilan, Willcocks, Leslie P. (eds.) Global Sourcing 2014. LNBIP, vol. 195, pp. 18–34. Springer, Heidelberg (2014)
39. Lin, T.: It outsourcing at the stage of psychological contract: governance-in-practice and governance-in-contract. In: ECIS 2013 Proceedings (2013)
40. Silverman, D.: Interpreting Qualitative Data: Methods for Analyzing Talk, Text, and Interaction, 3rd edn. Sage Publications, London (2006)
41. Walsham, G.: Interpretive case studies in IS research: nature and method. Eur. J. Inf. Syst. **4**, 74–81 (1995)
42. Flyvbjerg, B.: Five misunderstandings about case-study research. Qual. Inq. **12**(2), 219–245 (2006)
43. Klein, H.K., Myers, M.D.: A set of principles for conducting and evaluating interpretive field studies in information systems. MIS Q. **23**(1), 67–93 (1999)
44. Eriksson, P., Kovalainen, A.: Qualitative Methods in Business Research. Sage Publications, London (2008)
45. Myers, M.D., Newman, M.: The qualitative interview in IS research: Examining the craft. Inf. Organ. **17**(1), 2–26 (2007)
46. Fink, L.: Information technology outsourcing through a configurational lens. J. Strateg. Inf. Syst. **19**(2), 124–141 (2010)
47. Sabherwal, R.: The role of trust in outsourced IS development projects. Commun. ACM **42**(2), 80–86 (1999)
48. Rousseau, D., Parks, J.: The contracts of individuals and organizations. Res. Organ. Behav. **15**, 1–43 (1993)
49. Orlikowski, W.J.: Practice in research: Phenomenon, perspective and philosophy. In: Golsorkhi, D., Rouleau, L., Seidl, D., Vaara, E. (eds.) Cambridge Handbook of Strategy as Practice, pp. 23–33. Cambridge University Press, Cambridge (2010)

Using E-markets for Globally Distributed Work

Jos van Hillegersberg and Chintan Amrit[✉]

IEBIS, University of Twente, P.O. Box 217, 7500 AE Enschede, The Netherlands
{j.vanHillegersberg,c.amrit}@utwente.nl

Abstract. For over a decade, dedicated E-markets have been facilitating globally distributed systems development by enhancing the traditionally high-risk global sourcing processes. At the same time, the success and potential of E-markets for sourcing project globally can be questioned, as E-markets embody a variety of temporal, geographical and socio-cultural gaps. To study the effectiveness of the mechanisms offered by the E-markets, we ran a field experiment in which four development teams worked for 10 weeks to have a software development product designed, programmed and tested by remote developer(s) using an E-market. Three out of the four teams managed to deliver a successful product within time and budget. This result exceeded our expectations and contradicts the critical observations and opinions in several blogs and news articles. We find that for effective e-Market sourcing a skilled customer team with competences including vendor selection, software contracting, software requirements specification, development methods, cross-cultural and virtual communications, use of various cloud based tools, frequent functional and non functional testing are necessary.

Keywords: Global outsourcing · E-markets · Outsourcing risks

1 Introduction

The risks associated with globally distributed development of software have been extensively studied. Risks specific to the globally distributed setting are often classified based on the temporal, geographical and social cultural dimensions and their potential impact on Communication, Coordination and Control [1, 2]. Examples of Communication risks include lack of synchronous communications (temporal), limited face-to-face meeting time (geographical) and cultural diversity (socio-cultural) [1]. Coordination risks include lack of overlapping work hours (temporal), unclear task responsibilities (geographical) and insufficient knowledge and information sharing (socio-cultural) [1, 3]. Finally, Control risks include delayed feedback (temporal), challenges in maintaining stakeholders' commitment (geographical) and lack of equal domain knowledge (socio-cultural) [1]. Traditionally, mitigation strategies have focused on decreasing the gaps by carefully selecting vendors in lengthy bidding processes to assess socio-cultural fit and appropriate domain knowledge. During development, project partners have attempted to lower risks by investing in building relationships and trust between dispersed team members. Measures include frequent site visits, cross cultural training, social events, and placing individual developers for longer periods at the remote site.

© Springer International Publishing Switzerland 2015
I. Oshri et al. (Eds.): Global Sourcing 2015, LNBIP 236, pp. 206–227, 2015.
DOI: 10.1007/978-3-319-26739-5_12

While sometimes effective, these practices take considerable time and significantly increase costs. In extreme cases, mitigation costs may completely ruin the potential cost and efficiency gains of distributed development. Furthermore, these practices are mainly fit for larger projects where supplier and vendor will work intensively together for longer periods of time. There is clearly a need for more efficient and effective mechanisms for small to medium sized projects with short-term duration.

For several years, dedicated E-markets have been targeting at facilitating globally distributed systems development. E-markets support key sourcing processes such as vendor search, contractor and contractee ratings, matching, bidding, communicating about requirements, defining milestones and deliverables, conflict and dispute resolution, escrow services and settling payments. Through these services, E-markets claim to greatly enhance the traditionally high-risk global sourcing processes. Dedicated E-markets for sourcing distributed work have been around for years and have seen their business growing. Well-known examples of E-markets for sourcing of online work are Elance, Odesk, Guru and Freelancer. Elance was founded in 1999, Odesk in 2005. The two companies merged early 2014 into Elance-Odesk, generally seen as the global leader in online work. Elance-Odesk facilitates a community of 9 million freelancers and 3.7 million businesses. Elance-Odesk claims 2.7 million annualized job postings with workers making $900 million in annualized earnings [4].

At the same time, the success and potential of E-markets for sourcing project globally can be questioned. In 2013, Elance-Odesk holds less than 1 % of the overall global staffing market ("Why Freelancers Are Dismayed At Elance's Merger With oDesk," n.d.). Their share of the market is only a fraction of the total software development business. A simple calculation demonstrates that on average the 9 million freelancers make only 100$ annually. It is very likely many of the accounts are dormant or hardly get any business while bidding fruitlessly on posted projects.

In recent blog post and magazine articles, the usefulness of E-markets to run high-quality software development projects has been questioned. For example, a blog post on http://blog.launchastartup.com/ lists several drawbacks in the current practices of using E-Markets. First companies do no spent time to properly describe jobs and post ill-defined projects. In an attempt to bid fast, and spent very little time, vendors offer low quality bids. Quality bids may get lost in the high volume of bids sometimes even automatically generated. Price tends to dominate and results in a non-ideal match between contractee and the contractor. Both parties muddle through towards a solution, unwilling to go into the time intensive bidding process again, but at the same time remain unhappy with the current progress. Developers from low cost countries, working for as little as 2 to 3 dollars an hour, scare away freelancers with higher hourly rates. Outsourcers complain that it is very hard to find both high quality and reliable developers. They question how the high reputations scores have been built up. The low chance of winning a project may ultimately cause the more serious vendors to lose their interest. George Anders in a recent Forbes article writes: "These hubs for freelancers rely too much on the joyless mechanics of market matching ... and not enough on the quieter, friendlier dynamic of developing long-term trust between select employers and specialists who get to know one other" [5].

Thus, currently it is highly debated whether the mechanisms E-markets offer to bridge temporal, geographical and socio-cultural gaps that lead to successful system development projects and bring value to both outsourcers and vendors. As our literature review will show, researchers have not adequately addressed these questions.

In this paper we study the potential of E-markets to mitigate the common risks faced by globally distributed software development teams working on complex and domain specific requirements under high time and budget pressure. To study the effectiveness of the mechanisms offered by the E-markets, we ran a field experiment in which four development teams worked for 10 weeks to have a software development product designed, programmed and tested by remote developer(s) using an E-market. While each team worked on exactly the same initial project definition, budget, deadline and scope, they choose to make use of different leading E-markets, like Freelancer, Guru and Odesk. The teams were also given the freedom in how they used the E-market support for finding an appropriate vendor, communicating requirements and controlling progress. During the project, the teams kept a log of their experiences in tackling the typical risks in global sourcing. Three out of the four teams managed to deliver a successful product within time and budget. In this paper we discuss how various E-market features were used and evaluated by the development teams. We review the strategies used to select a trusted vendor and build a fruitful relationship, and reflect on the current features and differences among the three E-markets that were used. We then discuss how E-markets could enhance their support for distributed software development even further to facilitate ever larger and more complex projects, while successfully mitigating the risks of temporal, geographical and socio-cultural distance.

2   Related Literature

Software development was a popular activity already with the first emerging E-Markets for global work and services in the early 2000s. : shows the key features an E-Market facilitating the customer and service provider relationship [6]. The service provider builds up its profile consisting of his own company information and skills and project evaluations that are built up over time, provided by earlier customers and verified by the Electronic Services Market (ESM). As the E-Market also handles payments, the business results (such as annual reports) can also be generated by the E-Market and consulted by the customer. The contract is the result of a fully open or by-invitation bid process and kept by E-market specifying price, duration and important milestones and payment terms. Not shown in Fig. 1, but available in several E-markets is the feature to rate customers by providers. With this feature providers have information available to evaluate if they want to work for a customer.

Aguinis and Lawal discuss the "ELancing" phenomena, the various features of E-Markets and its implications for research [7]. Based on the E-market features, they argue that none of these are present in traditional outsourcing, offshoring, temporary work, teleworking and independent contracting. Thus, sourcing work through E-Markets is truly different from other modes of sourcing work and has its own set of practical challenges and research questions. "The marketplace plays a key role in

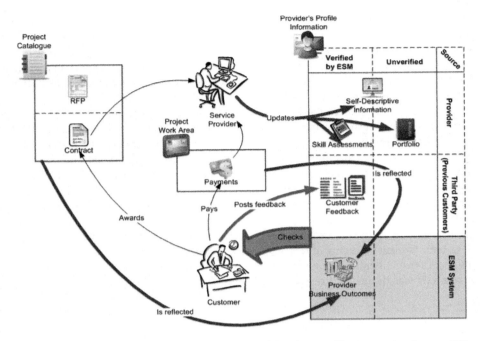

Fig. 1. E-Market services facilitating Customer and Service provider interaction (source [6])

matching employer with employee, assigning work, reviewing performance, and allocating rewards. This is why the marketplace keeps a portion of the profits" [7]. E-markets compete in various ways, e.g. by varying their commission rates, typically between 5 – 15 % of the total transaction value to be paid by the contractor. E-markets have started to also offer hourly rate projects in addition to the fixed price model. To address the large volume and fierce competition in open auctions, E-markets have started to offer private auctions by invitation. E-markets also vary in the richness of the profile information they provide including various statistics on earnings, repeat business and customer ratings of past projects. Several E-markets offer communication tools and work monitoring tools. Furthermore, they offer ever more advanced payment schemes and customizable milestones. Escrow services are offered by most E-markets, sometimes with mediation facilities in case of disagreement.

Most studies have examined the workings E-Markets from an outside perspective; looking at the number of providers and customers, transactions, features, use of profiles, etc.

Taking a provider-centric perspective [6], develop and test a model of the potential impact of provider profiles on their business outcomes. Based on an analysis of business results of providers active on a large E-market with more than 50.000$ turnover in 2011, they find that external profile information positively impacts business results, while internal information did not impact results. External information components mainly imply the possession of technical abilities, and experience by the provider, as specified by the provider. Internal information constitutes feedback ratings, recommendations and text comments submitted by a provider's previous customers.

Gefen and Carmel (2008) examined the proposition that information technology providers from low-wage nations can now underbid providers from high-wage nations and win contracts [8]. They study an online programming marketplace and analysed the history of transactions [8]. They find that the strongest determinant of the winning bid still is client loyalty: the client gives very strong preference to a provider with whom there has been a previous relationship, regardless of whether the provider is offshore or domestic.

Walter (2013) explores the importance of E-markets characteristics and software development project success factors on project success in his thesis on "Success Factors in Leveraging Freelance Marketplaces in Software Development Projects" [9]. He analyses the literature and dozens of blog posts on the use of E-markets for sourcing software development, both from the buyer and contractor perspective. Based on this data Walter develops an E-market software development project success model [9] (Fig. 2). The model is tested using a survey among users of E-markets. The initial results point at Cost control factors, Project efficiency factors, Qualifications of the buyer and Focus on product quality, as the important project success factors. For the E-market characteristics, both Website functionalities and Terms agreed upon mattered. However, the number of respondents to the survey was small (36 respondents) and obviously the depth of analysis was limited as a result of the length of the questionnaire.

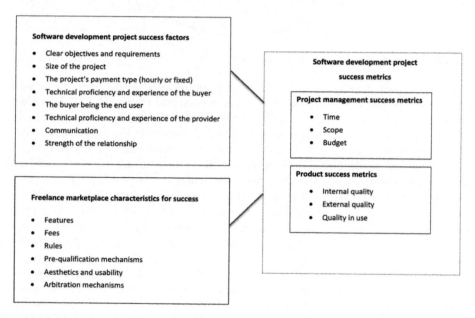

Fig. 2. A model to study project success of software development using E-markets. Source [9]

In our research we explore the relationships between E-market characteristics, software development project success factors and project success in more depth using a field experiment. The experiment and the results are described below.

3   Research Method: Field Experiment

To get more insight in project success factors and the role of E-markets in achieving sourcing success, we designed a field experiment to gain detailed experience with software development using E-markets. In the field experiment, four teams of 5 to 6 advanced MSc students enrolled in our Global Project Management course of the Business & IT MSc program were given the assignment to develop a system using a software development vendor via an E-market. Each of the teams was given the same assignment to develop a software game called Xchange. At the first course session (April 2014), the instructors played a paper-based version of the game with the group to illustrate the game and its mechanics. Next, the teams were told that they had 10 weeks development time and were allowed to spend €500 each to develop a web based version of the game using an E-market. The teams were given the freedom in what market to use, what tools to use and how to organize the development process. However, they were not allowed to spend more than the budget or to overrun the schedule. Also they were not allowed to code by themselves, as the goal was to gain experience in transferring requirements offshore online, and to effectively manage a global project using E-market functionality and other online communication and project management tools.

Each team was required to maintain a detailed log of their experiences and lessons learned. At the final course session (June 2014), the four teams presented the working game software developed and the process experiences, assessed product quality and lessons learned. The two instructors assessed the software products and project reports of the four teams and the software products that had been developed. Given the stringent parameters, it was surprising that three out of four teams managed to deliver good quality working software within time and budget, while one team delivered a partially working product. Considering our initial scepticism of sourcing using E-markets, the rich requirements and limited budget of only 500 euro and tight schedule of only 10 weeks, the results greatly exceeded our expectations. Below we highlight the experiences of the four teams based on the rich materials about their projects that they delivered. We have structured the results inspired by the research model by Walter [9] and the sourcing phases as described in [6], organizing the findings of each team in the following area's:

1. Choosing a platform and contractor
2. Contracting
3. Specifying Requirements
4. Development process
5. Project Success

We present the findings in each of this area's below.

3.1   Sourcing Field Study Team Experiences

Team 1. The experiences of team1 are illustrated by the excerpts from their logs and final report and summarized here as first person accounts:

Choosing a Platform and Contractor. We decided to use oDesk as a platform, since it was the only platform where we were able to find developers capable of working with the rapid prototyping framework MeteorJS. We received the first applications within a few minutes. We responded to serious offers and also invited some developers directly to our job description which we already found using the oDesk search engine. After filtering out some "bad apples" and excesses in price offerings, we arrived at a short-list of two candidates. We set up a Skype meeting with both to discuss in more detail our offer, inquiring about their application and asking them to provide an outline of their work during the development. In this way, we enabled them to decide on deliverables at milestones themselves, to put them in charge of their own agenda. Deciding ourselves on deadlines that are impossible for a developer to reach is useless, as the developer might be culturally restricted to refuse which eventually leads to failing deadlines and miscommunication. The final candidates (with their info-line on oDesk) were:

1. Nivov H.: Furniture Assembly Expert.Theoretical Physicist.JavaScript Developer
2. Poojan S.: Full Stack Developer: Node.js, AngularJS, Android, PHP, DB, Linux.

We did a little background research on both:

Nivov H. seems not to use his real name on oDesk, comments left by others named him Mushex or Allesandro. We did found his LinkedIn and GitHub account, where he posted some interesting stuff but not very professional, like a Web 1.0 theme for the Twitter Bootstrap Framework (http://code.divshot.com/geo-bootstrap/).

Poojan S. impressed us with a free demo. He kind of had to, because this would be his first project on oDesk. His written English vocabulary was impressive, however, during our Skype conversation he sometimes had trouble finding the right words. He did use his real name though, and has an impressive GitHub portfolio while his LinkedIn-profile looked professional with a clear picture of himself. We ultimately decided for Poojan S. as a contractee. Nivov H.'s way of implementation was not in MeteorJS, but an equivalent which was less known and he did not provide us with similar projects as reference. In our last interview before we contracted Poojan, we asked him by when would he be able to complete the assignment, to which he said he would be done within a week. We were a little sceptical about that deadline, so we asked him to keep the next weeks also available for bug fixing. Also, we supplemented our requirements to provide more or less as a contract, based on his promise.

The candidate we chose was from Nepal and had no former experience on oDesk, which could be a potential threat. Because his other Internet profiles (LinkedIn, Google Plus, Github, Facebook) seemed consistent and he made a demo for us, we chose to work with him. Getting in touch was very easy and he responded fast to our questions/ remarks, except when they were too critical.

Contracting. We agreed with the developer on the following terms of payment:

- 50 % upfront
- 50 % when all of the following is true (we define the following as "complete")

1. We have received the code of the product.
2. We have verified the code of the product.

3. All functionalities and other requirements of the product as described in this specification document are implemented and working.
4. If anything above is not met, the product will be developed until all holds true before June 10th, 2014.

Specifying Requirements. Because we did not have any knowledge about what quality we could expect from the applicants, we decided to approach this outsourcing assignment in as simple a way as possible. With the limited budget, time and need for high quality code this seemed the best choice to us. We wanted to implement the basic features including some extra requirements we made using simple visuals in order to enable the programmer to spend more time on the code quality than in understanding the game itself. We provided the outsourcee with a 26-pages long requirements document.

We specified the system boundary, rules, task descriptions, mock-up and some quality requirements. This way it was clear for both parties what we wanted in the game. Our software developer also said he had a clear understanding of what had to be done. The other applicant on our outsourcing platform was also impressed by our specifications, although this can be a result of the politeness of the candidates.

Another important aspect was that it seemed like the developer did not get the exact idea behind the game. He understood simple functionalities and was able to program them, but he had more trouble with correctly implementing more business-like functionalities closely related to the game rules, like when something is a profit or a loss. Our job was to be very specific and explicit about the more complex functionalities, in order that he could just follow detailed instructions instead of implementing high-level goals.

Development Process. Before the decision to contract the developer was made, we decided to use a waterfall approach. We agreed to not use an agile approach because it seemed to be more time consuming and we thought was possibly less suited for small software projects, like our game. We already completed most of our requirements, and as we were able to complete the requirements within a week so we chose to continue with the waterfall approach. After the outsourcing project started by providing Poojan the final requirements specification document (including the formal contract requirements), our team awaited the first delivery were he said to be done with everything. This milestone was not met, and we waited for a few more days. After this extended milestone was also incomplete (there has been source code committed, but not yet functional nor testable), we reminded him of the contract requirements in terms of delivery. We initiated a Skype meeting with our team and Poojan, in order to enable him explaining the situation to us and give us the reason of his delay. He was not very talkative after our reminders, and promised us (again and again) to keep working, giving all his time, and finishing the whole project within a couple of days. After missing the second deadline, nobody believed his deadline promises anymore, but it worked to keep him developing and enable us to review his progress each couple of days. It was quite a challenge to have a conversation with him. This was because his spoken English level was quite low, and it seemed that he did not always understand what we meant, as he was just responding with a short "ok" several times. He mainly blamed slow deployment and testing on a slow Internet connection. While he became aware of his delay, we decided to report missing functionality, issues and quality considerations by using the GitHub issue tracker, which proved to be working extremely well.

After this meeting on the first of June, Poojan showed incredible performance, it appeared like he was working day and night on our project and directly solved newly reported issues really fast. We were able to constantly monitor progress and test on the live environment he provided (upon each code commit, he also deployed the current version on the Meteor live site). This allowed us to verify if issued were solved. Ultimately he delivered according our own requested delivery date and additionally implemented some quality issues we reported. Neither of us explicitly mentioned it, but we regarded this reasonable since he exceeded his own promised delivery dates several times. When looking at the requirements we did specify, we quite benefitted from the established, explicit contract requirements detailing our general game specifics and quality requirements.

Use of Tools.

- Balsamiq - For Mock-ups supplementing the Requirements Specification
- oDesk – Outsourcing platform, contract agreements & Issue solving
- Skype – Communication with applicants
- GitHub –Version Control platform, issue management
- MeteorJS – Web Framework based on JavaScript
- JSHint - Code quality verification tool
- Facebook Group - Own primary communication channel
- WhatsApp Group - Secondary communication channel
- Google Chrome Developer Console-Simple debugging when testing delivered work.

Everyone in our team was familiar with Balsamiq mock-ups, so we could easily create simple interfaces for our Requirements document for this (Fig. 3).

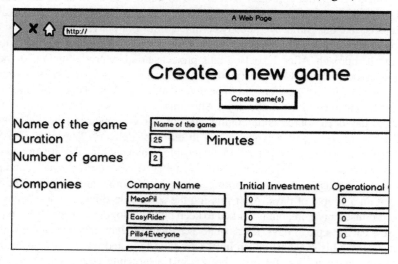

Fig. 3. Sample screen design in balasamiq (Team1)

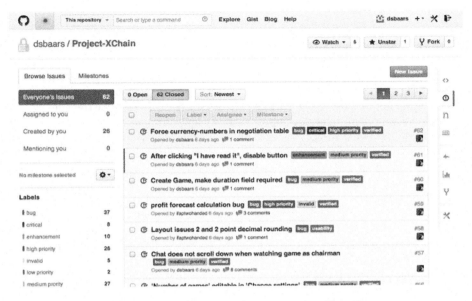

Fig. 4. Use of GitHub for issues reporting (Team1)

We used GitHub as code platform and issue tracker. This went very well, especially the simple tagging system helped mark the priority of issues and the status of verification (Fig. 4).

Sometimes we used Skype to talk to the contractor. Sometimes the sound quality was not that good, but fortunately our programmer responded on oDesk very fast when he was available. We used JSHint to detect errors and potential problems in the written JavaScript code. The final delivered code did not contain errors, but during the projects we sometimes checked specific commits, which were not always without errors. For our own documents we used Google Drive to work with multiple people in one document.

We used a Facebook Group as our main communication channel, and scheduled meeting. For urgent matters we also used a WhatsApp group.

Project Success. After some intensive 1, 5 weeks of programming in the beginning of June, the last issues were resolved on June 11, and on June 13 (after final testing) we were able to confirm the delivery of our project according to our specification. Reflecting back on the method we initially used, we switched our waterfall method after the first "function complete" deliverable to an agile way of working, using milestones as equivalent to Scrum sprints. Although the basic development method was still a waterfall, we did not come up with extra requirements or functionalities during the design (except for frequent quality issues), our communication and collaboration was quite agile due the high intensity of developing features and testing these immediately.

Team 2.

Choosing a Platform and Contractor. A short version of the requirements was created and uploaded on Guru.com together with a description of the game in order to find a developer. The selection of the offshore developer team was a difficult and challenging task with the limited amount of budget and strict deadline. With our advertisement on Guru.com, we got 21 quotes initially. It was a tricky task to discover the right developer/development team with right development ability and communication skills. With the number of quotes, we also got a large set of questions to answer which resulted in an immensely time consuming task. Several developers and companies reacted to the project on Guru.com. Most companies we negotiated with required compensation far above our budget. At last, with the discussion, communication and negotiation, we finalised the negotiation with one development company called GlobusSoft from India that agreed with our limited budget and timeline. Globussoft was the only company that was willing to develop the game for us for the budget of 500 euros. Due to the time constraints we decided to go with this company. A Skype call was made with Globussoft to make sure the developer and our group had a common understanding of the game to be developed. Globussoft made a video showing the functionality of an initial version of the game. GlobusSoft is a company, which started in 2009 and is located in Bhilai, India.

We used Guru.com as a platform to attract our developing party, as we were very satisfied with the platform. Not only did it offer us a marketplace, it also offered basic project management functionality. This made the use of a tool like Basecamp redundant, so we ditched that as soon as we saw the same functionality in Guru.com. Guru.com also offered a safe payment method, though it was a bit more expensive than direct transfer, it did help raise trust from the developing party that if they would do a good job, the money would be paid. It was also possible to pay parts, like per milestone (Fig. 5). We found it very important to check the skills of the programmer before hiring him, by checking his or her previous jobs.

There were a total six people in offshore team. Two of them were developers and one was a support person. For our frequent discussion, we had mostly interacted with these two developers. Communication with support people was only done at the start and at the end of the project.

Contracting. Payment was decided to be 500 divided by the number of iterations (denoted by P). After the first iteration, if the result were not to our satisfaction, we would pay the vendor half of P. He would then have the choice to continue working on the project or to quit. If he wanted to continue and his argument is to our satisfaction, we would continue working with him. Why should we pay the developer half of P if his work is not satisfactory? A number of reasons: (a) it is only fair, the developer has spent time on the project and (b) if we would not have paid him, we would be disrespecting his work leading to a negative comment on our profile, this could potentially result in no developers willing to work for us. To verify that the developer was reliable and capable, we tested him by asking to implement a part of the game in an hour or two. We

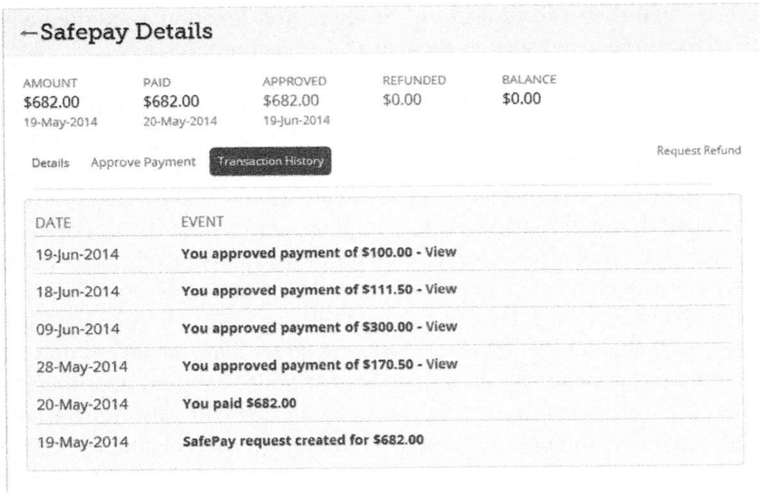

Fig. 5. Safepay payment schedule in Guru.com (Team2)

paid the dues after each milestone and kept the last 100 dollars until the moment that we thought we were satisfied with the game.

The payment plan and iteration planning did work as expected. The developing party even was consistently a week ahead of schedule. This made us happy to pay them for their services. At the beginning of the negotiation with the programmer we had some difficulty in knowing if the price for him was right. We needed to repeat our questions several times because he was never replying with a direct yes/no. To avoid misunderstandings about the price, we learned that it is better to be very clear from the beginning of the project about the maximum price we are going to pay.

When we hired GlobusSoft, we decided upon a price for fulfilling the requirements, but we forgot to make clear agreements on when payment will take place and when the code must be handed over. This resulted in the developers repeatedly asking for part of the payment and us repeatedly asking for some of the code. In the end, we received the code, but we were unable to have a look at the code before the entire project was finished and the full payment was done.

Specifying Requirements. In addition to screen mock-ups, we provided UML based activity and class diagrams to specify the design of the system. At the beginning of the project, it was difficult to communicate with the developers, as there were many questions and a lot of confusion about the financial data sheets implementation. But, with the start of the development process, the problems got mitigated. The weekly video demo from the offshore team and the feedback from our team to the offshore team had been useful to keep the developers on track and our team satisfied. We made a big requirement design, very detailed, in the beginning. Also we specified a lot of non-functional requirements in the beginning, some of them were not useful because they were too specific and, after the beginning of the programming part, we found out that they were not that usable. We learned that it is better to have fewer non-functional requirements in the beginning of the project and specify them as the project progresses.

Development Process. We devised the development process as a combination between the waterfall and the agile approach. Because of the challenges posed by the global aspect of the development of the game, such as the time difference, cultural difference and language barriers, waterfall has the advantage that specifying and designing the game beforehand thoroughly before actual implementation, the developer knows what has to be developed. This will not leave room for the developer to come up with his own ideas for the game, which could be considered a disadvantage as well as an advantage. As requirement engineers and designers are not fully aware of all technical capabilities, the agile approach enables the developer to come up with his own ideas and (possible) improvements for the game. By going completely agile, we think that the challenges posed by the global aspect of the development of the game will outweigh the advantages of agile. Agile requires frequent communication between all stakeholders of the development of the game. This can get time consuming because of the fact that much of the communication will be asynchronous.

We received a 2nd video with a demo from Globussoft to show the progress of their work. We had a feedback call with Globussoft to discuss the progress that was showed in the videos. After multiple iterations (an iteration taking roughly a week), the game was finished and installed on our server. On June 13th we received a link to play the game and on June 19th code was delivered when the last payment was made.

We were a very heterogeneous group composed by people from different nationalities, different backgrounds and therefore different ways of thinking. This was an advantage, on one hand, because we had different perspectives and different opinions about the job, but on the other hand it was a disadvantage due to the difficulty to come to an agreement in some circumstances. We improved the relationship with the programmer by replying quickly to every question that he had. We also gave feedback on the software's milestones in a complete and quick way. We found out that it is important to make a connection with the programmer (by talking about non work related topics).

Use of Tools. We let the developer decide the tools to be used, as we did not force any tooling upon the developer and let him use the tools he is familiar with. We used various media to communicate with the developer. For face-to-face communication and for feedback sessions we used Skype. We used the project management tool called Basecamp to communicate the project details. We attached documents from Google Drive to Basecamp. We used Google Drive to share documents for the project internally. These consisted of requirement documents, sketches of the interface, etc. Some of these, not all, were shared through Basecamp with the developer. We contacted them for every scheduled meeting on a weekly basis with a Skype call and privately with text messages using Skype. We reported our remarks during the call, but we also used an Issue Tracker that we shared with them on the Google drive. We always used a mix of synchronous (Skype calls) and asynchronous (e-mails) for our communication, both of them were very useful.

Project Success. It was aimed to construct a global team consisting of developers of the developing party and our team, in order to enable the developers in the team to come up with new ideas and possible improvements. This construction of a global team materialise, as there was a clear distinction between them and us. They were hired to develop, and we were their customers. In general, we found it easy to communicate with the developers and explain our concerns. However, we faced difficulties in vocal communication. Written chat was more effective in our case than the voice chat. A possible reason could be the language and diverse accents. We noticed that it was difficult for the offshore team to understand our accent and vice versa. However, from our team's perspective, this problem was somehow less severe as one member from our team was able to understand and capture the offshore teams' accent and speed of speech. After the communication and language, the major coordination issue was difference in time zones. The problem of time zone difference between our team and the offshore team was less intense because of two major reasons. Firstly, the time zone difference between India and The Netherlands is not that large and was successfully synchronized. In addition, we observed that the offshore developer maintained a very professional (boss-employee) relationship with our team where communication was quite precise.

The assessment of software quality metrics such as source code usability, reusability, maintainability, complexity and a number of other metrics of code, are important. This is especially the case since another party has created the code, it is important that the code is understandable, in order to be able add functionality and perform maintenance.

The code for the game was written in Java. The code was imported in Eclipse to be able to run some metrics on it. When importing and looking at the code, a big downside was discovered immediately. There was no documentation in the code whatsoever. For the purpose of the source code quality assessment, we used the Eclipse Metrics plugin tool that. The quality of source code was measured on a number of different general metrics e.g. number of packages, number of methods, number of interfaces, lines of code to the specific quality metrics e.g. McCabe cyclomatic complexity, weighted methods per class (WMC), lack of cohesion of methods (LCOM), etc. The final assessment of the code quality was not so good. The metrics indicated some weak points. Even though the results from the metrics were not dramatic, it was obvious that it will be hard to add functionality to this code or maintain or update it in any way. This was caused by the complete lack of documentation Javadoc in the code. The delivery of proper documentation was not put clearly in the requirements, which apparently was needed to get proper code quality.

Team 3.

Choosing a Platform and Contractor. We quickly found out that Odesk was our preferred website for the rest of the project. Most of the replies on our first Odesk posting came from Indian and Pakistan developers. After several Skype sessions we selected a programming agency, called Websumster Technologies. Initially, we thought we hired a female programmer, but after the first Skype session our contact changed to a manager from the same company. It took some time for us to clarify that we wanted our first sprint needed to be finished within one week. During this week the manager told us that they were working on the project, and every time we spoke he said 'within two days you can see some progress'. However, after 1.5 weeks we did not see any progress at all, and started pushing them to show us something. It took two hours, but then they sent us a URL to an online environment where we could see their progress. When we took a closer look, it turned out the code was copied from a chat box tutorial at CSSTricks.com. That was reason for us to stop working with this company, because they could not give us a reasonable explanation for copying the code. We told our story to the Odesk customer service, and they have banned the initial developer's account. After 1.5 weeks we had to start our programmer selection process all over again. This time we changed our approach, and asked developers to show us something (e.g. a html conversion of the mock-ups) before we decided to hire them. This led to one Ukrainian programmer who built almost 50 % of the total functionality of the first sprint in just a few hours, in order to convince us to hire him. After a compelling Skype conversation we chose to hire this programmer. He delivered the sprints as promised, and even surprised us by hiring a special designer to redesign the whole layout without us having to pay more. The Ukrainian developer was quite young, was experienced with web development and asked the right questions. Cultural differences were not present: just like our local team members, he was straightforward, did not need small talk and kept his promises. Another advantage was the fact that we could always access his server, so we could have an update whenever we wanted.

Contracting. Odesk was the platform of our choice to recruit and pay our programmer(s). Before we made a decision about the platform, we posted jobs on five different platforms. On almost all of the platforms, we got bids or offers, but we saw the most potential in the Odesk platform. Programmers reacted quickly and provided realistic offers. The fee Odesk charges is at the higher end, but very clear: 10 % of the amount is paid to Odesk. Programmers can add 11.11 % to their price for the final price. For us, this fee was a nice bargaining leverage. Overall, Odesk worked quite intuitively, it was easy to access and handle complaints.

Specifying Requirements. We would be lying if we said we had no problems in the area. There were a couple of really basic things we overlooked in the first meetings with our foreign programmers. The lesson we learned from this was fourfold. (1) Make sure that the home-team has reached a complete consensus on what agreements need to be made and what the negotiation scope is. Write it down and use it as a guide through the meeting. Possible elements could be price, deadlines, getting updates, availability for questions, tools, delivery of end product etc. (2) Use video meetings as a way to bond with your away-team and do not worry about getting a bit informal. These moments create trust amongst each other and create a better working environment. I.e. we used some Ukrainian friends to write texts to our programmer in Russian. (3) When agreements are not met, take action. Be respectful, but very clear about what the expectations are. Think about how you would react if the same situation would happen in your home-team and use it as a guide to overcome the challenges. Be quick to act if the challenges are not being tackled and resort to plan B. (4) Do not position yourself as dependant on the away-team. Setup your project in way that allows you to change plans and switch programmers if necessary. Using this as requirements makes it clear for both sides.

Development Process. The project was divided into five steps, and in the week of May 2nd, we posted the first step on several websites. Within the group there was a consensus for the approach, which was to use the agile approach. Continuing on this road we wrote the specification on a 1.5 A4 sheet of paper with the design of the game in terms of the end result. This description made it very clear for every group member on what our objective for the development: the developer had to deliver functionality in sprints, with the most value first. The rationale in favour of this approach was to get a better measure of progress, as opposed to a waterfall-like approach, where all requirements are specified up front and handed over to our developer. We thought that a more rigorous process might give us a false promise of progress where a lot of work that should have been addressed earlier becomes apparent near the deadline. Continuously adjusting the process enabled us to find the appropriate amount of formality in controlling the developer. In addition, the continuous adjustments allowed us to find the appropriate degree of formality in communicating the requirements for each sprint that was appropriate for the developer depending on what he understood and the degree of freedom he could handle.

Use of Tools. When managing an outsourced project, we learnt that one should not use tools for the sake of using specific tools. I.e. we set out to use Freedcamp in order to manage our milestones and use it as a communication platform. In hindsight, it was not used a lot, but the project communication did run more smoothly over Skype. We did not have much experience with project management tools and working with Freedcamp was the first for all of us. We mainly used Freedcamp to initialise our project, create a planning and set-up all the necessary to-do's. The programmers were able to look at the entire environment except our to-do's. Both our initial Indian programmers and our Ukrainian developer were added to the project and we tried to use Freedcamp as a communication and planning platform. Both programmers said they had some experience using Freedcamp or similar tools i.e. Basecamp. When looking in hindsight at the project, we can clearly say that the potential of Freedcamp was not completely used. It was mainly used as a repository of sprint specifications and deadlines, which worked quite efficiently.

Real-time collaboration on documents amongst all group members was made possible using Google Drive. Because documents where always 'in sync' at every location, consistency of all requirements was ensured. Skype was used as the main medium of communication with the developers. We used Skype in combination with a small tool called 'Skype Auto Recorder' to record all audio conversations. Not all group members had the time to join the interviews, so using the recordings everybody could listen back to the conversations that had taken place. Quickly, it became clear that it's easier to communicate using Skype's chat function than using audio or video conversations. Both with our Indian as well as our Ukrainian programmer, we experienced low audio quality, and thus decided to communicate using chat. However, we used the video chat option to initialise some sort of bond. MockFlow was used in all sprints to created mock-ups and to illustrate clearly what had to be built. MockFlow is a cloud-based tool to create mock-ups. This tool provides all the necessary elements of a web-page, such as tables and buttons, which can be easily 'dragged and dropped' to a canvas. The free version provided enough functionality to create all the necessary mock-ups.

Project Success. The final product of this outsourcing project was delivered on time and having the functionality specified in the requirements. We qualitatively analysed the delivered software using the ISO 9126 standard. We were confident that the software functionality is sufficient to play the game. All requirements had been incorporated into the application. The outputs of the program were exactly like the requirements stated and as the project group intended. The application had a pleasant layout and beautiful scaling. This increased the attractiveness for users.

For the interactions between the front-end and the server JavaScript was used. The code is based on JQuery, a popular JQuery Library. The specific code written by our programmer had been assessed using JSHint, a community-driven tool to detect errors and potential problems in JavaScript. The results of the JSHint test are shown below (see Fig. 6).

Metric	Value
Lines of code	447
Number of functions	14
Highest number of arguments for a function	2
Median number of arguments for a function	0
Highest number of statements within one function	6
Median number of statements within one function	1
Highest cyclomatic complexity	3
Median of cyclomatic complexity	1
Number of warnings	52 (due to mixing up spaces and tabs)

Fig. 6. Code quality assessment using JSHint (Team3)

Using PHPLoc we were able to analyse the size and structure of the project. Overall the code quality can be classified as good. Since all code was put in classes (except for the code in the index.php, the file to launch the system) we can conclude that the developer adhered well to our requirement of using object-oriented design. Also the average cyclomatic complexity, which is 3.28, shows that most methods have low complexity.

Team 4.

Choosing a Platform and Contractor. For this project we used freelancer.com to find a suitable programmer and Freedcamp to keep track of the progress made. Freelancer is a platform for both developers and project owners. The project owners are able to upload their project, which is then readable for developers. The project owners find and invite developers to look at their project. The developers are able to search for projects and place a bid. Freelancer requires you to upload a project description, the required skills of the programmer and a project name. Additional details can be added using a pdf file. We asked for bids for the entire project regardless of the hours needed. This created a situation where it was the responsibility of the developer to create the software within budget. Additional details were added containing all our requirements.

We were quite satisfied overall with Freelancer, as it got us in touch with the programmer. Despite the relatively short time we needed to find an adequate programmer, there were some major issues to the platform. First of all, upon placing a project we received about eight proposals within the first three minutes. These were all automatically generated and at seemingly random rates. Despite their randomness, they all had 5/5 ratings and admiring comments. However, fake users placed all these comments and ratings. This was tiresome and annoying to say the least, but on a more serious note, it also made us doubt the great ratings that real users had. As a final remark, it should be noted that there are some really strange features in the site. It does not allow you to edit the project name, but you can edit the project description etc. You cannot edit the final deadline, even when you've already handed the project over to a programmer and you have mutually agreed that it should be postponed. This can only be done with the help of the support team. Upon placing a fake project to test the website, it turned out that 'deleting' the project would result in a 5$ fee, while 'closing' the project was free. The only difference between these solutions was the fact that 'deleting' would also make it undiscoverable through the Google search engine.

Contracting. Freelancer takes up part of the money because we had to pay project fees (10 %).

As our project cost was 660$, our programmer only got 600$ of the total amount. Also.

Freelancer kept a percentage (2 %) of the amount of money transferred per transaction. This is something we found out once we paid the first milestone. In the future, to choose a platform we probably would check this first and compare the different platforms on their revenue model.

Specifying Requirements. We made functional, non-functional and technical requirements that were supported by mock-ups, UCD and UML. Not only did we get insights into the difficulty of managing the process of working together at a large distance, but we also got to experience first hand what it took to write real requirements. After an iteration, we gave our programmer feedback as soon as possible. He was very open towards receiving feedback. As soon as he received the feedback the programmer started revising the game. When he was ready he let us know straight away so we could test what he had developed. In the beginning we had some trouble communicating between our group and the programmer, this was mainly due to the fact that we work in a different time zone and the effects of working in a flexible and agile way, as this required more input from our side than we had anticipated. After switching to Skype on mobile, this problem was quickly resolved.

Development Process. Even though many papers would suggest on to go with a fully agile approach for such a small project, we decided we would not. One of the big benefits from agile is the reduced time in documenting, which means increased time for programming. In this project, we were not allowed to contribute to the code, which meant that we had 5 people out of 6 in the team that had plenty of time to do proper documentation. At the start, this meant a very extensive requirements document, which you would not normally find in agile development. The document included information about the entire application, thus it seemed as if we were following the waterfall model, despite of the fact that we had told our developer that we would test what he had made every week and we might change some of our requirements; a rather agile approach. We found multiple benefits of starting the project in a waterfall manner. The first is that it was clear to the programmer what the idea behind each milestone was and where the development was heading. The second advantage was that the programmer was able to agree on a price for the entire program. We have seen in the other student groups that the programmer wanted more money after each sprint, after discovering that the group became dependent of him. They worked it out, but we think the agile sprints did put them in a difficult position. The third advantage was that our programmer worked at unusual hours (weekends and night), which caused problems for providing synchronous feedback. By giving him the entire project in one document, he was able to work at some other part of the software when he was stuck. The next morning we were able to help him, which ensured minimal delay. The last advantage was that our large team of 5 had discussed the entire project before it would start. This minimized discussion and design problems later on and ensured the programmer was able to talk to all of us and get the same answers.

A disadvantage for the waterfall start was that the project needed two weeks before it could be posted on freelancer. We also needed to make sure the developer did not get obsessed with the document too much, and that it was merely a guideline for the situation when he got stuck and when we were not available. We made sure that his progress was visible to us, and that miscommunication or faults in the documents were found quickly. To conclude, we started in a waterfall manner to get clarity on what needed to be done and how much it would cost and from that point onwards we worked agile, to ensure the project was heading in the right direction. We are very glad we did so, because there were many miscommunications at the start and further on in the project and we discovered that the initial document was neither complete nor completely right on some aspects.

Use of Tools. Freedcamp was used to keep track of our progress. Freedcamp can help one monitor one's entire project with posts, to-do's, milestones and files. For informal and fast feedback Skype is the ideal tool, especially in an international working environment. Next to synchronous calls and chat, the chat function also provides asynchronous communication. By using Skype on mobile, both the developer and our team were available every day of the week. We created a new Skype account so that we would not be involved privately. Google Drive was mainly used for file sharing within our team, but some documents (e.g. bug lists and data file examples) were shared with the developer as well. Initially, we started using Freedcamp for setting milestones and to-do lists. However, later on we shifted to Skype and Google Drive for the communication and file sharing. Although we see the positive aspects of Freedcamp when working in larger projects, in our case we basically worked with the one external programmer. Within our group we communicated through WhatsApp and one of us communicated the outcome of our discussion to the programmer.

The group members, who were available when the code was delivered, performed the testing. One of us logged in as the administrator and invited the rest to play the game. While playing the game we mentioned it to each other on Skype if we encountered bugs. We all were listing our bugs in a Google spreadsheet that was shared with the programmer later on.

Project Success. The software worked well for its purpose, but could be designed and documented better. For checking syntax we have use the tool PHP Code Sniffer. This command line tool analyses all PHP, CSS and JS files and checks the syntax. Most errors and warnings are because of syntactical errors, nothing too serious. Furthermore the level of documentation is not very high which might cause some trouble in the future when maintaining or extending this tool.

4   Conclusions and Discussion

While E-markets for global sourcing of projects have been established for over a decade and more recently the market has consolidated by mergers of several leading players, the phenomena is still under researched and its potential to source small and medium sized software development projects is being debated. Extant research has mainly focused on macro characteristics of E-markets. Detailed insight into successful practices for developing software using E-markets is lagging. In this research we aim to provide more insights into the potential of E-markets to successfully source software development projects. Through a field experiment in which four teams develop a software product using identical initial requirements (budget and time schedule, but are otherwise free to select an E-market, tooling, development process and vendor), we aim to gain more insight in factors that determine success and the role of the E-market to facilitate this success.

The research model developed by [9] provided a useful framework for our analysis. Overall, our findings suggest that E-markets can be used to successfully develop a small sized software system in quite spectacular timeframe and very limited budget. Three out of four teams managed to have a working product according to the initial requirements specifications. This result exceeded our expectations and contradicts the critical observations and opinions in several blogs and news articles.

From the detailed experience reports and log files of the four teams several lessons can be drawn that can aid buyers on E-markets to achieve success:

Choosing a Platform and Contractor: All platforms selected by the teams (Odesk, Guru and Freelancer) did fulfil their key features. Still, a key issue is that too many bids are either not legitimate or are automatically generated. Customer ratings seem to be no guarantee. This in-turn makes the selection process cumbersome and time intensive. Additional research on the developers and careful selection are a key requirement for success.

Contracting: The E-markets all offer useful services through predefined payment conditions, where escrow services and guaranteed payments security is provided to both the vendor and customer. However, sometimes hidden fees are applied and also some vendors perceive the fees for each transaction as too high.

Specifying Requirements: Even more than in traditional outsourcing, it appears that having very clear initial requirements and continuous communication about the requirements is key. Cloud based document sharing tools and mock-up tools to visualize screenshot designs are a useful addition. Conceptual models such as UML based activity and class diagrams also proved useful. Non-functional requirements such as performance and code quality are key as well, while these can be specified at a later stage, they have to be clearly communicated and reviewed similar to the review of the functional requirements.

Development Process: A full waterfall nor an agile process did function well for sourcing a small project through an E-market. Carefully mixing the strengths of both approaches worked best, using the waterfall style milestones, precise requirements and contract specifications, combined with more agile rapid adaptation and frequent communications between 'product owners' and developers.

Use of Tools: E-markets have come a long way in supporting more than just vendor search, contracting and payment, and also offer communication tools and project management support. Still, several other tools for communications, requirements specification, modelling and code quality tests proved their value in reaching success, as shown in previous research [10]. Cloud based tools to draw mock-ups greatly enhanced communications. Use of video demo movies communicated intermediate results between the remote and on-site teams. Skype was frequently used especially its basic chat functionality. Remote access to the development server requires high mutual trust, but allowed for frequent testing and feedback. Finally, the use of code quality assessment tools enabled the customer team to assess code quality objectively.

Project Success: It is important to adopt a balanced view towards product success. Usage of standards, like ISO 9126, facilitates a balanced view on product success, including non-functional product quality. Even assessment of comments in the source code should not be forgotten. When the customer has a tight budget and schedule, the focus can be easily drawn to deliver functionality in time. By dividing roles at the customer site to assess different quality aspects, the variety of quality attributes can be guarded.

Gary Swart, CEO of Odesk writes on the company's website communication on the Odesk-Elance vision of the new combined company: "Just as Amazon reinvented retail, and Apple iTunes transformed the music industry, together oDesk and Elance will revolutionize the way we work. This merger will create unprecedented freedom for people to find job opportunities regardless of their location, and will allow businesses of all sizes to more easily access the best available talent".

Indeed our research confirms that it is feasible to run small sized systems development projects successfully through E-markets like Odesk-Elance. However, several factors need to be taken into account and a skilled customer team with competences including vendor selection, software contracting, software requirements specification, development methods, cross cultural and virtual communications, use of various cloud based tools, frequent functional and non functional testing are necessary. Other factors such as socio-technical coordination [11, 12], also have to be taken into account for large projects with multiple vendors or a vendor company employing multiple developers. By no means is the use of these E-markets a guarantor for success. Future research could focus on collecting more experiences and developing guidelines for enhancing the chances of success for small and also larger development projects.

Acknowledgements. The authors would like to express their gratitude to the dedicated work of the software vendors quoted in this paper and the skilled efforts and detailed high quality reporting by the four project teams of class 2014 of the Global Project Management Course at the University of Twente.

References

1. Sakthivel, S.: Managing risk in offshore systems development. Commun. ACM **50**, 69–75 (2007)
2. Persson, J.S., Mathiassen, L., Boeg, J., Madsen, T.S., Steinson, F.: Managing risks in distributed software projects: an integrative framework. IEEE Trans. Eng. Manag. **56**, 508–532 (2009)
3. Amrit, C.: Coordination in software development: the problem of task allocation. In: ACM SIGSOFT Software Engineering Notes, pp. 1–7. ACM, (Year)
4. http://techcrunch.com/2014/11/25/elance-odesk-30m-benchmark/
5. Anders, G.: Why Freelancers Are Dismayed At Elance's Merger With oDes (2013)
6. Assemi, B., Schlagwein, D.: Profile information and business outcomes of providers in electronic service marketplaces: an empirical investigation. In: Proceedings of the 23rd Australasian Conference on Information Systems 2012, ACIS 2012, pp. 1–10. ACIS (Year)
7. Aguinis, H., Lawal, S.O.: eLancing: a review and research agenda for bridging the science–practice gap. Hum. Resour. Manag. Rev. **23**, 6–17 (2013)
8. Gefen, D., Carmel, E.: Is the world really flat? a look at offshoring at an online programming marketplace. MIS Q. **32**, 367–384 (2008)
9. Walter, A.: Success Factors in Leveraging Freelance Marketplaces in Software Development Projects. University of Ottawa (2013)
10. Katsma, C., Amrit, C., van Hillegersberg, J., Sikkel, K.: Can agile software tools bring the benefits of a task board to globally distributed teams? In: Oshri, I., Kotlarsky, J., Willcocks, L.P. (eds.) Global Sourcing 2013. LNBIP, vol. 163, pp. 163–179. Springer, Heidelberg (2013)
11. Amrit, C., van Hillegersberg, J.: Coordination implications of software coupling in open source projects. In: Ågerfalk, P., Boldyreff, C., González-Barahona, J.M., Madey, G.R., Noll, J. (eds.) OSS 2010. IFIP AICT, vol. 319, pp. 314–321. Springer, Heidelberg (2010)
12. Amrit, C., van Hillegersberg, J., Kumar, K.: Identifying coordination problems in software development: finding mismatches between software and project team structures. arXiv preprint. (2012) arXiv:1201.4142

Building a Supply Chain Ecosystem: How the Enterprise Connectivity Interface (ECI) Will Enable and Support Interorganisational Collaboration

Simon Dalmolen[1,2(✉)], Hans Moonen[1,2], and Jos van Hillegersberg[1]

[1] School of Management and Governance, University of Twente, P.O. Box 217, 7500 AE Enschede, The Netherlands
{s.dalmolen,hans.moonen,j.vanhillegersberg}@utwente.nl
[2] CGI, Business Consulting, George Hintzenweg 89, 3068 AX Rotterdam, The Netherlands

Abstract. This chapter proposes a model how to setup IT supported interorganisational collaboration in the current world where IT and business collaboration is intertwined. Businesses have been struggling to achieve supply chain integration for both technical and organizational reasons. This hinders effective collaboration with partners: vertical collaboration with suppliers and customers, as well as horizontal collaboration with competitors. This paper gives a literature overview of the current challenges within supply chain collaboration. The suggested Enterprise Connectivity Interface approach is inspired on the popular API model that enables connectivity between software systems. We reflect how such quick connectivity can be applied also on a business level.

Keywords: Supply chain collaboration · Enterprise connectivity interface · Agile supply chain · Supply chain integration · Ecosystem · Interorganisational

1 Introduction

For both technical and organizational reasons, businesses have been struggling to achieve supply chain integration. This hinders effective collaboration with partners: vertical collaboration with suppliers and customers, as well as horizontal collaboration with competitors. Furthermore for many organizations it is challenging to generate value from their IT investments [1]. Peppard [1] concludes 40 % of all investments in IT to be lost, due to legacy thinking and practices. Luftman and Derksen [2] researched the main IT managerial concerns in the decade spanning from 2003 till 2012. Their top two challenges for organizations are business productivity & cost reduction, and IT and business alignment. In line with these challenges, Van Heck and Vervest [3] envisioned a "business operating system". This business operating system is a layer on top of the transactional layer that steers the operational (physical) layer of an organization, it makes it possible to abstract processes from individual implementation details. They state that quick connectivity is required to share information among business partners. Unfortunately, Van Heck and Vervest solely present the vision and the challenges, not at all hinting in the direction of specific technologies, next steps in research, or changes which are needed.

© Springer International Publishing Switzerland 2015
I. Oshri et al. (Eds.): Global Sourcing 2015, LNBIP 236, pp. 228–239, 2015.
DOI: 10.1007/978-3-319-26739-5_13

The last few years we saw a trend in the B2C (business-to-consumer) application domain. Increasingly standard protocol, named API (application programming interface) are utilized to integrate products and services. With the use of an API quick connectivity can be accomplished and therefore information can be shared among products and services. Furthermore, with this model new products and services can be developed e.g. to compose novel services by integrating social media (Twitter, LinkedIn, Facebook), travel-, or weather service API's, to name a few. As such API's are much more than just technical standards, it enables new business strategies for quick novel service composition. However, we notice that research into their nature, impact and potential is still rather scarce and yet to be embraced in B2B (Business-to-Business) environments.

Inspired by the success of this API model, this chapter proposes the novel Enterprise Connectivity Interface (ECI) approach to enable quick business connectivity, in line with the ideas presented by Van Heck and Vervest [3]. This provides organizations the ability to operate more agile and dynamic in their daily business processes, and to more dynamically outsource processes or services. To support agile business networks this requires a new type of ICT architectures. Dalmolen et al. [4] mention key requirements to support agile business networks:

(1) Modularization of Services, Product, Process Services,
(2) Coordination and Collaboration Capability,
(3) Quick connect capability,
(4) Relationship Management Capability,
(5) Risk Management Capability.

The research in this paper combines literature review with a design science approach following Hevner et al. [5]. Fed by a series of supply chain collaboration case studies we have worked on in recent years we were able to distill a number of lessons learned in establishing supply chain collaboration (horizontal, vertical, network). The so-called "Enterprise Connectivity Interface", which details and prescribes how to set up supply chain collaboration between organizations, is the result of our design. It is divided in four building blocks, supply chain, organizational, semantic, and technical.

2   Literature

Rigid ERP Systems Hinder Supply Chain Integration. Many companies have struggled with longer and more difficult implementation trajectories for their enterprise software, specifically ERP, than foreseen. It is not the process that changed the software, but the software that changed the process. Enterprise Resource Planning systems (ERPs) are generally *"tightly integrated and monolithic systems that reflect and respect traditional company boundaries"* [6]. A particular challenge for these systems is to enable flexibility and interconnectivity between information systems throughout the supply chain. Indeed, Lee and Myers [7] have demonstrated that ERP likely results in a lock-in into relatively inflexible business processes. Van Hillegersberg et al. [8] specifically illustrate the difficulties of ERP-type styled centralized systems, or marketplaces/hubs, in going inter-organisational. One result is that many workers experience the systems as inconvenient, not user friendly, and not future proof. The correct data are therefore not always available in the current information systems, but reside in the minds of employees. Important side effect is that, as a result, the sharing of this information beyond organizational walls is a challenge. Akkermans et al. [9] revealed the key limitations of ERP systems. There is a lack of functionality in enabling supply chain collaboration crossing organizational boundaries. Many companies have long and difficult implementation projects behind regarding ERP software. The software even has a huge impact on the business and the internal processes. The goal of an ERP system in general is providing functionality and support for internal processes. It was not designed for sharing information across organizational boundaries. In practice cross-domain collaboration use custom made interfaces for bulk exchanges and furthermore people sharing information via email, phone, fax or source-documents.

Table 1. Challenges when establishing supply chain collaboration.

Category	Challenge	References
Supply chain	Agility & flexibility is a challenge	[2, 12, 13].
Supply chain	Fragmented market (multiple small/medium enterprises)	[14]
Supply chain (alignment)	Enabling more transparency and control; Information sharing; Coordination of supply chains; Collaborative supply chains.	[15–19].
Semantic	Lack of standards, Organization of data, Interpretation of data	[20–26].
Technical (development)	Wide use of old fashioned software development methods (e.g. waterfall) less suitable for rapid development	[27, 28].
Technical	Accessibility of data	[29, 30].
Technical	Legacy systems (difficult to access, support and maintain)	[31, 32].
Technical	Closed systems become disconnected information silo's/business value of IT; No B2B API driven innovation and connectivity	[33, 34].

Logistics is a Fragmented Market with Small Parties with Limited System Capabilities. Producers, brand-owners, and retailers generally do not consider transportation their core competence. They often outsource this work to specialized firms, referred to as Third Party Logistics (3PL) or Logistics Service Providers (LSP) [10]. LSPs are generally not seen as very strategic supply chain partners. One factor that illustrates this is the fact that the most important factor for selecting an LSP still is price, the quality of its logistics services ranks only second [11]. Logistics in The Netherlands is a highly fragmented market, with many small firms or so-called "one–pitters" carrying out transportation. The 2015 standard practice for these small firms still is that orders arrive by phone or fax and are entered manually into the LSP's system. This is far-off from real-time information sharing. As margins are thin, we cannot expect any major IT implementations from these firms. This hinders innovation.

A series of challenges for supply chain collaboration is identified, see Table 1. The outcome of the categorized literature review underpin the need for an agile business network [3] what is in line with the key requirements of Dalmolen et al. [4]. Currently quick connectivity is hard, because of the fragmented market and closed systems. Secondly, coordination and collaboration requires transparency, information sharing mechanisms. Chae et al. [35] mention that various studies suggest that information technology (IT) is critical to the development of collaboration between supply chain partners. IT is often viewed as enabler for supply chain integration and studies reported positive effects of ITs on collaboration, partner relationship, supply chain performance. Yet, an analysis of existing partner relationships and their impact on the effect of collaboration and supply chain performance is needed. If such an analysis is not carried out, this may lead organizations to form the misconception that any investment in IT technology will automatically bring higher supply chain performance [35].

3   The Enterprise Connectivity Interface (ECI)

In optimizing supply chains, the sharing of data and information is crucial. A (virtual) ecosystem in which each organization uses procedures, rules, and standards for sharing information could provide a solution to address a series of challenges. Intensified and agile collaboration between organizations can only be successful if we manage to increase the connectivity between information systems cross-domain.

The ECI model; see Fig. 1 is a derivative of the literature review above. It prescribes rules and procedure for collaboration. It supports multiple maturity collaboration types e.g. outsourcing, process/IT integration. The current business environment requires a greater flexibility from organizations in order to increase efficiency/effectiveness of scarce resources. This is due to an increase of ICT systems and globalization.

Agile business networks require new generation technologies (Internet of Things, API), but it's not just technologies. Trust and willingness to share information between organizations is mandatory. Collaboration e.g. outsourcing, integration via an agile, flexible manner is not common. Furthermore, on the topic of collaboration and integration we found that organizations lack knowledge and skills.

The ECI models consist of four layers, namely supply chain, organizational, semantic and technical layer. For each building block we've composed procedures, rules and instruction which are helpful to set up supply chain collaboration e.g. on the supply chain layer entry and exit instructions for organization who want to join or leave the ecosystem.

Supply Chain layer. This is the overall layer and shows the collaborative goals of the ecosystem. For example, reduce the costs of the current supply chain via collaboration,

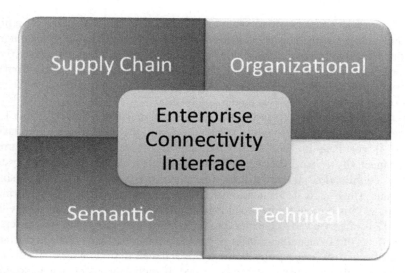

Fig. 1. The Enterprise Connectivity Interface composed out of four different layers together supporting supply chain collaboration.

reduce empty running, increase shelf availability. In short what is the joint value creation (synergy)? Secondly, what value can each partner add to the ecosystem? For example a logistic service provider (LSP) can add specific lanes, trucks where a shipper can give insight in their order flow.

This is the so-called matching part, where can be seen if there is synergy for collaboration.

They have to agree on the why (what is it going to bring) and the how/what (what info to share, what purpose to fulfill) – trust is the result of a joint ambition and the matching activity to match synergies Trust is an important pre-condition; this can be partly addressed via non-disclosure agreements. Are the partners in the ecosystem willing to share information e.g. order or truck planning towards competitors for the greater good.

It is important to create an overview of the ecosystem specific key performance indicators (KPI) to monitor the performance in achieving the collaborative goals. What are the most important KPI's to steer on within the ecosystem? As soon as synergies are identified, KPI's can be generated to steer the system upon.

Supply chains are demanding more and more collaboration, also from competitors. Horizontal collaboration is seen more and more where competitors share assets for mutual benefits, however this requires a lot of trust and willingness to share information to enable collaboration. Therefore gain-sharing is a hot topic. How will the located synergy flow back to each individual organization? Currently, concepts from cooperative game theory are adopted e.g. Shapley value [36, 37] to address this challenge.

If the collaboration synergy is addressed, the willingness to collaborate exists, and there is an agreement on the KPIs and the sharing the gains and pains the supply chain ecosystem layer is complete to become operational, however an ecosystem is not a static concept. Partners will come and go in the ecosystem. It can occur that a new LSP wants to join the ecosystem or a partner leaves the ecosystem.

A final procedure should be filled in, namely the "Entry/exit procedure", within the ecosystem partners should get an agreement how new partners can enter the ecosystem and on which terms organizations can leave the ecosystem.

Organization Layer. Within this layer all the procedures of an individual organization are categorized.

First, what value can it deliver towards the ecosystem? Secondly, which KPIs are important for the individual organization? And are the KPI beneficial towards the ecosystem. And are they in line with the agreed overall KPIs. With a high alignment the collaboration complexity will be reduced.

Furthermore, the organizational capabilities and limitations should be addressed. For example, retail supply chain; what are the time slots and can they be stretched?

Semantic Layer. The goal of this layer is providing interoperability via a flexible and responsive manner [30]. In short exchanging different types of data.

It is all about connectivity in flexible and secure manners. Connecting organizations that are willing to collaborate. Connectivity is an important pre-condition for operational cooperation and collaboration between organizations. In practice, this is very difficult. The discussion goes beyond lack of functionality of IT systems, for example, the interpretation of data. Organizations that want to collaborate should be aware of how to present their data:

- Joint agreement on the interpretation of data
  - What is an order? Size of the pallet - Chep or EURO?
  - What will be the estimated time of arrival (ETA)? Is the ETA the time an order arrives at the destination, if so at the gate, or at the door, or even when the actual unloading starts? This can have huge impact on the operational supply chain process.
  - Et cetera.
- Joint agreement on the organization of data
  - Will the data be copied every time and for each process where the data is required?
  - Or is the data to be stored in one central place?
  - How long is data to be stored?
  - What parties have access to what data?
  - Is anonymized use of the data, for example for benchmarking purposes, allowed?

Technical Layer. Within this layer the challenge should be addressed of how to access data per individual organization.

- Accessibility of data
  - How can the data be accessed? What will be the format of the data?
  - Who is allowed to get access to the data?

IT investments are lost and supply chains need to be more flexible see Table 1. IT should support or enable supply chain collaboration and integration. With current legacy systems and methods, it is very challenging. Future IT systems/platforms need to offer API functionality. So more flexibility is gained and business functionality can be extended. Using an API will help other organizations in implementing their information needs for their own process, instead of one bi-lateral hard interface.

Within this layer each organization should be aware of which information is necessary for the ecosystem. What data will be exchanged and what will be the time interval. Then, how can the data being accessed by the ecosystem partners? Within this layer we propose to adopt the successful API mechanism as used by Twitter and Facebook on a business-to-business level.

By building a single enterprise API that is able to connect with external services/products two out of the three challenges of data will be addressed, namely the organization of data and the accessibility. The third one is interpretation of data.

Gonzalez-Rodriques et al. propose to come up with a common language:

"Although several standards from the logistics world are used for message exchange, there is still a need of agreement on using the same language while preserving the internal way of operation at each company. The solution to this need opens a new horizon in providing access to information in a common language (taking advantage of existing standards). This common language would allow deploying real-time cooperative planning algorithms to find the best route attending to criteria such as the most green, quick, economic and/or safe route as well as algorithms able to react to real-time events (e.g. delays, accidents, breakdowns)." [26]

3.1   Ecosystem Enabling Supply Chain Collaboration

Due to the high overlap of the semantic and technical layer an example is given. The virtual ecosystem supports cross chain collaboration in transportation of containers and products, see Fig. 2. It is possible for one or more containers to create a digital shadow where the information can be categorized virtually. This virtual container uses an e-dossier. It contains the characteristics of the load, the location, but also the limitation/boundaries of the cargo, such as to maintain constant temperature and humidity. The partners are allowed to access the data, depending on their access rights in the dossier or certain parts of the dossier. This digital shadow can also be used for trucks and ships. This means that organizations have the control of who may view (access) their data, preventing their information from falling into the wrong hands [30].

An advantage of this entity centric approach is that it is about control physical freight flows instead of focusing on all kind of processes. By organizing information via a smarter way, there is now a one version "truth" about the status of the container, truck or ship. Organizations can (un-)subscribe itself on a digital shadow, whereby the owner of the data can give this organization access or not. This stands in sharp contrast to the current information sharing mechanisms, many organizations manage the same order, but different versions of the truth exist, and the data gets both redundant, inaccurate and worst out-of-date.

Companies have the ability of sharing crucial information through the ecosystem. This information can be used for making better decisions in optimizing the supply chain e.g. when it comes to truck utilization and CO_2 reduction across organizational boundaries.

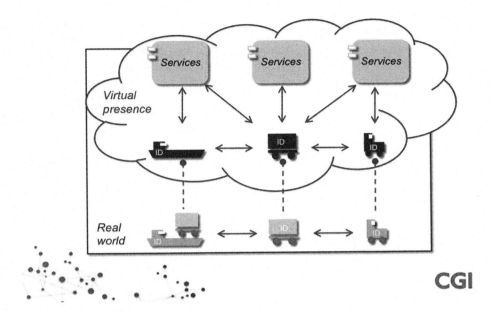

Fig. 2. Virtual ecosystems based on digital shadows

4 Conclusion and Discussion

Enterprises that are able to achieve operational collaboration with partners in a quick manner can exploit more business opportunities e.g. Prakash and Deshmukh [38] identify that collaboration is mainly optimized within one single organization and that collaboration in supply chains mainly takes the form of vertical collaborations. Frisk et al. [39] demonstrate that better planning systems and processes within companies can result in a saving of 5 % and that collaboration with supply chain partners can add another 9 %, which accumulates to a total of 14 %. Similar numbers are reported by Palmer and McKinnon [40], who derive to a reduction of nearly 18 % external cost and 14 % CO_2 reduction. Collaboration is crucial for enterprises. API thinking can be used for faster and more controlled integration.

The ECI model prescribes rules and procedure for collaboration. It supports multiple maturity collaboration types e.g. outsourcing, process/IT integration.

The current business environment requires more flexibility from organizations. The ECI model describes how to enable a more agile business network to increase efficiency/effectiveness of the scarce resources. Secondly, it enables a new functionality for an ecosystem of organizations who are willing to collaborate, namely - orchestration within the ecosystem. Agile business networks require the application of new generation technologies (IoT, API, etc.), but that's not the only answer. Trust and willingness to share information between organizations is mandatory. Collaboration e.g. outsourcing, integration via an agile, flexible manner is not common. Organizations, lack of knowledge and skills to make it happen.

Supply chains are complex by itself, this is due to the fragmentation of the market. Secondly, current IT infrastructures are mostly single-enterprise focused and intentionally not developed for exchanging information cross-domains. Where logistic service providers (LSP) are willing to collaborate instead of competing each other which is called horizontal collaboration, however in practice, setting up a horizontal collaboration is challenging [41]. Nearly 70 % of LSP companies in Benelux indicated that they have either already implemented horizontal cooperation or plan to do so within the next 4–5 years [42].

The theoretical relevance is two-folded. Näslund [43] shows that nearly 7 % of all articles in major logistics journals used case studies to develop new theories and models. Secondly, API driven development used for supply chain innovation is not yet researched. Using search engines such as Scopus, Web-of-Science and Google scholar give not any relevant articles about API driven development in encouraging supply chain collaboration & innovation, however service oriented architecture (SOA) is well known and often researched.

The current research is an outcome of studying supply chains for several years. The derived model is an outcome of several lessons learned. It is mostly validated in the Fast Moving Consumer Goods (FMCG) supply chain. Validation of the whole model is still limited.

Interorganisational systems is not a new field of research, however with the upcoming of the Internet of Things and API's interorganisational systems will change. The Internet of Things will enable collecting a huge amount of data with sensors. However it will demand a new way of thinking in retrieving all these heterogeneous types of data. This will also affect the manner of outsourcing. It will enable or support more tech-savvy companies to outsource more easily.

The proposed ECI model will open up the complex task of supply chain collaboration via the four-layer model. Each layer gives an overview of the given challenges and how they can be addressed. Within current (virtual) supply chains flexibility and agility is key. And the highly IT intertwined environment demands new solutions to become more agile as a supply chain. This research addresses the procedures how to collaborate on a ecosystem/supply chain level, but in more detail how individual organization can prepare themselves for this type of collaboration. Start thinking in services and semantics and how data should be interpreted and organized. By using APIs organization can control the accessibility of their data towards the ecosystem.

4.1　Limitations

The current research is still in progress. We have seen that the standard legacy thinking approach is not working. This is due to, less IT agility and extensibility.

Further research is required about open innovation platform based on API's. And about organizations creating their own API. It supports organizations to translate their processes into services, that they can offer to their customers. The way of service thinking, (open) data, to increase flexibility to integrate data and information can be translated in to a more agile ecosystem of partners that collaborate in a supply chain. Also more research is necessary about monitoring the use of an API, version control and backwards-compatibility.

Acknowledgments. This work was partly supported by the Dinalog 4C project, www.dinalog.nl. The results presented in this paper build on the current research-taking place within the EU iCargo project, which is funded by the European Union, http://www.i-cargo.eu/.

References

1. Peppard, J.: The pervasive IS organization. J. Strat. Inf. Syst. (2013)
2. Luftman, J., Derksen, B.: Key issues for IT executives 2012: doing more with less. MIS Q. Executive **11**, 207–218 (2012)
3. van Heck, E., Vervest, P.: Smart business networks: how the network wins. Commun. ACM **50**, 28–37 (2007)
4. Dalmolen, S., Moonen, H., van Hillegersberg, J.: Towards an information architecture to enable cross chain control centers. In: de Kok, T., van Dalen, J., van Hillegersberg, J. (eds.) Cross-Chain Collaboration in the Fast Moving Consumer Goods Supply Chain, University of Eindhoven, pp. 111–122. (2015)
5. Hevner, A.R., March, S.T., Park, J., Ram, S.: Design science in information systems research. MIS Q. **28**, 75–105 (2004)
6. Sharman, G.J.: E-supply chain management: venturing beyond e-commerce. In: 2001 Annual Conference Proceedings (2002)
7. Lee, J.C., Myers, M.D.: Dominant actors, political agendas, and strategic shifts over time: a critical ethnography of an enterprise systems implementation. J. Strat. Inf. Syst. **13**, 355–374 (2004)
8. Hillegersberg, J., Tseng, J.C., Zuidwijk, R.A., van Oosterhout, M., van Nunen, J.: Hub to higher performance?-an internet hub for the Vos Logistics supply chain. In: ISPE CE, pp. 435–443 (2003)
9. Akkermans, H.A., Bogerd, P., Yucesan, E., Van Wassenhove, L.N.: The impact of ERP on supply chain management: exploratory findings from a European Delphi study. Eur. J. Oper. Res. **146**, 284–301 (2003)
10. Christopher, M.: Logistics and supply chain management: strategies for reducing cost and improving service (1999)
11. Langley, C.J. Jr., Allen, G.R.: Third-Party Logistics Study Results and Findings of the 2006 Eleventh Annual Study. Capgemini US LCC and FedEx Corp. (2006)
12. Van Oosterhout, M., Waarts, E., Van Heck, E., Van Hillegersberg, J.: Business agility: need, readiness and alignment with IT strategies. Agile Inf. Syst. 52–69 (2007)
13. Swafford, P.M., Ghosh, S., Murthy, N.: Achieving supply chain agility through IT integration and flexibility. Int. J. Prod. Econ. **116**, 288–297 (2008)
14. Cruijssen, F., Dullaert, W., Joro, T.: Freight transportation efficiency through horizontal cooperation in Flanders. Int. J. Logistics: Res. Appl. **13**, 161–178 (2010)
15. Van Laarhoven committee: LOGISTIEK EN SUPPLY CHAINS: Innovatieprogramma (2008)
16. van Hillegersberg, J., Moonen, H., Dalmolen, S.: Coordination as a service to enable agile business networks. In: Kotlarsky, J., Oshri, I., Willcocks, L.P. (eds.) Global Sourcing 2012. LNBIP, vol. 130, pp. 164–174. Springer, Heidelberg (2012)
17. Van der Vorst, J., Duineveld, M.P., Scheer, F.-P., Beulens, A.J.: Towards logistics orchestration in the pot plant supply chain network. In: Electronic Proceedings of the Euroma 2007 Conference, 18–20 June 2007, Ankara, pp. 1–10. Ministry of Economic Affairs (2007)
18. Kumar, K., Van Dissel, H.G.: Sustainable collaboration: managing conflict and cooperation in interorganizational systems. Mis Q. **20**(3), 279–300 (1996)

19. Simatupang, T.M., Sridharan, R.: The collaborative supply chain. Int. J. Logistics Manag. **13**, 15–30 (2002)

20. De Corbière, F.: Interorganizational information systems and data quality improvement: the case of product information in the French large retail industry. In: Proceedings of the 12th International Conference on Information Quality (ICIQ), Cambridge (2007)

21. de Corbiere, F., Rowe, F.: From ideal data synchronization to hybrid forms of interconnections: architectures, processes, and data. J. Assoc. Inf. Syst. **14**, 550–584 (2013)

22. Dabhilkar, M.: One standard fits all? Disentangling multi-vs. single-brand retail supply chains, visibility benefits, and the role of GS1 global standards (2013)

23. Steinfield, C., Markus, M.L., Wigand, R.T.: Through a glass clearly: standards, architecture, and process transparency in global supply chains. J. Manag. Inf. Syst. **28**, 75–108 (2011)

24. Markus, M.L., Steinfield, C.W., Wigand, R.T.: Industry-wide information systems standardization as collective action: the case of the US residential mortgage industry. Mis Q. **30**, 439–465 (2006)

25. Folmer, E., Luttighuis, P.O., van Hillegersberg, J.: Do semantic standards lack quality? A survey among 34 semantic standards. Electron. Market. **21**, 99–111 (2011)

26. Gonzalez-Rodriguez, M., Vennesland, A., Dalmolen, S.: A common language for logistics services interoperability. In: 2015 4th International Conference on Advanced Logistics and Transport (ICALT), pp. 70–75. IEEE (2015)

27. VanderLeest, S.H., Buter, A.: Escape the waterfall: agile for aerospace. In: IEEE/AIAA 28 th Digital Avionics Systems Conference, DASC 2009, p. 6–D. IEEE (2009)

28. Sureshchandra, K., Shrinivasavadhani, J.: Moving from waterfall to agile. In: Agile, AGILE 2008 Conference, pp. 97–101. IEEE (2008)

29. Dalmolen, S, Moonen, H.M, Cornelisse, E: Information architecture using a cargo centric approach – digital shadows of real world objects. Presented at the e-Freight Conference (2012)

30. Dalmolen, S., Moonen, H.M., van Hillegersberg, J., Stoter, A.J.R., Cornelisse, E.: Supply chain orchestration and choreography: Programmable logistics using semantics. In: 2015 4th International Conference on Advanced Logistics and Transport (ICALT), pp. 76–81. IEEE (2015)

31. Evangelista, P., McKinnon, A., Sweeney, E.: Technology adoption in small and medium-sized logistics providers. Indus. Manag. Data Syst. **113**, 967–989 (2013)

32. Alanne, A., Pekkola, S., Kähkönen, T.: Centralized and distributed ERP development models: operations and challenges (2014)

33. Fielt, E., Gregor, S.: Towards simple rules heuristics for IT business value

34. Bharadwaj, A., Sawy, O.A.El, Pavlou, P.A., Venkatraman, N.: Digital business strategy: toward a next generation of insights. MIS Q. **37**, 471–482 (2013)

35. Chae, B., Yen, H.J., Sheu, C.: Information technology and supply chain collaboration: moderating effects of existing relationships between partners. IEEE Trans. Eng. Manag. **52**, 440–448 (2005)

36. Shapley, L.S.: A value for n-person games. DTIC Document (1952)

37. Vanovermeire, C., Sörensen, K., Van Breedam, A., Vannieuwenhuyse, B., Verstrepen, S.: Horizontal logistics collaboration: decreasing costs through flexibility and an adequate cost allocation strategy. Int. J. Logistics Res. Appl. **17**, 339–355 (2014)

38. Prakash, A., Deshmukh, S.: Horizontal collaboration in flexible supply chains: a simulation study. J. Stud. Manufact. **1**, 54–58 (2010)

39. Frisk, M., Göthe-Lundgren, M., Jörnsten, K., Rönnqvist, M.: Cost allocation in collaborative forest transportation. Eur. J. Oper. Res. **205**, 448–458 (2010)

40. Palmer, A., McKinnon, A.C.: An Analysis of the Opportunities for Improving Transport Efficiency through Multi-lateral Collaboration in FMCG Supply Chains. University of Southampton, Southampton, LRN, UK (2011)
41. Cruijssen, F.C.A..: Horizontal cooperation in transport and logistics. Open Access Publications from Tilburg University (2006)
42. EyeForTransport: European horizontal collaboration in the supply chain (2010)
43. Näslund, D.: Logistics needs qualitative research–especially action research. Int. J. Phys. Distrib. Logistics Manag. **32**, 321–338 (2002)

The Importance of IT Energy Efficiency in Outsourcing Decision Making: A Survey in the Dutch Outsourcing Infrastructure Market

Erik Beulen[✉]

Department of Information Management, Faculty of Economics and Business Administration, Tilburg University, Warandelaan 2, PO Box 90153, 5000 LE Tilburg, The Netherlands
erik.beulen@tilburguniversity.edu

Abstract. There is a growing corporate interest in IT energy efficiency. This will potentially impact also outsourcing decision making. In infrastructure, suppliers are focusing on increasing the IT energy efficient of their solutions. In this research 166 Dutch IT executives indicated the importance of IT energy efficiency in outsourcing decision making for infrastructure services. Is IT energy efficiency a decisive selection criteria in outsourcing decisions? The expectation is that the importance of IT-energy efficiency in outsourcing decisions increase for organization with a larger revenue, with a larger revenue outside the Netherlands, with a larger revenue outside the Europe, with a larger IT spend and larger external spend of organizations. In this research also test the expectation the importance of IT-energy efficiency in outsourcing decision making, is larger for organizations which apply for European tendering than for organizations which don't apply for European tendering. The expectations are tested by the Chi-squared test and the Cochran-Armitage test for trends. In additional to the statistical tests also survey data is qualitatively analysed. The data indicates the importance of IT energy efficiency in outsourcing decision making as 37 % of the organizations of the respondents include IT energy efficiency in outsourcing decision making. In one out of four organizations IT energy efficiency was discriminator in the selection of the infrastructure services supplier.

Keywords: Chi-squared test · Cochran-Armitage test · Green IT · IT energy efficiency · Outsourcing

1 Introduction

Companies measuring and report on sustainability. One of the most important index is RobecoSAM and S&P Dow Jones Indices (www.sustainability-indices.com). Also green IT contributes to sustainability. Molla [1] defines Green IT as "a systematic application of ecological-sustainability criteria (such as pollution prevention, product stewardship, use of clean technologies) to the creation, sourcing, use and disposal of the IT technical infrastructure as well as within the IT human and managerial components of the IT infrastructure, in order to reduce IT, business process and supply-chain related emissions, waste and water use; improve energy efficiency and generate Green economic rent" [1, p. 757].

© Springer International Publishing Switzerland 2015
I. Oshri et al. (Eds.): Global Sourcing 2015, LNBIP 236, pp. 240–250, 2015.
DOI: 10.1007/978-3-319-26739-5_14

There is currently still only limited research in this area [2–4]. The scope of green IT is wider than the scope of this research. This research is only focusing on the energy consumption of IT. The life cycle of IT [5, 6] has been taken into account in this research (energy consumption related to manufacturing, use and dispose). Measuring green IT requires standards such as ISO 14031 (environmental management) and frameworks such as the Integrated sustainable-value framework [7], Green Information Technology (IT) framework [8] and the Green Hardware IT Infrastructure (GHITI) frame work [9].

There are three types of energy consumptions energy for the manufacturing, the use and/or the disposal of the device. Therefore this is not limited to Power Usage Effectiveness (PUE) [10]. Manufactures provide information related to the energy consumption of all three types of energy consumption. This information is certified by independent third parties such as TUV and MET Laboratories, using international standards such as STAR Energy.

It is important to state that IT energy efficiency is not always extent their environmental efforts to the IT department. This also applies to outsourcing contracts with external suppliers [11, 12]. The IT-energy efficiency is becoming an emerging decision criteria in outsourcing [13]. Eco-efficiency and eco-effectiveness motives amongst others the increase of the adoption of technologies that enhance the energy efficiency of infrastructure services and that decrease IT related emissions [14]. Traditional decision criteria for outsourcing are cost, quality, innovation, continuity of the service provisioning and reputation of the supplier [15, 16]. In the market suppliers and manufacturers are increasingly focusing on IT energy efficiency as an important theme. Some suppliers and manufacturers focussen on individual bid, where the more mature suppliers and manufacturers are focusing on increase the energy efficiency of their portfolio. Infrastructure services consists of infrastructure management, network management and desktop management. In addition cloud services (IaaS, PaaS and SaaS) have an infrastructure component, organizations might consider to also include the energy consumption of cloud services as a selection criteria for cloud services. Cloud service providers are also exploring options to make their services more green and energy efficient [17–19].

2   Research Questions

The main research question is the importance of IT energy efficiency in outsourcing decisions. The number of companies that include IT energy efficiency in their outsourcing decisions drive the importance (related to question 7 of the questionnaire: inclusion increases the importance).

The effect of organizational characteristics will be investigated. The five organizational characteristics are revenue (question 2), geographical spread (question 3), IT spend (question 5), external IT spend (question 6) and if European tendering is applicable (question 4). This results in six research questions (1, 2a, 2b, 3, 4 and 5). These research questions and their rational are detailed below.

Research question 1:

H_0: Pr(IT energy efficiency is taken into account in outsourcing decision making by small organizations) = …. = Pr(IT energy efficiency is taken into account in outsourcing decision making by large organizations)

H_1: Pr(IT energy efficiency is taken into account in outsourcing decision making by small organizations) < …. < Pr(IT energy efficiency is taken into account in outsourcing decision making by large organizations)

Rational: the larger the revenue of an organization the higher the potentially benefits from IT energy efficiency.

Research question 2a:

H_0: Pr(IT energy efficiency is taken into account in outsourcing decision making by national organizations) = …. = Pr(IT energy efficiency is taken into account in outsourcing decision making by multinational organizations)

H_1: Pr(IT energy efficiency is taken into account in outsourcing decision making by national organizations) < …. < Pr(IT energy efficiency is taken into account in outsourcing decision making by multinational organizations)

Research question 2b:

H_0: Pr(IT energy efficiency is taken into account in outsourcing decision making by European organizations) = …. = Pr(IT energy efficiency is taken into account in outsourcing decision making by multinational organizations)

H_1: Pr(IT energy efficiency is taken into account in outsourcing decision making by European organizations) < …. < Pr(IT energy efficiency is taken into account in outsourcing decision making by multinational organizations)

Rational for research questions 2a and 2b: the more international footprint of an organization the higher the likelihood of peer pressure to focus on IT energy efficiency.

Research question 3:

H_0: Pr(IT energy efficiency is taken into account in outsourcing decision making by organizations with a small IT spend) = …. = Pr(IT energy efficiency is taken into account in outsourcing decision making by organizations with a large IT spend)

H_1: Pr(IT energy efficiency is taken into account in outsourcing decision making by organizations with a small IT spend) < …. < Pr(IT energy efficiency is taken into account in outsourcing decision making by organizations with a large IT spend)

Rational: the larger the IT spend of an organization the higher the potentially benefits from IT energy efficiency.

Research question 4:

H_0: Pr(IT energy efficiency is taken into account in outsourcing decision making by organizations with a small external IT spend) = …. = Pr(IT energy efficiency is taken into account in outsourcing decision making by organizations with a large external IT spend)

H_1: Pr(IT energy efficiency is taken into account in outsourcing decision making by organizations with a small external IT spend) < …. < Pr(IT energy efficiency is taken into account in outsourcing decision making by organizations with a large external IT spend)

Rational: the larger the external IT spend of an organization the higher the potentially benefits from IT energy efficiency and the focus of suppliers on IT energy efficiency is larger than the focus of internal IT-departments/IT shared service centers.

Research question 5:

H_0: Pr(IT energy efficiency is taken into account in outsourcing decision making by organizations which are not hold to European Tendering regulations) = Pr(IT energy efficiency is taken into account in outsourcing decision making by organizations which are hold to European Tendering regulations)

H_1: Pr(IT energy efficiency is taken into account in outsourcing decision making by organizations which are not hold to European Tendering regulations) < (IT energy efficiency is taken into account in outsourcing decision making by organizations which are hold to European Tendering regulations)

Rational: organizations to which the European Tendering regulations apply, have more focus on Corporate Social Responsibilities (CSR) strategies than organization which are not hold to European Tender regulations. IT energy is one of the options organizations have to implement and execute their CSR strategy.

3   Research Method

The data for this research is collected by a survey. The survey was submitted to community of ICT Media[1], a Dutch organization that facilities IT decision makers in the Netherlands. The members of this community are Chief Information Officers and their direct reports. The response rate was 5 % (166 response on 3.622 invitations). The survey was an anonymous survey. Therefore it is not possible to conclude on the representativeness of the sample (166 responses versus to total community of 3.622 members). However the spread over the different sectors and spread of the size of the organizations the respondents represent don't indicate that the respondents are not representative for the community, also which was confirmed by ICT Media.

The survey is conducted in Dutch (see appendix). The participants completed their response via a portal. The responses were collected from 25 August 2014 to 2 September

---

[1] The mission of ICT Media is to facilitate Dutch IT decision makers. The community of ICT media consists of Chief Information Officers and the their direct reports. The community is supported by a knowledge portal and business magazines. ICT Media also regularly facilitates round tables, such as round tables on IT energy efficiency (2011 and 2012). ICT Media has an active community which represents the Chief Information Officers community in the Netherlands.

2014. The potential participants received one friendly reminder are the first week the survey was introduced.

To investigate the importance of IT energy efficiency in outsourcing decisions the Chi-squared test is applied (tests of goodness of fit and tests of independence). If there is in the Chi-squared test an association and independency for an organizational characteristic the Cochran-Armitage test for trends is conducted (research questions 1 to 4 only). Applying the Cochran-Armitage test [20, 21] is used to perform a categorical data analysis to assess for the presence of an association between the importance of IT energy efficiency in outsourcing decision making and five organizational characteristics: revenue, Dutch revenue – rest of the world revenue, European revenue – rest of the world revenue, IT spend and external IT spend. This test has a higher power than the Chi-squared test when the suspected trend is correct. This test modifies the Chi-squared test to incorporate a suspected ordering in the effects of the k categories in the second variable [22]. This trend test is often used as a genotype-based test for case control genetic association studies and applied in this study on the importance of IT energy efficiency in outsourcing decision making and an organizational characteristic. For the data set we except for all test a linear trend and used the weights t = (0,1,2).

4 Statistical Analysis

Research question 1:

H_0: Pr(IT energy efficiency is taken into account in outsourcing decision making by organizations <=10 m Euro revenue) = ... = Pr(IT energy efficiency is taken into account in outsourcing decision making by organizations > 1.000 m revenue)
H_1: Pr(IT energy efficiency is taken into account in outsourcing decision making by organizations <=10 m Euro revenue) < .... < Pr(IT energy efficiency is taken into account in outsourcing decision making by organizations > 1.000 m revenue)

Test Statistic (Chi-Squared Test – Goodness of Fit): 13,8167 (N = 163 - df = 5). At a 5 % significance level there is enough evidence to reject the null hypothesis for the Chi-Squared test – goodness of fit.

Test Statistic (Chi-Squared Test – Test of Independency): 3,7404 (N = 163 - df = 5). At a 5 % significance level there is not enough evidence to reject the null hypothesis for the Chi-Squared test – test of independency.

Research question 2a:

H_0: Pr(IT energy efficiency is taken into account in outsourcing decision making by organizations with <=25 % of their revenue in the Netherlands) = ... = Pr(IT energy efficiency is taken into account in outsourcing decision making by organizations with > 75 % of their revenue outside the Netherlands)
H_1: Pr(IT energy efficiency is taken into account in outsourcing decision making by organizations with <=25 % of their revenue in the Netherlands) < .... < Pr(IT energy

efficiency is taken into account in outsourcing decision making by organizations with > 75 % of their revenue outside the Netherlands)

Test Statistic (Chi-Squared Test – Goodness of Fit): 12,0920 (N = 154 - df = 3). At a 5 % significance level there is enough evidence to reject the null hypothesis for the Chi-Squared test – goodness of fit.

Test Statistic (Chi-Squared Test – Test of Independency): 2,8914 (N = 154 - df = 3). At a 5 % significance level there is not enough evidence to reject the null hypothesis for the Chi-Squared test – test of independency.

Research question 2b:

H_0: Pr(IT energy efficiency is taken into account in outsourcing decision making by organizations with <=25 % of their revenue in Europe) = ... = Pr(IT energy efficiency is taken into account in outsourcing decision making by organizations with > 75 % of their revenue outside Europe)

H_1: Pr(IT energy efficiency is taken into account in outsourcing decision making by organizations with <=25 % of their revenue in Europe) < .... < Pr(IT energy efficiency is taken into account in outsourcing decision making by organizations with > 75 % of their revenue outside Europe)

Test Statistic (Chi-Squared Test – Goodness of Fit): 10,7071 (N = 154 - df = 3). At a 5 % significance level there is enough evidence to reject the null hypothesis for the Chi-Squared test – goodness of fit.

Test Statistic (Chi-Squared Test – Test of Independency): 1,4167 (N = 154 - df = 3). At a 5 % significance level there is not enough evidence to reject the null hypothesis for the Chi-Squared test – test of independency.

Research question 3:

H_0: Pr(IT energy efficiency is taken into account in outsourcing decision making by organizations with a < 1 % IT spend) = ... = Pr(IT energy efficiency is taken into account in outsourcing decision making by organizations with a > 10 % IT spend)

H_1: Pr(IT energy efficiency is taken into account in outsourcing decision making by organizations with a < 1 % IT spend) < .... < Pr(IT energy efficiency is taken into account in outsourcing decision making by organizations with a > 10 % IT spend)

Test Statistic (Chi-Squared Test – Goodness of Fit): 18,0551 (N = 158 - df = 4). At a 5 % significance level there is enough evidence to reject the null hypothesis for the Chi-Squared test – goodness of fit.

Test Statistic (Chi-Squared Test – Test of Independency): 8,471 (N = 158 - df = 4). At a 5 % significance level there is not enough evidence to reject the null hypothesis for the Chi-Squared test – test of independency. However at a 10 % significance level this is enough evidence to reject the null hypothesis for the Chi-Squared test enough evidence to reject the null hypothesis for the Chi-Squared test – test of independency.

Test Statistic (Cochran-Armitage Test): 0,9080 (N = 158). At a 5 % significance level there is not enough evidence to reject the null hypothesis for the Cochran-Armitage test.

Research question 4:

H_0: Pr(IT energy efficiency is taken into account in outsourcing decision making by organizations with a <=10 % IT spend) = ... = Pr(IT energy efficiency is taken into account in outsourcing decision making by organizations with a > 75 % spend)
H_1: Pr(IT energy efficiency is taken into account in outsourcing decision making by organizations with a <=10 % IT spend) < .... < Pr(IT energy efficiency is taken into account in outsourcing decision making by organizations with a > 75 % IT spend)

Test Statistic (Chi-Squared Test – Goodness of Fit): 16,9744 (N = 160 - df = 4). At a 5 % significance level there is enough evidence to reject the null hypothesis for the Chi-Squared test – goodness of fit.

Test Statistic (Chi-Squared Test – Test of Independency): 6,390 (N = 160 - df = 4). At a 5 % significance level there is not enough evidence to reject the null hypothesis for the Chi-Squared test – test of independency.

Research question 5:

H_0: Pr(IT energy efficiency is taken into account in outsourcing decision making by organizations which are not hold to European Tendering regulations) = Pr(IT energy efficiency is taken into account in outsourcing decision making by organizations which are hold to European Tendering regulations)
H_1: Pr(IT energy efficiency is taken into account in outsourcing decision making by organizations which are not hold to European Tendering regulations) < (IT energy efficiency is taken into account in outsourcing decision making by organizations which are hold to European Tendering regulations)

The reduces number of respondents are related to the large number or respondents which selected "other" for the sector. Only the responses with pre-populated sectors have been taken into account.

Test Statistic (Chi-Squared Test – Goodness of Fit): 4,000 (N = 108 - df = 1). At a 5 % significance level there is enough evidence to reject the null hypothesis for the Chi-Squared test – goodness of fit.

Test Statistic (Chi-Squared Test – Test of independency): 1,6662 (N = 108 - df = 1). At a 5 % significance level there is not enough evidence to reject the null hypothesis for the Chi-Squared test – test of independency.

5   Qualitative Analyses

In addition to the statistical tests the context information provided by the respondents is analyzed to understand the importance of IT energy efficiency in outsourcing decision making better. It is relevant to understand the aspects of energy efficiency that organizations take into account. Also for organizations who are taking IT energy efficiency into account it is relevant to understand the weighting of IT energy efficiency. Finally it is relevant to understand if IT energy efficiency is discriminator in outsourcing decisions.

Scope. There are three types of energy consumptions energy for the manufacturing, the use and/or the disposal of the device. Most of the respondents indicate that their organization includes the energy consumption during "use": 55 respondents out of 61 respondents. The Table 1 below indicated the spread of the responses (multiple responses are possible). The limited focus on the manufacturing and the disposal of the device might be related to the emerging IT energy efficiency maturity of the organizations of the respondents. As the energy related to the manufacturing and the disposal of devices is substantial, organizations might consider to include this their evaluation of IT energy efficiency.

Table 1.   Different categories of energy consumptions taken into account in IT energy consumptions.

Importance of IT energy efficiency in outsourcing decision making	Energy related to manufacturing of the device	Energy related to the use of the device	Energy related to the disposal of the devie
IT energy efficiency included in outsourcing decision making, however not discrimitor	15	39	4
IT energy efficiency included in outsourcing decision makingand discrimitor	9	16	3
Total number of respondents	24	55	7

Weighting. The weighting of IT energy efficiency drives the importance of IT energy efficiency in outsourcing decision making. In general the weighting of IT energy efficiency doesn't exceed 15 %. This is set as the threshold for the responses that have been taken into account. From the 61 respondents, who's organization take IT energy efficiency into account in outsourcing decision making, completed 17 respondents this question with responses a weighting that didn't exceed the 15 % for all reported infrastructure services. Eight respondents have enter 0 % or no response for all infrastructure services. This could indicated that these organizations have not included a specific weighting for IT energy efficiency. It is remarkable that a large number of these response are linked to cloud computing (IaaS, PaaS and SaaS). This might be explained by the inclusion of IT energy efficiency in the value propositions of most cloud service providers. As this embedded in their solutions the IT energy efficiency might be perceived a necessity instead as a differentiator. The remaining responses are predominantly 5 % and 10 %.

As most outsourcing competitive biddings are decided on relatively small differences (less than 10 % difference between winner and second best supplier). There are hardly any 10 %–15 % weighting percentage response. Which could be explained by the relatively small differences in outsourcing decisions. There is no need to increase the weighting percentage for IT energy efficiency, weighting ranging from 5 % to 10 % is sufficient to meaningful include IT energy efficiency in outsourcing decision making (Table 2).

Table 2. Weighting percentage of IT energy efficiency in outsourcing decision making.

Weighting % IT energy efficiency in outsourcing decision	Number of respondents						
	Infra. Man.	Network Services	Desktop Services	IaaS	PaaS	Saas	Total
15%	2	0	0	0	0	0	2
10%	9	7	10	4	2	2	34
8%	1	0	0	1	1	0	3
5%	5	6	4	1	1	1	18
2%	0	1	0	0	0	0	1
0%	0	2	3	7	9	10	31
no value	0	1	0	4	4	4	13
Total	17	17	17	17	17	17	102

Furthermore there was also one respondent who's organization has added a knock-out criteria related to IT-energy efficiency. Potential suppliers had to be ISO certified. This is an interesting strategy. This strategy avoids that in the evaluation there have to be a percentage allocated to IT energy efficiency. If this knock out criteria, instead of a certification only, is described as requirement, the importance of IT energy efficiency will increase further. Maximum thresholds for IT-energy consumption and saving patterns can be included in the IT energy efficiency requirements. However it is also fair to say that there are still issues in measuring the IT energy, as the frameworks are more process frameworks than measurement frameworks. In future the feasibility of this strategy most likely will increase.

Discriminator. The differences in the evaluation in competitive bidding processes is mostly very limited. Depending on the weighting, as detailed in the previous section, IT energy efficiency can make the difference. From the 61 respondents who take IT energy efficiency into account in more than one of four of the outsourcing decisions IT energy efficiency made the difference (N = 16). In this discriminator group of respondents the governmental sector (N = 8) as well as the sector utility and telecom (N = 4) are well represented.

For the governmental sector the obligation to contract by European tendering might explain the outcome. In European tendering the criteria for selecting a supplier have to be documented in advance. If IT energy efficiency is a defined criteria, the evaluators have to include this criteria as detailed. In European tendering there are limit options to alter the criteria after the submission to suppliers. Also the sector utility and telecom is a highly structured sector. This characteristic might be in favor of the including IT energy efficiency in outsourcing decision making.

6   Limitations

This research is conducted in the Netherland only and also only including 166 respondents. Also, although the spread of the respondents in terms of revenue and sectors didn't raise a concern, the participating IT executives might have a larger interest in IT energy efficiency and therefore more likely include IT energy efficiency in outsourcing decision making. A larger and more international survey mitigates these concerns. Also the supplier perspective of IT energy efficiency is missing. Suppliers might be able to add additional insights in the importance of IT energy efficiency in outsourcing decision making.

7 Conclusions

The data didn't support the expectation that the importance of IT-energy efficiency in outsourcing decisions increase for organization with a larger revenue, with a larger revenue outside the Netherlands, with a larger revenue outside the Europe, with a larger IT spend and larger external spend of organizations. Also the data didn't support the expectation the importance of IT-energy efficiency in outsourcing decision making, is larger for organizations which apply for European tendering. However the qualitative analyses provided valuable insights to understand the importance of IT energy efficiency in outsourcing decisions better. The focus of IT energy efficiency is on the energy consumption during the use.

Organizations need to consider if and how they would like in to incorporate IT energy efficiency in their outsourcing decisions. When the measuring of IT-energy consumption is improved, organizations might consider to include IT-energy efficiency as a knock out criteria in outsourcing decision making, For now organizations are advised to limit the weighting of IT-energy efficiency to a weighting of maximum 10 %. A clear and in advance communication to the market is helpful. Also suppliers can include IT energy efficiency not only in their proposal but more important in their product and service portfolio. The importance of IT energy efficiency will only significantly increase in the future if IT energy efficiency is strongly embedded in the product and service portfolio of a supplier.

Organizations might consider to include also the energy consumption for the manufacturing and the disposal in outsourcing decision making. This will increase the urgency for suppliers and manufacturers to reduce the energy consumption. It also became clear that organization which qualify for European tendering have an increased focus on IT energy efficiency. Suppliers have to take this into account when they are participating in a European tendering bidding process.

Acknowledgements. The author would like to thanks Rob Beijleveld, Jorick van der Vlies and Arnoud van Gemeren from ICT Media (www.ictmedia.nl) for inviting the members of the ICT Media community to participate in the survey and for facilitating the execution of the survey. The author would also like to thank Pierre Gorissen and Neel Bhagodia for sharing their valuable insights.

References

1. Molla, A.: The reach and richness of green IT: a principal component analysis. In; 20th Australasian Conference on Information Systems, pp. 754–764 (2009)

2. Melville, N.: Information systems innovation for environmental sustainability. Manage. Inf. Syst. Q. **34**(1), 1–21 (2010)
3. Jenkin, T., Webster, J., McShane, L.: An agenda for 'Green' information technology and systems research. Inf. Orga. **21**(1), 17–40 (2011)
4. Chowdhury, G.: An agenda for green information retrieval research. Inf. Process. Manage. **48**(6), 1067–1077 (2012)
5. Murugesan, S.: Harnessing Green IT: principles and practices. IEEE IT Prof. **10**(1), 24–33 (2008)
6. Molla, A., Cooper, V.: Green IT readiness: a framework and preliminary proof of concept. Australas. J. Inf. Syst. **16**(2), 5–23 (2010)
7. Dao, V., Langella, I., Carbo, J.: From green to sustainability: information technology and an integrated sustainability framework. J. Strateg. Inf. Syst. **20**(1), 63–79 (2011)
8. Uddin, M., Talha, M., Rahman, A., Shah, A., Ahmed, J., Memon, J.: Green information technology (IT) framework for energy efficient data centers using virtualization. Int. J. Phys. Sci. **7**(13), 2052–2065 (2012)
9. Punte Kalsheim, J., Beulen, E.: Framework for measuring the environmental efficiency of IT and setting strategies for green IT: a case study providing guidance to chief information officers, chapter 7 in green ICT & ENERGY: From smart to wise strategies. In: Appelman, J.H., Warnier, M., Osseyran, A. (eds.) Sustainable Energy Developments serie (#5), pp. 77–96. CRC Press (2013)
10. Kipp, A., Jiang, T., Fugini, M., Salomie, I.: Layered green performance indicators. Future Gener. Comput. Syst. **28**(2), 478–489 (2012)
11. Cone, E.: The greening of the CIO. CIO insights (2006). (http://www.cioinsight.com/c/a/Trends/The-Greening-of-the-CIO/)
12. Babin, R., Nicholson, B.: Sustainable global outsourcing: achieving social and environmental responsibility in global IT and business. Palgrave Macmillan, Basingstoke (2012)
13. Bai, C., Sarkis, J.: Green information technology strategic justification and evaluation. Inf. Syst. Front. **15**(5), 831–847 (2013)
14. Molla, A., Abareshi, A.: Organizational green motivations for information technology: empirical study. J. Comput. Inf. Syst. **52**(3), 92–102 (2012)
15. Lacity, M., Willcocks, L.: Information systems and outsourcing: studies in theory and practice. Palgrave, Basingstoke (2008)
16. Beulen, E., Ribbers, P., Roos, J.: Managing IT Outsourcing Relationships. Routledge, UK (2011)
17. Chowdhury, C.R., Chatterjee, A., Sardar, A., Agarwal, S., Nath, A.: A comprehensive study on cloud green computing: to reduce carbon footprints using clouds. Int. J. Adv. Comput. Res. **3**(1), 78–85 (2013)
18. Jain, A., Mishra, M., Peddoju, S., Jain, N.: Energy efficient computing-green cloud computing. In: 2013 International Conference on Energy Efficient Technologies for Sustainability (ICEETS), pp. 978–982. IEEE Conference Publications (2013)
19. Jing, S.Y., Ali, S., She, K., Zhong, Y.: State-of-the-art research study for green cloud computing. J. Supercomput. **65**(1), 445–468 (2013)
20. Cochran, W.: Some methods for strengthening the common chi-squared test. Biometrics **10**(4), 417–451 (1954)
21. Armitage, P.: Test for linear trends in proportions and frequencies. Biometrics **11**(3), 375–386 (1955)
22. Agresti, A.: Categorical Data Analyses. Wiley & Sons, New Jersey (2002)

Author Index